The EU and the Political Economy of Transatlantic Relations

P.I.E. Peter Lang

Bruxelles · Bern · Berlin · Frankfurt am Main · New York · Oxford · Wien

Finn LAURSEN (ed.)

The EU and the Political Economy of Transatlantic Relations

"European Policy"
No. 51

The book is published under the auspices of the EU Centre of Excellence at Dalhousie University with financial support from the European Commission.

© P.I.E. PETER LANG S.A.
Éditions scientifiques internationales
Brussels, 2012
1 avenue Maurice, B-1050 Brussels, Belgium
info@peterlang.com; www.peterlang.com

ISSN 1376-0890
ISBN 978-90-5201-900-0
D/2012/5678/108

Printed in Germany

Library of Congress Cataloging-in-Publication Data
The EU and the political economy of transatlantic relations / Finn Laursen (ed.).
p. cm. -- (European policy ; no. 51)
Includes bibliographical references and index. ISBN 978-90-5201-900-0 (alk. paper)
1. European Union countries--Foreign economic relations--North America.
2. North America--Foreign economic relations--European Union countries.
3. European Union countries--Commercial policy. 4. North America--Commercial policy. I. Laursen, Finn.
HF1531.Z4N748 20123   37.1'42097--dc23   2012038257

CIP also available from the British Library, UK.

Bibliographic information published by "Die Deutsche Nationalbibliothek". "Die Deutsche Nationalbibliothek" lists this publication in the "Deutsche Nationalbibliografie"; detailed bibliographic data is available on the Internet at <http://dnb.de>.

Contents

Preface

This book is about political aspects of transatlantic relations. Most of the chapters were first presented at the fifth annual conference of the European Union Centre of Excellence (EUCE) at Dalhousie University, Halifax, Nova Scotia, Canada, 10-12 April 2011. The conference also had panels dealing with security aspects of transatlantic relations. Afterwards selected papers were revised for publication. Those dealing with political economy questions appear in this book.

Obviously security and political economy interact and can sometimes be difficult to separate. The chapters in this book cover especially the financial crisis, trade relations, competition policy and environmental issues.

The papers dealing with security questions will be published in a separate volume, also to be published by PIE Peter Lang.

Finn Laursen
Halifax, NS, Canada, March 2012

Acknowledgements

This book is published under the auspices of the EU Centre of Excellence (EUCE) at Dalhousie University, Halifax, Canada. The EUCE receives financial support through a 3-year agreement with the then Directorate-General for External Relations (DG Relex) of the European Union (Grant Agreement No. SI2.541580) signed on 4 December 2009, now administered by the European External Action Service (EEAS). Without this support the conference that brought most authors together in April 2011 as well as the subsequent production of this book would not have been possible. The financial support from the EU is gratefully acknowledged. Needless to say, the EU is not responsible for any information or views in this book.

The editor, who currently directs the EUCE at Dalhousie, also wants to acknowledge the contribution of Tatiana Neklioudova, the Administrative Secretary of the EUCE until June 2011. She took care of the logistics in connection with the 5th annual conference in April 2011.

Thanks also to Dr. Robert Summerby-Murray, Dean, Faculty of Arts and Social Sciences at Dalhousie for welcoming the participants and colleagues and students who participated at the conference, especially Professors Robert Finbow and Ruben Zaiotti who contributed with papers and chaired panels.

The language check and copy-editing was done efficiently by Phyllis Singer, senior editor at GreenPoint Global, and my assistant at Dalhousie University Carolyn Ferguson has done the typesetting, the list of abbreviations as well as the index. I am grateful to both Phyllis and Carolyn for their professional and efficient help with this book.

Finally I want to thank PIE Peter Lang, Brussels, for agreeing to publish this book. In particular I thank the director, Emilie Menz, and the editor of the "European Policy" series, Pascaline Winand, for excellent cooperation.

Finn Laursen

List of Abbreviations

AC	Andean Community
ACN	Andean Community of Nations
ACP	African, Caribbean, and Pacific countries
ASEAN	Association of Southeast Asian Nations
ATC	Advisory Technical Committee
B2B	Business to Business
B2C	Business to Consumer
BoP	Balance of Payments
BRIC	Brazil, Russia, India, China
BSC	Banking Supervision Committee
CAFTA-DR	Dominican Republic-Central America-United States Free Trade Agreement
CAP	Common Agricultural Policy
CCP	Common Commercial Policy
CSDP	Common Security and Defence Policy
CERT	Canada Europe Round Table for Business
CETA	Comprehensive Economic and Trade Agreement
CFSP	Common Foreign and Security Policy
CO_2	Carbon Dioxide
CRTC	Canadian Radio-Television and Telecommunications Commission
CSA	Canadian Standards Association
CSD	Civil Society Dialogue
CUPE	Canadian Union of Public Employees
EBA	European Banking Authority
EBRD	European Bank of Reconstruction and Development
ECB	European Central Bank
ECHO	European Community Humanitarian Office
ECIP	European Community Investment Partners
ECJ	European Court of Justice

ECODIR	European Consumer Dispute Resolution
ECOFIN	Council of Economic and Finance Ministers
ECU	European Currency Unit
EEAS	European External Action Service
EEC	European Economic Community
EFC	Economic and Financial Committee
EFSF	European Financial Stability Facility
EFSM	European Financial Stabilization Mechanism
EFTA	European Free Trade Association
EIB	European Investment Bank
EIOPA	European Insurance and Occupational Pensions Authority
EMS	European Monetary System
EMU	Economic and Monetary Union
ERM	Exchange Rate Mechanism
ESAs	European Supervisory Authorities
ESC	Economic and Social Committee
ESFS	European System of Financial Supervision
ESM	European Stability Mechanism
ESMA	European Securities and Markets Authority
ESRB	European Systemic Risk Board
ESRC	European Systemic Risk Council
EU	European Union
EU-LAC	European Union, Latin America and the Caribbean
FARC	*Fuerzas Armadas Revolucionarias de Colombia*
FDI	Foreign Direct Investment
FSOC	Financial Stability Oversight Council
FTA	Free Trade Agreement
FTAA	Free Trade Area in the Americas
GAAP	Generally Accepted Accounting Principles
GATS	General Agreement on Trade in Services
GATT	General Agreement on Tariff and Trade
GDP	Gross Domestic Product
GEA	Green Energy Act
GHG	Greenhouse Gas

GPE	Global Political Economy
GSP	Generalized System of Preferences
HR	High Representative
ICSID	International Centre for Settlement of Investment Disputes
ICT	Information and Communication Technologies
ILO	International Labour Organization
IMF	International Monetary Fund
IP	Intellectual Property
IPE	International Political Economy
IPR	Intellectual Property Rights
ITC	Information Technology and Communication
JCC	Joint Co-Operation Committee
MARPOL	International Convention for the Prevention of Pollution from Ships
MEFTA	Middle East Free Trade Agreement
MEP	Member of the European Parliament
MERCOSUR	*Mercado Común del Sur*
MFN	Most-Favoured Nation
NAFTA	North American Free Trade Area
NATO	North Atlantic Treaty Organization
NGO	Non-governmental Organization
NTA	New Transatlantic Agenda
NTB	Non-Tariff Barriers to Trade
ODR	Online Dispute Resolution
OECD	Organization for Economic Cooperation and Development
OEEC	Organization for European Economic Cooperation
PIPEDA	Personal Information Protection and Electronic Documents Act
PTA	Preferential trade agreement
QMV	Qualified Majority Voting
QR	Quantitative Restrictions
ROO	Rules of Origin
SAQ	*Société des Alcools du Québec*

SEA	Single European Act
SEC	Securities and Exchange Commission
SIA	Sustainability Impact Assessment
SPS	Sanitary and Phytosanitary
TAD	Transatlantic Declaration
TBT	Technical Barriers to Trade
TEC	Transatlantic Economic Council
TEP	Transatlantic Economic Partnership
TIEA	Trade and Investment Enhancement
TPP	Trans Pacific Partnership
TRIMS	Trade-Related Aspects of Investment Measures
TRIPS	Trade-Related Aspects of Intellectual Property Rights
UNCITRAL	United Nations Commission on International Trade Law
UNCTAD	United Nations Conference on Trade and Development
USTR	United States Trade Ambassador
WCO	World Customs Organization
WSRCPA	Wall Street Reform and Consumer Protection Act
WTO	World Trade Organization

PART I

INTRODUCTION

The EU and Transatlantic Economic Relations

Interdependence and Shifting Regime Constellations

Finn LAURSEN

Introduction

This book is focusing on transatlantic economic relations. These relations form an important part of the external relations of the European Union (EU). They include trade, money and finance, foreign direct investments (FDI), competition policy, and other economic relations, but they largely exclude security-related relations, even if security relations can affect economic relations in various ways. Some would argue that security relations form a certain space within which economic relations can develop. If security relations are benign, economic relations can prosper. In the title of this book I have used the term "political economy". This indicates that we are at the intersection of politics and economics, where states and markets interact. There is an academic tradition of studying International Political Economy (IPE), now sometimes called Global Political Economy (GPE) to indicate that it is also transnational, involving more actors than states (Gilpin 1987; Strange 1988; Laursen 1995; Gilpin 2001; Laursen 2009; Walter and Sen 2009; and Verdun 2011). Authority and exchange would be two other concepts that could indicate what kind of relationships we are interested in.

In the North Atlantic area, the North Atlantic Treaty Organization (NATO) has been a central organization in the area of security, but there has been no comparable organization in the economic area. True, the Organization for European Economic Cooperation (OEEC) was established in 1948. At the beginning, it had 18 Western European members. A major purpose in the early years was the distribution of the Marshall Aid from the United States to Western European after World War II. It became the Organization for Economic Cooperation and Development (OECD) in 1961, with a broader membership and mandate. The United States and Canada joined at that time. Later other mostly industrialized countries joined, including Mexico in 1964.[1] Today, the OECD has become a kind of think tank for the industrialized countries. It gives advice to the governments but it does not form what scholars in the 1960s and 1970s started calling an international regime.

Krasner defined a regime as "implicit or explicit principles, norms, rules and decision-making procedures around which actors' expectations converge in a given area of international relations" (Krasner 1982; see also Little 2005). The study of international regimes was an important part of the so-called neo-neo debate in the 1980s and early 1990s. Neo-realists took a fairly sceptical view to the possibility of creating strong international regimes while neo-liberal institutionalists were more optimistic (Keohane 1986; Baldwin 1993). Neo-realists tended to focus on relative gains, while neo-liberal institutionalists focused on absolute gains. At the end of the debate, both groups agreed that states are the main actors and that states behave rationally (Jackson and Sørensen 1999).

The political economy of transatlantic relations is dominated by complex interdependence (Keohane and Nye 1977). In efforts to manage this interdependence, the states in the region face collective action problems. In the main areas studied in this book, namely trade, money, and environment, there are temptations to defect from agreements, in the form of protectionism, competitive devaluations, and pollution, as well as distribution problems, where some states may benefit more than others. Both global and regional regimes have been created in efforts to deal with these collective action problems. But with the two main actors, the EU and the United States, often having diverging interests, it is difficult to create and maintain efficient and equitable common institutions. Without such institutions unilateral action – and power – become ingredients in otherwise close relations. In the following, I shall give an overview of multilateral as well as more region-specific regimes and trace the development of EU competences and decision-making procedures in these areas.

Multilateral Regimes

Regimes that affect the transatlantic area tend to be wider than the Atlantic area, in some cases near-global in coverage. Right after World War II, the International Monetary Fund (IMF) established the monetary regime, and the General Agreement on Tariffs and Trade (GATT) was the trade regime. The United States played a leading role in establishing

---

[1] Information on the OECD is available on the website: <http://www.oecd.org/home/0,2987,en_2649_201185_1_1_1_1_1,00.html>. [Accessed 11 February 2012].

these so-called Breton Woods institutions, including also the World Bank.

The central currency in the monetary regime was the US dollar. Many national currencies were pegged to the dollar at a fixed exchange rate. The dollar itself in turn was linked with the price of gold. This system came under pressure in the late 1960s, partly because of US spending in the Vietnam War (Verdun 2011). In 1971, US President Nixon cut the link with gold and let the dollar float. This led to efforts in Europe to create currency stability though various forms of co-operation, including the so-called "snake in the tunnel" in the first part of the 1970s and later the European Monetary System (EMS) from 1979. The Maastricht Treaty establishing the EU (1993) included the plan for Economic and Monetary Union (EMU), which created the single currency, the euro in 1999.

The GATT, on the other hand, was based on various principles and rules: most-favoured nation (MFN) treatment, prohibition of quantitative restrictions (QR), gradual reduction of tariffs through rounds of trade negotiations, and national treatment of foreign products (no tax discrimination, for instance). Deviations from MFN treatment were allowed for customs unions and free trade agreements (FTAs). This allowed the European Economic Community (EEC) to establish a customs union and some countries, which did not join the EEC at the outset, to form the European Free Trade Association (EFTA) in 1960.

The Uruguay Round of the GATT (1986-93) expanded the agenda of international trade policy to include agriculture, services, and trade-related aspects of intellectual property rights (TRIPS). It strengthened the dispute settlement system in the new World Trade Organization (WTO), which emerged from the round in 1994. Today, the WTO arguably includes three regimes: the GATT, as well as the General Agreement on Trade in Services (GATS) and the TRIPs agreement.

Since the EU and the North American states all are members of the WTO, transatlantic trade relations are governed by WTO principles: MFN treatment, national treatment, etc. Having an international regime does not hinder trade conflicts. As a matter of fact, there have been a number of transatlantic trade conflicts, some referred to as trade wars, through the years, starting with a chicken war (1963-64), relatively soon after the creation of the EEC in 1958 (Piening 1997). Bilateral negotiations are one way of dealing with trade conflicts. Another is dispute settlement through GATT/WTO, and this road has become more common in recent years, especially after a strengthening of dispute settlement under the WTO.

EU Policies and Decision Making in External Economic Relations

The EU's latest constitutive treaty, the Lisbon Treaty, which entered into force in December 2009, includes the concept of "external action", which covers external economic relations as well as the Common Foreign and Security Policy (CFSP), which in turn includes the Common Security and Defence Policy (CSDP). The guiding idea was to bring more coherence and efficiency to the EU's external action. The treaty created the post of High Representative (HR) of the Union for Foreign Affairs and Security Policy. The HR is a vice president of the European Commission, chairs the Foreign Affairs Council, and heads the newly established European External Action Service (EEAS). The current HR is Lady Catherine Ashton. However, decision making for external economic relations and CFSP remain different, the former largely using what used to be called the Community method, while the latter remains intergovernmental. The Community method gives the Commission an exclusive right of initiative, allows for qualified majority voting (QMV) in the Council, and the European Court of Justice (ECJ) is competent to judge cases. In CFSP, the Member States remain the decisive actors, normally unanimity is required, the Commission has less influence, and the ECJ is excluded except when it comes to judging the borderline between CFSP and external economic relations (Laursen 2012).

The Common Commercial Policy

The Common Commercial Policy (CCP) was from the beginning an exclusive competence of the European Economic Community (EEC), which became part of the first pillar of the EU created by the Maastricht Treaty in 1993. The Treaty of Rome establishing the EEC in 1958 gave the Commission an exclusive right of initiative in trade policy. It established a trade policy committee (Art. 113 Committee) of senior national trade officials and included QMV in the Council of Ministers. Interestingly enough, it did not mention the European Parliament. International trade agreement negotiations would be conducted by the Commission in co-operation with the special trade policy committee on the basis of a mandate from the Council (Woolcock 2000).

Trade policy at the time basically meant trade in goods. The treaty specifically said that the CCP "shall be based on uniform principles, particularly in regards to changes in tariff rates, the conclusion of tariff and trade agreements, the achievement of uniformity in measures of liberalization, export policy and measures to protect trade such as those taken in the event of dumping or subsidies" (Art. 113).

The scope of trade policy in the Treaty of Rome covered what GATT dealt with at the time. But international developments were gradually expanding the scope of international trade policy. Non-tariff barriers to trade (NTBs) got on the GATT agenda in the 1970s. The outcome was the rather weak Tokyo Codes dealing with some of these (Winham 1986). About the same time, the EEC Member States started realizing that it is not enough to abolish tariffs and QRs within the customs union to realise free internal trade. Here too, NTBs became an obstacle, which was subsequently dealt with through the Internal Market Plan in the 1980s (Young and Wallace 2000).

The founding fathers had foreseen that harmonisation of national legislation was necessary to create an internal market. The Treaty of Rome included an article that required unanimity for such harmonisation (Art. 100). It turned out that it was often impossible to reach agreement on the necessary legislation. Sometimes the ECJ stepped in and made rulings. This included the famous Casis de Dijon ruling, which established the principle of "mutual recognition" for the internal market in 1979 (Hix 2005, p. 124). Eventually, the Single European Act (SEA) in 1987 introduced a new Article 100a, which allowed for QMV, with some exemptions, to harmonise legislation. This gave European integration a new momentum in the run up to 1992, the official deadline for completing the internal market. The Commission had concluded that nearly 300 directives were necessary to realise the four freedoms of the internal market, namely free movement of goods, services, capital, and people (Young 2010).

At about the time when the SEA was negotiated, the Uruguay Round of GATT got started. The agenda now included agriculture, a sensitive topic for the EEC, services, trade related aspects of intellectual property rights (TRIPS), trade-related aspects of investment measures (TRIMS), and dispute settlements. The Common Agricultural Policy (CAP) increasingly produced a surplus that was dumped on the world market with EEC subsidies, something resented by a number of producers of agricultural products in third countries. In the end, the EU had to reform the CAP in order for the Uruguay Round to be concluded in 1993. The decisive agreement on CAP reform was reached with the United States at the Blair House in Washington in 1992, only to have France claim that the Commission had gone beyond its mandate. Subsequently, some side-payments to France had to be produced internally in the EU (Paemen and Bensch 1995).

The external dimension of the internal market was ignored by the Commission at the beginning. Trading partners, including the United States and Japan, started talking about "Fortress Europe", claiming the EEC was protectionist and inward looking. Eventually, towards the end of 1988, the Commission responded and claimed that Europe 1992 would be a World Partner (European Commission 1988). The same point was repeated by the heads of state or government when they met in the European Council at the Rhodes Summit in December 1988:

> The Single Market will be of benefit to Community and non-Community countries alike by ensuring continuing economic growth. The Internal Market will not close in on itself. Europe 1992 will be a partner and not a "Fortress Europe". The Internal Market will be a decisive factor contributing to greater liberalization in international trade on the basis of the GATT principles of reciprocal and mutually advantageous arrangements. The Community will continue to participate actively in the GATT Uruguay Round, committed as it is to strengthen the multilateral trading system. (In Laursen 1991, p. 8)[2]

The conclusions from Rhodes went on to say, *inter alia*, "The Community will continue to work closely and cooperatively with the United States to maintain and deepen the solid and comprehensive transatlantic relationship" (*ibid.*).

When the Uruguay Round was concluded, the question came up whether it was a trade agreement that the EU as such could ratify or whether the Member States had to ratify it too. The Commission sought an answer to the question from the ECJ, which determined that GATS and TRIPS were shared competences. So the agreement was a mixed agreement that also required ratification by the Member States. In the treaty reforms that followed the Uruguay Round, therefore, there were efforts to extend the definition of trade in the EU treaty to include services and intellectual property. They were included by the Treaty of Amsterdam, but decisions had to be by unanimity. The Treaty of Nice introduced QMV for services and intellectual property. However, the sensitive areas of "cultural and audiovisual services, educational services, and social and human health services" would still require unanimity (Art. 133 TEC).

The Treaty of Lisbon retains QMV for services and intellectual property and extends it to the new category of foreign direct investment (Laursen 2012). However, it retains unanimity for cultural and audiovisual services ("where these agreements risk prejudicing the Union's cultural and linguistic diversity") as well as social, education, and health services ("where these agreements risk seriously disturbing the national organisation of such services and prejudicing the responsibility of Member States to deliver them"). So, with exceptions, the recent treaty changes have enlarged the exclusive commercial policy competence of

---

[2]   Also online at <http://aei.pitt.edu/1483/1/rhodes_june_1988.pdf>. [Accessed 3 February 2012].

the EU. Finally, the Lisbon Treaty introduces the ordinary legislative procedure for commercial policy, thus giving the EP a strong role in commercial policy (Art. 207 TFEU). Making the EP a co-legislator in trade policy is one of the more important innovations of the Lisbon Treaty. It may lead to a greater concern for human and labour rights, as well as consumer protection and safety (Meunier and Nicilaïdis 2011, p. 282; Niemann 2012).

Despite having built up a pyramid of relations with third countries, including preferential treatment of neighbouring countries and former colonies in the African, Caribbean, and Pacific (ACP) countries through the Lomé Convention of 1975, now Cotonou Agreement from 2000, the EU has traditionally emphasized multilateralism and GATT/WTO treatment of at least its major industrialised trading partners. So countries like the United States and Canada were at the bottom of the hierarchy of trade preferences, based on MFN treatment and other GATT principles, but not offered preferential treatment. This may be changing now, partly because of the lack of progress in the WTO's Doha Development Round. In 2006, Trade Commissioner Peter Mandelson announced a new policy called "Global Europe", in which the possibility of more bilateral agreements, also with industrialised countries, was announced: "Our core argument is that rejection of protectionism at home must be accompanied by activism in creating open markets and fair conditions for trade abroad" (European Commission 2006, p. 6). Some of the emerging economies were seen as rather protectionist. The multilateral trading system was viewed as important, and the EU remained committed to the WTO and was working for resumed negotiations. But,

> Free Trade Agreements (FTAs), if approached with care, can build on WTO and other international rules going further and faster in promoting openness and integration, by tackling issues which are not ready for multilateral discussion and by preparing the ground for the next level of multilateral liberalisation. Many key issues, including investment, public procurement, competition, other regulatory issues and IPR [intellectual property rights] enforcement, which remain outside the WTO at this time can be addressed through FTAs. (*Ibid.*, p. 10)

The document specifically mentioned ASEAN, Korea, MERCOSUR, India, Russia, and the Gulf Co-operation Council as potential FTA partners. The North American partners were not (yet) mentioned as potential FTA partners. In a section on Transatlantic Trade and Competitiveness it was stated:

> The transatlantic trading relationship is by far the largest in the world and at the heart of the global economy. The economic gains from tackling non-traditional behind-the-border barriers are potentially significant in the EU

and US. We have been seeking to do so for some time, most recently through the Transatlantic Economic Initiative launched in 2005, and a range of regulatory dialogues. Despite some progress, this has proven to be difficult territory and further injection of momentum is necessary. (*Ibid.*, p. 12)

But no Transatlantic FTA was proposed. Soon, however, it was to get on the agenda with Canada, but not the United States. Mexico already had a kind of FTA negotiated in the late 1990s and in force since 2000.

Economic and Monetary Union

The Economic and Monetary Union (EMU) is an exclusive competence for the Member States that have adopted the single currency, the euro. EMU was an important part of the Maastricht Treaty creating the EU. There had been monetary co-operation before among EC states. The Treaty of Rome called for macro-economic co-operation, especially concerning conjunctural policy (Art. 103) and balance of payments (Art. 104) and established a Monetary Committee with advisory status (Art. 105). According to Article 104, it was up to the Member States to "pursue the economic policy needed to ensure the equilibrium of its overall balance of payments and to maintain confidence in its currency, while taking care to ensure a high level of employment and a stable level of prices".

The idea of EMU was subsequently proposed at The Hague Summit in 1969 and a plan, the Werner Plan, was worked out. It foresaw the establishment of EMU during the following decade. This was at about the time that the Breton Woods system was starting to crumble. But the Werner Plan was too ambitious at the time. Instead, some Member States in 1972 started cooperating about limiting currency fluctuations, within the "snake", limiting exchange rate fluctuations to max. ± 2.25 per cent. This co-operation had its limits and flaws, so in 1979, the European Monetary System (EMS) was initiated. EMS established an Exchange Rate Mechanism (ERM) and a European Currency Unit (ECU) based on a basket of currencies. Currency movements were limited to 2.25 per cent around parity (Hodson 2010; Verdun 2011).

EMS was successful in creating macro-economic convergence in the 1980s, and EMU got on the agenda again, as a next step. The SEA added a new Article 102a about co-operation in economic and monetary policy. It mentioned "Economic and Monetary Union" for the first time, but in a bracket. Although EMU was on the agenda, the Member States were not yet ready for treaty-based commitments. "In order to ensure the convergence of economic and monetary policies which is necessary for the further development of the Community Member States shall cooperate". The experience acquired within the EMS should be taken into account. Should institutional changes be necessary, it would require another treaty amendment, it was said. Such treaty amendment followed with the Maastricht Treaty. In the meantime, a committee chaired by Commission President Jacques Delors had prepared a report in 1988, which outlined three phases towards EMU. These phases became part of the Maastricht Treaty. The third phase saw the creation of the European Central Bank (ECB) and the introduction of the common currency, the euro, from 1999.

To qualify for taking part in the euro, the Member States had to fulfil certain so-called convergence criteria:

- *Price stability*: Inflation rate may not be higher than 1.5 per cent of the average inflation rate of the three best performing Member States.

- *Sound public finance*: The government deficit may not exceed 3 per cent of the GDP.

- *Sustainable public finance*: The government debt may not exceed 60 per cent of GDP.

- *Durable convergence*: Nominal long-term interest rate may not be higher than 2 per cent of the average of the three best performing Member States in terms of price stability.

- *Exchange rate stability*: Observance of normal fluctuation margins in the European Exchange Rate Mechanism (ERM), without devaluation for at least two years (Art. 109j and Protocol No. 6 on the Convergence criteria; Hodson 2010, p. 162).

After the entry into force of the Maastricht Treaty, the Germans, in particular, wanted to establish stricter rules for fiscal policy, which basically remained a national responsibility according to the Maastricht Treaty. Some governments hesitated, including the French government. These governments wanted to be able to use fiscal policy to create jobs, especially as they lost their monetary policy autonomy. The outcome was the adoption of the Growth and Stability Pact at the time when the negotiations of the Amsterdam Treaty were concluded in June 1997. The main elements were:

- Governments will aim to achieve a balanced budget.

- Countries with a budget deficit exceeding 3 per cent of GDP will be fined up to 0.5 per cent of GDP.

- These fines will not be applied if there are exceptional circumstances, such as a natural disaster or a decline in GDP of more than 2 per cent in one year.

- In cases where the drop in GDP is between 0.75 per cent and 2 per cent, the application of the fine will be decided by EcoFin [the Council of Economic and Finance Ministers] by a QMV.[3]

The Growth and Stability Pact was not part of the treaty but a separate resolution. Subsequently, it was complemented by two regulations (McNamara 2005). Regulations are legally binding. However, the commitments were insufficient. In connection with the economic slowdown in 2001-2, several governments started borrowing in excess of 3 per cent, including Germany and France. EcoFin failed to act on Commission recommendations. A softer version was adopted in 2005, and excessive deficit procedures against Germany and France revoked in 2007, after fiscal improvement in 2006 (Hodson 2010, pp. 172-173).

The collapse of the US sub-prime loan market in August 2007 had serious repercussions in Europe. For the first time, the euro area entered into recession, a number of European banks had to be rescued, and some national governments stepped in to assist their banks. The ECB also injected liquidity into the monetary markets, and in October 2008, the first of a number of interest cuts took place. In March 2009, a high-level group headed by Jacques de Larosière recommended major changes in the EU financial mechanisms. This led to the creation of the European Systemic Risk Board (ESRB) (Hodson 2010, pp. 176-178).[4]

But that was not the end of the story. The sovereign debt crisis followed, especially with Greece being unable to finance or refinance its debt. This exposed the asymmetrical nature of EMU, with a centralized monetary policy and decentralized fiscal policy. To make things worse, the Maastricht Treaty had a no-bailout clause (Art. 104b in the Maastricht Treaty, now Art. 125 TFEU), so rules had to be bent to assist Greece, but the situation was further complicated by strong political resentment against the southern members of the euro zone who faced the debt crisis: Portugal, Italy, Greece, and Spain (by some named the PIGS, or PIIGS, if Ireland is included). The idea behind the no-bailout clause was to avoid so-called "moral hazard", i.e., a temptation to engage in imprudent fiscal policies (Verhelst 2011, pp. 9-10).

A rescue package of €750 billion was approved by EcoFin in May 2010 through the new temporary European Financial Stability Facility

---

[3] Additional information at: <http://europa.eu/legislation_summaries/economic_and_monetary_affairs/stability_and_growth_pact/l25021_en.htm>. [Accessed 18 February 2012].

[4] The ESRB website: <http://www.esrb.europa.eu/home/html/index.en.html>. [Accessed 19 February 2012].

(EFSF).[5] On 16 December 2010, the European Council agreed to amend the Lisbon Treaty to allow for the creation of a permanent bailout mechanism, the European Stability Mechanism (ESM) to replace the temporary EFSF beginning in 2013. In March 2011, the EMS was approved by the European Parliament (Hall and Barber 2010).

Another package was agreed by the euro zone leaders in October 2011, increasing the EFSF to about €1 trillion. At the same time, banks were asked to accept a 50 per cent write-off of Greek debt.[6]

To get financial help, the debt-ridden countries had to adopt austerity measures that were extremely unpopular. In the process, most of the countries changed governments, in some cases because of elections, but in the cases of Greece and Italy, the external pressure brought technocrats into the governments. The crisis of some euro zone members became a crisis for the whole euro zone; some would say the whole EU political project.

The crisis led to calls for fiscal union, where the euro zone countries would give up sovereignty over taxation and budgetary policy and accept enforcement mechanisms through the European Commission. Especially German Chancellor Angela Merkel demanded such a fiscal union. On the other hand, however, she was not willing to accept the idea of Eurobonds issued by the ECB to mutualise part of the sovereign debt. Commission President José Manuel Barroso on 21 November 2011 suggested that Eurobonds, which he called "stability bonds", could be a good way to deal with the crisis (Taylor 2011).

On 9 December 2011, the European Council again had a meeting dealing with the crisis.[7] All 17 members of the euro zone as well as most other EU Member States agreed to work out an intergovernmental treaty creating a fiscal compact. Given a veto from the British Prime Minister David Cameron, this will not be a revision of the EU treaty, but a new separate treaty.[8] In the end, it was signed by all EU Member States expect the UK and the Czech Republic on 2 March 2012 (Mahony 2012). Since the focus is on fiscal discipline, it does not help the coun-

---

5 "About EFSF", <http://www.efsf.europa.eu/about/index.htm>. [Accessed 19 February 2012].

6 "Europe's rescue plan", *The Economist*, 29 October 2011, <http://www.economist.com/node/21534849>. [Accessed 18 February 2012].

7 For conclusions, see <http://europa.eu/rapid/pressReleasesAction.do?reference=DOC/11/8&type=HTM>. [Accessed 18 February 2012].

8 For an account of the meeting, see "Eurozone crisis live: Germany wins battle on tighter fiscal rules for the euro", <http://www.guardian.co.uk/business/2012/jan/30/debt-crisis-greece>. [Accessed 18 February 2012].

tries facing the debt crisis in the short run. So the EU still needs to do more about economic growth and job creation.

The pertinence of the euro zone crisis for transatlantic relations became clear when President Obama in his press conference on 6 October 2011 warned against European "gridlock": "The problems Europe is having today could have a very real effect on our economy at a time when it is already fragile". In a similar way, US Treasury Secretary Timothy Geithner told the US Senate Banking Committee: "Europe is so large and so closely integrated with the US and world economies that a severe crisis in Europe could cause significant damage by undermining confidence and weakening demand" (quoted from Phillips 2011).

Environmental Policy

Environmental policy is an example of a shared competence. The EU competence developed gradually through time. The founding Community treaties in the 1950s did not explicitly include provisions relating to the environment, but the treaties were sufficiently flexible for the development of an environmental policy to start early on, rather explicitly from 1972 when a summit in Paris singled out the environment as being important (Sbragia 2000). This was also the year of the UN environment conference in Stockholm. In Paris in July 1972, the EC leaders declared that particular attention should be given to the environment as a way to improve the quality of life.[9]

In 1970, in the so-called ERTA case, the ECJ had concluded that "the system of internal Community measures may not be separated from that of external relations" (quoted from Vogler 2011, p. 354). So the moment the EC/EU develops an internal competence it also has an external competence in that area.

Early developments included the EC becoming a party to the Paris Convention for the Prevention of Marine Pollution from Land-based Sources in 1975 and a contracting party to the Barcelona Convention for the Protection of the Mediterranean Sea against Pollution in 1977. The Amoco Cadiz disaster in 1978 led to an accelerated ratification of the 1973 Convention for the Prevention of Pollution from Ships (MARPOL).

Environmental policy was given an explicit treaty basis in the Single European Act (SEA) in 1987. Article 130r stated that action by the Community relating to the environment shall have the following objectives:

---

[9]   <http://europa.eu/legislation_summaries/institutional_affairs/treaties/amsterdam_treaty/a15000_en.htm>. [Accessed 18 February 2012].

(i) to preserve, protect and improve the quality of the environment;
(ii) to contribute towards protecting human health;
(iii) to ensure a prudent and rational utilization of natural resources.

And the SEA introduced the subsidiarity principle for the environment: "The Community shall take action relating to the environment to the extent to which the objectives referred to in paragraph 1 can be attained better at Community level than at the level of the individual Member States' (Art. 130 r (4)).

According to Article 130s of the SEA, environmental legislation would require unanimity in the Council. However, if the legislation was part of harmonisation of domestic legislation to realize the internal market, the use of a QMV was possible (Art. 100a).

The Maastricht Treaty subsequently strengthened environmental policy in the treaty. As a general rule it was moved to QMV. However unanimity still applied to sensitive areas:

– provisions primarily of a fiscal nature;

– measures concerning town and country planning, land use with the exception of waste management and measures of a general nature, and management of water resources;

– measures significantly affecting a Member State's choice between different energy sources and the general structure of its energy supply (Art. 130s(2)).

Given the shared nature of environmental competences, international negotiations can be complicated. They follow the treaty provisions on international agreements. The old Article 300 TEC, now Article 218 TFEU (Lisbon) applies: QMV in Council, EP consultation, co-decision or consent, depending on the issue. The Commission gets a mandate to negotiate. But separate Commission and Member State delegations take part in international negotiations, and each can speak within its sphere of competence (usually the presidency for the Member States, sometimes also for Commission). Much depends on the leadership role of the presidency.

In recent years, the EU has especially been actively involved in climate policy. The UN Framework Convention on Climate Change, 1992, led to the Kyoto Protocol in 1997. The EU played an important role in getting sufficient ratifications to the protocol. It entered into force 2004. It provided for a 5.2 per cent reduction in developed world of "greenhouse gases" (especially carbon dioxide). The EU commitment was 8 per cent (to be shared unevenly among the Member States). The US commitment was 7 per cent, and Japan's 6 per cent. Subsequently, the Bush administration reneged on the US commitment in 2001 (Bretherton and Vogler 2006, p. 108).

In recent efforts to renew the Kyoto Protocol, the EU has so far been less successful. The global summit meeting in Copenhagen in December 2009 ended with a disappointing result seen from the EU perspective. US President Barack Obama turned up in Copenhagen and spoke mostly with the Chinese and other leaders from BRIC countries. The fact that the EU was represented by the Commission President Barroso, the Swedish President in Office Reinfeldt, as well as national leaders, including those representing France, Germany, and the UK, did not make the situation easier (Vogler 2011, pp. 370-73).

Towards Stronger Transatlantic Regimes?

There are now ongoing negotiations between the EU and Canada about a Comprehensive Economic and Trade Agreement (CETA) which could change that.[10] And Mexico signed a trade agreement with the EU in the late 1990s. Should the negotiations with Canada succeed, the question will be, what about the United States? And if the EU and the United States were to start negotiating an FTA, the next question would be: How would that affect the multilateral trade regimes?

EU-US Relations[11]

The United States has traditionally been the EU's largest trading partner, and there are important flows of Foreign Direct Investments (FDI) both ways. This has created a high degree of interdependence between the two sides of the Atlantic. Together the EU and the US account for about 40 per cent of world trade.

US-EU trade relations have gone through a number of disputes since the early 1960s. An early dispute was the famous Chicken War, 1963-64. A more recent conflict was the one concerning European subsidies to Airbus, 1986-92. A dispute about hormones in beef has been running since 1987, with WTO dispute settlement decisions siding with the US and Canada. Sometimes, the United States threatened to use Section 301 of the US Trade Act, which allowed the US to use unilateral action outside GATT in response to unfair trade practice. In some cases, GATT/WTO panels have contributed to the settlement of trade disputes (Piening 1997, pp. 105-108). A long running conflict about bananas was

---

[10] For a listing of EU external relations legislation affecting North America, see: <http://eur-lex.europa.eu/en/legis/latest/chap114040.htm>. [Accessed 12 February 2012].

[11] This section partly relies on the introductory chapter in Laursen 2009.

eventually solved in 2001 with the EU losing WTO cases finding the EU's preferential treatment of bananas from the ACP countries in violation of GATT (BBC News 2001).

During the 1990s, there were several efforts to institutionalise EU-US relations. In 1990, the EU and the US agreed on a Transatlantic Declaration (TAD). It was complemented with a New Transatlantic Agenda (NTA) signed in Madrid in December 1995. The NTA itself was formulated in very general terms, mentioning four areas of co-operation: peace and democracy, global challenges, world trade, and bridges across the Atlantic. The section on "contributing to the expansion of world trade and closer economic relations" referred to strengthening the multilateral trading system, implementing the Uruguay Round results, and completing unfinished business – in particular, telecommunications and maritime services (Piening 1997, pp. 108-112).

Discussions about a more formalized relationship between the EU and the US has had relatively limited results so far. Proposals for transatlantic free trade have come up against protectionist forces on both sides as well as a feeling that transatlantic relations should not undermine the multilateral system. A Commission proposal for a New Transatlantic Marketplace (NTM), which would create free trade in services and abolish industrial tariffs by 2010, ran into stiff French opposition at a Council meeting in April 1998. The US wanted NTM talks to include agricultural subsidies and audio-visual trade, both very sensitive issues in France (Smith and Steffenson 2011).

Instead, the EU-US summit in London in May 1998 adopted a joint statement on a Transatlantic Economic Partnership (TEP), the purpose of which was to intensify and extend co-operation in the fields of trade and investment (Smith and Steffenson 2011).[12] In the multilateral area, regular dialogue was foreseen. The bilateral agenda included regulatory co-operation, mutual recognition, alignment of standards and regulatory requirements, consumer product safety, services, procurement, etc. The list suggests the importance of behind-the-border issues in the relations among industrialized countries.

In 2007, a Transatlantic Economic Council (TEC) was created to accelerate government-to-government co-operation with the aim of advancing transatlantic economic integration.[13] According to an EU source, the TEC brings "together governments, the business community and consumers to work on key areas where greater regulatory conver-

[12] <http://ec.europa.eu/external_relations/us/docs/trans_econ_partner_11_98_en.pdf>. [Accessed 11 February 2012].
[13] <http://ec.europa.eu/enterprise/international_relations/cooperating_governments/usa/usa_tec_en.htm >. [Accessed 11 February 2012].

gence can reap rewards on both side of the Atlantic".[14] Clearly, the main agenda points in EU-US relations concern NTBs. It has been estimated in a study carried out for the European Commission that the United States benefits from abolishing NTBs could be €41 billion annually, and the EU benefits could be €122 billion annually.[15]

EU-Canadian Relations[16]

The early period of European-Canadian relations, at the start of the European integration process, is sometimes called the period of indifference. European integration in the 1950s created some unease in Canada because of the Canadian preference for North Atlantic free trade (Muirhead 1992, Ch. 6). The fact that Canada's most important trading partner in Europe, the United Kingdom, was not a member of the European Community at the beginning eased the Canadian situation. Although the United Kingdom first applied for membership in the European Economic Community (EEC) in 1961, the bid for membership was vetoed by General de Gaulle in 1963 and again in 1967. UK negotiations had the Canadian government of Prime Minister John Diefenbaker very worried. What would happen to the Commonwealth's preferences?

The United Kingdom finally joined in 1973. Before then, another event was to influence Canadian thinking, the so-called Nixon shocks in 1971, when the US government put a 10 per cent surcharge on imports and made no exemption for Canada. Canadian politicians began considering how to diversify trade in order to become less dependent on the United States. Three options were discussed in 1972 (Potter 1999, pp. 35-36). The first option was to do nothing and resign to "continentalism", the term used for developing relations first of all with the United States. The second option considered was to embrace continentalism and seek more integration with the United States. The third option was to diversify trade using the EC as a counterweight. It was supported by the government of Pierre Trudeau during the 1970s.

Since 1972, when the EC enlargement was confirmed, there have been high-level bilateral consultations between the EC and Canada. Since 1973, Canada has had an ambassador to the EC, and since 1974, parliamentarians have met regularly. Since 1976, Canada has had a

---

[14] *EU Focus*, December 2010, <http://www.eurunion.org/eu/images/stories/eufocus-eu-usrels-dec-2010.pdf>. [Accessed 12 February 2012].

[15] "Non-Tariff Measures in EU-US Trade and Investment – An Economic Analysis", <http://trade.ec.europa.eu/doclib/docs/2009/december/tradoc_145613.pdf>. [Accessed 12 February 2012].

[16] This section partly relies on Laursen 2010.

Framework Agreement for Commercial and Economic Cooperation with the EC.[17] It created what was called a contractual link. It confirmed the MFN treatment and spoke in general terms about commercial and economic co-operation. Institutionally, it created a joint co-operation committee (JCC) to "promote and keep under review the various commercial and economic co-operation activities envisaged" The JCC would normally meet at least once a year. (Interestingly, the United States did not get a similar contractual link with the EC at the time.) But the outcome was modest (Rempel 1996, Ch. 5).

Given the meagre results of the third option, the second option, continentalism, increased in importance. In the 1980s, the government of Brian Mulroney promoted the Canada-US Free Trade Agreement (1988), and then, in 1993, it was expanded to include Mexico, to form the North American Free Trade Area (NAFTA). These developments, of course, further increased Canada's trade dependence on its southern neighbours.

In the late 1980s and the 1990s, the internal market plan in Europe affected EU-Canada relations as the creation of the customs union had done at the beginning, but it actually affected FDI flows more than trade. A number of Canadian companies, especially the bigger ones, made important investments in Europe at this point.

At the end of the Cold War, the idea of free trade was again promoted by some Canadian politicians, and the Americans also became interested in developing relations with the EC. In both cases, the new interest led to a Declaration on Transatlantic Relations (TAD), which introduced increased policy consultation and co-ordination and further developed the institutional framework. The Canadian TAD began by adding summit meetings between the prime minister of Canada on one side and the president of the European Council and the president of the European Commission on the other. However, the TAD was vague on specifics.[18]

Later in 1996, a joint political declaration and an Action Plan were adopted. The objective was to strengthen bilateral relations and to enhance economic and security co-operation. Although the Action Plan dealt with a number of issues, including new trade policy issues, such as the environment, investment, competition, labour standards, and intel-

---

[17] For text, see: <http://eur-lex.europa.eu/LexUriServ/LexUriServ.do?uri=CELEX: 21976A0706%2801%29:EN:NOT>. [Accessed 11 February 2012].

[18] For text, see: <http://eeas.europa.eu/delegations/canada/eu_canada/political_relations /bilateral_agreements/1990_declaration/index_en.htm>. [Accessed 12 February 2012].

lectual property rights, commitments were not very specific.[19] The economic section mentions the negotiation of a trade and investment enhancement agreement and the development of a voluntary framework for regulatory co-operation.[20]

In January 2007, Premier Jean Charest of Quebec spoke out in favor of an FTA with the EU. At the time, the EU Member States were divided. But a joint study by the European Commission and the government of Canada, which was published before the EU-Canada summit in Quebec City in October 2008, suggested important gains for both sides by addressing tariff barriers and nontariff barriers, including discriminatory regulations and standards, as well as liberalizing trade in services (Canada and European Union 2009). The summit meeting, therefore, agreed to explore the idea of a "stronger, ambitious and balanced economic partnership".[21] The following EU-Canada summit in Prague, on May 6, 2009, then decided to launch negotiations towards a "comprehensive economic partnership agreement".[22] These negotiations are still ongoing.

EU-Mexican Relations

Mexico got a trade agreement with the EEC in 1975. It was adapted in 1989, and a new one was signed in 1991 but was still only a trade cooperation agreement (Sberro 1999). After two years of negotiations, Mexico entered a so-called Global Agreement with the EU in 1997.[23] The full name is Economic Partnership, Political Coordination and Comprehensive Agreement between the European Community and its Member States, of the one part, and the United States of Mexico, of the other part. Since it was a mixed agreement, going beyond trade, it also involved the Member States as parties. The very first article committed the parties to fundamental human rights, a conditionality clause now becoming standard in EU agreements with third states, something Mexico was not so happy about. The agreement included political cooperation, but from the perspective of this book, a central objective was

---

[19] For text, see: <http://eeas.europa.eu/delegations/canada/eu_canada/political_relations /bilateral_agreements/1996_action_plan/index_en.htm>. [Accessed 11 February 2012].

[20] For text, see: <http://eeas.europa.eu/canada/docs/partnership_agenda_en.pdf>. [Accessed 12 February 2012].

[21] See: <http://eeas.europa.eu/canada/sum10_08/index_en.htm>. [Accessed 11 February 2012].

[22] See: <http://europa.eu/rapid/pressReleasesAction.do?reference=IP/09/701&format =HTML&aged=0&language=EN&guiLanguage=en>. [Accessed 11 February 2012].

[23] For text, see: <http://eur-lex.europa.eu/LexUriServ/LexUriServ.do?uri=CELEX: 22000A1028%2801%29:EN:NOT>. [Accessed 11 February 2012].

to "establish a framework to encourage the development of trade in goods and services, including a bilateral and preferential, progressive and reciprocal liberalisation of trade in goods and services, taking into account the sensitive nature of certain products and service sectors and in accordance with the relevant WTO rules" (Art. 4). Notice the word "preferential". A Joint Council was established to

decide on the arrangements and timetable for a bilateral, progressive and reciprocal liberalisation of tariff and non-tariff barriers to trade in goods, in accordance with the relevant WTO rules, in particular Article XXIV of the General Agreement on Tariffs and Trade (GATT), and taking account of the sensitive nature of certain products (Art. 5).

The Global Agreement entered into force in 2000. Article XXIV is the one authorizing FTAs.

As a result of the Global Agreement, Mexican industrial products have had free access to the EU market since 2003, and EU products have had free access to the Mexican market since 2007.[24] By being a comprehensive agreement, the scope went beyond the WTO. It included the so-called Singapore issues of investment, competition, transparency and trade facilitation (Ciambur n.d.).

No doubt Mexico's participation in NAFTA was one of the reasons for the EU to seek closer relations with Mexico. Trade diversification was important for Mexico, and Europe could be used as a counterweight to the United States (Sberro 1999). For the EU, Mexico's proximity to the US was attractive, and European investments in Mexico could be a way to gain access to the US market. Further, the agreement included EU access to public procurement and services in Mexico on conditions similar to NAFTA conditions. Concerning the timing, it is also worth remembering that 1994 was the year of the Summit of the Americas where a Free Trade area in the Americas was proposed (FTAA) (Dominguez 2006).

The latest development in EU-Mexican relations followed in 2008, when the EU and Mexico established a Strategic Partnership. The agenda is rather broad:

1. Political issues, such as multilateralism, democracy, human rights, rule of law, cultural dialogue, Latin America, regional integration, Rio Group;

2. Security issues, such as the fight against terrorism, organised crime, drug and human trafficking;

---

[24] "The EU's External Relations with Latin America", <http://oui-iohe.org/blogoui/en/2010/10/29/essential-reference-the-eu%E2%80%99s-external-relations-with-latin-america/>. [Accessed 11 February 2012].

3. Environmental issues, such as climate change, natural disasters, fight against overexploitation of fish stocks;

4. Socio-economic issues, such as development policy, investment and social responsibility, innovation and intellectual property rights, open markets, social policies, decent work/social protection, migration, poverty, global macro-financial stability, good governance in the tax area, energy security, sustainability and improved efficiency, food prices.[25]

In 2010, the parties adopted a Joint Executive Plan of the Strategic Partnership. Again, the broad agenda is clear. The section on trade is relatively short. It refers to the trade part of the Global Agreement as an FTA and claimed that it "has led to a major increase in trade and investment flows in both directions, making the European Union Mexico's second largest trading partner" (p. 18).

Maybe it should be added here that the United States and Canada are also considered strategic partners of the EU, a concept that is still not very well-defined.

Overview of Book Chapters

In the chapter that follows this introductory chapter, former US Congressman Joseph J. DioGuardi warns about the looming crisis. Focussing at the outset on the United States, he argues that accumulated debt has made the situation financially unsustainable. He partly blames inadequate accounting principles used in the US budget process but also efforts by politicians to disguise deficit spending to get re-elected. DioGuardi sees an urgent need to reduce federal spending, but getting the bipartisan compromise needed will be difficult in an election year. Turning to Europe, there too he finds a debt crisis of enormous proportions. When we learned in the spring of 2011 that Greece's debt equalled 150 per cent of its GDP, the problem became very clear. But several other EU Member States face sustainability problems.

The next chapters also deal with issues of economic challenges and governance in Europe and the United States.

Ferran Brunet argues that both the United States and the EU face the challenges of financial stabilization and structural reforms. In the US case, there is a twin deficit: fiscal and current accounts deficits. In the EU case, there is a quadruple deficit, adding what he calls an employment deficit and an economic governance deficit. Unemployment rose

---

[25] For more information, see: <http://eeas.europa.eu/delegations/mexico/eu_mexico/political_relations/strategic_partnership/index_en.htm >. [Accessed 11 February 2012].

on both sides of the Atlantic after the financial crisis started in the United States in 2007 and reached Europe in 2010. In some European countries, extremely high levels of unemployment were reached, and the EU economic governance system can be cumbersome and inefficient. Structural reforms of the labour markets in many European countries are urgently needed to increase competitiveness. Growth levels have been very low, if not negative. And the macro-economic convergence between the two sides of the Atlantic and among EU countries that existed until the 1990s has stopped. Especially among the euro zone countries, gaps have been increasing, and the various measures introduced to deal with the problems have so far been inadequate.

Priyan Nandita Pooran looks at the reforms introduced in the United States and the EU to deal with systemic risk in response to the financial crises. It was realised on both sides of the Atlantic that systemic risk assessment and monitoring should play a greater role in the future to assure financial stability. On the EU side, the institutional innovation was the European Systemic Risk Board (ESRB), under the auspices of and with the logistical support of the ECB. It is a component of the wider European System of Financial Supervision (ESFS), which came into force in December 2010. It was largely based on the so-called De Larosière Report issued in February 2009, subsequently endorsed by the Commission and European Council in May 2009. The ESRB can issue recommendations and warnings, which are nonbinding. In the United States, the Wall Street Reform and Consumer Protection Act 2010 – also known as the Dodd Frank Law – was passed and signed into law in July 2010. It set up the Financial Stability Oversight Council (FSOC) with a number of functions and tasks designed to monitor financial institutions and make recommendations to reduce risks. The US reform also included the establishment of a new Bureau of Consumer Financial Protection.

The following chapters deal with trade issues, beginning with Maria Behren's chapter on Free Trade Agreements (FTAs) and the emergence of what she calls the transnational competitive state. Recent years have seen a strong turn to the negotiation of bilateral FTAs and both the United States and the EU have taken part in this process, especially negotiating FTAs with developing countries, where they have exploited "asymmetrical interdependence" to their advantage. Using a neo-Gramscian perspective, it is argued that the two big trade policy actors gain economic political power, institutional power, and legitimacy at home through the support from civil society. Their power position allows them to protect non-competitive domestic sectors (such as agriculture) by exclusion from the agreements, but at the same time they can force developing countries to accept the inclusion of labour rights and environmental provisions and open up these countries for foreign investments and access to public procurement. Liberal institutionalism cannot explain these turns in global trade policy. But given the high transaction costs of the many FTAs – including administration of complicated rules of origin – the world may eventually turn to a multilateral approach again.

In the following chapter, Robert Finbow looks at the Comprehensive Economic and Trade Agreement (CETA) currently being negotiated between the EU and Canada. In this case, we are dealing with two industrialised actors, so the degree of asymmetry presumably is less, than say, between the EU and the Mediterranean non-Member States or the African, Caribbean, and Pacific (ACP) states taking part in the Cotonou agreement. However, Finbow suggests that in the EU-Canada relationship, the EU is the stronger partner, possibly allowing the EU to push changes on Canada that could affect social and environmental policies. It is argued that the EU has become more commercial and less social in its policies towards third countries in recent years. A fear is expressed that Canada may benefit in areas of the old economy (fossil fuels, agriculture, aerospace, chemicals, fish, automobiles, and car parts) while the EU would benefit in the areas of the new economy (including high technology, investments, intellectual property, government procurement, and services). A number of critics have pointed to these problems, but it seems that the Canadian government, which now has a parliamentary majority, is rather determined to move ahead. And even if some European MEPs are concerned about seal hunting, oil sands, and other existing irritants, the EP does have a pro-trade majority.

Nanette Neuwahl and Nicolas Vermeys look at a particular aspect of CETA, namely e-commerce. The chapter situates e-commerce in the wider perspective of CETA. There are three main aspects of e-commerce that have to be dealt with, namely, privacy, information security, and consumer protection. Based on various documents, including a leaked draft from 2010, the authors discuss these issues. We learn about existing legislation in Canada and the EU as well as past co-operation. It seems that protection of privacy and personal information are reasonably well-covered, while the conduct of secure electronic commerce is a more difficult issue, involving issues of authentication, certification, use of electronic signatures, and co-operation to combat illegal activities. Consumer protection especially includes online dispute resolution, which the EU has dealt with, and there are also OECD guidelines. Further, there is ongoing work in wider international fora, such as the United Nations Commission on International Trade Law (UNCITRAL). Another issue is spam, where the EU developed legislation relatively early, followed by Canada recently. Overall, the authors see the CETA chapter on e-commerce as a solid achievement. It is expected to consolidate and reinforce current practices.

In the following chapter, Roberto Dominguez looks at what he calls the other transatlantic relationship, namely EU-Latin American relations. He does so at three different levels: region to region, EU to sub-region and EU to individual states. In the inter-regional section, he mainly looks at the biregional summits that have taken place regularly since 1999. Overall, it seems that the outcomes have been rather limited. Relations with sub-regions, such as MERCOSUR, the Andean Community, and Central America have had relatively high priority for the EU. But efforts to export the EU model has had limited results. Efforts to negotiate inter-regional agreements took place with MERCOSUR from 1999-2004 and resumed in 2010. Negotiations with the Andean group started in 2007 but were unproductive at the inter-regional level due to disagreements among the Andean countries. In the end, separate bilateral FTAs were reached with Colombia and Peru in March 2011. Negotiations with the Central American group starting in 2007 did produce an Association Agreement in 2010. In the section on relations with individual countries, the focus is on Mexico, Chile, and Brazil, with Mexico getting an Association Agreement in 2000 and Chile in 2005. Brazil, which is the biggest member of MERCOSUR, does not have a similar agreement, but due to its status as a BRIC country, it was included in the EU's group of strategic partners in 2007. Mexico also became a strategic partner of the EU in 2008. Interestingly, EU efforts to negotiate FTAs with Latin American groups or countries largely followed previous steps in that direction by the United States.

The following two chapters look at aspects of competition policy, increasingly on the international trade agenda. Declan Walsh looks at antitrust policy on the two sides of the Atlantic and co-operation among competition authorities. There are divergent approaches to anti-cartel policy in the United States and the EU but also a fair amount of co-operation given the global effect of major cartels. Both sides agree on the importance of investigating cartels and sanctioning them. Cartels are outlawed by both US and EU law, but cartels can be sophisticated when it comes to avoidance of detection. This makes co-ordinated investigations particularly important. Some differences when it comes to sanctions are due to cultural differences. In the EU, sanctions are civil in nature and subject to public enforcement. In the United States, public enforcement may lead to criminal convictions, and private actions for damages are common. The possibility that the EU will move in the direction of the US approach is there, but it remains to be seen how far. At the same time, global co-operation is expected to increase.

Next, Christian Marfels and James Sawler compare merger control policies in the EU and Canada. In both cases, it took quite some time to develop merger policies. We get well into the 1980s before merger control is strengthened as part of the wider competition policies. The authors trace similarities and differences in merger control policy in Canada and the EU. The argument is that differences can be costly. These costs may become more visible if the CETA is concluded successfully.

Rafael Leal-Arcas then looks at climate change policy, focussing on the three largest emitters of CO_2, the United States, China, and the EU. In this area, the Westphalian state system is challenged. The issue is: Can the world agree on limiting greenhouse gas (GHG) emissions sufficiently? During the Clinton administration, the United States signed on to the Kyoto Protocol, but the George W. Bush administration did not seek ratification of the agreement. The EU went ahead together with some other industrialised states and ratified. Now the challenge is bringing the United States and the developing countries, in particular, the emerging economies like China and India, into a new agreement. Hope that the Obama administration would change US policy was dashed at the Copenhagen climate summit in 2009, which only produced a non-binding agreement. China has, however, turned to more green policies domestically, partly because of the extreme pollution in major cities and health costs associated with pollution. To get an agreement involving both developed and developing countries, equity concerns will have to be addressed.

Next, Anders Hayden asks why Canada and the EU attack each other's green-energy initiatives. The context is international climate policy. The EU has tried to be an international leader while Canada has been a laggard. Behind this is the fact that Canada has huge oil reserves in tar sand in Alberta. But the exploitation of this reserve is heavy on CO_2 emissions, a problem that modern technology cannot solve, at least in the short run. The EU has, therefore, been very critical of Canadian policy. Canada has responded by lobbying European institutions. The issue gets linked to the CETA negotiations, creating splits in the European Commission between commissioners responsible for climate and trade. Canada also finds more sympathy in the UK and the Netherlands, home to BP and Shell, than in most other Member States, which have embraced ecological modernization. In parallel, Ontario's Green Energy Act (GEA) has also become an issue, not because of its purpose to create green energy jobs and protect the environment but because it has local content requirements. Both the EU and Japan have taken the GEA to the WTO. Anders Hayden rightly notices that green policies in Europe have also had strong government support, including, for instance, high subsidies in former.

In the concluding chapter, the editor presents a broad analytical overview of the current situation and tries to look towards the future.

*   *

*

The complex nature of economic relations across the Atlantic Ocean clearly emerges from the above studies. But the bottom line is that both sides have common interests in promoting trade, currency stability, financial sustainability, and a clean environment. Building good institutions to facilitate those goals is part of the challenge for the governments in the region. As the largest and most powerful actor, it especially falls on the United States to exercise such leadership. But in economic areas the EU is a giant, too. So we also need EU leadership, which is more difficult to get since the EU is a rather decentralized polity and none of its leaders, the Commission President, the European Council President, or the High Representative of the Union for Foreign Affairs and Security Policy have the legitimacy provided by popular elections. Nor has the EU introduced a parliamentary system like the Canadian one.

References

BBC News (2001). "EU and US end banana war", 11 April. <http://news. bbc.co.uk/2/hi/business/1271969.stm> [Accessed 3 March 2012].

Baldwin, David (ed.) (1993). *Neorealism and Neoliberalism: The Contemporary Debate*. New York: Columbia University Press.

Bretherton, Charlotte and John Vogler (2006). *The European Union as a Global Actor.* 2nd ed. London: Routledge.

Canada and European Union (2009). *Assessing the Cost and Benefits of a Closer EU-Canada Economic Partnership.* A Joint Study by the European Commission and the Government of Canada. <http://www.international. gc.ca/trade-agreements-accords-commerciaux/assets/pdfs/EU-CanadaJoint Study-en.pdf>. [Accessed 11 February 2012].

Ciambur, Corina (n.d.). "The EU-Mexico Free Trade Agreement: Stepping Stone or Stumbling Bloc?" <http://www.atlantic-community.org/app/ webroot/files/articlepdf/EU-Mexico-SteppingStone-StumblingBloc.pdf>. [Accessed 11 February 2012].

Croci, Osvaldo and Livianna Tossutti (2009). "Canada and the European Union. A Story of Unrequited Attraction", in Finn Laursen (ed.), *The EU in the Global Political Economy.* Brussels: P.I.E. Peter Lang, pp. 149-176.

Dominguez, Roberto (2006). "New Generation of Agreements between the EU and Latin America: The cases of Mexico and Chile", in *Jean Monnet/Robert*

Schuman Paper Series, Vol. 6, No. 13 (June). Miami: Miami European Union Centre.

European Commission (1988). "Europe 1992: Europe World Partner", in *Europe Documents*, No. 1530 (25 October).

European Commission (2006). Global Europe Competing in the World: A Contribution to the EU's Growth and Jobs Strategy. Brussels. <http://trade.ec.europa.eu/doclib/docs/2006/october/tradoc_130376.pdf>. [Accessed 3 February 2012].

Gilpin, Robert (1987). *The Political Economy of International Relations*. Princeton: Princeton University Press.

Gilpin, Robert (2001). *Global Political Economy: Understanding the International Economic Order*. Princeton: Princeton University Press.

Hall, Ben and Tony Barber (2010). "Europe agrees rescue package", in *Financial Times*, May 10. <http://www.ft.com/intl/cms/s/0/f96a6c14-5b48-11df-85a3-00144feab49a.html#axzz1mlmDTh00>. [Accessed 18 February 2012].

Hix, Simon (2005). *The Political System of the European Union*. 2nd ed. Houndmills: Palgrave Macmillan.

Hodson, Dermot (2010). "Economic and Monetary Union: An Experiment in New Modes of EU Policy-Making", in Helen Wallace, Mark A. Pollack, and Alasdair R. Young (eds.), *Policy-Making in the European Union*. 6th ed. Oxford: Oxford University Press, pp. 158-180.

Jackson, Robert and Georg Sørensen (1999). *Introduction to International Relations*. Oxford: Oxford University Press.

Keohane, Robert O. (1984). *After Hegemony: Cooperation and Discord in the World Political Economy*. Princeton: Princeton University Press.

Keohane, Robert O. (ed.) (1986). *Neorealism and Its Critics*. New York: Columbia University Press.

Keohane, Robert O. and Joseph S. Nye Jr. (1977). *Power and Interdependence: World Politics in Transition*. Boston: Little, Brown.

Krasner, Stephen D. (1982). "Structural Causes and Regime Consequences: Regimes as Intervening Variables", in *International Organization*, Vol. 36, pp. 185-205.

Krasner, Stephen D. (ed.) (1983). *International Regimes*. Ithaca, NY: Cornell University Press.

Laursen, Finn (ed.) (1991). *Europe 1992: World Partner? The Internal Market and the World Political Economy*. Maastricht: European Institute of Public Administration.

Laursen, Finn (ed.) (1995). *The Political Economy of European Integration*. The Hague: Kluwer Law International.

Laursen, Finn (ed.) (2009). *The EU in the Global Political Economy*. Brussels: P.I.E. Peter Lang.

Laursen, Finn (2010). "EU-Canada Relations: A Case of Mutual Neglects?", in Federiga Bindi (ed.), *The Foreign Policy of the European Union: Assessing*

Europe's Role in the World. Washington, DC: Brookings Institution Press, pp. 230-238.

Laursen, Finn (ed.) (2012). *The Lisbon Treaty: Institutional Choices and Implementation.* Farnham: Ashgate.

Little, Richard (2005). "International Regimes", in John Baylis and Steve Smith (eds.), *The Globalization of World Politics. An introduction to International Relations.* 3rd ed. Oxford: Oxford University Press, pp. 369-386.

McNamara, Kathleen (2005). "Economic and Monetary Union", in Helen Wallace, William Wallace, and Mark A. Pollack (eds.), *Policy-Making in the European Union.* 5th ed. Oxford: Oxford University Press, pp. 141-160.

Mahony, Honor (2012). "Twenty five EU leaders sign German-model fiscal treaty", in EUobserver, 2 March. <http://euobserver.com/843/115460>. [Accessed 3 March 2012].

Meunier, Sophie and Kalypso Nicolaïdis (2011). "The European Union as a Trade Power", in Christopher Hill and Michael Smith (eds.), *International Relations and the European Union.* 2nd ed. Oxford: Oxford University Press, pp. 275-298.

Moravcsik, Andrew (2010). "US-EU Relations: Putting the Bush Years in Perspective", in Federiga Bindi (ed.), *The Foreign Policy of the European Union: Assessing Europe's Role in the World.* Washington, DC: Brookings Institution Press, pp. 203-208.

Muirhead, B.W. (1992). *The Development of Postwar Canadian Trade Policy: The Failure of the Anglo-European Option.* Montreal: McGill-Queen's University Press.

Niemann, Arne (2012). "The Common Commercial Policy: From Nice to Lisbon", in Finn Laursen (ed.), *The EU's Lisbon Treaty: Institutional Choices and Implementation.* Farnham: Ashgate, pp. 205-227.

Paemen, Hugo and Alexandra Bensch (1995). *From the GATT to the WYO: The European Community in the Uruguay Round.* Leuven: Leuven University Press.

Phillips. Leigh (2011). "US warns against European 'gridlock'", in <http://euobserver.com/19/113853>. [Accessed 18 February 2012].

Piening, Christopher (1997). *Global Europe: The European Union in World Affairs.* Boulder: Lynne Rienner Publishers.

Potter, Evan (1999). *Trans-Atlantic Partners: Canadian Approaches to the European Union.* Montreal: McGill-Queen's University Press.

Rempel, Roy (1996). *Counterweights: The Failure of Canada's German and European Policy 1955-1995.* Montreal: McGill-Queen's University Press.

Sberro, Stephan (1999). "Mexico/EU relationship, bridge or exception in North America?" Paper for ECSA Conference, Pittsburgh, June. <http://aei.pitt.edu/2377/1/002913_1.PDF>. [Accessed 11 February 2012].

Sbragia, Alberta M. (2000). "Environmental Policy: Economic Constraints and External Pressures", in Helen Wallace and William Wallace (eds.), *Policy-*

Making in the European Union. 4th ed. Oxford: Oxford University Press, pp. 293-316.

Sbragia, Alberta (2010). "The EU, the US, and trade policy: competitive inter-dependence in the management of globalization", in *Journal of European Public Policy,* 17: 3 (April), pp. 368-382.

Smith, Michael and Rebecca Steffenson (2011). "The EU and the United States", in Christopher Hill and Michael Smith (eds.), *International Relations and the European Union.* 2nd ed. Oxford: Oxford University Press, pp. 404-431.

Strange, Susan (1988). *States and Markets.* London: Pinter.

Taylor, Simon (2011). "Barroso says Eurobonds will 'be seen as natural,'" in *European Voice,* 17 November. <http://www.europeanvoice.com/article/imported/barroso-says-eurobonds-will-be-seen-as-natural-/72630.aspx>. [Accessed 18 February 2012].

Verdun, Amy (2009). "The EU as a Global Actor. The Role of EMU and the Euro", in Finn Laursen (ed.), *The EU in the Global Political Economy.* Brussels: P.I.E. Peter Lang, pp. 45-63.

Verdun, Amy (2011). "The EU and the Global Political Economy", in Christopher Hill and Michael Smith (eds.), *International Relations and the European Union.* 2nd ed. Oxford: Oxford University Press, pp. 246-274.

Verhelst, Stijn (2011). *The Reform of European Economic Governance: To-wards a Sustainable Monetary Union?* Egmont Paper 47. Brussels: Royal Institute for International Relations.

Vogler, John (2011). "The Challenge of the Environment, Energy, and Climate Change", in Christopher Hill and Michael Smith (eds.), *International Relations and the European Union.* 2nd ed. Oxford: Oxford University Press, pp. 349-379.

Walter, Andrew and Gautam Sen (2009). *Analysing the Global Political Economy.* Princeton: Princeton University Press.

Winham, G. (1986). *International Trade and the Tokyo Round Negotiation.* Princeton: Princeton University Press.

Woolcock, Stephen (2000). "European Trade Policy: Global Pressures and Domestic Constraints", in Helen Wallace and William Wallace (eds.), *Policy-Making in the European Union.* 4th ed. Oxford: Oxford University Press, pp. 373-399.

Young, Alasdair R. (2010). "The Single Market: Deregulation, Reregulation, and Integration", in Helen Wallace, Mark A. Pollack, and Alasdair R. Young (eds.), *Policy-Making in the European Union.* 6th ed. Oxford: Oxford University Press, pp. 107-131.

Young, Alasdair R. and Helen Wallace (2000). "The Single Market: A New Approach to Policy", in Helen Wallace and William Wallace (eds.), *Policy-Making in the European Union.* 4th ed. Oxford: Oxford University Press, pp. 85-114.

The Looming Crisis

The Fiscal Unsustainability of Western Governments

Joseph J. DIOGUARDI

As the first practicing certified public accountant elected to the US Congress, I have been sounding the alarm for more than two decades about the inadequate accounting principles used in the US budget process to measure annual deficits and national debt.[1] After leaving the US House of Representatives in 1989, I set up a foundation, Truth in Government, because I believe that America, along with every other country, needs an independent, oversight group to provide the real numbers when it comes to the financial results of government operations. Many governments, including the United States, do not publicize their total debt and obligations for all to see. Thankfully, in this time of economic crisis, a genuine debate is starting in the US Congress about the unmanageable increases in the annual budget deficit as a percentage of Gross Domestic Product (GDP), and, as a result, America's financial unsustainability as a nation whose economy is built much more on debt, consumption, and imports than on investment, production, and exports. Because of the current concern that major bond rating agencies could downgrade the AAA rating of US Treasury securities (one well-known rating service has done so already), members of the House and Senate (and state comptrollers) are now recognizing that the government has to consider unfunded pension liabilities and obligations for other entitlements that, in the past, were not considered to be part of the national debt. Publicly traded companies have always been required by the Securities and Exchange Commission (SEC) to calculate and report all these obligations in order to protect corporate stockholders. The question today is: Will the US government do the same to protect American taxpayers, even those in future generations?

In 1992, I published *Unaccountable Congress: It Doesn't Add Up* to make the case that there should be no double standard when it comes to federal accounting, financial management, and financial reporting. I updated and republished the book in May 2010, and I chose an apoca-

---

[1] Joseph J. DioGuardi was a member of the US House of Representatives representing New York's 20th District from 1985-1989.

lyptic-looking cover for the new edition – one that includes "a national debt card" on the backs of young people and the Capitol of the United States in flames. I wanted to draw attention to the unsustainable fiscal picture that I see emerging in the next 10 years. A partisan, uncompromising political fight on whether to raise taxes or cut spending has been raging since then. (This continuing partisan conflict took us to the edge of a shutdown of the US government during the summer of 2011 when the statutory debt ceiling for the US bonded debt of $14.3 trillion was reached.) As we go into a presidential election year in 2012, we see no resolve to do anything but political posturing on both sides of the aisle.

President Barack Obama came to office with a message of hope and change. But many Americans, both Democrat and Republican, say that he has not delivered. Out of the eighty-seven new members of Congress, seventy are either identified with the Tea Party or are fiscally conservative. The Tea Party is a new movement calling for limited government and dramatic spending cuts without raising taxes at the federal level. In order to get elected in November 2010, they promised their constituents that they would shut down the government if deficit spending and the national debt were not dramatically reduced. No one wants to see the US government shut down. Nevertheless, the United States cannot continue with current debt levels and deficit spending. Much attention has been given to the European debt crisis, but the crisis that is now looming in the United States is not disconnected from what is going on with Greece, Portugal, Italy, Spain, Ireland, and France today, and may even be worse once the real numbers are known. (Alarmingly, the US government's deficit is currently reported to be $1 trillion 300 billion for the fiscal year ending 30 September 2011. This was the third year in a row that spending exceeded revenue by more than a trillion dollars, adding to an already bloated national "bonded" debt, which is now approaching 100 per cent of US GDP.)

The current problem will only grow because the US government must raise the debt ceiling limit again in 2012 in order to keep the government going. (Under US law, when the legal borrowing limit runs out, Congress cannot spend more money until it passes a law raising the statutory debt ceiling.) In the past, Congress has not been serious about the consequences of raising the debt ceiling. Every time the government ran out of money, Congress automatically raised the debt ceiling in order to avoid any restraints on its spending and, in the process, increased the national debt without much reflection or resistance. To make matters worse, Congress only takes into consideration the bonded debt when raising the debt limit – not obligations for unfunded entitlements like Social Security and Medicare. This is also true in many other countries, and this is why we need to develop better global accounting standards for governmental entities. International accounting standards are emerging to ensure that publicly traded corporations protect the business assets of shareholders, but they have yet to emerge in the public sector. This remains a big challenge for the United States and the European Union in the future in order to gauge which countries are fiscally sustainable and can continue to borrow when funds are needed to cover a nation's annual operating budget deficit and to pay promised retirement and health care benefits, which are usually not officially recognized as part of the annual deficit or national debt.

When it comes to spending taxpayer dollars and borrowing money responsibly, most governments have a credit card mentality. Certainly the United States does, and that is why, when I first published *Unaccountable Congress: It Doesn't Add Up*, I put what I called a "congressional credit card" on the front cover. (I felt strongly that it represented a congressman's or congresswoman's plastic voting card, which is inserted into a computer terminal at the end of each row of seats in the House of Representatives in order to record a member's vote.) In one of my first speeches on the US House floor, I held up my voting card and called it "the most expensive credit card in the world" and said that every time we members use our cards in the computer terminal to vote on spending, we were raising the annual deficit and the national debt. I pointed out that a personal credit card has a limit – one that you cannot change unless you convince the bank to raise it based on objective criteria like increased personal income – while the "Congressional credit card" has no effective limit. Even in 1986, under Ronald Reagan, a president who called himself a staunch fiscal conservative, the United States had a $200 billion deficit. That is why Congress passed the "Gram Rudman" bill (H.R. 3520) in 1986, which was a formulaic approach to reduce the deficit and balance the budget during four years. When Congress was failing to reach that target in four years, they changed it to five years, and then ultimately abandoned it altogether. And during the last 40 years, the US Congress has been changing the budget process to meet the desires of politicians who want to disguise deficit spending to get re-elected, not the needs of citizens who deserve a fiscally sound and economically sustainable government.

The fiscal crisis that America is facing today is the same one that the 17 eurozone countries are facing. Politicians are controlling the budget process and under-reporting liabilities for pensions and other entitlements, passing them on to future generations. The US Congress uses what is called a "cash basis" accounting system for the budget – not generally accepted accounting principles (GAAP) that the SEC requires for publicly traded corporations. The "cash basis" of accounting is easily manipulated because one does not need to record an expense until one writes a check, not when one gets the bill. (Under GAAP, an expense must be recorded as soon as a bill is received or a liability to pay is incurred.) In an economic sense, GAAP gives a sound picture of where a government stands financially. And yet, Congress is still using the cash basis for budgeting (raising the debt ceiling whenever it needs more money to spend) and passing a huge national debt on to the next generation, with interest.

The Founding Fathers of the United States envisioned a limited federal government. Listening to the Obama administration today, one would think that the federal government created the states when, in fact, the states created the federal ten years concerns the urgent need to reduce federal spending and to decide what the role of the federal government should be today and in the future. The United States is a democracy, but it is also a republic in which each state is sovereign. But through the years, the US government has raised taxes from the states, and Washington has become the paymaster for many programs like health care, education, and retirement benefits. In the process, we have put government too far from the people, creating an inefficient and uncontrollable bureaucracy. The question now is whether we will bring government closer to the people, so we can measure how effective or inefficient government expenditures are. As a fiscal conservative, I believe in the vision that the Founding Fathers had of a smaller government in Washington, leaving it to the states (and their localities) to decide how to serve the everyday needs of the people.

On 7 April 2011, Congressman Paul Ryan, chairman of the House Budget Committee, initiated an important debate about the role of the federal government when he unveiled his budget proposal for cutting federal spending by $5.8 trillion during the next decade. Earlier, in December 2010, President Obama's Debt Commission, a bipartisan commission on fiscal responsibility and reform that was chaired by two highly regarded former senators – Alan Simpson, a Republican from Wyoming, and Erskine Bowles, a Democrat from North Carolina – put forward a plan that never even made it into the Obama administration's 2012 proposed budget. Now that Congressman Ryan, the Debt Commission, and most recently, the failed Congressional Super Committee on deficit reduction have sounded the alarm, the 2012 budget hopefully will be based on a bipartisan vision that results in a decreasing annual deficit and national debt for a fiscally sustainable America.

A bipartisan debate and compromise on government spending is important because the fast-rising national debt curve must be bent downward. As of this writing, it is projected to go dramatically upward during the next five years, further threatening the Triple-A Treasury bill and bond ratings of the United States. The projected increase in America's national debt will create such high interest expenditures that all discretionary spending in the next five to ten years will be in jeopardy. (Interest paid on the public portion of the national debt has never been as low as it is now because the Federal Reserve Bank, "the Fed", has lowered the short-term interest rate to practically zero to keep the United States from plunging into a major recession.) As soon as interest rates rise – as they are expected to do because of inflation – there will be an immediate, negative impact on the budget of the United States.

Last year, the price of cotton doubled to $1.90 a pound. The cost of food and other household staples in the United States rose steeply. The price of oil hit more than $100 a barrel, contributing to high gasoline prices at the pump. As a result, many believe that the Fed will have to increase interest rates gradually to keep inflation under control. This is what happened in the late 1970s, when President Jimmy Carter's "stagflation" (a stagnant economy with high inflation) resulted in a prime interest rate of 21 percent. The Fed will not go to this extreme, but it, nevertheless, will be forced to raise interest rates in the next five to ten years to, I believe, somewhere between 6 and 10 per cent in order to cope with the legally permitted national debt that is estimated by the Obama administration to be $20 trillion by 2017. (At the end of fiscal year 2011, the bonded debt subject to the statutory debt limit reached approximately $15 trillion.) If the interest is calculated on only the public portion of the projected national debt by 2017 (approximately 60 per cent of the total bonded debt of $20 trillion, equalling $12 trillion), the interest cost at 6 per cent would be more than $700 billion dollars and would wreak havoc on future discretionary spending for defence, education, and aid to the states. (It should be noted that the public portion of the debt does not include Treasury securities in the so-called trust funds for which interest is accrued for future payment and not paid out currently.)

The 2012 edition of the *Pocket World in Figures* published by *The Economist* lists the world's gross domestic product (GDP) at about $63 trillion or approximately $11,000 per person in 2010. Since America's GDP should approximate $15 trillion by the end of 2011, this means that the United States is responsible for about one-quarter of the sum of economic activity in the world, or about $48,000 per American. The eurozone, which now includes 17 European countries, is roughly equal to the United States in total and per person GDP. China has a GDP of approximately $5 trillion, which is now in excess of Japan's. Nevertheless, China's GDP per person is estimated at only $6,800 because of the enormity of its underutilized population.

Looking at the 10-year average annual growth rate by country through 2009, China is indexed at 10.3 per cent and India at 6.9 per cent, because both countries are trying to boost their domestic economies as well as their exports. The United States has a projected growth rate of only 2.5 per cent, although this rate is projected by many economists to increase as long as the country does not slide into a double dip recession. It should be noted that, when population growth is taken into consideration, Japan (and potentially some Western countries) has a big problem: Its population is aging and its birth rate is not increasing; thus a smaller workforce will be required to supply the pension benefits for a growing retired and elderly majority. Japan has the world's oldest population according to the 2012 edition of *The Economist's Pocket World in Figures*, and this, together with high debt levels of 200 per cent of GDP in 2010 and a weak domestic economy showing no economic growth, could result in a deflationary spiral leading to a significant economic depression.

Against the backdrop of this global perspective, the US economy plays and will continue to play an important role in the future. In June 2003, I published an article, entitled "Cooking the Nation's Books", in *The National Law Journal*. Because there are laws that affect the budget and accounting process in the United States, I wanted to have my opinions vetted by lawyers, not just by accountants. I especially wanted to make the legislative branches in the states and in Washington (where lawyers predominate) aware of the role that they have played in disguising the fiscal problems that America faces today and how they can fix them by reforming the budget process. They especially need to review the accounting principles used in the budget process to make sure that all spending and commitments to spend in the future are recognized in the annual financial statements of the US government.

One must recognize that the political parties represent very different philosophies in Washington. Liberal Democrats will say that the federal government should keep spending money in order to keep the unemployment rate down. While that may be a good thing to do initially, at what point does the nation focus on the fact that the national debt is becoming so large that just spending more and paying the interest on that debt can soon bankrupt America?

Europe is also facing a debt crisis of enormous proportions. Greece, Iceland, Ireland, and Portugal have technically defaulted on their debts. The extent of the problem was made clear when we learned in the spring of 2011 that Greece's debt equalled 150 per cent of its GDP. Meanwhile, although the United States has a recognized national debt of approximately $15 trillion, amounting to approximately 100 per cent of its GDP, the real debt is much larger. In addition, actuaries have computed unfunded pension and entitlement liabilities for the United States as follows: $8 trillion for Social Security and $37 trillion for Medicare

Parts A, B, and D. When this $45 trillion total is added to $15 trillion, the national debt of the United States is approximately $60 trillion, which is an amazing 400 per cent of America's GDP.

Whether we are talking about the European debt crisis or the US national debt, the key word is "sustainability". Are Europe and America economically sustainable? Is a country able to sustain a certain level of debt based on its economic activity? In response to these questions, Stanford University sponsored a research project that came up with a sovereign fiscal responsibility index. Compared to 34 other countries, the United States was ranked low at 28. But if the budget reforms that Congressman Ryan and President Obama's Debt Commission have recommended were implemented, the United States would be ranked at 16, as stated in the Sovereign Fiscal Responsibility Index 2011 produced by Stanford University's Public Policy and International Studies Program (see Table 1).

According to the Stanford study, there are several factors that go into determining a country's sovereign fiscal responsibility index. There is a "fiscal path", which describes how a country's debt level is managed through time. "Fiscal status" concerns the level of a nation's debt and how it is determined. And, finally, "fiscal governance" describes the financial structure of a government and its budgeting and accounting processes in order to ascertain whether a country is fiscally responsible and transparent. Australia and New Zealand, for example, are ranked number 1 and 2, respectively, because they use GAAP accounting and have financial management systems and controls that restrain unnecessary spending and borrowing. By contrast, Greece has a zero "sovereign fiscal responsibility index", and it is ranked last at 34 because it is technically in default and in need of a massive bailout. In short, Greece cannot borrow from others, is completely unsustainable as a nation, and is in dire need of massive external help and significant internal fiscal reforms.

The debate that is taking place in America about the fiscal crisis and the national debt needs to take place in every country. The United States is spending money that it does not have and borrowing from foreign countries that do not share its commitment to democracy and human rights. (Major European countries like Spain, France, and Italy are heading down the same economically disastrous path.) As a result, the United States is threatening the very foundation of its democracy and the prospects of the next generation to achieve the American dream of self-development and prosperity. That dream motivated my father to immigrate to the United States in 1929 at the age of 15 from a poor farming village in Italy. As his oldest child, I have benefitted from the opportunity America offered my father and mother. The challenge that

Americans face today is keeping the promise of America alive. That will not only be good for the future economic, political, and social sustainability of the United States but will serve as a shining example to other developed and less-developed countries around the world. I believe that this can be done only if the politicians tell the truth about what they are spending and if people learn to live within their means, work hard, and create a self-sustaining economy currently and for the future.

References

Augustine, T.J. *et al.*, under the guidance of David M. Walker (2010). *Sovereign Fiscal Responsibility Index 2011*. Stanford: Stanford University and the Comeback America Initiative. <www.tcaii.org/pefs/SFRI_Final_Report_Executive_Summary.pdf.>

DioGuardi, Joseph J. (2003). "Cooking the Nation's Books", *The National Law Journal*. 23-30 June.

DioGuardi, Joseph J. (2010). *Unaccountable Congress, It Doesn't Add Up*. Revised edition. New York: Amazon.

The Economist (2012). *Pocket World in Figures 2012 Edition*. London: Profile Books, Ltd.

Appendix

Table 1
Sovereign Fiscal Responsibility Index 2011 (Overall SFRI Rankings)

Country	Fiscal Space (% of GDP, 2010)	Fiscal Path (# of years)	Fiscal Governance (pts out of 100)	Overall Rank
Australia	168.2	40+	65.9	1
New Zealand	163.6	38.0	68.5	2
Estonia	138.1	40+	61.7	3
Sweden	153.7	40+	59.0	4
China	184.9	40+	49.4	5
Luxembourg	178.0	22.0	61.8	6
Chile	193.3	40+	45.9	7
Denmark	153.1	34.0	54.7	8
United Kingdom	90.8	27.0	66.4	9
Brazil	102.3	39.0	56.9	10
Canada	106.0	39.0	51.5	11
India	97.3	40+	56.3	12
Poland	94.9	31.0	58.0	13
Netherlands	92.7	12.0	72.3	14
Norway	171.6	22.0	47.9	15
Slovak Republic	107.7	33.0	50.9	16
Korea	124.9	40+	27.5	17
Mexico	112.1	30.0	50.7	18
Israel	113.0	40+	40.5	19
Slovenia	105.2	21.0	54.3	20
Austria	76.4	12.0	67.8	21
Finland	99.2	13.0	57.9	22
France	58.7	15.0	62.8	23
Spain	81.5	12.0	60.7	24
Germany	75.7	18.0	57.4	25
Belgium	42.3	8.0	61.2	26
Italy	17.8	7.0	59.2	27
United States	62.4	16.0	46.0	28
Hungary	53.2	12.0	46.1	29
Ireland	38.1	6.0	48.4	30
Japan*	49.0	5.0	47.2	31
Iceland**	17.1	20.0	20.2	32
Portugal	27.8	5.0	45.1	33
Greece	0.0	0.0	45.0	34

* Japan's debt rating has just been downgraded.

** Iceland has already defaulted, and its Sustainable Fiscal Path reflects reforms made since default occurred.

Source: Stanford University and the Comeback America Initiative (CAI). 23 March, 2011. Stanford University Public Policy and International Studies Programs. Prepared by T.J. Augustine, Alexander Maasry, Damilola Sobo, and Di Wang, under the guidance of David M. Walker, founder and CEO of the Comeback America Initiative and former comptroller general of the United States.

PART II

TRANSATLANTIC RELATIONS, ECONOMIC GOVERNANCE, AND SYSTEMIC RISKS

·

The American and European Challenges

Financial Stabilization and Structural Reforms to Avoid
Collapse, Limit Recession, and Promote Competitiveness

Ferran BRUNET[1]

Introduction

America and Europe are faced with stiff challenges of competitiveness and solidarity. With the financial crash and the rescue of banks,
industries, and sovereign debt, governments are mired in the recession
and its attendant gloomy perspectives, procrastinating about stabilisation and structural reforms.

This chapter puts forth an analysis of the twin American deficits, the
quadruple European deficits, and the economic policies developed to
address them. The global imbalances have turned into euro imbalances.
The European employment deficit and the economic governance deficit
are hobbling any means of addressing the other disequilibria and are
prolonging the recession and its costs. In a non-optimal monetary area,
the economic success or failure of an economy hinges on its ability to
compete. Competitiveness, as well as productivity and the quality of
regulation that support it, appears to be the principal challenge. Clearly
there is a huge need for stabilization, for reforms and for Europe. The
United States, although it does not share the over-complexity of governance of its European counterparts, is still suffering from serious imbalances. Such conditions can only provoke a lengthy recession on both
sides of the Atlantic.

The dynamics of American and European economies converged until
1991. Although the catching-up process stalled during the new
knowledge economy, the biggest instability was to be found in the
United States (US), something which eventually provoked the 2007
financial crash. In the European Union (EU), the 2010 crash of the
peripheral eurozone economies is strong evidence for the limitations of
European integration. In place of the twin American deficits, the EU has

[1] Thanks are due to Shuo Wang, Zhejiang University, for his helpful comments on an
earlier version of this chapter. The usual disclaimers apply.

a quadruple deficit: trade and fiscal deficits are complemented by the employment and the economic governance deficits.

When the balancing credit fails, the inability of many euro economies to compete in a non-optimal monetary area generates suspicion about the euro area (EA). The stabilization and structural reforms needed to restore competitiveness and to confront the European challenges should be powered by European economic governance that commits the Member States' (MS) governments to a number of virtuous policies (see Table 1).

Table 1
The American and European Models: Some Dialectic Elements

America – US	Europe – EU
American Dream, American Way of Life, American Spirit	European Dream, European Style of Life, European Spirit
Limited Government, Freedom	Public Intervention, State Property, Regulation
Religion, God	Laicism, Politics
Liberalism	Interventionism
Confidence on Economy and Market	Confidence on State and Public Intervention
Limited Government, Minimum Taxation	Public Administration, Public Services
Work Passion	Leisure Preference
Competition	Solidarity
Production, Economy	Distribution, Social
Realism, Special Mission, Hegemony, Modernity	Soft Power, Conditionality, Post-Modernity
Stock Market	Banks
Federation	European Integration, Common, Confederal Governance, Multilevel Governance
War, Hard, Man from Mars, Unilateralism	Peace, Soft, Woman from Venus, Euro-centrism, Hegemony, Consensus
Racial Discrimination, 20th Century Imperialism	Political Violence: Mass Crimes, from Revolution to Totalitarianism; Communism, Fascism, Nazism; Colonialism and Imperialism
Large Territory, Small History	Small-Dense Territory, Large-Excessive History
Individual Rights	National, Regional, Ethnic Rights
Theory of America: Freedom; Immigration, Borders, Frontiers; Secession War; Civil Rights	Theory of Europe: Peace; Member States, Regions; Gradualism; Functionalism; Multiculturalism

Regions: New England, Middle Atlantic, South, Midwest, Southwest, West	Models: North-Baltic, Western, Continental, Mediterranean, Eastern; Catholic, Protestant, Orthodox; Liberal, Social Democratic; Transition

In Common
Civilization, Culture, Values (Human Dignity, Personal Freedom, Free Thinking) vs. Interests
Freedom, Representative Democracy, Division of Powers, Rule of Law
Non Discrimination by Race, Gender and Age; Minority Protection; Multiculturalism
Market Economy, Competition
High Material and Energy Consumption, High Productivity, Knowledge Economy, Innovation System, Mass Production, Mass Consumption, Sustainability
Advanced Economic Policy, Policy Mix, Labour Market Protection, Social Services, Compensatory Policies, Welfare State

Despite the unanimity among decision-makers on the need for stabilization and structural reforms to improve the competitiveness of the US and EU economies (and the general political and social stability that allow it), the measures implemented are macroeconomic – more specifically, a complacent monetary policy with quantitative easing and negative real interest rates.

The public debate about economic policy is broad, but clarity is scarce on the ground (République Française Sénat 2010; European Commission [EC] Directorate General for Communication 2011) (see Table 2). Thus, in the more developed societies based on a knowledge of economy and public intervention, the capabilities of the social sciences is quite limited, as is the effectiveness of the measures adopted.

This chapter proposes an analysis of the US and EU economies during the current crisis, the strong challenges they confront, and the sharp economic policy choices they are implementing. The EU can be an anchor for Member States' economic policy, thus reducing their deficits and favouring their competitiveness. But if the EU doesn't manage to generate enough confidence or avoid the rescue of the debt of the peripheral Member States, a lengthy recession will set in. For the peripheral Member States, as well as for the entire EU and Europe, there is a most pressing need for stabilization and for structural reforms (see Figure 1).

American and European Economies: Dynamics and Crisis

One, Two, Many Model(s)

From the days of Alexis de Tocqueville (La démocratie en Amérique 1835) right up to Jeremy Rifkin (The European Dream 2004), America and Europe have been a mirror of each other. Both are also a mirror of the rest of the world. The transatlantic flows between the United States and the EU are the main economic flows (Hamilton and Quinlan 2011), and between these advanced areas and the emerging countries and the rest of the world, these main economic flows are also to be found (International Monetary Fund [IMF] 2011a).

Figure 1
The Ceasing of the Catching-Up and the Dynamics of the Gaps
between Productivity and Living Standard

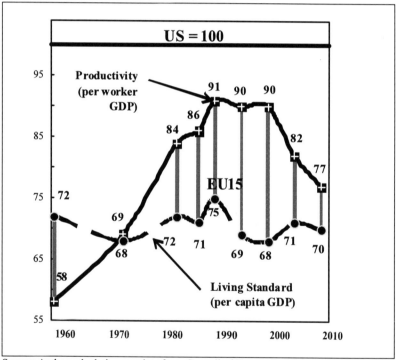

Source: Author calculations on data from Council of Economic Advisers (2011), fedStats (2011), Eurostat (2011), and OECD (2011).

Table 2
The American and European Performances

US		EU (15)
	Productive Model	
71.0%	Employment Rate	65.1%
5.5%	Unemployment Rate	8.3%
15.2%	Foreign Workers (as % total workers)	UK 5.6% & DE 9.1%
$21.3	Wage of Industrial Workers (per hour)	$20.1
$32.6	Cost of Industrial Workers (total per hour)	$35.9
	Model Performances	
$68,216	Productivity (per year and worker GDP)	$52,383
$39,700	Living Standard (per year and per capita GDP)	$28,700
3.2	GDP Growth (1992-2007 year average)	2.1
2.1	Price Inflation (annual %)	2.4
	Knowledge Economy	
2.8	R+D+D Total Investment (as % GDP)	1.9
30.1%	Creative Activities (as % of total employment)	UK 26.7% & DE 18.2%
17	No. of Universities among World Top 20	2 (UK)
40	No. of Regions among World Knowledge Competitiveness Top 50	8 (UK 3, Sweden 2)
	Institutional Model and Performance	
93.7	Regulatory Quality (by 100)	UK 98.0 & DE 91.2
-19.4	Competition Deficit (from 0.0 to -100)	UK -21.5 & DE -28.8
	Technological and Energy Model	
330	Energy Intensity	191
20.6	Contamination (CO$_2$ metric tons per inhabitant and year)	8.9
8	Human Development Index (World rank)	2 to 26

Source: Brunet (2010a and 2011a) and author calculations on data for year 2011 or closer and from European Central Bank (2011), Eurostat (2011), UN (2011) and fedStats (2011).

Low Growth, Global Imbalances, and Financial Crisis

The advanced economies are experiencing difficulties. Despite the high living standard, for a decade the annual growth of US and EU countries has been about 1-2 per cent (OECD 2010a and 2011, IMF 2011b).

Table 3
EU Dilemmas on Economic Governance

	Subject	
Consensus, unanimity		Majority, pondered vote
Intergovernmentalism		Community method
Summits, Council	Forms	Commission
Politics, politicians		Technical, ruled
Member States		EU, euro zone
By quantities (e.g. unemployment)	Economic Adjustment	By prices (e.g. wages)
Capitalism, banks, speculators, rating companies	Crisis' Causes	Competitiveness deficit, unruly policies
Wishful thinking		Realism, politically incorrect
Yes (permitted, desirable)	Public Deficit	No (no permitted, no desirable)
MS over-regulation		EU deficit of governance
Fiscal stimulus = deficit		Austerity: sustainability, consolidation
Macroeconomics		Microeconomics
Buying time, anaesthesia, procrastinating		Acting
Passive, policies contradicting the market	Economic Policy Orientation	Active, policies accompanying the market
Too big to fail		Too inefficient to survive with public financing
Rescue (with public help) = bailout		Bankruptcy, "bail-in" (a way of refinancing a bank without making it go bankrupt and without simply giving the bank public money)
No	Economic Policy by Rules	Yes — Only financial subjects / Also structural subjects
Discretionary, unlimited		Rules, benchmarking; limited
Quantitative Easing	Monetary Policy	Positive real interest rates
Objective: Employment, growth		Objective: inflation
Independent	Fiscal policy	Co-ordination, unique
ECB: unlimited		ECB: limited
European stabilisation Mechanisms: permanent	Institutions	European stabilisation Mechanisms: temporary
Protocols Annexed to Treaties	Law Instruments	Treaties (Treaty of Lisbon, Treaty of EU, Treaty on the Functioning of the EU)
Don't touch it	Welfare State, European Socio-economic Model	Reform to maintain

But the current economic crisis sprang forth from the United States (National Commission on the Causes of the Financial and Economic Crisis 2011), and its main impact is to be seen in the EU. The financial crash has proved to be an earthquake in terms of social relations, putting into grave danger both the American way of life and the European social model (Baldwin 2009; Gerson Lehrman Group 2010; Hamilton 2011). The crux is this: Behind the current phenomena of small or negative growth, unemployment, trade imbalances, and the financial crash, there are important challenges for America and Europe (Baily 2010). So far, neither has found a way of rebalancing its economy (Collignon 2010; *The Economist* 2011) (see Table 3).

The Stalled Catch-Up Process and the Euro Imbalances: From Convergence to Divergence

Between the end of World War II and the middle of the 1990s, the American and European economies were convergent. In the advanced Member States of the EU, GDP growth was bigger due to high levels of productivity (Eichengreen, Stiefel, and Landesmann 2008; Eichengreen 2011). But the New Economy, while more open, market-oriented, and knowledge-based, has not kept up this transatlantic convergence. The current crisis is also highlighting an important matter for Europe: Economic returns among the EU Member States vary wildly. The imbalances between them are growing and are no longer possessed of a tendency to converge in the higher levels of living standards. Among the bigger Member States, unemployment levels are quite varied, and they are evolving in disparate ways. The gaps in socioeconomic conditions and performance among the Nordic, Central, Western, Mediterranean, and Eastern Member States are considerable and growing (Nowotny, Mooslechner, and Ritzberger-Grünwald 2011).

So we see that for Europe there is a doubly big problem and a doubly big challenge:

a) The ceasing of the convergence with the United States: The closest the two came was in the 1990s, a moment in which the 15 Western Member States of the EU (EU 15) came to within 91 per cent of the productivity of the United States and 75 per cent of their living standard. Since then, productivity has fallen to 77 per cent and living standard to 70 per cent (Figure 1). The differences between American and European performances are large and becoming more so (Table 2).

b) The ceasing of the convergence among Member States. This is a key development because in the first stage of the euro (Pisani-Ferry and Posen 2009; Lorca-Susino 2010) as well as in later stages of the European integration process, the narrowing of dif-

ferences among Member States was one of the more positive results (Brunet 2012).

The American and European Crisis:
Impacts and Policy Responses

The American and European Crashes

The crisis began in the American financial sector, spread throughout
its economy and then throughout the entire world, the main chapters
being the 2008 financial crash in the United States and the 2010 euro
crisis. The magnitude of this crisis can be gauged by analyzing its
impacts on GDP growth, (un)employment, industrial production, and
trade. In advanced countries, growth was reduced by 3 per cent, employment by 2 per cent, industrial production by 26 per cent, and foreign trade by 11 per cent. To appreciate the scale of the impacts, they
are compared with those of the 1929 crisis and of other contemporary
crises: The current one appears to be more profound than most of the
previous: a financial crisis made manifest as a real crisis. Stabilisation
alone will not be sufficient to rebalance and recover; some structural
adjustments will be needed (Baily and Kirkegaard 2004; Anonymous
2010; Ahearn 2011).

Accumulating Deficits: The Triplet Deficit Skyline

The crisis makes itself evident as disequilibrium or an imbalance in
certain economic and social conditions (see Figure 2). Traditionally, the
basic economic disequilibria are related to:

– Employment, in the form of unemployment (Wyploz 2010;
Stiftung 2011).

– Public sector, in the form of fiscal deficit (Cohen and DeLong
2010).

– Foreign trade, in the form of current account deficit (Allen,
Carletti, and Corsetti 2011).

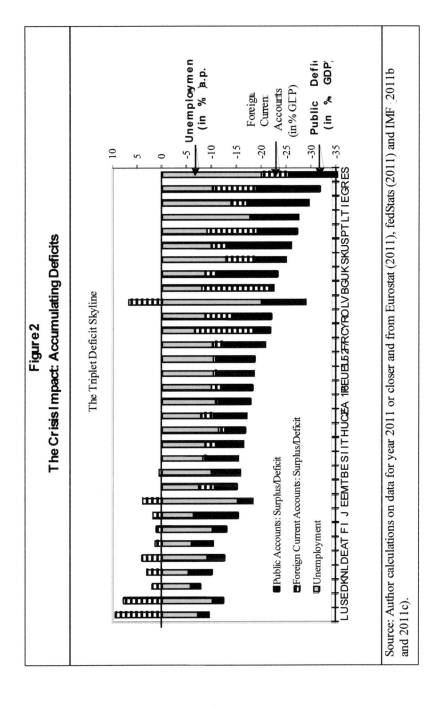

Figure 2
The Crisis Impact: Accumulating Deficits

The Triplet Deficit Skyline

Source: Author calculations on data for year 2011 or closer and from Eurostat (2011), fedStats (2011) and IMF (2011b and 2011c).

In the United States, unemployment has risen to 10 per cent of the total active population. In Europe, this main limiting factor of the European economy – employment – has devolved into huge unemployment rates, especially in those Member States with the worst labour market quality (World Bank 2011a). Unemployment surpassed the 20 per cent mark in Spain and is close to this level in other Mediterranean Member States (Balakrishnan and Berger 2009; Brunet 2011b).

Public accounts have evolved negatively after an era in which equilibrium was both much desired and highly attainable in the more advanced countries. But the fiscal scissors have made for a generalization of financing by issuing public debt. The trade balance is the other key disequilibrium. The crisis has limited trade (IMF 2011b), and the imbalances surpass 10 per cent of the GDP in many OECD countries, as it does in the United States.

The Competitiveness Deficit: from Global Imbalances to Euro Imbalances

Imbalances: Competitiveness versus Governance

In advanced countries, the crisis is underlining the constraints imposed by the dynamics of competitiveness and the limitations due to the complexity of economic governance. Even if one were to shower down money from a helicopter (Shiller 2008; Wolf 2008; Bernanke 2011), not everything is possible (Samuelson 2008; Roxburgh *et al.* 2010): The real sector has shown serious decreases in levels of activity, and there are well-established limits to indebtedness (James 2009; Reinhart and Rogoff 2009) (see Table 4).

Imbalances in foreign trade, public finance, and the labour market are the fruit of limitations of the advanced economies that have contributed to the huge impact of the current financial crisis. Financing of the twin American deficits is contributing to the global imbalances (Yamashita 2009; Posner 2009). In all probability, both the American and the global imbalances are related to overconsumption (because the regulations favour mass credit and social expenditures) in the United States and overinvestment in emerging countries (because of the novelty of high growth and limited social benefits) (European Commission Directorate General for Economic and Financial Affairs [EC-DGECFIN] 2009, 2010a, and 2010b; IMF 2011b; OECD 2011).

Table 4
Dynamics of the European Governance in Times of Crisis

	Pre-Existing (and substantially maintained)	New (additional)
Initiatives	European economic constitution (EU treaties and derived law). Competition policy and the other EU policies	European Recovery Plan
	EMU, Stability and Growth Pact (preventive and dissuasive arms; for each MS: stability program and convergence and structural reform program), excessive deficit procedure, early warning mechanism and policy advice. Broad economic policy guidelines, macroeconomic dialogue and multilateral supervision	Economic Governance Package: broader and enhanced surveillance, effective enforcement of budgetary surveillance in the EA; European semester on the MS budgetary framework; preventing and correcting macroeconomic imbalances (by the EC), enforcement mechanisms. Competitiveness Pact for the Euro → Euro Plus Pact. Surveillance of intra-euro area imbalances, alert mechanism through a scoreboard, excessive imbalance procedure (EIP, by peer pressure, and fine of 0,1% GDP). Reinforced multilateral surveillance
	Single market strategy	
	Employment Pact, European Employment Strategy, Flexisecurity, social agenda. Open method of co-ordination of economic and social policies	
	Lisbon strategy, structural policies co-ordination	Europe 2020.
	Balance of payments (BoP) assistance	BoP (following the Community method, administered by the European Commission): for Hungary, Latvia, and Romania.
	Macro-financial assistance to non-EU countries.	

Institutions and bodies	Council: ECOFIN. Commission: DG Eco Fin and the other DG related to the Economic Policies (competition, market, enterprise, trade, employment) European Central Bank (ECB). European Investment Bank (EIB). Economic and Social Committee (ESC).	European stabilization of finance actions: A. Institutions (agencies or bodies): European Financial Stabilization Mechanism (ESFM, from May 2010 until June 2011, under the Community method) European Financial Stability Facility (EFSF), created by the Euro area Member States (EA MS) as Luxembourg-registered company owned by the EA MS (under the Intergovernmental method). It has the mandate to safeguard financial stability in the euro zone by raising funds in capital markets to finance loans for the EA MS. Part of the overall rescue package of €750 billion, the EFSF is able to issue bonds for up €440 billion guaranteed by the EA MS, the other provided by the EU (€60 billion) and the IMF (€250 billion). The EFSF has been assigned the best possible credit rating (AAA, by S&P and Fitch Ratings, and Aaa by Moody's). European Stability Mechanism (ESM), substituting the EFSF from June 2013. It's a permanent body which aim is to prevent the crisis and reduce its probability. B. Packages of Financial and Economic Support: For Greece. For Portugal. For Ireland. For Italy and Spain.
	European Bank of Reconstruction and Development (EBRD). Economic and Financial Committee (EFC). Economic Policy Committee (EPC). Economic and Monetary Affairs Committee of the European Parliament.	
		Following the launch of the European Systemic Risk Board (ESRB) on 16 December 2010, three European authorities start their work for the supervision of financial activities with regard to banks, markets and insurances and pensions respectively: European Banking Authority (EBA). European Securities and Markets Authority (ESMA). European Insurance and Occupational Pensions Authority (EIOPA).
	Eurogroup (MS' ministries of Economy and Finance)	Task Force on Economic Governance chaired by the President of the European Council, Herman Van Rompuy.

Competitiveness Deficits

The twin American deficits born of the competitiveness deficits have been financed by the emerging countries with a surplus (Brunet 2008b). Financial conditions up until the financial crash, with very low nominal rates, sharply negative real interest rates, and a huge quantitative easing, have financed the balancing of the real deficits in competitiveness, trade, and government (Cecchetti, Mohanty, and Zampolli 2010; Krippner 2011) (see Figure 3).

Inversely, the crisis has reduced foreign trade and, thus, the foreign imbalances. European financial conditions were not quite so different from those of America. The financial conditions caused by the launching of the euro have permitted all EA Member States to finance over-consumption and imbalances in trade (see Figure 3).

The Great Recession and the Competitiveness and Governance Deficits

Low Growth, Systemic Risk, and Great Recession

After a decade of low growth and five years of systemic risk, the American and European economies are in the midst of a great recession. Macroeconomic measures and a monetary policy heavy on quantitative easing and real negative interest rates have proved their ability to lessen financial systemic risk. But these have served to perpetuate the imbalances in foreign current accounts and public budgets. The traditional question (Has the recovery been affected?) can be substituted by another question (Can a recovery be effected?). Is recovery possible without rebalancing? What's the place of governance in recovery? (Dyson and Quaglia 2010; Laurent and Le Cacheux 2010; Jabko 2011).

The Deficits on Competitiveness and the Quality of Regulation

The crisis has been exacerbating certain imbalances and divergences among countries. Their competitiveness and general abilities are under enormous pressure. There is a strong link among economic performances, conditions for competition, and the quality of regulation (Monti 2010; Executive Office of the President, Office of Management and Budget 2011; Kristensen and Lilja 2011; Brunet 2011b). The fiercest challenges are global, but the instruments to manage them are national.

Strong links exist between:

– Competitiveness and the quality of regulation (Figure 3, Panel A): R^2 is about 0,45.

– Current account balances and the competitiveness (Figure 3, Panel B): R^2 is about 0,43.

Despite these differences, there is always a great divide between Nordic and Central Member States and Mediterranean and Eastern Member States. The former have surpluses, the latter have deficits. The United Kingdom, the United States, Ireland, and sometimes France fall in between these two categories.

The European Economic Governance Deficit

Because of the gradual nature of the European integration process and the newness of the euro (Heipertz and Verdun 2010), there is a European economic governance deficit. This is clear when compared with US economic regulation and, more important, when compared with what is needed to ensure economic and financial stability.

The difficulties related to the euro and the rescues of Greece, Ireland, and Portugal have helped in the development of the instruments and institutions of a new European economic policy: the European Financial Stability Facility, the European Banking Authority, the European Securities and Markets Authority, and the European Insurance and Occupational Pensions Authority (EU 2010a; EC-DGECFIN 2010a, 2010b; EU Eurogroup 2010; Jabko 2011; Young 2011).

But this is not enough to reduce the euro imbalances. In all likelihood, a huge stabilization effort is needed in certain Member States to rein in the financial risks, as a step towards reforming the economic structures that are crippling their competitiveness (Zemanek, Belke, and Schnabl 2010; Sinn and Wollmershaeuser 2011). If in the last decade it was possible for the non-competitive Member States to borrow to stay afloat, now they are forced to be competitive to keep up their activity, employment levels, and living standard. Europe appears to be an anchor for these Member States.

The American Economic Policy Dilemmas

The American financial crash has been followed by a relatively short recession. The tendency of economic activity to fall was counterbalanced by the monetary and fiscal stimulus. Despite this recovery, the twin deficit remains in place. Economic policy has proved its capability of realizing its main objective: recovery. But the sustainability of the recovery is not clear (Krugman 2009; Stiglitz 2010; Trichet 2011). Can the stimulus be reduced, and can the economic policy pass smoothly into an austerity phase (McKinsey Global Institute 2010), promoting deleverage (Roxburgh *et al.* 2010) and structural changes?

It is a matter of time and cost: The financial alleviation is a way of buying time by paying a cost consisting of minus future growth. But the rebalancing of the American economy is a condition necessary for the shrinking of its twin deficits (Bergsten 2009; Baily 2010; Rajan 2010; Pisani-Ferry, Sapir, and Wolff 2011). America, along with Europe, is fighting to keep up its competitiveness, its level of activity and employment, and, ultimately, its people's welfare (see Table 5).

Conclusion

In the last half-decade, the American and the European economies have weathered a serious financial crash that has affected real activity levels. The rescue of financial intermediaries has avoided the systemic risk, but the rebalancing of the economy has been hobbled by competitiveness levels. In America, the twin imbalances continue, the public deficit is bigger, and the current account deficit smaller. In Europe, the imbalances are widening the differences among countries, some of them provoking severe unemployment and huge public and foreign deficits. As a consequence, the rescues of Greece, Ireland and Portugal are putting the euro in a very delicate situation.

After a decade of limited growth, certain countries are settling into a recession that could be considerable. The systemic risk has been extinguished by throwing money at negative real interest rates. But this quantitative easing only postpones the rebalancing of the economy. The unclear prospects of deleverage, competitiveness, delocation, downsizing, and unemployment are shadowed by the inability to pass the reform that can allow the system to rebalance itself, to ensure a competitive position, and safeguard the people's living standard.

Figure 3
Quality of Regulation and Competitiveness

Panel A. Quality of Regulation and Competitiveness

Panel B. Competitiveness and Current Account

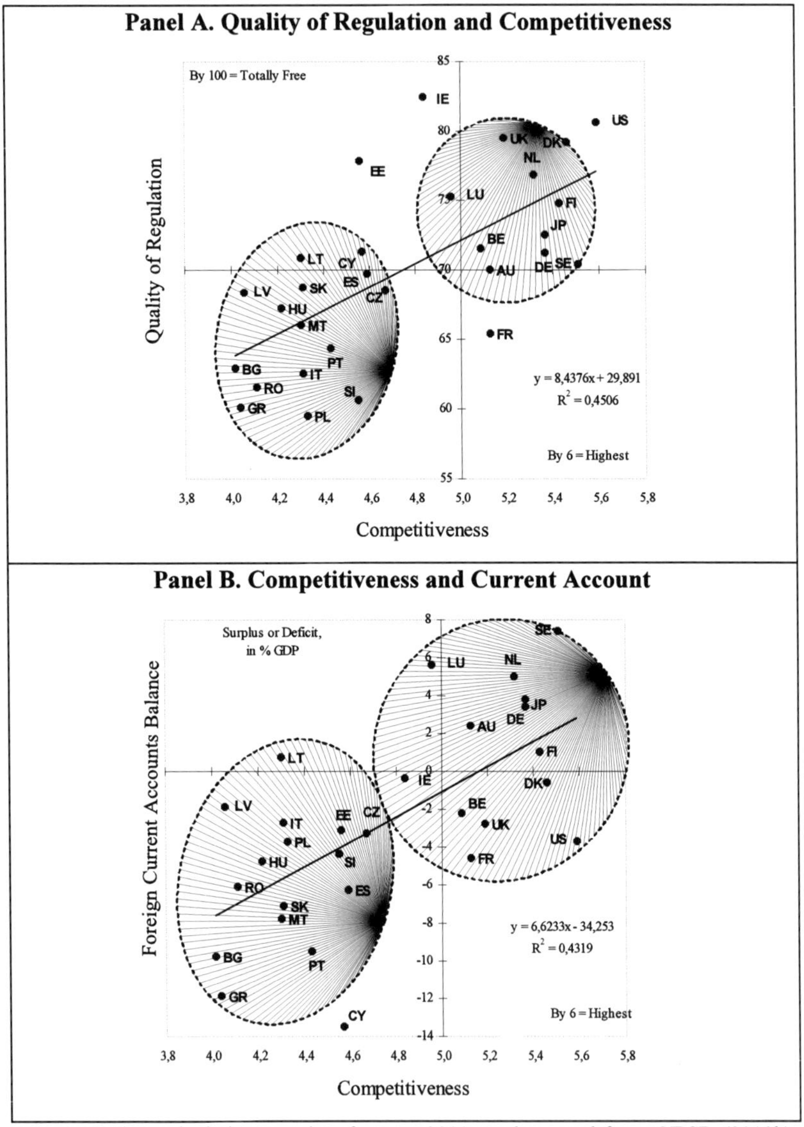

Source: Author calculations on data for year 2011 or closer and from OECD (2010b), World Bank (2011a, 2011b, and 2012), and World Economic Forum (2011).

Table 5
Some Economic Policy Subjects on Debate

Global					
Global Imbalances	Financial Bubble	Housing Bubble	Financial Crisis	Resources Shortage	Environment Pressures
Small Interest Rate	Bank Rescuing	Industries Rescuing	Currency War	Commodity Prices Rising	International Financial Architecture
Systemic Risk	Sustainability	Recovery	Recession	Distribution Divide	Economic Security
United States			European Union		
Twin Deficits	Quantitative Easing	Fiscal Stimulus	Austerity	Euro Imbalances	MS Disparate Positions
Health Reform	Dollar Exchange Rate	Protection	Unemployment	European Stabilization Mechanism	Stability, Competitiveness or Euro Pact
Common					
Growth and Employment	Stabilization	Competitiveness	Recovery Plans	Structural Reforms	Too... to...

References

Ahearn, Raymond J. (ed.) (2011). *The Future of the Eurozone and U.S. Interests*. Washington, DC: Congressional Research Service.

Allen, Franklin, Elena Carletti, and Giancarlo Corsetti (eds.) (2011). *Life in the Eurozone with or without Sovereign Default?* Philadelphia: FIC Press.

Anonymous (2010). "Prospects for real and financial imbalances and a global rebalancing", in *ECB Monthly Bulletin*, April, pp. 91-100.

Baily, Martin N. (2010). "The Next Economy and the Growth Challenge for the United States", paper prepared for the Scholars Strategy Network Conference, to be held at Tsai Auditorium, Harvard University, Cambridge, MA, 30 September. <http://www.brookings.edu/~/media/Files/rc/reports/2010/1001_next_economy_growth_baily/1001_next_economy_growth_baily.pdf> [Accessed 19 December 2011].

Baily, Martin N. and Jacob Funk Kirkegaard (2004). *Transforming the European Economy*. Washington, DC: Peterson Institute for International Economics.

Balakrishnan, Ravi and Helge Berger (2009). "Comparing Recessions in Germany, Spain, and United Kingdom", in *IMF Survey Magazine*, 18 November.

Baldwin, Peter (2009). *The Narcissism of Minor Differences, How America and Europe Are Alike*. New York: Oxford University Press.

Bergsten, C. Fred (ed.) (2009). *The Long-Term International Economic Position of the United States.* Washington, DC: Peterson Institute for International Economics.

Bernanke, Ben S. (2011). "The Effects of the Great Recession on Central Bank Doctrine and Practice", speech at the Federal Reserve Bank of Boston 56th Economic Conference, Boston, 18 October. <http://www.c.federalreserve. gov/newsevents>. [Accessed 18 October 2011].

Bertelsmann Stiftung (ed.) (2010), *Managing the Crisis. A Comparative Analysis of Economic Governance in 14 Countries.* Gütersloh: Verlag Bertelsmann Stiftung.

Brunet, Ferran (2008a). "The European Economic Constitution. An Analysis of the Constitutional Treaty", in Finn Laursen (ed.), *The Constitutional Treaty.* Leiden: Martinus Nijhoff, pp. 51-78.

Brunet, Ferran (2008b). "The European Competition Deficit", paper presented at the Annual Research Conference "Exchanging Ideas on Europe 2008 – Rethinking the European Union" of the University Association for Contemporary European Studies (UACES), University of Edinburgh, Europa Institute, 1 September.

Brunet, Ferran (2010a). "The European Imbalances: Competitiveness and Economic Policy in a Non-optimal Monetary Union and a Global Crisis – The Need for Europe, Stabilization and Structural Reforms", paper presented at the International Conference on the "The Economic Crisis and the Process of European Integration", European Parliament, Brussels, 2 June.

Brunet, Ferran (2010b). *Curso de Integración Europea.* 2nd ed. Madrid: Alianza Editorial.

Brunet, Ferran (2011a). "Regulatory Quality and Competitiveness in Europe", paper presented at the *International Seminar on European Regulatory Governance, Developments and Change*, Copenhagen Business School, 27-28 October.

Brunet, Ferran (2011b). "Calidad de la regulación y competitividad en los países euro-mediterráneos", in *Información Comercial Española*, No. 861, pp. 109-128.

Brunet, Ferran (2012). "An Economic Analysis of the Treaty of Lisbon", in Finn Laursen (ed.), *The Lisbon Treaty, Institutional Choices and Implementation.* Farham: Ashgate.

Cecchetti, Stephen G., M.S. Mohanty, and Fabrizio Zampolli (2010). "The future of public debt, prospects and implications", in *Bank for International Settlements Working Papers*, No. 300.

Cohen, Stephen S. and J. Bradford DeLong (2010). *The End of Influence. What Happens When Other Countries Have the Money.* New York: Basic Books.

Collignon, Stefan (2010). "Fiscal Policy Rules and the Sustainability of Public Debt in Europe", in *RECON Online Working Paper*, No. 2010/28.

Council of Economic Advisers (2011). *Economic Report of the President Transmitted to the Congress Together with the Annual Report of the Council of Economic Advisers.* Washington, DC: Government Printing Office.

Dyson, Kenneth and Lucia Quaglia (eds.) (2010). *European Economic Governance and Policies. Volume I, Commentary on Key Historical and Institutional Documents.* Oxford: Oxford University Press.

Economist, The (2011). "What's wrong with the America's economy", 30 April-6 May.

Eichengreen, Barry (2011). *Exorbitant Privilege. The Rise and Fall of the Dollar and the Future of the International Monetary System.* Oxford: Oxford University Press.

Eichengreen, Barry, Dieter Stiefel, and Michael Landesmann (eds.) (2008). *The European Economy in an American Mirror.* New York: Routledge.

European Central Bank (2011). *Statistical Data Warehouse.* <http//:ww.sdw.ecb.europa.eu>. [Accessed 23 October 2011].

European Commission Directorate-General for Communication (2011). "Economic Governance in the European Union", in *Eurobarometer*, No. 74.

European Commission Directorate General for Economic and Financial Affairs (2009). "Economic crisis in Europe, causes, consequences and responses", in *European Economy*, No. 7.

European Commission Directorate General for Economic and Financial Affairs (2010a). *Surveillance of Intra-Euro-Area Competitiveness and Imbalances.* Brussels: European Commission.

European Commission Directorate General for Economic and Financial Affairs (2010b). "Special issue, The impact of the global crisis on competitiveness and current account divergences in the euro area", in *Quarterly Report on the Euro Area*, Vol. 9, No. 1.

European Union (2010). "Council Regulation (EU) No. 407/2010 of 11 May 2010 establishing a European financial stabilisation mechanism", in *Official Journal of the European Union*, No. L 118, 12 May, pp. 1-4.

European Union Eurogroup (2010). "Surveillance of intra-euro-area. Competitiveness and macroeconomic imbalances. Conclusions, 15 March". <http://www.consilium.europa.eu>. [Accessed 3 December 2011].

Eurostat (2011). <eurostat.ec.europa.eu>. [Accessed 14 December 2011].

Executive Office of the President, Office of Management and Budget (2011). *Report to Congress on the Benefits and Costs of Federal Regulations and Unfunded Mandates on State, Local, and Tribal Entities.* Washington, DC: Office of Information and Regulatory Affairs.

FedStats (2011). <http://www.fedstats.gov>. [Accessed 14 December 2011].

Gerson Lehrman Group (2010). "Europe at the Crossroads, Too Unbalanced To Recover Without Policy Coordination". <http://www.glgroup.com>. [Accessed 25 March 2011].

Hamilton, Daniel S. (2011). *Europe 2020, Competitive or Complacent.* Washington DC: Center for Transatlantic Relations, Johns Hopkins University, Paul H. Nitze School of Advanced International Studies.

Hamilton, Daniel S. and Joseph P. Quinlan (2011). *The Transatlantic Economy. Annual Survey of Jobs, Trade and Investment between the United States and Europe.* Washington DC: Center for Transatlantic Relations, Johns Hopkins University, Paul H. Nitze School of Advanced International Studies.

Heipertz, Martin and Amy Verdun (2010). *Ruling Europe: The Politics of the Stability and Growth Pact.* Cambridge: Cambridge University Press.

Hull Kristensen, Peer and Kari Lilja (2011). *Nordic Capitalisms and Globalization, New Forms of Economic Organization and Welfare Institutions.* Oxford: Oxford University Press.

International Monetary Fund (2011a). "Euro Area Policies, 2011 Article IV Consultation – Lessons from the European Financial Stability Framework Exercise; and Selected Issues Paper", in *IMF Country Report*, No. 11/186, July.

International Monetary Fund (2011b). *World Economic Outlook. September 2011. Slowing Growth, Rising Risks.* Washington, DC: International Monetary Fund.

International Monetary Fund (2011c). *World Financial Instability Report. September 2011. Grappling with Crisis Legacies.* Washington, DC: International Monetary Fund.

Jabko, Nicolas (2011). "Which Economic Governance for the European Union? Facing up to the Problem of Divided Sovereignty", in *Swedish Institute for European Policy Studies*, No. 2, March.

James, Harold (2009). *The Creation and Destruction of Value, The Globalization Cycle.* Cambridge, MA: Harvard University Press.

Krippner, Greta R. (2011). *Capitalizing on Crisis. The Political Origins of the Rise of Finance.* Cambridge, MA: Harvard University Press.

Krugman, Paul (2009). *The Return of Depression Economics and the Crisis of 2008.* New York: W. W. Norton & Company.

Laurent, Éloi and Jacques Le Cacheux (eds.) (2010). *Report on the State of the European Union. Volume 3, Crisis in the EU Economic Governance.* New York: Palgrave Macmillan.

Lorca-Susino, Maria (2010). *The Euro in the 21st Century. Economic Crisis and Financial Uproar.* Burlington, VT: Ashgate.

McKinsey Global Institute (2010). *Beyond austerity, A path to economic growth and renewal in Europe.* <http://www.mckinsey.com>. [Accessed 8 June 2011].

Monti, Mario (2010). *A New Strategy for the Single Market at the Service of Europe's Economy and Society. Report to the President of the European Commission José Manuel Barroso.* <http://ec.europa.eu/bepa/pdf/monti_report_final_10_05_2010_en.pdf>. [Accessed 11 May 2010].

National Commission on the Causes of the Financial and Economic Crisis (2011). *Final Report of the National Commission on the Causes of the Financial and Economic Crisis in the United States. Submitted Pursuant to Public Law 111-21.* Washington, DC: Government Printing Office.

Nowotny, Ewald, Peter Mooslechner, and Doris Ritzberger-Grünwald (2011). *Post-Crisis Growth and Integration in Europe. Catching-up Strategies in CESEE Economies*. Cheltelham: Edward Elgar.

OECD (2010a). "Euro Area 2010", in *OECD Economic Surveys*, No. 2.

OECD (2010b). *Going for Growth*. Paris: OECD.

OECD (2010c). "United States 2010", in *OECD Economic Surveys*, No. 15.

OECD (2011). *Main Economic Indicators*. <http://www.oecd.org/dataoecd>. [Accessed 19 August 2011].

Pisani-Ferry, Jean and Adam S. Posen (eds.) (2009). *The Euro at Ten, The Next Global Currency?* Washington, DC: Peterson Institute for International Economics.

Pisani-Ferry, Jean, André Sapir, and Guntram B. Wolff (2011). "TSR External Study. An Evaluation of IMF Surveillance of the Euro Area". <http://www.imf.org/external/np/pp/eng/2011/071911.pdf>. [Accessed 20 July 2011].

Posner, Richard A. (2009). *A Failure of Capitalism. The Crisis of '08 and the Descent into Depression*. Cambridge, MA: Harvard University Press.

Rajan, Raghuram G. (2010). *Fault Lines. How Hidden Fractures Still Threaten the World Economy*. Princeton: Princeton University Press.

Reinhart, Carmen M. and Kenneth Rogoff (2009). *This Time Is Different: Eight Centuries of Financial Folly*. Princeton: Princeton University Press.

République française. Sénat (2010). "Rapport d'information fait [par Bernard-Reymond, Pierre et Richard Yung] au nom de la commission des affaires européennes sur la gouvernance économique européenne", République Française, Sénat, Session ordinaire de 2010-2011, enregistré à la Présidence du Sénat le 19 octobre avec le No. 49.

Rifkin, Jeremy (2004). *The European Dream*. Cambridge: Polity Press.

Roxburgh, Charles *et al.* (2010). *Debt and Deleveraging. The Global Credit Bubble and Its Economic Consequences*. London: MacKinsey Global Institute.

Samuelson, Robert J. (2008). *The Great Inflation and Its Aftermath. The Past and Future of American Affluence*. New York: Random House.

Shiller, Robert J. (2008). *The Subprime Solution. How Today's Global Finance Crisis Happened, and What to Do about It*. Princeton: Princeton University Press.

Sinn, Hans-Werner and Timo Wollmershaeuser (2011). "Target Loans, Current Account Balances and Capital Flows. The ECB's Rescue Facility", in *CESifo Working Paper*, No. 3500, 24 June.

Stiglitz, Joseph E. (2010). *Freefall: America, Free Markets, and the Sinking of the World Economy*. New York: W. W. Norton & Company.

Stiftung, Bertelsmann (ed.) (2010). *Managing the Crisis. A Comparative Analysis of Economic Governance in 14 Countries*. Gütersloh: Verlag Bertelsmann Stiftung.

Tocqueville, Alexis de (1835). *Democracy in America.* New York: Penguin, 2003.

Trichet, Jean-Claude (2011). "La compétitivité et le fonctionnement harmonieux de l'UEM. Intervention de Président de la Banque centrale européenne, Université de Liège, le 23 février". <http://www.ecb.europa.eu/ecb/legal/pdf/en_con_2011_13.pdf>. [Accessed 24 February 2011].

United Nations (2011). *Human Development Index.* <http://hdr.undp.org>. [Accessed 2 September 2011].

Wolf, Martin (2008). *Fixing Global Finance.* Baltimore: The Johns Hopkins University Press.

World Bank (2011a). *Doing Business 2010-2011.* Washington, DC: World Bank and International Finance Corporation.

World Bank (2011b). *Quarterly External Debt Statistics.* Washington, DC: World Bank.

World Bank (2012). *Worldwide Governance Indicators.* <www.info.worldbank/governance>. [Accessed 2 January 2012].

World Economic Forum (2011). *The Global Competitiveness Report 2010-2011.* Davos: World Economic Forum.

Wyploz, Charles (2010), "Germany, current accounts and competitiveness". <http://www.voxeu.org>. [Accessed 31 March 2010].

Yamashita, Eiji (2009). "The Comparison of Policy Responses to Financial Crises between the European Union Currently and Japan in 1990s", paper presented at the 3rd Annual Research Conference of the EU Centre of Excellence (EUCE), "The EU in a Comparative Perspective", Dalhousie University, Halifax, Canada, 26-28 April.

Young, Brigitte (2011). "Economic Governance in the Eurozone, A New Dawn", in *Economic Sociology*, Vol. 12, No. 3, March, pp. 11-16.

Zemanek, Holger, Ansgar Belke, and Gunther Schnabl (2010). "Current Account Balances and Structural Adjustment in the Euro Area", in *International Economics and Economic Policy*, Vol. 7, No. 4, pp. 83-127.

Transatlantic Perspectives on Systemic Risk after the Crisis

Twin Objectives or an Uneasy Marriage?

Priya Nandita POORAN

Introduction

The global financial crisis that erupted in 2008 was not caused by a singular failure. Instead, it reflected the cumulative effect of a myriad of weaknesses in the supervisory approach of the global financial system that was inadequately equipped to accommodate the modernization of international finance or to reflect the progression of transnational financial innovations, the cross-fertilization of sectors within the financial services industry and products that dominated the markets of the world's most advanced economies, and the rapid advances and mutations in risk management techniques that became enmeshed within the EU-US and global financial markets with even greater rapidity.

One central theme that has been accepted as a key policy objective is the need for a renewed focus on financial stability and the key role of systemic risk assessment and monitoring as a means of achieving greater national, transnational and global stability. In the transatlantic financial regulatory reform agenda of the past two years, few issues have received such attention as that of systemic risk. Academic and policy discussion has sought to further understand the intrinsic nature of systemic risk and to examine the role of systemic risk in facilitating the widespread disruptions in the global financial system, and reform efforts continue to seek an appropriate response to this in the post-crisis supervisory framework in particular, an effective institutional design that shall allow the necessary and optimum means of oversight and assessment of systemic risk in the financial system.

Given the centrality of the US-EU relationship, the treatment of this issue is of paramount importance, and the impact of the financial regulatory reforms on either side of the Atlantic is a key aspect of the continued dynamism of the transatlantic economy. Within this context, it is essential that the way in which both partners address financial stability and systemic risk is mutually supportive, serves the growth and development of the economies of the federal US and Single Market, promotes the stability of the shared US-EU financial system (and beyond), and serves the larger global financial system. Not only must the transatlantic regulatory reforms respond to the weaknesses of this recent crisis, but the changes must provide a forward-looking framework that will facilitate competition among financial institutions while providing reassurances of policyholder and investor protection to its primary stakeholders and enable timely warnings to be made of potential areas of weakness and vulnerability that may develop into damaging crisis events and enhance the stability of the financial system.[1] In this regard, the respective treatment of systemic risk is unparalleled in its role.

The Global Economic Crisis Revisited

In the aftermath of the global economic crisis, various investigations and analyses have revealed a number of weaknesses in the financial regulatory system that provided the enabling circumstances for the emergence of this crisis and, further, allowed the weaknesses to develop into a crisis event in such an unanticipated manner. A number of key regulatory deficiencies are now acknowledged as having exerted a significant influence in the build-up to the crisis. These include:

- an imbalance in the focus afforded to institutional safety and soundness by supervisory authorities as the dominant pre-crisis approach and renewed attention to this phenomenon as an inappropriate approach to promoting effective oversight of the financial markets and to the promotion of stability in the financial system;

- a lack of adequate, if any, attention to risk throughout the national and international financial system (and to the assessment of such risk);

- lack of effective corporate governance;

- inadequate capital requirements;

- lack of knowledge and attention by regulators as to financial market activities. In retrospect, this may be understood as too arms-length an approach by supervisors to provide the key in-

---

[1]   See, for example, *The Report of the High Level Group on Financial Supervision in the EU*, chaired by Jacques de Larosiere (25 February 2009) including the following: "A consensus, both in Europe and internationally, need so to be developed on which financial services regulatory measures are needed for the protection of customers, the safeguarding of financial stability, and the sustainability of economic growth". Other notable reports include *The Turner Review: A Regulatory Response to the Global Banking Crisis* (March 2009) and the Report of the Independent Commission on Banking (September 2011).

sights needed for effective analysis and understanding of the day-to-day activities of the financial markets; and

• very short-term profit models.

This chapter focuses on systemic risk and addresses recent efforts in the EU and the United States to introduce measures for addressing and providing oversight of systemic risk. The chapter presents the implications of post-crisis systemic risk assessment and the institutional frameworks that seek to capture this, from the transatlantic perspective.

Systemic Risk

Prior to the crisis, the relevance of systemic risk to the financial system was attributed little – and clearly inadequate – relevance. The importance of systemic risk frameworks and tools to the promotion of financial stability and to the prevention or early detection of vulnerabilities that could morph into financial crisis events is now accepted. The post-crisis reform efforts in this area have been significant in both the EU and the United States and are inextricably linked with the increased recognition of macro-prudential supervision in a post-crisis environment. Indeed, systemic risk lies at the heart of the concept of macro-prudential supervision, and advances in the latter inevitably require stringent attention to the nature of systemic risk and its occurrence in the financial sector.

In responding to the need for a shift to macro-prudential supervision, one of the major reforms in a post-crisis era is the heightened consideration and integration of systemic risk in the approach to regulating the international financial markets – and the introduction of the appropriate institutional structures to reflect this. Within this context, it has emerged that the new frameworks and institutional designs for protecting the financial system must necessarily reflect and incorporate systemic risk as a core aspect of modern day financial market surveillance. To this end, frameworks to better capture systemic risk have been evolving and moving forward in EU and US financial regulatory responses to the recent financial crisis.

Changes in the EU have occurred both at the regional and state level. For the purpose of this discussion, this chapter focuses on changes at the EU levels. The introduction of the European Systemic Risk Board (ESRB) and changes in the Lamfalussy structure are the primary institutional changes that have occurred.[2] In the United States, the post-crisis

---

[2] In addition, further changes have occurred at a Member State level in terms of allocation of supervisory responsibility, for example, in the United Kingdom where significant shifts have occurred between the FSA and Bank of England.

institutional changes primarily arise from the enactment of the Wall Street Reform and Consumer Protection Act, introduced in 2010, which includes the introduction of a Consumer Protection Bureau and the Financial Stability Oversight Council (FSOC) as significant institutional changes to be implemented following the global economic crisis.

Systemic risk is to a large extent still nebulous both in its conceptual understanding and its translation in policy and supervision. In the context of this chapter and from the perspective of the EU-US and global financial regulatory reforms, there is a need to distinguish the different contexts in which the term "systemic" arises. First, the term "systemic risk" has most justifiably and correctly assumed a place in the context of "contagion". This term should be understood as referring to the inter-connectedness of financial institutions and the potential for risks from one area to have disruptive consequences on separate areas. "Systemic" in this context refers to the contagion and domino effect that single event failures or weaknesses in the financial sector could have on the broader financial system or the translation of weaknesses in one sector on different sectors or institutions – and beyond the potential impact (of such events and weaknesses) on the broad financial sector. Second, "systemic" has arisen in the regulatory reform dialogues in the context of systemically relevant financial institutions. This use is rather distinct as it describes the theory that certain financial institutions, due to their size or other denominator(s), are more relevant than others from a financial regulatory perspective and for their economic effects and their potential for financial stability disruptions, most notably in the context of the failure of a member of this group. Third, "systemic" may be understood in terms of the relative economic power of different nations within the global economy. For the purpose of this chapter, the term is used primarily in this first aspect.

An Institutional Design for Systemic Risk

Following the financial crisis, the EU response to the need for such reform has resulted in the implementation of the European Systemic Risk Board. In the United States, the FSOC has been its counterpart and forms part of the extensive Dodd-Frank Law introduced in July 2010. Both have both been designed to respond to the need for financial regulatory systems to adopt macro-prudential supervision as a key supervisory approach to the promotion of financial stability on a trans-national level (Pooran 2009). This chapter assesses from a comparative perspective the respective developments in the United States and the EU for the monitoring and assessment of systemic risk. It addresses the implications of this institutional and regulatory development – arguably the most fundamental change to take place in a post-crisis financial regulatory environment – in terms of its effectiveness for enhancing stability in the respective systems for promoting financial stability as a key policy objective and for integrating systemic risk into financial regulation and policy.

The EU Response to Systemic Risk

Any discussion of the EU's post-crisis response and framework for systemic risk monitoring, which has resulted in the introduction of a new body, the ESRB, to address it, must by necessity refer to the process preceding this. In the case of the ESRB's evolution and final introduction, the process was a pivotal one. Accordingly, it is necessary to revisit the circumstances in which the new developments in this area have taken form.

Early Origins of the European Systemic Risk Board (hereafter the "ESRB" or the "Board")

The evolution of the ESRB can be traced to the early origins of the recent global crisis. In the wake of the recent global crisis, the De Larosiere Report, and the recommendations therein, provide a critical and pivotal point for the reforms subsequently launched in the EU and for the approach more broadly taken to regulatory reform for the Single Market (European Commission 2009). While the concept of macroprudential supervision predates the recent crisis, the origins of a systemic risk board as an institutional framework to bolster financial stability in the context of the recent crisis arises largely from the recommendations of the High Level Group on Financial Supervision in the EU, chaired by Jacques de Larosiere (hereafter, the "De Larosiere Report"). Against the background of the onset of the global financial crisis, the High Level Group was mandated by the European Commission in November 2008.[3] More poignantly, from the perspective of the broader vision and direction of the EU, against which this new institution has been necessitated, the report proposed the way forward by reference to the following two options: "We have two alternatives: the first '*chacun pour soi*' beggar-thy neighbour solutions; or the second – enhanced, pragmatic, sensible European cooperation for the benefit of all to preserve an open world economy. This will bring undoubted economic

---

[3] It is noteworthy that the *Avant-Propos* of this report notes the fragmentation in the existing structures, regulatory rulebook, and framework and set forth the objectives of: "a new regulatory agenda – to reduce risk and improve risk management; to improve systemic shock absorbers ... stronger coordinated supervision – macroprudential and microprudential. Building on existing structures. .... Much stronger, coordinated supervision for all financial actors in the European Un ion ... effective crisis management procedures". De Larosiere Report, p. 4.

gains, and this is what we favour" (*ibid.*, 4). The relevance of these remarks clearly goes beyond the measures finally proposed and introduced for systemic risk assessment but more broadly gives an indication of the context in which the present-day goals and vision of the European Union that such a reform seeks to promote.

The origins of the present systemic risk body in the EU lies in the origins of the recommendations of the De Larosiere Report. Among the recommendations of the De Larosiere was the establishment of an EU-level body with responsibility for oversight of risk in the broad financial system of the EU and not an approach fragmented into national or sectoral lines. On the issue of macro-prudential supervision, this report noted, *inter alia*, "an urgent need to upgrade macro-prudential supervision in the EU for all financial activities" (*ibid.*, 44 Paragraph 173) and proposed the following: "A new group, replacing the current Banking Supervision Committee (BSC) of the ECB, called the European Systemic Risk Council (ESRC) should be set up with a mandate to form judgments and make recommendations on macro-prudential policy, issue risk warnings, compare observations on macro-economic and prudential developments and give direction to these issues" (*ibid.*, Paragraph 177). The European Central Bank (hereafter, the "ECB") was proposed for this function (*ibid.*, Paragraph 175). The De Larosiere Report further noted,

> What could and should be prevented is the kind of systemic and inter-connected vulnerabilities we have seen and which have carried such contagious effects. To prevent the recurrence of this type of crisis, a number of critical policy changes are called for. These concern the European Union [… and] also the global system at large.

The recommendations of its final report were subsequently welcomed by the European Commission.[4] Following the endorsement of the De Larosiere Report by the European Commission and European Council in March 2009 and the subsequent publication of implementation details in May 2009, the recommendations of this report culminated in proposals for reforms in the area of financial stability and the establishment of the ESRB. The origins of the recently implemented ESRB lies in Recommendation 16 of the report, below which described the proposal for a systemic risk body for the Single Market in the following terms: "A new body called the European Systemic Risk Council (ESRC), to be chaired by the ECB President, should be set up under the auspices and with the logistical support of the ECB" (*ibid.*, 46 Recommendation 16). The reforms for macro-prudential oversight culminated in Regulation (EU) No. 1092/2010 of the European Parliament and of

---

[4] The final recommendations were issued in February 2009.

the Council establishing the ESRB. The European System of Financial Supervision (ESFS) comprises: (a) the ESRB (as discussed below); (b) three (3) new European Supervisory Authorities (ESAs); (c) the Joint Committee of the European Supervisory Authorities; and (d) the competent or supervisor authorities in the Member States (European Union 2010a Article 3).[5]

The ESRB that focused on the systemic risk element of the new supervisory framework is one constituent of the European System of Financial Supervision (hereafter, the "ESFS"). Legislation to establish the ESFS – of which the ESRB is a key component – came into force in December 2010, marking a key and historical moment not only in the evolution of the Single Market's response to the global crisis but also in terms of the evolution of its institutional framework in response to the global financial crisis.

From Theory to Practice

"A European Systemic Risk Board (ESRB) is established. It shall have its seat in Frankfurt am Main" (*ibid.*, Article 1(1)).

As noted above, legislation to implement the ESRB and the broader ESFS came into force on 16 December 2010.[67] In its implemented form,

---

5 The broader reforms would require (i) the continued execution [preservation] of ongoing supervision by national supervisory agencies and supervisory responsibility for domestic financial institutions; (ii) the creation of three new bodies – the European Banking Authority, the European Insurance and Occupational Pensions Authority, and the European Securities Authority to replace existing Level 3 committees (CEBS, CEIOPS, and CESR); and (iii) the establishment of colleges of supervisors for major cross-border institutions. Independence from but accountability to political authorities was deemed to be key to the effectiveness of the new system. Within the new system, the revised European Authorities would maintain their existing responsibilities but would be charged with further responsibilities considered more effectively performed at a regional (European) level. Such new tasks would with regard to macro-prudential oversight include co-operation and information sharing with the proposed systemic risk body, the European Systemic Risk Council.

6 The ESFS consists of the ESRB, the ESAs (3), the Joint Committee, and the national supervisory authorities of the EU Member States. See in particular, para. 14 of EU Regulation 1092/2010: "A European System of Financial Supervision (ESFS) should be established, bringing together the actors of financial supervision at national level and at the level of the Union to act as a network".

7 See in particular, Regulation (EU) 1092/2010 of the European Parliament and of the Council of 24/11/2010 on European Union macro-prudential oversight of the financial system and establishing a European Systemic Risk Board and Council Regulation (EU) No. 1096/2010 of 17/11/2010, conferring specific tasks on the ECB for the proper functioning of the Board.

the ECB is entrusted with the secretariat of the ESRB.[8] The inaugural meeting of the ESRB took place on 20 January 2011, and two subsequent meetings of the general board have occurred.[9] During the inaugural Rules of Procedure for the ESRB were established, and a meeting schedule for the forthcoming year set.

Purpose

The *raison d'être* of the ESRB as set forth in Article 3(1) of the implementing regulation is responsibility

for the macro-prudential oversight of the financial system within the Union in order to contribute to the prevention or mitigation of systemic risks to financial stability in the Union that arise from developments within the financial system and taking into account macroeconomic developments, so as to avoid periods of widespread financial distress. It shall contribute to the smooth functioning of the internal market and thereby ensure a sustainable contribution of the financial sector to economic growth. (*Ibid.*)[10]

For this purpose, its tasks are set forth as follows:

(a) determining and/or collecting and analysing all the relevant and necessary information, for the purposes of achieving the objectives described in paragraph 1;

(b) identifying and prioritising systemic risks;

(c) issuing warnings where such systemic risks are deemed to be significant and, where appropriate, making those warnings public;

(d) issuing recommendations for remedial action in response to the risks identified and, where appropriate, making those recommendations public;

(e) when the ESRB determines that an emergency situation may arise [...] issuing a confidential warning addressed to the Council and providing the Council with an assessment of the situation in order to enable the Council to assess the need to adopt a decision addressed to the ESA's determining the existence of an emergency situation;

---

[8] And is responsible for the provision of "analytical, statistical, administrative and logistical support" as well as human and financial resources. See Article 2, EU Regulation 1096/2010.

[9] Subsequent Board meetings have occurred on 22 June 2011 and 21 September 2011.

[10] See also para. 11 of EU Regulation 1092/2010: "The present arrangements of the Union place too little emphasis on macro-prudential oversight and on inter-linkages between developments in the broader macroeconomic environment and the financial system. Responsibility for macro-prudential analysis remains fragmented, and is conducted by various authorities at different levels with no mechanism to ensure that macro-prudential risks are adequately identified and that warnings and recommendations are issued clearly, followed up and translated into action. A proper functioning of Union and global financial systems and the mitigation of threats thereto require enhanced consistency between macro- and micro-prudential supervision".

(f) monitoring the follow-up to warnings and recommendations;

(g) co-operating closely with all the other parties to the ESFS; where appropriate, providing the ESA's with the information on systemic risks required for the performance of their tasks; and, in particular, in collaboration with the ESA's, developing a common set of quantitative and qualitative indicators (risk dashboard) to identify and measure systemic risk;

(h) participating, where appropriate, in the Joint Committee;

(i) co-ordinating its actions with those of international financial organizations, particularly the IMF and the FSB as well as relevant bodies in third countries on matters related to macro-prudential oversight;

(j) carrying out other related tasks as specified in Union legislation (*ibid.*, Article 3(2)).

Structure and Decision Making

The EU systemic risk body is substantial in its composition and comprehensive in breadth. It consists of a general board (described below), steering committee,[11] secretariat, an advisory technical committee (hereafter, the ATC)[12] and an advisory scientific committee.[13] Decision-making as to the core tasks allocated to this body is conferred on the general board, which consists of 65 members. The tasks of the ESRB are to be, in essence, carried out by the general board. It is chaired by the president of the ECB, Jean-Claude Trichet, and its vice chair is the governor of the Bank of England, Mervyn King, following his election to this position on 16 December 2011.[14]

The following members of the general board have voting rights: the president and vice president of the ECB; the governors of national central banks; one member of the European Commission; each of the chairpersons of the EBA, the EIOPA, and the ESMA respectively; the chair of the advisory scientific committee as well as its two vice chairs; the chair of the advisory technical committee. Its non-voting members are the president of the economic and financial committee as well as one high-level representative for each Member State of the competent supervisory authority.

The ESRB's powers are non-binding. It shall issue recommendations[15] and warnings (*ibid.*, Article 16(2)). The possible recipients of such warnings and recommendations are the Member States (an indi-

---

[11] 14 members.
[12] 65 members.
[13] 15 members.
[14] By the General Council of the ECB.
[15] Includes "legislative initiatives" per Article 16(1) EU Regulation 1092/2010.

vidual state or a number of Member States), the EU, one or more ESAs, and the national supervisors. The conditions in which the issuance of such warnings and recommendations are envisaged are circumstances in which risks to financial stability are assessed pursuant to the aims of the body as established in the legislative mandate of the body.[16] From a purely legalistic and enforcement perspective, its findings are not mandatory or legally binding. The degree of importance to be attributed to this feature of the ESRB has attracted some attention. It is submitted that despite the non-binding nature of the ESRB's warnings, this feature of its design shall not detract from the effectiveness of the body that lies more in its decision-making power and singular ability to provide determinations as to vulnerabilities in the EU financial system rather than from its ability to enforce measures. Indeed, it is worth considering that this very feature of the ESRB offers a delicate balance between the opportunity for EU-wide surveillance of risks and vulnerabilities combined with continued responsibility at a state level for the design of policies and measures to take appropriate measures in response to such perceived threats to financial stability and the opportunity for Member States to retain ownership of the response mechanisms. The new system *prima facie* includes, however, appropriate mechanisms for accountability by requiring information as to actions and inaction following ESRB advice to be provided to the body and, if necessary, made public. Its effectiveness, instead, shall derive more from its moral suasion, the substantive merit of its analytical findings, and its ability to provide preemptive warnings to countries within the EU or to the Single Market in a way that would not be easily accomplished in any other institutional framework and which carries the potential for vast rewards in economic governance, crisis aversion, and financial stability.

In his comments on the implementation of the ESRB, Chair Jean-Claude Trichet commented:

> The macro-prudential activities of the ESRB are now starting at the operational level...The General Board of the ESRB has agreed to have a look at systemic risks in the EU's financial system each quarter. It may however also study long-term structural issues relevant for financial stability, in as much as they may create future risks (Hearing on the ESRB 2011).

With regard to the decision-making and analytical framework for its deliberations, an area likely to require further development, he has also further stated: "The ESRB will make use of a wide set of quantitative and qualitative indicators as well as analytical tools. They will include financial stability indicators, early-warning signal indicators and models, contagion and spill-over models as well as stress tests" (*ibid.*). The

---

[16] Per Article 3(1) EU Regulation 1092/2010.

latter, in particular, the policy instruments and the analytical tools used in the exercise potentially provide the greatest area for further work in this field.

The ESRB may be viewed as a key measure and potentially radical shift to bolster financial stability and enhance systemic risk monitoring with implications that clearly go beyond the recent crisis to larger questions of supervisory focus and power, centralization, and responsibility in financial market and supervisory policy-making in the EU. It represents the culmination of efforts initiated at the onset of the global crisis to identify the weaknesses and shortcomings in financial regulation and supervision of financial institutions that enabled the recent crisis and the failure of instruments and institutions to predict this or provide more timely policy directives that may have mitigated the onset or extent of the crisis, prevented its occurrence, or diluted its effect throughout the international financial system.

US Reforms: The Financial Stability Oversight Council

The US response to the global financial crisis has produced one primary piece of federal legislation: the Wall Street Reform and Consumer Protection Act 2010 (commonly referred to as the Dodd-Frank reforms), signed into law on 21 July 2010. This aims at addressing and responding to the multiple deficiencies and subsequent areas of reform, including but not limited to systemic risk monitoring, that are considered to have contributed to the global financial crisis.[17] The need for further supervisory attention to systemic risk and the emerging concept of a cross-jurisdictional, multi-sectoral systemic risk board has been one of the numerous features of the reforms incorporated in the US legislation (Wall Street Reform and Consumer Protection Act 2010 Title I). Another far-reaching institutional reform that the Dodd-Frank reforms introduce is a new Bureau of Consumer Financial Protection (*ibid.*, Title X). The latter is also a new post-crisis institution and introduces novel regulatory measures into the US system.

In the case of its response to systemic risk, the United States provides that its systemic risk body, the Financial Stability Oversight Council is charged with:

(1) the identification of risks to US financial stability potentially arising from the failure, ongoing operation or material financial distress of large, interconnected bank holding companies or non-bank financial companies, (or from outside the financial services marketplace);

---

[17] In contrast to the approach to the reforms in the EU in which a number of separate bills targeting different areas. This difference is unlikely to have any impact on the effectiveness of the reforms and may be more a question of form than of efficacy.

(2) the promotion of market discipline, by eliminating expectations on the part of shareholders, creditors, and shield them from losses in the event of failure; and

(3) responding to emerging threats to the stability of the United States financial system. (*Ibid.*, Section 112)

It consists of ten voting members and five non-voting members. The voting members of the FSOC are the secretary of the treasury (also the chairperson), the chairman of the Board of Governors of the Federal Reserve System, the comptroller of the currency, the director of the Bureau of Consumer Financial Protection, the chairman of the Securities and Exchange Commission, the chairperson of the Federal Deposit Insurance Corporation, the chairperson of the Commodities Futures Trading Commission, the director of the Federal Housing Finance Agency, the chairman of the national Credit Union Administration Board, and an independent member with insurance expertise. The latter is necessitated by the absence at present of a federal supervisory authority in the United States for the insurance sector. The FSOC's non-voting members are the director of the Office of Financial Research, the director of the Federal Insurance Office, a state insurance commissioner, a state banking supervisor, and a state securities commissioner (*ibid.*, Section 111).

The tasks of the FSOC are:

(A) collation of information from member agencies, other Federal and State financial regulatory agencies, the Federal Insurance Office and, if necessary to assess risks to the United States financial system, direct the Office of Financial Research to collect information from bank holding companies and non-bank financial companies;

(B) provide direction to, and request data and analyses from, the Office of Financial Research to support the work of the Council;

(C) monitoring of the financial services marketplace to identify potential threats to the financial stability of the United States;

(D) monitoring of domestic and international financial regulatory proposals and developments and provision of advice to Congress and issuance of recommendations in such areas that will enhance the integrity, efficiency, competitiveness, and stability of the U.S. financial markets;

(E) facilitate information sharing and coordination among the member agencies and other Federal and State agencies regarding domestic financial services policy development, rulemaking, examinations, reporting requirements, and enforcement actions;

(F) recommend to the member agencies general supervisory priorities and principles reflecting the outcome of discussions among the member agencies;

(G) identify gaps in regulation that could pose risks to the financial stability of the United States;

(H) require supervision by the Board of Governors for non-bank financial companies that may pose risks to the financial stability of the United;

(I) make recommendations to the Board of Governors concerning the establishment of heightened prudential standards for risk based capital, leverage, liquidity, contingent capital, resolution plans and credit exposure reports, concentration limits, enhanced public disclosures, and overall risk management for non-bank financial companies and large, interconnected bank holding companies supervised by the Board of Governors;

(J) identify systemically important financial market utilities and payment, clearing, and settlement activities;

(K) make recommendations to primary financial regulatory agencies to apply new or heightened standards and safeguards for financial activities or practices that could create or increase risks of significant liquidity, credit, or other problems spreading among bank holding companies, non-bank financial companies, and United States financial markets; the Commission and any standard-setting body with respect to an existing or proposed accounting principle, standard, or procedure; (L) provide a forum for – (i) discussion and analysis of emerging market developments and financial regulatory issues; and (ii) resolution of jurisdictional disputes among the members of the Council; and (M) annually report to Congress on – (i) the activities of the Council; (ii) significant financial market and regulatory developments, including insurance and accounting regulations and standards, along with an assessment of those developments on the stability of the financial system; (iii) potential emerging threats to the financial stability of the United States. (*ibid.*, Section 112(A))

The legislation requires the FSOC to make annual recommendations to discharge its mandate. It is required to hold quarterly meetings. According to the FSOC's annual report, meetings were held on 1 October 2010, 23 November 2010, 18 January 2011, 17 March 2011, 24 May 2011, 13 July 2011, and 18 July 2011 (Financial Stability Oversight Council 2011). Pursuant to the 2011 Annual Report, the FSOC has fulfilled its mandate (above) by "recommending (1) heightened risk management and supervisory attention in specific areas; (2) further reforms to address structural vulnerabilities in key markets; (3) steps to address reform of the housing finance market; and (4) coordination of financial regulatory reform".[18]

---

[18] See 2011 Annual Report, p. 11 for further details of the specific recommendations in these areas.

Challenges for the FSOC

The ambit of the FSOC is, therefore, broader than that employed in the EU. It is noteworthy that while EU implementing regulations, notably Regulations (EU) 1092/2010 (European Union 2010a) and 1096/2010 (European Union 2010b) bringing into force the new institutional measure, specifically address the need for increased macro-prudential oversight as a key focus of the reforms and new legislation, in the case of the United States, a broader set of objectives has been identified as the driving force of the Dodd-Frank Law.[19] At an extreme, it may be said that the latter is more akin to a list of policy goals that seeks to address a myriad of issues requiring reform in the financial regulatory system; systemic risk monitoring is addressed in this context. On a pessimistic note, the treatment of systemic risk in the US financial system may be viewed as subsumed in this way. The passage of secondary legislation and guidelines addressing in detail the requirements and implementation of systemic risk oversight is one option that can provide the required specification. The need for more detailed and targeted reform in this area is acknowledged and shall provide more effective conditions for optimal implementation. Such further specification, as acknowledged by the supervisory agencies, remains a significant area where further progress continues to be made.

Further challenges are likely to be encountered in the case of the FSOC. These arise from the existing supervisory structure in the United States. The latter consideration is an important element of the new supervisory structure within which the macro-prudential body will operate. In this regard, for example, the insurance sector, which continues to be supervised on a state-by-state level in the United States, is likely to present particular supervisory (and policy) challenges. There are likely to be challenges in forming opinions as to risks on a sectoral level. The translation of weaknesses into system-wide disruptions in the absence of more cohesion and centralization in the micro-prudential function may be a necessary precondition for the effective implementation of the Financial Stability Oversight Council and for effective macro-prudential supervision more broadly. Due to the fragmentation in the US financial system and the underlying need for resolution of fundamental supervisory issues, including the continued state-by-state form of supervision for the insurance sector, it would appear that further work is beneficial in this area for the FSOC to perform the optimal level

---

[19] The Preamble of WSRCPA addresses the need for financial stability throughout increased transparency and accountability – as distinct as throughout greater measures for systemic risk monitoring but arguably includes a longer laundry list of reforms specifically targeting bailouts and abusive consumer protection practices.

of system-wide surveillance across the US financial system and for the FSOC to make the level of recommendations that macro-prudential oversight would require.[20] The FSOC requires the resolution of such sectoral and state level issues to be capable of comprehensive system-wise surveillance of the US financial sector and further to assess the inter-play between weaknesses in this area and the economy. There is a need for these existing supervisory issues to be addressed in order for the US reform in this area to move as envisaged.

In both systems, there remains a need for considerable further work in the development of macro-prudential instruments and tools to translate these policy objectives into a pragmatic, workable regulatory approach for both regulated institutions and regulators in the respective EU and US financial systems. Time is needed for the underlying supervisory structure, the micro-prudential framework, in particular in the US, to adapt to a more centralized style of oversight. Changes in the actual conduct of (micro) prudential analysis by national supervisory authorities in each system are not required in this regard, but improvements in the structure of the over-arching supervisory system and framework could strongly improve the level of oversight provided by the FSOC.

The reforms are clearly intended to enable more effective crisis mitigation and appropriate policy interventions to safeguard the financial system and avoid a system of oversight that depends too heavily on a micro-prudential approach to financial market governance, that is too sectoral in its view of risks to the broader economy, that is too limited in jurisdictional terms, and too nationalistic in the reach and scope of its supervisory authorities. It is arguable that in the case of the United States, the legislation highlights and seeks to address the perceived cumulative failings in diverse areas that enabled the global economic crisis while the EU reforms achieve that objective by focusing more strongly and with greater precision on the institutional reforms that would achieve such change. The EU reforms may be viewed in this way as more advanced than their counterparts in the United States in terms of achieving more targeted reforms to address the weaknesses in the shared global financial system and in bringing about enhanced systemic risk monitoring that could serve the interests of promoting financial stability.

---

[20] It must be noted, however, that the underlying issues requiring resolution for greater progress on the implementation of a systemic risk body may have its roots in historical underpinnings rather than a lack of political will.

Concluding Remarks

The implementation of the ESRB and the legislative enactment in the United States are representative of the political will on either side of the transatlantic partnership to effectively change the approach to supervision of financial institutions and the institutional framework used for determining financial institution strength, the basis for policy determinations in the financial systems, and represent the integration of a macro-prudential approach to supervision. The concept further raises questions as to the balance of supervisory power and policy among (member) states and the federal government or council in each system, the differences and co-existence of existing national supervisory agencies, and the new supervisory structure and the inter-relationship among national and supra-national regulators with the potential implications for extra-territoriality that this may have.

The EU and US reform packages respond to the need for far-reaching changes in the supervision of financial institutions and recognise the need for introducing and integrating systemic risk assessment into the mechanisms for exercising surveillance of the financial system to implement a macro-prudential approach to financial market supervision. Both jurisdictions have moved forward in acknowledging and incorporating systemic risk in the new supervisory framework through respective systemic risk boards – the ESRB and FSOC. It would appear that while the most significant institutional reform to result from the recent crisis has in the case of the EU been the introduction, design, and swift, effective implementation of the ESRB, in the United States, the implementation of a council to address this may be hampered by underlying structural and supervisory issues. Accordingly, in the US system, the most significant institutional advance in financial regulatory reform thus far has been the new Bureau of Consumer Financial Protection. The FSOC may be more embryonic and requires the resolution of sectoral and state level issues to be capable of truly comprehensive system-wide surveillance of the US financial sector and effective macro-prudential oversight. Accordingly, it would appear that while both the EU and the United States have made significant progress in their respective and shared financial regulatory systems in response to the onset of the global economic crisis, the US reforms have more fundamentally addressed the need for enhanced consumer protection while in the EU, greater progress has been made in integrating systemic risk in supervision. At an institutional level, the Bureau of Consumer Protection represents a more fundamental advance for the United States while the ESRB is more highly developed in the EU. Further, the EU reforms would at this stage appear to be more comprehensive in addressing the new institutional framework in the area of systemic risk from the Mem-

ber State level through to the ESRB, while in the United States, fundamental, persistent state level issues require political and regulatory
resolution for the FSOC to truly operate as envisaged, in a way that
would in practice complement its EU counterpart with consistency,
cohesion, and parity in institutional and regulatory function. Ultimately,
the latter is necessary for a truly integrated EU-US financial supervisory
architecture that would most effectively protect the financial institutions, whether or not operating on a transatlantic level, and consumers
and enable continued growth and development of this integral market
and serve the transatlantic interest of financial market growth and
development, as well as that of future financial stability.

References

European Commission (2009). "Report of the High Level Group on Financial
Supervision in the EU". http://ec.europa.eu/internal_market/finances/docs/
de_larosiere_report_en.pdf.

European Union (2010a). "Regulation (EU) No. 1092/2010 of the European
Parliament and of the Council of 24/11/2010 on European Union macro-
prudential oversight of the financial system and establishing a European Systemic Risk Board". *Official Journal of the European Union*, L 331,
15 December, pp. 1-11. <http://www.esrb.europa.eu/shared/pdf/ESRB-
en.pdf?2ccd405d7216f4baa605c2f92fef979e>.

European Union (2010b). "Council Regulation (EU) No. 1096/2010 of
17/11/2010 conferring specific tasks upon the European Central Bank concerning the functioning of the European Systemic Risk Board". *Official
Journal of the European Union* L 331. 15 December, pp. 162-164.
<http://www.esrb.europa.eu/shared/pdf/ESRB-ECB-
en.pdf?9d4cb41f9f6571bed985d131fb55a301>.

Financial Stability Oversight Council Annual Report (2011).
<http://www.treasury.gov/initiatives/fsoc/Documents/FSOCAR2011.pdf>.

High-Level Group on Financial Supervision in the EU (2009). Brussels
25 February. <http://www.esrb.europa.eu/shared/pdf/de_larosiere_report_en.
pdf?694f9f09ffc6d335c2bd251a136cfb77>.

Pooran, Priya Nandita (2009). "Macro-Prudential Supervision – A Panacea for
the Global Financial Crisis?" *Law and Financial Markets Review*, November
2009.

Wall Street Reform and Consumer Protection Act (2010). <http://www.gpo.
gov/fdsys/pkg/CRPT-111hrpt517/pdf/CRPT-111hrpt517.pdf>.

PART III

TRANSATLANTIC RELATIONS AND TRADE

Beyond the Competition for Liberalisation

Free Trade Agreements and the Emerging of the Transnational Competitive State

Maria BEHRENS

Introduction

According to proponents of liberal institutionalism, the globalisation process limits the acting capability of states, a decline they can only make up for by pooling their sovereignty on an international level. In the post-national constellation of international relations – as Zürn (2002) has labelled it – international institutions promote the co-ordination and harmonisation of politics among different states through principles, norms, rules, and decision-making processes. In this process, the state is continuously internationalised. Given the augmented requirement for rules and regulations that help solve problems arising during a collision of norms, and furthermore to ensure rules are adhered to, international institutions are transforming from intergovernmentalism to supranationalism and – when including transnational actors – towards transnationalism (Knodt and Jachtenfuchs 2002, p. 16). Due to these changes, states continuously lose their dominance in foreign policy in favour of international/regional organizations and transnational actors. This development will lead to a process of constitutionalism in world politics in which a transformation of the state from a monopolist to a manager of political authority will take place (Genschel and Zangl 2009).

From this functionalist perspective, the world trade regime may be regarded as an empirical success story. While the old intergovernmental GATT-1947 channelled interests among states primarily through diplomatic means, the World Trade Agreement of 1994, within the Uruguay Round framework, strengthened the World Trade Organization's (WTO's) dispute settlement mechanism by establishing legal and judicial elements. The panel's decisions can now only be blocked by a resolution member states unanimously support. Hence, states lost the possibility of politically tilt panel-decisions and are left with the sole option of submitting objections to the permanent Appelate Body. The new regulations enforced the mandatory nature of WTO-rules (Keohane *et al.* 2000), a transformation that is interpreted as a limited supra-nationalization (Neyer 1999). The stalemate of the world trade round in Doha, Qatar, is blamed on the difficulty to convey interests within a heterogeneous structure of members. From this point of view, the political order of the world trade regime is not endangered, but we are dealing with a seemingly solvable conflict on regulation matters.

The regionalism of the 1990s/2000s – NAFTA (North American Free Trade Agreement), MERCOSUR (Common Southern Market), ASEAN (Association of Southeast Asian Nations) – may be regarded through the integration-theoretic lens and perceived as complementary to the world trade regime: Transaction costs may be reduced through regional co-operation by dismantling trade barriers. Furthermore, the small number of co-operation partners simplifies the implementation of steps towards liberalisation and widens their scope. Accordingly, regional free trade agreements (FTAs) are spearheads or building blocks forming a larger structure of an additional liberalisation of world trade. Article XXIV of the WTO is based on these assumptions and allows the signing of FTAs under certain circumstances. The exponential increase of bilateral FTAs since the early 1990s (see Figure 1) cannot, however, be explained by resorting to liberal institutionalism theory: The new bilateral FTAs are detached from the regional context and are, *ergo*, not integrational projects in the common sense. Furthermore, one can observe a notable increase in the number of FTAs signed between developed and develop-ing countries, characterised by asymmetrical rather than symmetrical relationships of interdependence. Based on these findings, several questions arise: How relevant is the rise of bilateral FTA numbers for world trade? What characterises a typical bilateral FTA under the conditions of asymmetrical relationship of interdependence? And final-ly: How do bilateral FTAs affect the world trade regime?

This chapter is based on the thesis that the macroeconomic welfare effects of bilateral FTAs with developing countries are not seen as the only reason by the United States and the European Union to sign one. In the asymmetric relationship of interdependence, the aspect of power is also influential as it enables states to further and implement their strategic goals not only in economic fields, but also in noneconomic areas. Therefore, it is to be expected that the structures of dependence will deepen more, instead of – as the classic liberal economic theories assume(d) – being dismantled by free trade's welfare effects. Instead, the stronger states enforce protectionism, hollowing out and weakening the world trade regime. Concerning the transformation of statehood, the competition between large trade powers, such as the US and the EU, incrementally will lead to a transnational competitive state. But, transnational is not to be confused with transnationalism in terms of

Knodt and Jachtenfuchs (2002). The term "transnational competitive state" as used in this chapter is referring to the "national competitive state" as proposed by Hirsch (1998).[1] A national competitive state thus is characterized by the competition for the most attractive industrial locations compared to other states.

Figure 1
FTAs Registered with the WTO (1990-2011)

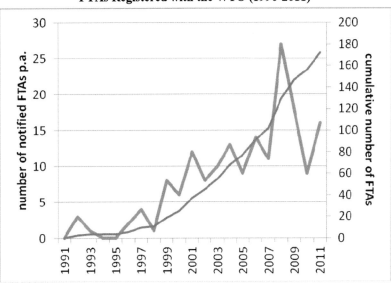

Source: WTO, RTA Database (wto.org, accessed 17 January 2012).

An attribute of the transnational competitive state is its outward strategy of creating necessary institutional conditions in weaker states, in order to open and ensure foreign markets for its own domestic enterprises (such as protection of investment and public procurement) and also to protect domestic sectors that are unable to compete on an international level. While a transnational enterprise, as an economic actor, (re)settles its commodities and services to foreign markets, the transnational competitive state, as a political actor, imposes its national regulations on other political systems. Additionally to gaining economic power, the state also raises its institutional power level. Regarding the functional

---

[1]   According to Hirsch (1998), the national competitive state is characterised by its task to optimise the conditions under which capital is exploited, meaning to render the terms and conditions on-site as attractive as possible (see, as well, Strange 1996). Optimising the terms and conditions on-site leads to an enlargement of the economic and social inequalities within the national societies as well as on an international level.

process of transformation, the transnational competitive state can thereby count on the support of domestic enterprises and groups of civil society, as well as on the assistance of transnational enterprises. In this way, the transnational competitive state expands the output legitimacy of its power. Precondition for domestic support and increased legitimacy is either way the existence of an asymmetrical interdependence in international relations. The input legitimacy becomes more and more decentralized, shifting towards local authorities (Strange 1996).

The first section of this chapter introduces an evaluation of the trade political conflicts from a critical realist perspective on which the definition of the transnational competitive state is based. The second section delves into the development of bilateral FTAs. US and EU political trade motives for signing FTAs are analysed by means of our own empiric investigations.[2] The third section includes an analysis of the effects these new US and EU foreign trade strategies have on the design of FTAs negotiated with developing countries. Finally, section four discusses possible consequences of previous points of the chapter for the world trade regime and contains the presentation of results from studies conducted by economic science on the efficacy of FTAs. The results are examined for potential implications they might have on political power.

Trade Conflicts in the World Economic System from a Theoretical Perspective

Until the end of 2011, agreement on central questions between developed and developing countries – such as the dismantling of agrarian subsidies – was not reached within the Doha world trade round. Even the Uruguay round seemed short of failure in 1988 and 1990. However, on a structural level and in view of the current goals, fundamental differences between the current Doha round and the Uruguay round can be noted. On a structural level, the power relations between the US and the EU changed. Due to its eastward enlargement, the EU rose to be a similarly strong economic power able to compare to the US. From a realistic perspective, the US has consequently lost hegemonic power. Additionally, one should consider the new challenges posed by the emerging markets of China and India. We can thus speak of observing the structural transformation of a now bipolar world trade system that was formerly unipolar. According to the hegemonic stability theory, hegemony promotes multilateral free trade because of the stark profit it

---

[2] For "the transnational competition-state" research project (ongoing), we performed eighteen semi-structured expert interviews with government officials in Mexico and Chile.

can count on from doing so. In his study, Mansfield (1992) proves the correlation between power constellation and the signing of trade agreements. In case of a hegemonic power decline, he concludes that a stronger protectionism will be implemented. The decreasing hegemonic position of the US can, in turn, be explained by resorting to the hegemonic stability theory and can also give the new regionalism context. Nonetheless, Mansfield's study (1992) related to the old regionalism and does not distinguish among the different types of states' agreements that might be preferentially signed. FTAs closed under the conditions of an asymmetrical relationship of interdependence are, hence, not specifically referred to in the study, and, thus, no explanations on the effects of these agreements on the multilateral trade regime are presented.

According to Susan Strange (1989, pp. 24 ff.), in addition to material or relational power, structural power is another factor of hegemonic predominance. For Strange, structural power is "the power to shape and determine the structures of the global political economy within which other states, their political institutions, their economic enterprises and (not least) their scientists and other professional people have to operate". Robert W. Cox (1981) uses a comparable definition that lists material resources, institutions, and ideas as essential factors of power. These powers may be translated into the areas of international economic politics as the Economy, Politics and Society (Hummel 2000). Cox postulates the existence of a consensus among the elites of these three areas: that they have a common opinion concerning the direction of economic policy. Translated to the transnational level, this concept is understood as a hegemonic consensus. Neoliberalism was implemented towards the end of the 1970s and is regarded as a hegemonic consensus of the world economic relations, a consensus institutionalised in the WTO. The current stalemate of the Doha/Qatar world trade round would be an expression of the dissolution of consensus encompassing society within the US and the EU, a common opinion on the future direction of world trade policy. The increased pressure of unions within the US shows that they are no longer willing to continue promoting world trade policy's neoliberal direction. The "Occupy Wall Street" movement in 2011 seems to be another indicator for the erosion of the neoliberal consensus (Mallory 2011). Also, EU Member States are increasingly faced with social protests and pressure from NGOs that insist on social justice not only on a national but also on an international level (a well-known example concerning the World Trade Regime were the protests during the Ministerial Conference in Seattle in 1999).

The problem of legitimacy and the shift in power relations between the US and the EU contributed to the disintegration of the transatlantic alliance in foreign trade politics. This alliance, founded on a neoliberal consensus, worked as glue bridging the conflicts between industrial and developing countries. Should the findings verify the thesis that consensus on the future direction of world trade policy is crumbling, the stalemate within the world trade round would not only be a conflict concerning regulation, but it would also be a conflict on order and will, in consequence, lead to either a failure or a transformation of the world trade regime. Following these postulations, the recent development of bilateral trade agreements will be empirically examined. To assist this effort, Cox's hegemonic power factors will be applied to US and EU foreign trade strategies and translated into f, institutional power and power of legitimacy.

The Strategy of Bilateral Trade Agreements

To not hinder the European integration process, Article 24 of the WTO permits the signing of regional FTAs under certain circumstances: An FTA may not position higher tariffs or other non-tariff trade barriers than those agreed within the world trade framework. FTAs aim at erecting free trade areas. FTA-members commit to mutually abolish all tariffs and non-tariff trade barriers within ten years (Paragraph 5c of Article 24 of the WTO). Compared to the US negotiating only FTAs, an FTA of the EU is part of an association agreement including a political dialogue and co-operation.

During its eastward and southern enlargement, the EU signed some FTAs, whereas the US rejected the option of regional and bilateral FTAs, claiming these agreements contributed to the weakening of the multilateral world trade regime. In fact, by 2001, the US had only finalized two (Israel and Canada) of the 130 FTAs it had registered with the WTO (Schott 2004).

From 2000 onward, powers within the US gained leverage. They voiced concern that the EU and its planned enlargement eastward might outweigh the US economically and in economic-political terms (Fergusson 2006). During the following years, the US closed a number of FTAs and is negotiating with different states (Cooper 2006). The EU responded to US participation in the race for FTAs from 2000 onward by publishing the foreign trade policy strategy paper *Global Europe* in 2006, which stresses the intention to continue signing bilateral contracts with new intensity (EU-Commission 2006a). "The Commission will propose a new programme of bilateral free trade agreements with key partners in which economic criteria will be a primary consideration" (EU-Commission 2006b).

Since then, a race to open new markets has ensued between the US and the EU. FTAs that the EU has already agreed to concentrate regionally on the Mediterranean countries (Tunisia 1998, Israel 2000, Morocco 2000, Jordan 2002, Lebanon 2003, Egypt 2004, Algeria 2005). Further agreements were signed with South Africa (2000), Mexico (2000), Croatia (2002) and Chile (2003). Since 2007, there have been negotiations with countries of Central America (Guatemala, El Salvador, Honduras, Nicaragua, Costa Rica, and Panama) and with countries of the Andean Community (Bolivia, Colombia, Ecuador, and Peru). The negotiations between Peru and Colombia were concluded successfully in March 2010 (USTR 2011). Furthermore, since 1999, the EU aimed to implement an interregional FTA with the countries of MERCOSUR, but the negotiations are difficult and lengthy. For this reason, the EU Commission made on the European Union-Latin America Summit in Madrid 2010 some pressure for concluding the negotiations.

Emerging markets in Asia are also of special interest to the US. An FTA with Singapore has existed since 2004. Talks with Thailand (since 2003) ceased in the fall of 2006, after the military coup. In South Korea, the US was able to sign an FTA on 30 June 2007 and thus outran the EU. South America is highest on the US' FTA priority list. The attempt to create a holistic Free Trade Area of the Americas (FTAA) failed in 2006 because of resistance by MERCOSUR. However, the US signed bilateral FTAs with Chile (2004), Panama (2006), Peru (2006, and Columbia (2006). In 2004, the US, Costa Rica, the Dominican Republic, El Salvador, Guatemala, Honduras, and Nicaragua signed a regional FTA (CAFTA-DR). Another regional focus of US efforts to close FTA deals is the Middle East. After signing FTAs with Jordan (2001) and Morocco (2006), FTAs in Bahrain (2006) and Oman (2006) were particularly seen as an anchor for the US in this region. By 2013, it was planned to implement the Middle East FTA (MEFTA), including all countries in the region (USTR 2007). The US started negotiations about a FTA with the UAE in 2005. But the negotiations seem not to be successful because no further negotiations with countries of the Middle East and North Africa followed.

Since 2010, the US has been negotiating with four member countries of the Trans Pacific Partnership (TPP) – Brunei, Chile, New Zealand, and Singapore – and also with Australia, Malaysia, Peru, and Vietnam about an expansion of the existing regional FTA. Furthermore, Mexico and Canada intend to join the negotiations. The ambitious negotiations for the TPP correspond to the changing strategy of US President Obama and his US Trade Ambassador (USTR) Ron Kirk to concentrate more on Asia. It is planned to finalize an agreement in 2012.[3]

---

[3]   See <http://www.ustr.gov/tpp>. [Accessed 26 April 2012].

Figure 2
FTAs Sorted by State Groups[4]

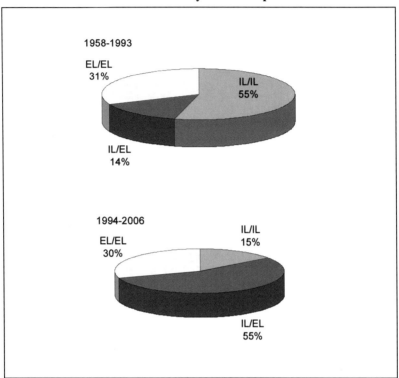

Distinguishing among different types of state groups, as depicted in Figure 2, confirms the increase of FTAs signed between developing and industrial countries since the mid-1990s. In comparison, the FTAs signed within the state group of developing countries and within the group of industrial countries are much lower.[5] In FTAs signed between developing and industrial countries, however, the economic interdependence is substantially lower, as is the case of FTAs signed between industrial countries as well. For example, exchange of goods between the EU-27 and its free trade partners is worth a mere one per cent –

WTO, Regional trade agreements. <http://www.wto.org/english/tratop_e/region_e/region_e.htm>. [Accessed 3 March 2007], graphic by the author.

5   FTAs between transitional countries were not considered for these numbers, even if they make up about one-fourth of all FTAs. However, these states already co-operated prior to the implosion of the Soviet Union. Through FTAs these co-operative relations are only renewed.

excluding India, South Africa and South Korea.[6] The numbers in the case of the US are similar (Ludema 2007, p. 1219). This raises the question: Why do the US and the EU sign FTAs with countries whose economic welfare effects are negligible? An analysis that differentiates according to sectors, however, shows that the imports from developing countries concentrate on few sectors, most often on the agrarian. Next to the Singapore Issues, such as investment, trade and competition policy, and transparency in government procurement, the US and the EU insist on adhering to environmental and social standards. This positive rule-making is labelled by William Dymond and Michael Hart (2000, p. 2138) as an attribute of a "post-modern trade policy", which – according to Falke (2005) – stands in particular for the European foreign trade policy within the multilateral negotiation system (compare also the debate about Normative Power Europe, Manners 2002; Sjursen 2006). The EU tried with little success to include environmental and social standards on the agenda of the world trade round, but failed because of resistance by the US and developing countries. In contrast, in its bilateral FTAs, the EU strives to implement its norms: "In considering new FTAs, we will need to work to strengthen sustainable development through our bilateral trade relations. This could include incorporating new co-operative provisions in areas relating to labour standards and environmental protection" (EU-Commission 2006a, p. 12).

Falke considers this post-modern trade policy to be an element of a concept of global governance that relies on positive rule-making (2005, p. 341). Instead, the economic sciences label this phenomenon as "export protectionism": According to this definition, the introduction of environmental and social standards deprives developing countries of their comparative cost advantages. This is done with the goal of protecting the non-competitive sectors within the EU from cheap imports (Bhagwati 2007, p. 13).

The US' new trade policy does not concern itself with questions of global governance, but as is also the case within the EU, its own interests are shaped by inner political forces. On 11 May 2007, both congressional parties and the administration presented a joint proposal for a "New Trade Policy for America". This proposal bridges the differing Republican and Democratic approaches toward globalisation and laid an existing schism within Congress to rest. The administration's interest to reach an agreement with Congress is easily explained, since the Trade Promotion Authority was up for renewal. The new trade agenda of 2007 was a shift in a new direction of the former trade policy by the Bush

---

[6] See Eurostat, External Trade, <http://epp.eurostat.ec.europa.eu/>. [Accessed 2 November 2007].

administration. For example, the administration had still refused to include environmental and socio-political standards on the agenda of the world trade round until recently.

The new US trade agenda now considers social and environmental standards – in accord with international regimes – in FTA negotiations. Thus, the following environmental conditions are now part of a bilateral trade agreement: "Each Party shall adopt, maintain, and implement laws, regulations, and all other measures to fulfill its obligations under the multilateral environmental agreements listed in Annex 17.2" ("covered agreements").[7]

For labour, the following conditions are part of a FTA: "Each Party shall adopt and maintain in its statutes and regulations, and practices thereunder, the following rights, as stated in the ILO Declaration on Fundamental Principles and Rights at Work and its Follow-up".[8]

In the US FTAs, a party can accuse the other for non-compliance with the multilateral environmental and labour agreements, because they are part of the dispute settlement mechanism of a FTA. In contrast to the FTAs of the United States, social and environmental standards in the Association Agreements of the EU are commitments and not obligations, thus not coming under the dispute resolution procedure.

Such norm-setting abroad as here described reveals that contract partners are negotiating in an asymmetrical relationship of interdependence: The new FTAs only require compulsory adherence to multilateral labour and environmental conventions which the US has already ratified. Conventions that remain unratified by the US, but which the FTA-contract partner might have ratified (for example, the Cartagena Protocol on Biosafety in the case of Peru) are not listed in the FTAs.

An analysis distinguishing among different types of contract partners shows that the asymmetrical relationship of interdependence functions as an enabler, allowing the US to promote its political security interests, as well. In a speech at the Institute for International Economics in May 2003, then-Trade Representative Robert Zoellick stressed that FTA-negotiations with the US would be linked to preconditions. Not only supporting US foreign political interests would be expected during the current world trade round, but also supporting its security policy. Deciding on a country's eligibility for FTA negotiations is based on a thir-

---

[7] Multilateral environmental agreements are, for example, the Montreal Protocol on Substances that Deplete the Ozone Layer or the Convention on International Trade in Endangered Species of Wild Fauna and Flora; see United States-Panama Trade Promotion Agreement 2007, Chapter 17, Environment, 17-1, ustr.org [Accessed 21 January 2012).

[8] *Ibid.*, Chapter 16, Labor, 16-1.

teen-point catalogue. Criteria include the FTA's influence on democratic development and economic reform processes of the negotiating country. Another standard for eligibility is the state's geostrategic relevance. The bilateral FTA with Bahrain, for example, is seen as an anchor in the Middle East, ensuring further regional access. Zoellick (2003) clarified that it is not simply a "competition for liberalization", but future trade partners also undergo a highly selective process based on their strategic security criteria before being chosen. In a speech at the University of South Carolina in May 2003, US President Bush stated that the US was striving to implement a Middle East Free Trade-Agreement (MEFTA) by 2013. Hereby, US economic interests in this region are secondary, as the entire GDP of the Arabic states in sum is lower than that of Spain on its own. The following quote illustrates clearly that security policy interests dominate the motivation behind these steps: "We're determined to help build a Middle East that grows in hope, instead of resentment. Because of the ideals and resolve of this nation, you and I will not live in an age of terror. We will live in an age of liberty".[9]

Bush's proposition of building a Middle East Free Trade Zone was supported by Congress. Republican senator John McCain and Democratic Senator Max Baucus jointly submitted the Middle East Trade and Engagement Act of 2003 (1121) to the Senate. The legal text underlines in Article 2.2 that "Congress views democratization and economic progress in the countries of the greater Middle East as important elements of a policy to address terrorism and endemic instability".

When signing Trade and Investment Framework Agreements (TIFAs), which function as a precondition prior to negotiating for an FTA, states have to agree to support the US security policy (particularly in the Middle East conflict).[10] Also, Preferential Treaties (Generalized System of Preferences – GSP) are linked to preconditions. GSPs – in the sense of the word – are limited to decrease tariffs on selected products. GSPs are supposed to support the economic growth of developing countries by trading tariff-free products with the US. Nonetheless, within the treaties, parties agree on extended regulations concerning noneconomic areas such as worker's rights, protection of investment, tax and customs, protection of the environment, human rights, and intellectual property rights. Linking economic matters of the FTA to security aspects are part of the preconditions a state has to fulfil before

---

9 White House, Office of the Press Secretary, President Bush Presses for Peace in the Middle East, <http://www.whitehouse.gov/news/releases/2003/05/20030509-11.html>. [Accessed 11 March 2007].
10 See Middle East Trade and Engagement Act of 2003, p. 1121.

it is even considered a negotiation partner. States ineligible for negotiations (Federal Register, 69(126), 2004, 39997) are those ruled by a communist regime (1), those which deprive the international trade from vitally important commodities or offer these at an unreasonable price (2a), offer products specified in a preferential agreement to a developed country other than the US, leading to significant disadvantages for the US economy (3), those which support individuals or groups involved in international terrorism, by offering them protection from legal prosecution on their soil or have not taken steps to support the US in the War on Terror (6). Not only the US, but also the EU, uses the asymmetrical relationship of interdependence to promote noneconomic interests. In an analysis comparing the different EU bilateral trade agreements, Hettne and Söderbaum conclude the EU proclaims to support its goal of carrying EU values such as human rights, democracy, law, and good governance into the world by means of regional agreements. In contrast to the EU-candidate negotiations, they observe a strategy of soft imperialism in the treaties with developing countries: "The latter [soft imperialism] refers to an asymmetric relationship and the imposition of norms in order to promote the EU's self-interest rather than a genuine (interregional) dialogue as a foundation for sustainable global governance" (2005, p. 549).[11]

The EU could increase the legitimacy of its power within its own ranks by demanding adherence to environmental and social standards. NGOs, and also enterprises unable to compete on an international level, as well as unions, welcome the EU's post-trade policy. On this basis, the EU has created a consensus on its foreign trade strategy in bilateral trade agreements.

The trade powers examined in this chapter, the US and the EU, offer the possibility of transferring their respective norm and rule system onto the weaker contract party due to the asymmetrical relationship of interdependence and implement this ability by signing bilateral FTAs with developing countries: Positive rule-making enables them to open new markets for their national enterprises (Singapore Issues) and in the same breath, allows them to protect domestic markets from cheap imports from developing countries by demanding they implement environmental and social standards.

In form of the strategy that Hettne and Söderbaum (2005, p. 549) labelled as soft imperialism – or with the term "export protectionism" hailing from the economic sciences – the transnationalisation of norms and rules of the EU and the US is taking place in developing countries. The transnationalisation of norms and rules is characteristic of the

---

[11]   See also Meunier and Nicolaidis 2006.

emerging transnational competitive state, which not only continues to strengthen its economic power by liberalizing the world trade in form of negative rule-making, but which also uses the protectionist characteristic of positive rule-making at the same time in order to increase the legitimacy of its power within society.

But which effects does the transformation of the national competitive to the transnational competitive state under the conditions of asymmetric interdependence have on developing countries as well as on the world trade regime? The following two sections seek to answer these questions.

Bilateral Trade Agreements Conditioned by an Asymmetrical Relationship of Interdependence

While for industrial countries the signing of FTAs with developing countries are of subordinate importance on a macroeconomic level, developing nations promise themselves better access to industrial nations' markets and their technological know-how by signing FTAs with developed countries. For most developing countries, the US and the EU are already today the most important market(s) for agrarian produce and for commodities with a low production level. General statements on the long-term effects of FTAs on the relationship of dependence between industrial and developing countries are currently not possible as the duration of most FTAs is still too brief. However, some studies suggest an increase in asymmetrical interdependence due to FTAs. Analysing the FTA NAFTA, one can see the increase of interregional trade and a rise of Foreign Direct Investment (FDI) on the one hand, especially for Mexico. Simultaneously, on the other hand, the concentration of Mexican exports on the US market increased: While the contingent of Mexican exports to the US was at an average of 62 per cent per annum in the 1980s, it rose to about 80 per cent between 1990 and 1995, and in the period between 2001 to 2006 even to a contingent of 86 per cent of total Mexican exports.[12] In turn, Mexico's dependence on the US as its most important export market heightened.

Mexico tried to reduce this dependence by signing further FTAs. In fact, it was Mexico's strategy to decrease its dependence on the US through closing further FTAs – alas with little success. In negotiations with the EU concerning an FTA, it became apparent that the EU was promoting its non-trade-related demands: In April 1997, the European Council accepted guidelines included the liberalization of intellectual property rights, movement of financial capital as public procurement, as

---

[12]   IMF, *Direction of Trade Statistics*, database; see also: UNCTAD 2007, p. 70.

well as regulations on environmental issues and adhering to human rights and the promotion of democracy. After Mexico initially refused to accept the democratic clause, the country eventually decided to accept EU demands (Szymanski and Smith 2005).

From a normative perspective, linking FTAs to norms and rules – such as abiding by human rights and environmental and social standards – is to be welcomed as the debate concerning European normative power shows (see Behrens 2011). Yet, for developing countries, this type of positive rule-making implies a loss of national capability and its scope of action, as clarified in an example by Mahnkopf in the case of NAFTA: Most bilaterally negotiated agreements on investment within the FTA framework surpass WTO regulations, which are supposed to determine guidelines in a state-to-state dispute settlement process. But now, bilaterally signed investment agreements also allow enterprises to sue states. A Spanish investor sued Mexico at the International Centre for Settlement of Investment Disputes (ICSID) of the World Bank for five million US dollars because the Mexican government – pressured by local and environmental political protests – did not extend the license for a landfill (Mahnkopf 2005). By enabling private foreign investors to sue a host state, the distinction between private and public law gets blurred. This new phenomenon is broadly discussed in juridical studies under the phrase of a "regulatory turn in international law" (Cogan 2011). It describes a power shift in favour of companies. So, Brown and Stern feared (2011, p. 341) that bilateral investment agreements as part of FTAs "could place serious constraints on the freedom of host governments to pursue certain policies, such as those affecting the environment or the health of the population".

Besides the power shift between developing countries and foreign investors, another indicator for the uneven distribution of power between developing and developed countries is the exceptions the more powerful country can insist on: In negotiations, the US and the EU are not only able to promote their interests through positive rule-making, but can also exclude sensitive areas from FTA reign – such as the agrarian sector – or by inhibiting certain sector's liberalization by writing exemption clauses into the agreements.

Also, developing countries are disadvantaged in asserting the norms and rules of an FTA. Paying the high administrative costs to ensure rules of origin are adhered to, for example, is much more intensive, higher and more difficult for institutionally weaker developing countries than it is for developed countries. Additionally, rules of origin leave a lot of room to be arbitrary. In his study on the effect of institutions in FTAs, Borrmann *et al.* (2006) conclude that states with a weak institutional system profit less from free trade than states with a strong(er) institutional system do. At the same time, they warn against simply endorsing the opinion that developing nations can just copy industrial nations' institutions to make up for this deficit/gain equally: "Institutions that are effective in industrial countries can have quite different outcomes in developing countries, which, for example, have fewer complementary institutions, weaker administrative capacity, higher per-capita costs, lower human capital levels, different technology, and different levels and perceptions of corruption" (p. 364).

The United Nations Conference on Trade and Development (UNCTAD) Trade and Development Report of 2007 also indicates the danger of bilateral FTAs for developmental measures on the political level. Referring to the Singapore Issues, the report clarifies that developing countries have a significantly smaller scope of action in FTAs signed with industrial nations – particularly concerning the promotion of specific sectors or in trying to increase certain enterprises' competitiveness (on an international level) – in comparison to the scope's width under current WTO rules. Thus, the UNCTAD recommends developing countries not only consider the positive trade effects or the rise of FDIs, but also to think about "the impact of these agreements on their ability to use alternative policy options and instruments in the pursuit of a longer term development strategy" (UNCTAD 2007, p. 65).

FTAs not only narrow the developing countries' developmental scope of political action, but studies have proven that bilateral FTAs lead to an erosion of regional integration projects such as MERCOSUR (Ribeiro-Hoffmann and Kfuri 2007) or ASEAN (Dieter 2005). Under the condition of an almost wholesome symmetrical interdependence, FTAs may definitely create positive welfare effects. Instead, in asymmetrical relationships of interdependence, the power factor exerts more influence, and, in consequence, developing countries' dependence on industrial nations strengthens a change that will not remain without effect on the world trade regime.

The Effects of Bilateral Trade Agreements on the World Trade Regime

The debate on the effects of FTAs in the economic sciences has a long tradition. There have been many economic scientific model calculations that will not be described further in this chapter. These studies centre on the question of whether FTAs contribute to trade creation, trade diversion or even to trade deflection. Most examinations are founded on Viner's study conducted in 1950, in which he questioned the efficiency of customs unions for the liberalization of world trade in his two-commodity model. The results of these studies differ greatly from one another. The question, if FTAs are stumbling stones or build-ing blocks contributing to a larger world trade regime, is not explicitly answered anywhere (Lloyd and Maclaren 2004). Differing results can *inter alia* be explained by stating that the asymmetrical relationships of interdependence are not included in these models and thereby neglect the power aspect. More recent studies, however, do include the asym-metrical relationships of interdependence.

Nuno Limão's study (2007) is particularly noteworthy. On the basis of mathematic models, Limão proves that linking economic and none-conomic interests effectively blocks the multilateral trade regime. Linking these two fields is most often found in trade agreements be-tween large and small states. FTAs signed between the US and smaller states or developing countries cannot be explained with the regular economic models of welfare effects for the US, as its effects are just marginal. Rather, these agreements are driven by noneconomic forces (worker's rights, war on drug production and trade). Limão points out an interesting phenomenon: Large states buy the noneconomic conven-iences by receiving advantages in customs on certain commodities by granting developing countries tariff levels below the multilateral tariff applicable to all other WTO members. Yet this implies that large states are not interested in promoting lower tariff levels on these commodities within the framework of the multilateral regime as doing so would lower the accessible tariff level due to the negotiation process with developing countries and the trade agreements signed with them. Limão's study feasibly proves the blocking effect of bilateral FTAs for the world trade regime.

Another argument for the blocking effect is the interests of the US and the EU within their societies that they can more easily promote in a bilateral FTA. Apart from protests by unions and NGOs, which mas-sively helped the implementation of social and environmental standards in FTAs, it is particularly enterprises – who are unable to compete on an international level – who are interested in bilateral FTAs as they create access to new markets. Due to the lower tariff levels agreed on in an FTA, these enterprises are granted the opportunity to establish business in a market in which they would have immediately failed without the FTA and the protectionist measures benefitting the stronger contract party the agreement entails (trade diversion).

These enterprises, therefore, prefer FTAs to the promotion of liberal-ization within the multilateral world trade regime framework as these would imply economic disadvantages for them (Kono 2007). This effect can be noted in FTAs under conditions of an asymmetrical relationship but also in FTAs with a symmetrical relationship of interdependence.

FTAs render a special-interest structure that contributes to a weakening of the world trade regime. Strong economic powers, such as the US and the EU, can better further their interests in FTAs under the conditions of an asymmetrical relationship than they can in the WTO comprising 150 member states. Different from bilateral negotiations, in multilateral negotiations, developing countries do have the opportunity to enter into strategic alliances (Payne 2010). FTAs, particularly those signed with Asian states, offer the possibilities for the US and the EU to open new markets for their transnational enterprises and to expand their economic power at the same time. In order to benefit from first-comer effects, the US and the EU have just about begun a race for the signing of FTAs. In this race, it is vital to expand economic political power. In FTAs with developing countries, the US and the EU can much more easily take advantage of their institutional benefits (agrarian clauses) as with Asian states and may continue fostering their institutional power (Singapore Issues) by taking their norm- and rule-system to the transnational level. Finally, the US and the EU can regain legitimacy within their societies by including social and environmental standards, clauses concerning human rights and good governance, and re-attain and increase legitimacy in face of domestic enterprises that are unable to compete on an international level as well as in the eyes of NGOs. In summary, the US and the EU can catch three flies with one swat: Power on the economic, institutional and legitimacy level rises simultaneously. Hence, the US and the EU renouncing from bilateralism is quite unlikely in the mid- to long term. This changed strategy in foreign trade policy is carried out on the back of the world trade regime and hollows this structure out continuously.

Do all of these developments imply the end of the WTO? Not at all. It is definitely thinkable that on a long-term-basis the transaction costs of bilateral FTAs will exceed the benefits of their use. The processes required to adhere to the rules of origin are incredibly complicated and linked to high administrational expenses. Furthermore, the spaghetti-bowl full of FTAs is ever more difficult to overlook. Parallel to the increase of transaction costs for the US and the EU (but also for their respective enterprises), an erosion of regional integration projects by FTAs is occurring. Eventually, the more developing countries accept social and environmental standards within an FTA framework, the more likely these standards will be integrated into the norm system of the WTO on a long-term basis.

Conclusion

The steep increase of bilateral FTAs since the beginning of 2000 cannot be fully understood by theories of liberal institutionalism. As

FTAs have detached from their regional context, integration theory approaches of explanation no longer hold as a justification. Alas, the new types of FTAs are not a "competition for liberalization" converging with the world trade regime and, therefore, cannot be accounted for from a liberal perspective. The attribute of this bilateral FTA is rather the following: They are highly motivated by protectionism and linked to noneconomic interests.

Protectionist phases in the world trade system are not a new phenomenon. Instead, they mark a state of upheaval in international relations and entail high insecurities for states. A phase of upheaval, for example, is the end of the East-West conflict. The US lost its hegemonic position of predominance as the EU grew stronger. The US, as well as the EU, is confronted with new challenges due to the emerging markets of China and India. These shifts in the structure led to an erosion of the former neoliberal consensus in world trade policy. The US and the EU now both attempt to promote their individual power interests by signing bilateral FTAs.

So, in world trade policy, a transformation of the state from a national competitive state to the transnational competitive state can be observed, a change facilitated by the existing asymmetrical interdependence in international relations. Differentiating the term of power in allusion to approaches of realistic and neo-Gramscian theory towards economic political power, institutional power and power of legitimacy renders it possible to specify the transformation processes more clearly: In bilateral FTAs, the US and the EU can expand not only their economic political power, but also their institutional power, by transferring their norms and rules beyond their own borders into other states.

Thus, not only an internationalisation of state sovereignty is occurring, but in parallel a process of transnationalisation is taking place. By means of the integration of noneconomic norms and rules in FTA – negotiations – such as social and environmental standards or human rights – the US and the EU can count on an almost wholesome support by Western civil society and hereby increase their power of legitimacy. Through these noneconomic norms and rules, the US and the EU simultaneously protect their domestic sectors and enterprises not fit enough to compete on an international level ("export protectionism").

While the large trade powers gain power in all three dimensions (economic, institutional and legitimacy), developing nations are counted among the losers. They lose not only comparative cost advantages (albeit normatively questionable), but also their scope of action, for development policy measures are reduced. Based on these findings, it is to be expected that developmental disparities will increase, and asymmetrical interdependence will strengthen.

Simultaneously, the world trade regime is weakened as the US and the EU align their foreign trade strategies less multilaterally and choose to point it towards a transnational direction. However, it is imaginable on a long-term basis that a new consensus on the direction of world trade policy will crystallise, a consensus which could be a "re-embedded liberalism" as current discussions about measures to overcome the world financial and economic crisis indicate. These might be multilaterally institutionalised in a reformed world trade regime. However, currently the world economic policy is changing, and further development is to be awaited.

References

Behrens, M. (2011). "Die Außenwirtschaftspolitik der Europäischen Union im Vergleich mit den USA", in G. Simonis and H. Elbers (eds.), *Externe EU-Governance*, Wiesbaden: VS-Verlag für Sozialwissenschaften, pp. 241-266.

Bhagwati, J. (2007). "America's bipartisan battle against free trade", in *Financial Times London*, 9 April, p. 13.

Borrmann, A., M. Busse, and S. Neuhaus (2006). "Institutional Quality and the Gains from Trade", in *KYKLOS*, Vol. 59, No. 3, pp. 345-368.

Brown, A.G. and R.M. Stern (2011). "Free Trade Agreements and Governance of the Global Trading System", in *The World Economy*, Vol. 34, No. 3, pp. 331-354.

Cogan, J.K. (2011). "The Regulatory Turn in International Law", in *Harvard International Law Journal*, Vol. 52, No. 2.

Cooper, W.H. (2006). "Free Trade Agreements: Impact on U.S. Trade and Implications for U.S. Trade Policy", in *CRS Report for Congress*, RL31356, 1 August.

Cox, R.W. (1981). "Social Forces, States and World Orders: Beyond International Relations Theory", in *Millennium: Journal of International Studies*, Vol. 10, No. 2, pp. 126-155.

Dieter, H. (2005). "Bilateral Trade Agreements in the Asia-Pacific: Wise or Foolish Policies?" *CSGR Working Paper Series*, No. 183/05, December, University of Warwick: Centre for the Study of Globalisation and Regionalisation.

Dymond, W. and M.M. Hart (2000). "Post-Modern Trade Policy Reflections on the Challenges to Multilateral Trade Negotiations after Seattle", in *Journal of World Trade*, Vol. 34, No. 3, pp. 21-38.

EU-Commission, External Trade (2006a). *Global Europe, competing in the world, a Contribution to the EU's Growth and Jobs Strategy*, 4 October.

EU-Commission, External Trade (2006b). *Global Europe*, Executive Summary.

Falke, A. (2005). "EU-USA Trade Relations in the Doha Development Round: Market Access versus a Post-modern Trade Policy Agenda", in *European Foreign Affairs Review*, No. 10, pp. 339-357.

Fergusson, I. F. (2006). "Trade Negotiations during the 109th Congress", *CRS Report for Congress*, RL33463, 6 July.

Genschel, Ph. and B. Zangl (2009). *Transformation of the State – From Monopolist to Manager of Political Authority*, paper written for the ISA 2009 Convention, New York.

Hettne, B. and F. Söderbaum (2005). "Civilian Power or Soft Imperialism? The EU as a Global Actor and the Role of Interregionalism", in *European Foreign Affairs*, No. 10, pp. 535-552.

Hirsch, J. (1998). *Vom Sicherheits- zum nationalen Wettbewerbsstaat*. Berlin: ID-Verlag.

Hummel, H. (2000). *Der neue Westen, Der Handelskonflikt zwischen USA und Japan und die Integration der westlichen Gemeinschaft*. Münster: Agenda.

Keohane, R.O., A. Moravcsik, and A.-M. Slaughter (2000). "Legalized Dispute Resolution: Interstate and Transnational", in *International Organization*, Vol. 54, pp. 457-488.

Knodt, M. and M. Jachtenfuchs (2002). "Regieren in internationalen Institutionen", Introduction, in M. Jachtenfuchs and M. Knodt (eds.), *Regieren in internationalen Institutionen*, pp. 9-28, Opladen: Leske+ Budrich.

Kono, D.Y. (2007). "When Do Trade Blocs Block Trade?", in *International Studies Quarterly*, No. 51, pp. 165-181.

Limão, N. (2007). "Are Preferential Trade Agreements with Non-trade Objectives a Stumbling Block for Multilateral Liberalization?", in *Review of Economic Studies*, No. 74, pp. 821-855.

Lloyd, P. and D. Maclaren, (2004). "Gains and Losses from Regional Trading Agreements: A Survey", in *The Economic Record*, Vol. 80, No. 251, pp. 445-467.

Ludema, R.D. (2007). "Allies and Friends: The Trade Policy Review of the United States, 2006", in *Journal of World Economy*, Vol. 30, No. 8, pp. 1209-1221.

Mahnkopf, B. (2005). "Investition als Intervention: Wie interregionale und bilaterale Investitionsabkommen die Souveränität von Entwicklungsländern beschneiden", in *Internationale Politik und Gesellschaft*, No. 1, pp. 121-141.

Mallory, F. (2011). "Occupy Wall Street ... Next Stop, Athens?", in *Forbes*, Vol. 188, No. 9, p. 40. 2011.

Manners, I. (2002). "Normative Power Europe: A Contradiction in Terms?", in *Journal of Common Market Studies*, Vol. 40, No. 2, pp. 234-258.

Mansfield, E. D. (1992). "The Concentration of Capabilities and International Trade", in *International Organization*, Vol. 46, No. 3, pp. 731-764.

Meunier, S. and K. Nicolaidis (2006). "The European Union as a conflicted trade power", in *Journal of European Public Policy*, Vol. 13, No. 6, pp. 906-925.

Neyer, J. (1999). "Legitimes Recht oberhalb des demokratischen Rechtsstaates? Supranationalität als Herausforderung für die Politikwissenschaft", in *Politische Vierteljahresschrift*, Vol. 40, No. 3, pp. 390-414.

Payne, A. (2010). "How many Gs are there in 'global governance' after the crisis? The perspectives of the 'marginal majority' of the world's states", in *International Affairs*, Vol. 86, No. 3, pp. 729-740

Ribeiro-Hoffmann, A. and R. Kfuri (2007). *The role of external actors upon regional integration: the US, the EU and Mercosur*, ECPR, Helsinki, May 7-12, unpublished paper. <http://www.essex.ac.uk/ecpr/events/jointsessions/helsinki/ws_list.aspx>.

Schott, J.J. (ed.) (2004). *Free Trade Agreements, US Strategies and Priorities*. Washington, DC: Institute for International Economics.

Sjursen, H. (2006). "The EU as a 'Normative' Power: How Can This Be?", in *Journal of European Public Policy*, Vo. 13, No. 2, pp. 235-251.

Strange, S. (1989). *States and Markets. An Introduction to International Political Economy*. London: Pinter.

Strange, S. (1996). *The Retreat of the State: The Diffusion of Power in the World Economy*. Cambridge: Cambridge University Press.

Szymanski, M. and M.E. Smith (2005). "Coherence and Conditionality in European Foreign Policy: Negotiating the EU-Mexico Global Agreement", in *Journal of Common Market Studies*, Vol. 43, No. 1, pp. 171-192.

UNCTAD (2007). *Trade and Development Report 2007*, Chapter III, The "New Regionalism" and North-South Trade Agreements, pp. 53-85.

USTR (2007). *2007 Trade Policy Agenda and 2006 Annual Report of the President of the United States on the Trade Agreements Program*, Washington, March.

USTR (2011). Press release: Statement by US Trade Representative Ron Kirk on Congressional Passage of Trade Agreements, Trade Adjustment Assistance, and Key Preference Programs. 12 October. <http://www.ustr.gov/about-us/press-office/press-releases/2011/october/statement-us-trade-representative-ron-kirk-congres>.

Zoellick, R.B. (2003). "Zoellick Says FTA Candidates Must Support U.S. Foreign Policy", in *Inside U.S. Trade*, 16 May.

Zürn, M. (2002). "Zu den Merkmalen postnationaler Politik", in M. Jachtenfuchs and M. Knodt (eds.), *Regieren in internationalen Institutionen*, Opladen: Leske+ Budrich, pp. 215-234.

Embedding Liberalisation
Will CETA Undermine the Social Dimension of Transatlantic Integration?

Robert FINBOW

Comparisons of Europe and North America often highlight their different approaches to labour and social affairs; some scholars consider the European Union social dimension a more inclusive model for regional integration than the liberalizing free trade in NAFTA. But the EU stance on the link between trade and social impacts has evolved. This chapter will analyse the Canada-EU negotiations on a Comprehensive Economic and Trade Agreement (CETA) and assess the liberalizing nature of the EU's proposals. Canadian progressives initially welcomed the CETA talks as a means to move Canada closer to Europe's vision of a social dimension to integration. This reflects an impression of Europe as a model for an alternative means of regulating environmental and social matters (Croci and Tossutti 2009, p. 171). But many CETA proposals would strengthen European corporations in transatlantic trade at the expense of social standards, environmental protection, and consumer well-being. In combination with the liberalizing approach of Canada's Conservative government, CETA could hamper policies to attenuate the worst impacts of market liberalization.

Europe is using CETA to move forward on issues that are stalled multinationally at the WTO – trade in services, public procurement, and intellectual property protections – as a prototype for a partnership with the United States. "Europe needs to look beyond tariff reduction to the trade barriers that lie behind borders. As tariffs fall, these barriers – such as restrictive regulations or standards – become increasingly important" (European Commission 2006). Hence, changing the behaviour of trade partners and subnational units is central to EU trade strategy to complement WTO mechanisms with bilateral deals with transborder juridical authority until the WTO is back on track. Since the collapse of the Doha round, commercial and economic goals are the priority in Europe's bilateral FTAs.

The EU trade agreements have "three broad commercial motivations": "neutralizing potential trade diversion resulting from FTAs between third countries; forging strategic links with countries or regions experiencing rapid economic growth; and enforcement of international trade rules" (Woolcock 2007, p. 3). While trade diversion in Canada's bilateral trade deals like NAFTA is a concern, Europe mainly seeks to strengthen "the implementation of existing international trade rules, such as intellectual property rights" in CETA (Woolcock 2007, p. 3). This colours Europe's proposals on intellectual property in pharmaceuticals, geographic indicators, and procurement. This accord between two developed partners differs from EU FTAs with emerging states. Canada has proposed some liberalizing elements, such as "negative list" exclusions for public services. But as the stronger trade partner, the EU can push changes on a weaker Canada, in a manner arguably not conducive to long-term social sustainability.

The EU has altered its social dimension since enlargement, with a liberalized approach in new Member States and monetarist orthodoxy via the European Monetary Unit (Hermann 2007). This is evident in transatlantic talks, where the EU approach to social matters has a *"laissez-faire"* quality. This differs from past negotiations when the EU joined with US Democratic regimes to promote a link between trade and labour issues in the WTO. European negotiators argue that "the goal of promoting labour standards remains the same, but that the ILO constitutes a more suitable organisation to discuss it" (Orbie *et al.* 2005). This study considers EU motives and Canadian responses in CETA talks to evaluate the implications for social aspects of trade and the viability of distinct federal, provincial, and municipal policies in labour and environmental and social matters. It will assess CETA's prospects in the framework of the Lisbon Treaty, which expands EU competence in investment and trade, increasing the Commission's ability to promote neoliberal approaches without interference from Member States, but with potentially enhanced scrutiny by the parliament at Strasbourg. Notwithstanding rhetorical commitments to a social dimension, CETA could increase liberalization in trade at the expense of social, labour, and environmental standards in both trade partners.

The European Union's "Next Generation" FTAs

Analysts agree that liberalization is now the motive for the deepening and broadening of the European Union and that the social dimension has become marginal. The first bilateral FTAs with neighbouring countries focused on political stability and illegal migration. To achieve "the EU's political objective of regional hegemony", these deals extended European rules of origin and made the euro the dominant currency in neighbourhood states (McQueen 2002, p. 1371). The EU next sought

FTAs on economic grounds with emerging partners like Mexico and MERCOSUR (Common Southern Market, currently including Argentina, Brazil, Paraguay, and Uruguay, with Venezuela in the process of joining). Business lobbies sought enhanced international competitiveness, deregulation in services, and an emphatic external trade strategy to eliminate barriers to EU firms. For critics, the

> Lisbon Strategy aims to increase European competitiveness both through external aspects, i.e. increased global market access for European TNCs, and internal aspects, i.e. creating "flexible labour markets". In effect, this means reducing labour standards in the EU. Ultimately, the EU's drive for competitiveness means that the interests of big business will come first – while social and environmental standards, as potential "barriers" to competitiveness, are left behind. (Deckwirth 2005, p. 4)

When the WTO process stalled, European trade bureaucrats saw bilateral deals with strategic partners as an alternative means to accomplish these goals.

European policymakers argue that the global economy requires agreements that include regulatory co-ordination and investor protection. The EU's new generation FTAs are based on economic advantage and are not broader political agreements to promote values and social conditions. "Two economic criteria were used to prioritise the EU's new generation FTA partners: market potential (market size multiplied by growth rate) and protected markets (both tariff and non-tariff barriers)" (Guerin 2008a). This new trade strategy was spelled out in the EU's *Global Europe* initiative:

> [R]ejection of protectionism at home must be accompanied by activism in creating open markets and fair conditions for trade abroad. This improves the global business environment and helps spur economic reform in other countries. It reinforces the competitive position of EU industry in a globalised economy and is necessary to sustain domestic political support for our own openness. (European Commission 2006, p. 6)

The EU extended new generation FTAs into new spheres:

> [A]s tariffs fall, non-tariff barriers, such as unnecessarily trade-restricting regulations and procedures become the main obstacles. These are often less visible, more complex and can be more sensitive because they touch directly on domestic regulation. Regulating trade is necessary, but it must be done in a transparent and non-discriminatory manner, with the least restriction on trade consistent with achieving other legitimate policy objectives. (European Commission 2006, p. 6)

Negotiators have "a sharper focus on market opening and stronger rules in new trade areas of economic importance to us, notably intellectual property (IPR), services, investment, public procurement and competition" (European Commission 2006, p. 7).

The substance of the EU's "next generation" FTAs is extensive; "the new areas of competition policy, public procurement and investment are WTO-plus" covering issues left out of the GATS and the Uruguay Round. Europe's "next generation" FTAs may "give a further impetus to regionalisation worldwide" (Lloyd and MacLaren 2006, p. 431). The EU seeks a rival "hub and spoke" trade system to counter the US, as it seeks to shape the WTO agenda after the deadlock (Lloyd and MacLaren 2006, pp. 433-34). These deals could fragment the global system, provoke damaging regional competition and divert energies to less efficient bilateral deals. "There is a risk that the success of certain big *demandeurs* [like the EU] in obtaining significant commitments in PTAs reduce somewhat their appetite for multilateral negotiations on services", regulation and investment (Martin *et al*. 2007, p. 187). The Commission promised to ensure that its bilateral deals reinforced multilateral efforts (European Commission 2006, p. 11).

After the 2008 economic crisis, the EU pursued even more "super-FTAs" which went well beyond tariff reductions, to cover "market access for services and investment, opening public procurement, better agreements on and enforcement of protection of IPR, unrestricted supply of raw materials and energy", "overcoming regulatory barriers including via the promotion of international standards" and facilitating temporary movement of business employees (European Commission 2010a, p. 4). A recent deal with South Korea covered financial services, marine transport, telecommunications, and e-commerce; "for the first time in the history of modern-day free trade agreements there are strong and precise clauses on the elimination of some selected non-tariff barriers (safety standards and accreditation procedures) in automobiles and electronics" (Dreyer 2010). Advances were made on rules of origin, competition, intellectual property, geographic indications, and sanitary and phytosanitary measures. This deal included a dispute resolution mechanism modelled on the US bilateral arbitration system (Dreyer 2010). European firms in pharmaceuticals, petrochemicals, electronics, shipping, agricultural exports, and financial and legal services sectors were poised to gain from this new deal.

Like past EU deals, it included reference to human rights, labour, and environmental accords that Korea was expected to ratify. But the deal showed "that the EU is becoming more commercially assertive" with provisions based on US trade pacts; "the filet is américain" [including core issues like tariffs, services, intellectual property, and disputes settlement], but the sauce is 'à l'européenne'" on geographic indicators, and the "precautionary principle" in setting standards (Dreyer 2010). The Korean deal passed the EU parliament in February 2011. Accords with MERCOSUR, Ecuador, Peru, India, and ASEAN (Association of Southeast Asian Nations) are also making headway. While sustainability is mentioned in these FTAs, commercial interests are paramount and imposed in asymmetrical regimes since developing states are largely "takers" of EU terms.

These agreements test the institutional matrix of the Lisbon Treaty. The European Commission has secured competence in international trade and investment and can act as a cohesive negotiator without reference to national states' concerns. But the European Parliament has a role in ratification, and the process is potentially open to transparency and accountability, though Parliament needs to improve its capacities before it can effectively scrutinize complex trade and investment policies (Woolcock 2010, p. 2). A lawsuit in the Indian case alleges biased access for business lobbyists, which suggests that the Commission has not been fully transparent so far (von Reppert-Bismarck 2011).

CETA as a "Next Generation" FTA

Canada's Conservative government shares similar priorities with liberalizers in the European Commission. *Seizing Global Advantage* outlined the interconnected supply chains of the global economy, which required new forms of commercial engagement. The government pledged to:

[b]oost Canadian commercial engagement in global value chains; [s]ecure competitive terms of access to global markets and networks for Canadian businesses; [i]ncrease foreign direct investment in Canada and Canadian direct investment around the world; and [f]orge stronger linkages between Canada's science and technology community and global innovation networks (DFAIT 2008, p. 4).

Canada first focused on emerging powers such as China, India, Brazil, and Russia and re-engaged with hemispheric partners in Latin America (Gecelovsky and Kukucha 2011, p. 45). It took efforts by business groups and the Quebec government, which lobbied Ontario and the EU, before the Conservative government agreed to talks as a response to global economic stagnation (Interviews 5, 8).

Some observers consider CETA as a "second-best" alternative for Europe and note that Canada has been historically more motivated to pursue trade with Europe to reduce dependence on the US market. This need to diversify was heightened with the "buy American" campaign and protectionist musings in Congress (Kitou and Philippidis 2010, p. 2). Business Europe promoted a transatlantic commitment to liberalization on "behind the border" issues and harmonized regulations.

Voluntary talks by business groups had proved fruitless, except for the Québec-France accord on professional mobility. European business sought a comprehensive deal (Interview 16). The EU sees CETA as a test run for a possible agreement with the Americans: "Ongoing negotiations between the EU and Canada over an ambitious and comprehensive FTA could also affect the US FTA debate. If a robust agreement is reached, the EU and the United States would then both have FTAs with Canada and Mexico, making the absence of a FTA between the United States and EU all the more glaring" (Ahearn 2010, 2). But there is no momentum for a US deal, as the two sides remain far apart on core issues; Canada is the best available alternative for Europe if CETA remains comprehensive (Interview 11).

CETA negotiators eschew the label "free trade" and refer to an "enhanced economic partnership". Negotiators are ambitious, as the "agreement between the EU and Canada is to go 'deeper' than NAFTA or any other preferential agreement either party has ever signed" (Guerin 2008b). Despite already low tariffs, the parties would gain from paring back other protectionist measures. The wide range of issues on the table includes:

- trade in goods including trade in industrial, agricultural, and fish products
- tariff and nontariff measures, trade defence instruments
- technical barriers to trade, sanitary, and phytosanitary measures
- trade in services, including cross-border delivery
- temporary presence for business or professional purposes
- customs/trade facilitation and rules of origin.
- investment, for services and non-services sectors, capital movements, and payments
- government procurement, including subnational units
- competition policy and regulatory principles.
- intellectual property
- trade and sustainable development (adapted from European Commission, DG Trade 2010, p. 8).

Advocacy for a deal in Canada is led by the Canada Europe Round Table for Business (CERT) whose chairman, former Liberal minister Roy MacLaren, touted the benefits in trade and investment, which could amount to $40 billion over seven years. Bilateral talks with Europe are consistent with the multilateral WTO Doha process. "The objectives and the benefits accruing from a Canada-EU free trade agreement are well within our reach. Moreover, it is squarely in-line with the growing recognition that deeper transatlantic co-operation is a precondition – not an alternative – to broader global cooperation" (MacLaren 2009). Canadian advocates agree that new broader FTAs are required for changing economic times. "No longer do companies solely produce goods at home and simply ship them to overseas. Businesses today invest overseas, developing a facility that either produces for the local market, or produces goods that are shipped to other facilities for final assembly. Investment has become a bigger part of the equation than trade" (CAIE 2010b).

Studies indicated that measures to promote trade in services and provide intellectual property protection would contribute to economic performance for both partners. This affects more domestic policies and sub-national issues in a federation like Canada. Issues like "labour mobility, government procurement and the elimination or harmonization of regulatory barriers to trade" (CAIE 2010b) involve provinces directly, so they have participated directly in the talks at the EU's insistence after Ottawa's initial resistance (Interview 8). Provinces are concerned with public procurement at all levels of government and investment in provincial jurisdictions, notably natural resources. Provinces have authority over labour markets, including mobility for professional, business, and skilled trades in an era of integrated transnational services (Vogel 2009). The EU seeks better intellectual property and patent protection, recognition of geographic trademarks (champagne, feta, cheddar, etc.), and co-ordinated industrial and financial regulations. European negotiators described Canada's intellectual property rules as "the weakest in the OECD" and a target for improvement (Interview 11).

Canadian and European negotiators sought to facilitate new economy exchanges and focussed on several issues. These included:

e-commerce (exclude all customs duties and other border charges on products delivered electronically), trade remedies (apply the WTO Anti-Dumping Code and the Subsidies and Countervailing Measures Agreement and exclude dispute settlement), regulatory cooperation (consultation mechanisms to promote cooperation and compatibility), customs and trade facilitation, competition (commitment to maintain competition laws, but excluding dispute settlement with respect to enforcement actions) and investment (standards for establishment, investor protection and investor-state dispute settlement, subject to determining scope of EU competence on investment matters relative to member states). (CAIE 2010a)

Supporters argue that, without a deal, "Canadians will lose out on freer access to a deep and wide range of trade opportunities that dwarf the widely reported $35-billion in annual Canadian product exports to the EU" (Goldfarb and Thériault 2010a).

CETA is expected to produce gains for both parties, if patterns based on NAFTA are evident (Guerin and Napoli 2008, pp. 22-23). But analysts disagree on the scale of costs and benefits for Canada. A joint study by the EU and Canadian government predicted higher gains for Europe but overall benefits for both partners if a broad range of goods and services are covered (Canada-EU 2008). The scoping exercise suggested "annual real income gains of approximately €11.6 billion for the EU and €8.2 billion for Canada within seven years" (Canada-EU 2009). Data has also been disaggregated to include less visible aspects of trade – "integrative commerce" encompassing services, skilled labour mobility, virtual commerce via the Internet or mobile phones, virtual goods, digital services, trade in technologies, investment flows, and sales by overseas corporate affiliates (Goldfarb and Thériault 2010). But when new economy issues are included, these reveal an even wider gap favouring the EU (Thériault 2010, Exhibits 1-2).

Canadian critics argue that talks are being conducted from a position of weakness. Canada focuses on old economy activities like fossil fuels, agriculture, aerospace, chemicals, forestry, fish, automobiles, and car parts and is weaker in emerging economic sectors (Ahearn 2010, 32). Critics fear the terms of trade would favour Europe, with Canada specializing in primary sector and old economy pursuits. This would augment Canada's persistent trade deficit with Europe (Byrd 2006). While some predict employment losses for Canada (Stanford 2010), others deny that Europe's gains in high technology and services would negatively affect Canada since both parties could gain (Leblond 2010).

EU and the Evolving Social Dimension of Trade

There has been a marked transition in attitudes towards labour and social aspects of integration since the expansion of the EU. From the 1970s, the European Commission sought the incorporation of a social clause in trade venues like GATT, the Lomé group, and Europe's general system of preferences. The proposals focussed on adoption and enforcement of International Labour Organization (ILO) standards by bilateral and multilateral trade partners. After 1978, the Economic and Social Commission encouraged the social element in European trade policy, "linking trade benefits to the compliance with four international labour standards, based on six existing ILO Conventions" (Orbie *et al.* 2005, p. 161). The Commission and Member States deferred serious consideration of a social clause for jurisdictional reasons:

> the Commission's initiative was basically blocked at the Council level [...]. The fact that the matter was not even examined by the Council indicates that the issue of labour standards in external trade relations was simply not con-

sidered to be an EC competence by the Member States. (Orbie *et al.* 2005, p. 161)

In the 1980s, pressure continued via the European Parliament for social clauses in commercial and trade agreements, but there was no serious consideration by the Council or Member States, except for environmental clauses.

With the American interest in the social dimension during NAFTA negotiations, EU states led by Belgium and France pressed for a social clause for the WTO, but with German and British resistance, there was no agreement on what form it should take (Orbie and Tortell 2008, p. 1). In the European GSP system, incentives and punishments (carrot and stick) for trade partners were introduced gradually, marking the first formal incorporation of a social dimension in European trade policy, though some states denied that labour standards even in a trade context fell under European Commission jurisdiction (Orbie and Tortell 2008, p. 1). Europe hesitatingly advocated a social clause in WTO negotiations, and labour matters were eventually left to the toothless ILO. The EU got members to support a "demand for a permanent joint WTO-ILO forum where the social issue would be discussed. As before, the emphasis was laid on stimulating measures and on the avoidance of protectionist misuse" (Orbie and Tortell 2008, p. 1).

The European Union later promoted a "social dimension of globalization" in bilateral and multilateral forums, "emphasizing that the EU could export elements of the European social model, which ensures that social and economic aims go hand in hand" (Orbie *et al.* 2009, p. 99). European leaders in the 1990s contemplated means to ensure that global integration included mechanisms to encourage social equity and investment in human well-being and sustainable development (Deacon 1999, p. 6). By pressuring states to eschew deficits, activist industrial strategies, progressive taxation, and corporate regulation, globalization undermined states' capacities to prepare citizens for global challenges. Yet, the "social consequences of globalization generated the need for more not less measures of social protection. Inequality requires more social redistribution, vulnerability requires the strengthening of social rights and entitlements and systems of social protection, social exclusion creates the need for strategies of empowerment" (Deacon 1999, p. 10).

Notwithstanding the increased need, the EU allowed the WTO-ILO link to atrophy and focused on voluntary ILO mechanisms without punitive enforcement on social and labour issues to match the strong penalties on commercial and trade matters. This "soft governance" approach removed concerns about enforcement by the WTO (and hence allowed trade talks to proceed) and focused on "private", nongovern-mental actions to support basic ILO norms. "Since 2001, the EU in-creasingly stressed the importance of dialogue, stimulation, the setting of standards and non-binding mechanisms, to the detriment of more or less binding trade mechanisms such as a social clause" (Orbie *et al.* 2005, p. 169). In the Doha "development round", "although the EU only made limited progress on environmental issues and no progress on labour standards at Doha, its rather strong position on these issues did not provoke the developing country outrage that previous American positions had" since it did not call for any real enforcement of such standards (Van den Hoven 2004, p. 265)

In its bilateral FTAs, the EU focused on a "social dimension of glob-alisation", including "[c]ore labour standards, the decent work agenda and corporate social responsibility" (Eichhorst *et al.*, 2010, p. 9). These involve voluntary agreements to ratify eight core ILO conventions; to encourage implementation of these standards through "decent work" initiatives promoted through "dialogue and technical assistance"; and to encourage multinational enterprises "to implement social standards via voluntary internal codes of conduct" (Eichhorst *et al.* 2010, p. 9). As in NAFTA, these are voluntary measures, which coexist alongside punitive guarantees for investor rights and goods and services access, which are implemented through binding arbitration and legalized disputes resolu-tion. The ILO summarizes current EU norms:

> The EU approach in its regional and bilateral arrangements is to focus more generally on social development objectives within a cooperative framework. EU agreements recognise and promote social rights and cooperation, including specific issues such as gender and health. The EU, however, does not pursue a trade sanctions-based approach to social and labour standards. Instead, it offers additional tariff preferences to countries which have signed and are effectively implementing the core UN/ILO human/labour rights international conventions (GSP system and GSP +). (ILO 2009)

This "soft governance" approach parallels the shift to "soft law" in European labour and social policy (Finbow 2010), as members resist extensions of Commission competence (Orbie and Barbarinde 2008, p. 460).

Commission documents do restate the EU goal of "sustainability" of trade deals in human and ecological terms. For instance, the 2020 trade strategy reaffirms the EU commitment to "promoting sustainable devel-opment, international labour standards and decent work also outside the EU" (European Commission 2010a, p. 8) accomplished in part by economic growth in developing states. One report argued that although the post-Lisbon trade policies have placed more emphasis on social elements, these are lacking in "coherence" and effectiveness, and "market-enhancing policies and competitiveness concerns are still prioritised over social policies" (Eichhorst *et al.* 2010, p. 9). Since the EU cannot act directly in labour and social matters, it has to work indirectly via its trade and development policies; despite "ambitious objectives" for the social dimension of globalization, the impact is limited and focused on developing states (Orbie and Barbarinde 2008, p. 461). The DG trade commitment to an ongoing civil society dialogue (CSD) is touted as evidence of an effort to ensure trade agreements embody appropriate social elements. Nonetheless, civil society actors have become disillusioned with this process and alternative mechanisms like the European Economic and Social Committee, which they claim provide legitimizing window-dressing, not meaningful involvement of social actors (Interview 15). Some groups boycott events because of a perceived bias in trade policy towards business. In "the absence of a formal systematic, inclusive, transparent and accountable process of consultation that can effectively open up the policy-making process of DG Trade and overcome the current privileged access to decision-makers enjoyed by business lobbies", several organizations withdrew from the CSD altogether (Seattle to Brussels Network 2009).

Critics suggest that the EU push for deregulation, flexibility, public-private collaboration, privatization, and reduced social services domestically, alongside the push for market access and resources internationally, reveals acute biases of policy in the context of global economic crisis: "European trade and investment policy has become dominated by a narrow set of interests. The EU needs to critically examine the developments over the past decade in the area of trade and investment policy. Now is the time to re-think the trade and investment model of the EU and promote policies that foster co-operation, solidarity and sustainable development and which are based on mutual support and public need, rather than competition and accumulation of profit" (Seattle to Brussels Network 2010). CETA is viewed in this same context;

> [U]nderlying this agreement is the ambition to create a vast free trade zone and, as stated in the EU's new trade strategy, to drive an insidious harmonisation of legislation between the USA, Canada and Europe towards a lower level of standards in social protections, environmental regulations, health and safety and other policies. As with other free trade agreements, CETA is being sold on the basis of benefits to the public (e.g. lower prices through competition), while in reality it poses numerous and grave threats to social and environmental standards and protections and public goods. (Seattle to Brussels 2011)

So far these critics have not influenced the direction of policy, though a sustainability impact assessment (SIA) and parliamentary scrutiny give some means of pressuring for more meaningful social, ecological, and labour clauses.

Potential Social Consequences of CETA

For a developed state like Canada, which is presumed to be meeting high standards despite globalization's weakening of social protection in all post-industrial societies, the EU focus is almost entirely on commerce, though a mandatory SIA is being completed that could affect European Parliamentary debates on CETA. Despite Canada's failure to ratify all the ILO core standards – owing to recalcitrance by many provinces – the EU has essentially taken a "hands-off" approach to labour and social elements, suggesting these are an internal matter for Canada's governments (Interview 5). The SIA found that Canada adhered to "decent work" standards, with a decline in numbers in poverty, though with a more rapid increase in income inequality than in most OECD states, with particular problems for women and aboriginal persons (European Commission, DG Trade 2010b) Given the conservative nature of recent federal regimes, Canada's already weaker social dimension can expect further pressure.

The EU SIA suggests Canada's terms of trade would be skewed with high technology and services trade increasingly favouring the Europeans with negative economic and ecological impacts on Canada. There is little evidence that intellectual property (IP) protection stimulates research spending or employment, and Canada would gain little new protection for its intellectual property (European Commission, DG Trade 2010b). Canada would face increased retail prices if IP provisions are strengthened. "IPR tend to increase consumer prices. Patents, copyrights, trademarks, geographical indications, plant breeder's rights, and other IPR confer exclusive rights, restrict competition and authorise holders to maintain higher prices" (Geist 2011). Canada's reliance on pharmaceutical imports from Europe means that intellectual protections for medicines could undermine the generic sector and increase costs for drug plans heightening demands on the health care system that is facing insistent corporate pressure for privatization. A stronger IPR regime could undermine Canadian cultural and industrial policy as well.

> Several exceptions and limitations to IPR provided in Canadian law are intended to maintain prices at reasonable levels. [...] If artistic works and data protection are protected for longer periods, the effective use of fair dealing exception is limited, protection for geographical indications and industrial designs are enhanced, and term extensions are made available for patents, it is very likely that CETA will create an inflationary pressure on consumer prices. (Geist 2011)

Academic models of services trade suggest that Canada will gain less and import more high-end telecommunications and business services from Europe in the future (Sandberg 2011).

European social groups support exemptions of public services from CETA to avoid subjecting them to privatization pressures; a cross-party group of MEPs hailed Canada's public services as a model to be protected (Public Services Intergroup 2011). If CETA weakens NAFTA exclusions for health services, pressures by European investors to erode Canada's health care model could arise (Sinclair 2011). Critics worry that allowing EU firms the right to bid for local and provincial contracts could increase pressures for privatization of public services, including water supplies (CUPE 2010). Provisions contemplated in CETA would encourage public-private partnerships and commercialization in public services and utilities while banning efforts to favour local workers, use local suppliers, or require high value added employment (Sinclair 2010). Opening procurement to Europeans would hinder local sustainable development strategies, especially if it extended to water supplies or sewage. Procurement provisions could allow companies to challenge local rules on issues like water conservation, bans on bottled water, and local source protections from development or pollutants. Access to resources may lead to loss of local control and damaging development; efforts to open up new resource supplies in minerals, forestry, etc. as part of the EU goal of securing resource supplies could have negative impacts on First Nations communities. Increased European access to sensitive resources like the fisheries could increase commercialization and overfishing, undermining the sustainability of this sector (Barlow 2011). CETA could promote environmentally unsustainable practices by encouraging EU investment in energy sources like the oil sands (Shrybman 2010).

Critics oppose investor-state disputes settlement mechanisms like Chapter 11 of NAFTA, which produced costly settlements for business challenges of environmental regulations. Investor rights give foreign firms a leg up over domestic competitors as some policies and regulations may be banned if they affect trans-ocean trade, even though practiced internally in either party (Drache and Trew 2010). These investor protections, coupled with procurement access "will clearly reduce regulatory flexibility in Canada, some of which will also constitute reductions in economic and social, and potentially environmental, policy space" (European Commission DG Trade 2011b, p. 15). Recent NAFTA challenges demonstrate the problems investor-state provisions can pose for policy in areas like renewable energy (McCarthy 2011). European challenges to Canadian marketing boards in wheat, alcohol, poultry, and dairy could undermine agricultural viability, forcing greater dependence on imports and corporate agribusiness at the expense of sustainable communities. All signs are that negotiators are avoiding this area altogether as this remains politically sensitive, but it could create frictions as talks proceed (Interviews 9, 11, 18).

These criticisms rely on hitherto secret drafts of the proposed CETA treaty, and only superficial briefings on negotiated areas are available publicly. Critics decry the secrecy surrounding the trade deal, given its coverage of broad areas of domestic policy, even though this secrecy has been defended as in keeping with trade and foreign policy negotiations historically (Interview 3). The "lack of transparency around these talks is preventing meaningful public debate on this agreement" (Wajeeha 2010) as politicians remain tight-lipped, and the media provides little coverage. The Canadian Union of Public Employees (CUPE) and the Council of Canadians declare that

> all levels of government must be transparent with Canadians about the effect that CETA will have on the provision of public services and development of social policy. They should seek informed consent from Canadians on what provisions a trade agreement with the EU should and should not include. (CUPE 2010, p. 2)

Civil society groups argue for transparent negotiations and full assessment of CETA effects on jobs, environment, poverty, gender, human rights, and culture.

In keeping with its other recent bilateral FTAs, although the EU considers Canada's practices relatively unproblematic, issues are raised about labour, social, and environmental realms, since Canada has not fully ratified ILO provisions and is a recalcitrant participant in global environmental forums. The SIA draft final report expresses the hope that:

> While labour standards in Canada and the EU are strong relative to most countries, greater commitment to the ILO's standards could help ensure greater implementation while helping to foster greater cooperation in international fora such as the WTO. Further, cooperation could help lead to eventual ratification of all Core Labour Standards that have not yet been ratified in Canada due to conflicts such actions would have with provincial labour laws. This could assist with improving rights of collective bargaining and association at the provincial level. (EU DG Trade 2011b, p. 53)

The SIA recommends that a "trade and sustainable development" clause be included in the agreement to require "effective implementation of core environmental regulatory measures" and "implementation [of] the ILO's core labour standards and Decent Work Agenda" (EU DG Trade 2011b, p. 53). The draft report suggests "cooperative activities" aimed at "increasing awareness of legal rights and obligations and fostering social dialogue" on bargaining rights and occupational injuries. It recommends a "Trade and Sustainable Development Monitoring Body" comprised of experts, government, business, and civil society groups to monitor the CETA. This "body would review sectoral labour and environmental commitments and related impacts as well as commitments and impacts in the areas of GP, IPR, investment, labour mobility, and competition policy" (EU DG Trade 2011b, p. 59).

European civil society groups worry that the inclusion of disputes resolution mechanisms allowing companies to sue for loss of "anticipated profits" from social and environmental regulations means that harmonisation would move in a downward direction and limit governments' ability to enact popular preferences for high social and ecological standards. The SIA addresses some concerns by arguing that provinces and municipalities should have room to protect their environmental well-being in setting policies and tendering procurement as long as these do not become disguised barriers to trade (EU DG Trade 2011b, p. 56). The draft report also notes that both "Canada and the EU made important progress in environmental regulation and awareness. The CETA can enhance this by calling for harmonisation of environmental regulation" (EU DG Trade 2011b, p. 53). But harmonisation is difficult in Canada as profound disagreements among provinces over ratification of the Kyoto protocol attest. Constitutional restrictions would preclude imposition of social standards upon provinces, making implementation of even this voluntary element of CETA problematic since Ottawa will be required to deal with violations and cannot impose compliance upon provinces (Interviews 6, 8).

Conclusions: Prospects for CETA

There remains a strong possibility that the CETA will be concluded in the next few months despite social concerns, which are less visible than similar criticism of past trade negotiations. At least some of the irritants have been cleared away with a recent settlement on imports of Canadian hormone-treated beef (EU DG Trade 2011). The willingness of the European Parliament to enact the Korean deal despite fears of unfair competition on automobiles indicates that ratification will be likely despite opposition from left, green, and socialist members since the benefits for European companies seem clear in this case. But there is also a possibility that CETA could be obstructed from the European side since it must clear a final sustainability impact assessment (SIA) and scrutiny in the European Parliament.

There could well be problems about issues close to the concerns of Canada's Conservative government. For instance, despite pledges to reduce greenhouse gas emissions from oil sands with new technologies like "carbon capture and storage", Canada has failed to meet these commitments, even while calling on the EU to defer clean-fuel standards that would label the oil sands as dirty fuel. The SIA outlined the European concern that the "oil and gas sectors, notably the tar sands industry in Alberta, are in part responsible for the important increase in Canadian greenhouse gas emissions. Where the CETA contributes to greater extraction and investment in the tar sands, it is likely that Canada's emissions of greenhouse gases will increase" (European Commission, DG Trade 2010b). The Europeans have enacted a directive on clean fuel that targets Canada's oil sands as a dirty fuel. This poses a potential problem for the CETA ratification, though Canada's negotiators reject an explicit linkage between these issues (Dowd 2011). Canada vigorously challenges the singling out of this fuel source, claiming it is no less clean than many more conventional fuel supplies (Interview 10). Despite vigorous Canadian lobbying at Brussels and Strasbourg, which has offended some, the EU will label oil sands "dirty", hampering European investments in this resource. Despite earlier denials, a leaked letter reveals that the Harper government considers a dirty oil label for oil sands a threat to improved trade relations (Harrison 2011). However, while Canada is lobbying hard to ensure oil sands are treated fairly relative to other fuel sources (Interview 10), those close to the talks suggest that EU action under the clean fuel directive, however vexing, is separate from trade and will not derail CETA. The directive would only minimally penalize energy imports – limited in volume –, which include tar sands products (Interview 9).

There is some municipal resistance on procurement access, but if they maintain a solid front, the provinces can overrule these. Difficult issues remain on farm subsidies and supply management in key sectors like dairy, poultry, and meat products. It appears such issues will be set aside as there are too many political minefields on both sides (Interview 8). There is concern respecting Canada's imposition of visa require-ments for persons from the Czech Republic to stem the flow of Roma refugee claimants – the first such imposition by any country with visa-free access to European states (Eggenschwiler 2010). While both nego-tiating teams insist that this will not interfere with CETA talks, the European Parliament passed a resolution expressing concern and assert-ing "that if the question of the breach of the mutual mechanism with respect to visas is not resolved soon, the corresponding retaliatory measures can be expected from the EU side"; the EU ambassador to Canada admits that the "visa issue might become an even bigger prob-lem once we have concluded the negotiations and the agreement has to be ratified" since this requires Czech approval in the Council (Kenety

2011). However, officials with the European Parliament feel the Czechs are likely to use their resistance to secure more favourable terms in areas such as development funds (Interview 17).

Green issues are of concern to parliamentarians, with criticism of the seal hunt, oil sands, and asbestos exports by some MEPs (Interview 17). European investment in uranium mining remains controversial, perhaps more so after the Fukushima incident. There are issues involving genetically modified organisms, which Europe has generally resisted, preferring instead chemically assisted agriculture more favourable to its agribusiness and chemical sectors. Other issues like the seal ban, Arctic sovereignty, fisheries access, animal rights concerns over furs, and similar irritants remain important regionally and particularly to First Nations communities. The European Parliament passed a resolution in June outlining support for the CETA but raising serious concerns about these issues. The resolution called for Canada to withdraw its WTO challenge to the EU ban on imported seal products as a condition for finalizing CETA (European Parliament 2011). But despite these rumblings, many close to Parliament (Interview 17), in the social dialogue (Interview 12), in NGOs (Interview 15), and close to the negotiations (Interview 11) believe these problems will be side-stepped and dealt with by separate means.

Recent EU studies seem to support the contention that benefits for Canada would be less while constraints would be greater, with some accusing the Harper government of a "political sales pitch" (O'Neil 2011). But that government is now strengthened by its majority position. If the EU does follow the SIA recommendations and insists on environmental clauses and labour and social elements (including ILO ratifications) that would be problematic for major provinces, then the motivations from Europe's side to sign an agreement may be tested. The European Commission will seek to address these issues outside CETA, which will leave NGOs and some in Parliament dissatisfied (Interview 13). The new regulations after Lisbon may reduce the Commission's ability to impose such solutions, if Parliament insists on adherence to policies tying trade to global agreements and norms like Kyoto (from which Canada has withdrawn) and ILO commitments (which several provinces have not ratified). But it is unclear if the Lisbon rules have empowered Parliament to assert itself, and the pro-trade majority in Strasbourg at present makes blocking of CETA unlikely (Interview 17). If there is a will to reach a deal, irritants will be set aside for the sake of economic gain, as neither side would let these issues undermine the overall relationship (Interviews 9, 18). The outcome could demonstrate how far Europe has evolved away from concern for a social dimension towards commercial goals in its trading partnerships. The exact nature of CETA's social impact cannot be fully ascertained until a final draft agreement is released sometime in 2012.

References

Ahearn, Raymond J. (2010). "Europe's Preferential Trade Agreements: Status, Content, and Implications". Washington: Congressional Research Service report for Congress, 7-5700. <http://www.fas.org/sgp/crs/row/R41143.pdf>.

Barlow, Maude (2011). "What you don't know about a deal you haven't heard of", in *Globe and Mail*, 6 January. <www.canadians.org/media/council/2011/06-Jan-11.html>. [Accessed 16 March 2011].

Burgoon, Brian (2004). "The Rise and Stall of Labor Linkage in Globalization Politics", in *International Politics* Vol. 41, No. 2, pp. 196-220.

Byrd, Craig (2006). "Canada's merchandise trade with the European Union, 1995 to 2004", Ottawa, Ont. Statistics Canada. <http://www.statcan.gc.ca/pub/65-507-m/65-507-m2006006-eng.pdf>. [Accessed 2 October 2010].

Canada Department of Foreign Affairs and International Trade (DFAIT) (2008). *Seizing Global Advantage: A Global Commerce Strategy for Securing Canada's Growth and Prosperity*, July. <http://www.international.gc.ca/commerce/assets/pdfs/GCS-en.pdf>. [Accessed 3 April 2011].

Canada-European Union (2008). *Joint Study on Assessing the Costs and Benefits of a Closer EU-Canada Economic Partnership*. <http://www.international.gc.ca/trade-agreements-accords-commerciaux/assets/pdfs/EU-Canada_Joint_Study-Introduction_Executive_Summary.pdf>. [Accessed 9 December 2010].

Canada-European Union (2009). *Joint Report on the EU-Canada Scoping Exercise* 5 March 2009. <http://www.international.gc.ca/trade-agreements-accords-commerciaux/assets/pdfs/Canada-EUJointReport2009-03-05.pdf>. [Accessed 9 December 2010].

Canadian Association of Importers and Exporters (CAIE) (2010a). "Update on the Canada-EU Trade Negotiations", in *ieNow*. <http://www.iecanada.com/ienow/2010/may_10/inside_1.html>. [Accessed 10 March 2011].

Canadian Association of Importers and Exporters (CAIE) (2010b). "CETA: A New Generation of FTA", in *ieNow*. <http://www.iecanada.com/ienow/2010/may_10/inside_4.html>. [Accessed 10 March 2011].

Canadian Union of Public Employees and Council of Canadians (2010). "Public Water for Sale: How Canada will privatize our public water systems". <http://canadians.org/trade/documents/CETA/water-report-1210.pdf>. [Accessed 15 March 2011].

Croci, Osvaldo and Livianna Tossutti (2009). "Canada and the European Union: A story of unrequited attraction", in Finn Laursen (ed.) *The EU in the Global Political Economy*. Brussels: P.I.E. Peter Lang, pp. 149-176.

Deacon, Bob with Morgan Killick (1999). *Socially Responsible Globalization: A Challenge for the European Union*, prepared by the Director of the Globalism and Social Policy Programme (GASPP), for the Ministry of Social

Affairs and Health of Finland. <http://gaspp.stakes.fi/NR/rdonlyres/ 75EC5345-2791-434D-B120-EA9CE6CAB91D/4822/eubook.pdf>. [Accessed 14 March 2011].

Deckwirth, Christina (2005). *The EU Corporate Trade Agenda: the role and the interests of corporations and their lobby groups in Trade Policy-Making in the European Union.* Brussels: Seattle to Brussels Network <http:// www2.weed-online.org/uploads/s2b_eu_corporate_trade_agenda.pdf>. [Accessed 19 August 2011].

Dowd, Alan (2011). "Canada says EU oil spat not linked to trade talks", Reuters online 23 Feb. <http://www.reuters.com/article/2011/02/23/us-eu-canada-crude-idUSTRE71M3UU20110223?feedType=RSS&feedName=GCA-GreenBusiness>. [Accessed 25 March 2011].

Drache, Daniel and Stuart Trew (2010)."The Pitfalls and Promises of the Canada-European Union Comprehensive Economic and Trade Agreement". SSRN: <http://ssrn.com/abstract=1645429>. [Accessed 16 March 2011].

Dreyer, Iana (2010). "What the EU South Korea Free Trade Agreement Reveals About the State of EU Trade Policy". European Centre for International Political Economy <www.ecipe.org/.../what-the-eu-south-korea-free-trade-agreement-reveals-about-the-state-of-eu-trade-policy>.

Eggenschwiler, Alejandro (2010). "The Canada-Czech Republic visa affair: A test for visa reciprocity and fundamental rights in the European Union", in *CEPS Liberty and Security in Europe.* <http://aei.pitt.edu/15125/>. [Accessed 30 March 2011].

Eichhorst, Werner *et al.* (2010). "External Dimension of EU Social Policy". I Z A Research Report No. 26. <www.iza.org/en/webcontent/publications/ reports/report.../iza_report_26.pdf>. [Accessed 15 March 2011].

European Commission DG Enterprise and Industry (2010). "International Affairs: Free Trade Agreements". <http://ec.europa.eu/enterprise/policies/ international/facilitating-trade/free-trade/index_en.htm>. [Accessed 15 March 2010].

European Commission DG Trade (2006). *Global Europe: Competing in the world. A Contribution to the EU's Growth and Jobs Strategy.* <http://trade.ec.europa.eu/doclib/docs/2006/october/tradoc_130380.pdf>. [Accessed 11 January 2011].

European Commission DG Trade (2010a). *Trade, Growth and World Affairs: Trade policy as a Core Component of the EU's 2020 Strategy.* <http://trade.ec.europa.eu/doclib/html/146955.htm>. [Accessed 22 March 2011].

European Commission DG Trade (2010b). "A Trade SIA relating to the Negotiation of a Comprehensive Economic and Trade Agreement (CETA) between the EU and Canada", Draft Inception Report. <http://trade.ec.europa.eu/ doclib/docs/2010/september/tradoc_146459.pdf>. [Accessed 15 March 2011].

European Commission DG Trade (2010c). "A Trade SIA relating to the Negotiation of a Comprehensive Economic and Trade Agreement (CETA) between the EU and Canada", Final Inception Report. <www.eucanada-sia.org/docs/ EU-Canada_SIA_Inception_Report_FINAL.pdf>. [Accessed 15 March 2011].

European Commission DG Trade (2011a). "A Trade SIA relating to the Negotiation of a Comprehensive Economic and Trade Agreement (CETA) between the EU and Canada", Draft Final Report – Summary Report March 2011. <http://trade.ec.europa.eu/doclib/docs/2011/march/tradoc_147754.pdf>. [Accessed 15 March 2011].

European Commission DG Trade (2011b). Press release: "EU Commission and Canada reach provisional solution in beef dispute", 17 March. <http:// trade.ec.europa.eu/doclib/press/index.cfm?id=685>. [Accessed 31 March 2011].

European Parliament (2011). "Resolution of 8 June 2011 on EU-Canada trade relations", 8 June. <http://www.europarl.europa.eu/sides/getDoc.do?type= TA&language=EN&reference=P7-TA-2011-0257>. [Accessed 29 July 2011].

Finbow, Robert (2010). "The Evolving Labour Relations Dimension of the European Regional System: a Model for North America?", in Finn Laursen (ed.), *Comparative Regional Integration: Europe and Beyond*. Farnham: Ashgate, pp. 101-130.

Geist, Michael (2011). "EU Report Says CETA IP Provisions Would Increase Consumer Prices, Royalty Deficit". <http://www.michaelgeist.ca/content/ view/5691/125/>. [Accessed 29 March 2011].

Gecelovsky, Paul and Christopher J. Kukucha (2011). "Foreign policy reviews and Canada's trade policy: 1968-2009", in *American Review of Canadian Studies*, 41, 1, pp. 37-52.

Goldfarb, Danielle and Louis Thériault (2010a). "Canada's 'Missing' Trade with the European Union". Ottawa, The Conference Board of Canada. <http://www.conferenceboard.ca/documents.aspx?did=3759>. [Accessed 11 January 2011].

Goldfarb, Danielle and Louis Thériault (2010b). "Canada's EU trade talks could fall apart", in *National Post*, 23 September. <http://sso.conferenceboard. ca/press/speech_oped/10-09-23/Canada_s_EU_trade_talks_could_fall_apart. aspx>. [Accessed 19 August 2011].

Guerin, Selen Sarisoy (2008a). "Prospects for the EU's New Generation of FTAs", *CEPS Commentary*. <www.ceps.eu/system/files/book/1648.pdf>. [Accessed 10 March 2011].

Guerin, Selen Sarisoy (2008b). "The mega new-generation deal with Canada", *CEPS Commentary*. <www.ceps.be/book/mega-new-generation-deal-canada>. [Accessed 10 March 2011].

Guerin, Selen Sarisoy and Chris Napoli (2008). "Canada and the European Union:Prospects for a Free Trade Agreement", *CEPS Working Document* No. 298. <http://www.ceps.eu/ceps/download/1514>. [Accessed 29 March 2011].

Harrison, Pete (2011). "Canada warns EU over oil sands", in *Globe and Mail*, 4 April 4. <http://www.theglobeandmail.com/report-on-business/canada-warns-eu-over-oil-sands/article1969643/>. [Accessed 5 April 2011].

Hermann, Christoph (2007). "Neoliberalism in the European Union", in *Studies in Political Economy*, 79, pp. 61-89.

International Labour Organization (2009). "European FTAs". <http://www.ilo. org/global/standards/information-resources-and-publications/free-trade-agreements-and-labour-rights/WCMS_115822/lang--en/index.htm#P4_728>. [Accessed 14 March 2011].

Kenety, Brian (2011). "UNHCR: Czech asylum bids to Canada plummet", in *Czechposition.com*. <http://www.ceskapozice.cz/en/asylum-seekers/unhcr-czech-asylum-bids-canada-plummet>. [Accessed 3 April 2011].

Kitou, Elisavet and George Philippidis (2010). "A quantitative economic assessment of a Canada-EU Comprehensive Economic Trade Agreement", paper presented at the Thirteenth Annual Conference on Global Economic Analysis Bangkok, <https://www.gtap.agecon.purdue.edu/resources/ download/4708.pdf>. [Accessed 29 March 2011].

Leblond, Patrick (2010). "Free trade with Europe will not destroy 150,000 jobs". Canada-Europe Transatlantic Dialogue Commentary. <http://canada-europe-dialogue.ca/publication/2010-11-LeblondCommentaryCETA.pdf>. [Accessed 13 March 2011].

Lloyd, Peter J. and Donald MacLaren (2006). "The EU's New Trade Strategy and Regionalisation in the World Economy", in *Aussenwirtschaft*, 61, 4, pp. 423-36.

MacLaren, Roy (2009). Speech to the Networking Session hosted by the Canada-Spain Chamber of Commerce, Madrid, Spain. <http://canada-europe. org/en/Resources/pdf/Roy%20MacLaren%20speech%20on%20Canada-EU%20free%20trade%20to%20the%20Spain-Canada%20Chamber% 20of%20Commerce%20-%2011%20March%202009.pdf>. [Accessed 29 March 2011].

Martin Roy, Juan Marchetti, and Hoe Lim (2007). "Services liberalization in the new generation of preferential trade agreements (PTAs): how much further than the GATS?", in *World Trade Review*, 6, pp. 155-192.

McCarthy, Shawn (2011). "Oil tycoon takes on Ontario Green Energy Act over wind farm", in *Globe and Mail*, 14 July. <http://www.theglobeandmail.com/report-on-business/industry-news/energy-and-resources/oil-tycoon-takes-on-ontario-green-energy-act-over-wind-farm/article2097575//>. [Accessed 5 July 2011].

McQueen, Matthew (2002). "The EU's Free-trade Agreements with Developing Countries: A Case of Wishful Thinking?", in *The World Economy*, 25, 9, pp. 1369-1385.

O'Neil, Peter (2011). "EU study: Canada free-trade deal far less lucrative than projected", in *Vancouver Sun*, 30 March. <http://www.vancouversun. com/business/study+Canada+free+trade+deal+less+lucrative+than+projected /4529510/story.html>. [Accessed 31 March 2011].

Orbie, Jan and Olufemi Babarinde (2008). "The Social Dimension of Globalization and EU Development Policy: Promoting Core Labour Standards and Corporate Social Responsibility", in *Journal of European Integration*, 30, 3, pp. 459-477.

Orbie, Jan and Lisa Tortell (eds.) (2008). The European Union and the Social Dimension of Globalization: How the EU Influences the World. London: Routledge.

Orbie, Jan *et al.* (2005). "EU trade policy and a social clause: a question of competences?", in *Politiqueeuropéenne*, 17, pp. 159-187.

Public Services Intergroup, European Parliament (2011). "Long live Canadian public services!" 8 June. <http://cupe.ca/updir/EU_PublicServices Article_EN.docx>. [Accessed 5 August 2011].

Sandberg, Oscar (2011). *Bridging the Atlantic: A Trade Effect Assessment of Services Inclusion in a Canada-EU Trade Agreement*, M.Sc. Department of Economics, Lund University, <http://lup.lub.lu.se/luur/download?func= downloadFile&recordOId=1963303&fileOId=1963304>. [Accessed 27 December 2011].

Seattle to Brussels Network (2009). Letter to Catherine Ashton, EU Commissioner for External Trade, 26 May.

Seattle to Brussels Network (2010). "The new EU's 2020 trade strategy will reinforce the policies responsible for the economic, social and environmental crises". <http://www.bilaterals.org/spip.php?article18438>. [Accessed 22 March 2011].

Seattle to Brussels Network (2011). "European civil society calls for a halt to negotiations for a Comprehensive Economic and Trade Agreement (CETA) with Canada". Brussels, 18 January.

Shrybman, Steven (2010). "Municipal Procurement Implications of the Proposed Comprehensive Economic and Trade Agreement (CETA) between Canada and the European Union", legal opinion prepared for the Centre for Civic Governance at Columbia Institute 28 May 2010. <http://cupe.ca/updir/FINAL-Shrybman_CETA_report.pdf>. [Accessed 22 January 2011].

Sinclair, Scott (2010). *Negotiating from Weakness: Canada-EU trade treaty threatens Canadian purchasing policies and public services*. Ottawa: Canadian Centre for Policy Alternatives. <http://www.policyalternatives.ca/ publications/reports/negotiating-%E2%80%89weakness>. [Accessed 29 March 2011].

Sinclair, Scott (2011). "The CETA and Health Care Reservations: A briefing note for the Canadian Health Coalition". Ottawa: Canadian Centre for Policy Alternatives. <http://www.policyalternatives.ca/publications/reports/ceta-and-health-care-reservations>. [Accessed 29 March 2011].

Stanford, Jim (2010). "Out of Equilibrium: The Impact of EU-Canada Free Trade on the Real Economy". Ottawa: Canadian Centre for Policy Alternatives. <http://www.policyalternatives.ca/sites/default/files/uploads/publications/Nat

ional%20Office/2010/10/Out_of_Equilibrium.pdf>. [Accessed 29 March 2011].

Thériault, Louis (2010). "Canada's 'Missing' Trade with the European Union", presented to the Conference on "A Canada-EU Free Trade Agreement: Public Good or Private Interest?", Centre for European Studies, Carleton University, Ottawa, 28 October. <http://canada-europe dialogue.ca/publication/Louis-Theriault-Panel-3.pdf>. [Accessed 15 January 2011].

Van den Hoven, Adrian (2004). "Assuming leadership in multilateral economic institutions: the EU's 'Development Round' discourse and strategy", in *West European Politics*, 27, 2, pp. 256-283.

Vogel, Toby (2009). "Talks to Start on Trade Deal with Canada", in *European Voice*, 15 October. <http://www.europeanvoice.com/article/imported/talks-to-start-on-trade-deal-with-canada/66131.aspx>. [Accessed 13 March 2011].

von Reppert-Bismarck, Juliane (2011). "EU hauled to court over secrecy in India trade talks", in Reuters Online, 15 February. <http://www.reuters.com/article/2011/02/15/eu-trade-transparency-idUSLDE71D1Q920110215>. [Accessed 29 March 2011].

Wajeeha, Rabeea (2011). "CETA: Is this Agreement Right for Canada?", in *Arbitrage*, <http://www.arbitragemagazine.com/topics/international-affairs/canada/ceta-agreement-canada/>. [Accessed 29 March 2011].

Woolcock, Stephen (2007). "European Union policy towards Free Trade Agreements", ECIPE Working Paper No. 3 <http://www.acp-eu-trade.org/library/files/Woolcock_EN_010307_ECIPE_EU-policy-towards-free-trade-agreements.pdf>. [Accessed 13 March 2011].

Woolcock, Stephen (2010). "The Treaty of Lisbon and the European Union as an actor in international trade", *ECIPE Working Paper*, No. 01. <http://www.ecipe.org/publications/ecipe-working-papers/the-treaty-of-lisbon-and-the-european-union-as-an-actor-in-international-trade/PDF>. [Accessed 29 March 2011].

Cited Interviews:

Interview 1: Official at EU delegation in Ottawa, 29 October 2010.

Interview 2: DFAIT official, 29 October 2010.

Interview 3: DFAIT official, 29 October 2010.

Interview 4: Official, NS Government negotiating team, 5 November 2010.

Interview 5: Official with Canada-EU business lobby group, 27 January 2011.

Interview 6: Official in Ontario ministry of economic development, 27 January 2011.

Interview 7: DFAIT official, 4 February, 2011.

Interview 8: Quebec delegation officer, Brussels, 6 June 2011.

Interview 9: Canadian delegation officer, Brussels, 6 June 2011.

Interview 10: Canadian delegation officer, Brussels, 6 June 2011.

Interview 11: Official at European Commission DG Trade, 7 June 2011.

Interview 12: Economic and Social committee official, 8 June 2011.

Interview 13 Trade union representative, 9 June 2011.

Interview 14: Economic and Social committee official, 9 June 2011.

Interview 15: NGO official, Brussels, 9 June 2011.

Interview 16: Business lobby group official, 10 June 2011.

Interview 17: Parliamentary officer, 10 June 2011.

Interview 18: European External Affairs Service official, 10 June 2011.

Interview 19: Officer at European Parliament, 10 June 2011.

Interview 20: Publications officer, European Commission, 14 June 2011.

Interview 21: Official at Council of Europe, 14 June 2011.

Interview 22: Official at European Parliament, 14 June 2011.

DFAIT briefing of Civil Society, 29 October 2010 (conference call).

DFAIT briefing of Civil Society, 4 February 2011 (conference call).

The EU-Canada Comprehensive Economic and Trade Agreement and E-Commerce

Nanette NEUWAHL and Nicolas VERMEYS

Introduction

Like most Internet-related concepts and constructs, electronic commerce or "e-commerce", a term said to have been coined by Kalakota and Whinston in 1996 (Romano 2001, p. 1), suffers from a lack of universally accepted definition (Vermeys *et al.* 2004, p. 648). What does e-commerce encompass? Online transactions? Surely. Online marketing? Probably. Offline delivery? Maybe. In fact, depending on the author, e-commerce can be limited to transactions completely executed online, or expanded to include any transaction where the Internet is used as a tool for the exchange or gathering of information. However broad or narrow a definition one chooses to use, the importance of e-commerce in a globalised world is undeniable. Although statistical evidence in the field remains somewhat unreliable, it does show a steady growth of e-commerce in the world (Amazon.com 2011 and Plunkett Research 2011). It is, therefore, not the least surprising that this matter is to be covered by the Comprehensive Economic and Trade Agreement (CETA) currently being drafted between Canada and the European Union, where it is defined as "commerce conducted through telecommunications, alone or in conjunction with other information and telecommunications technologies" (Canada and European Union 2010, p. 187). As defined, e-commerce is undoubtedly an important and growing avenue of trade in the relations between Canada and the EU: Through the Internet and by email, companies and private parties can advertise, exchange information, and conclude contracts concerning goods or services, such as banking, insurance, transport, and employment of personnel. Proper clauses in a bilateral agreement serve to regulate and protect businesses and consumers that are frequently engaging in cross-border transactions and, therefore, operating in a context of shifting vulnerabilities. Cross-border trade invariably exposes parties to the rules and requirements of more than one country, with the result that a transaction is more hazardous and unpredictable than when trading in a single geographical territory. Adequate and well thought-out regulation favours a sound development of trade as well as an adequate protection of the consumer.

This chapter analyses the chapter of the CETA dealing with e-commerce. As we shall demonstrate, the legal framework that appears to be emerging from the CETA is robust, and this can be explained by the fact that both the EU and Canada already possess well-developed legislation in the field. Our goal is not to address the adequacy or appropriateness of said legislation, but rather whether CETA discussions and objectives are realistic when considering the legal frameworks currently in place on both sides of the Atlantic.

The chapter begins with a brief description of the CETA, to put the e-commerce section in context. Thereafter, the chapter considers what the chapter of the CETA that deals with e-commerce adds, if anything, to the relevant existing legislation in Canada and the European Union. We will present our overall evaluation in the concluding section.

Notion, Content and Benefits of the CETA

Notion

The CETA that is currently being negotiated between Canada and the EU is an elaborate agreement covering such matters as tariffs, agricultural export subsidies, rules of origin, sanitary and phytosanitary issues, technical barriers, trade facilitation, customs procedures, cross-border trade in services, investment, government procurement, regulatory co-operation, intellectual property (IP), including geographical origin rules, movement of persons, competition issues, and sustainable development.

It was the intention of the parties that the CETA go further than the previous agreements between EU and Canada (Canada and European Union 2009), further than the existing multilateral treaties, and further than NAFTA. On almost all accounts, the negotiations are ambitious, going well beyond any previously existing agreements between EU and Canada. It also goes further than existing multilateral treaties involving both parties. It goes further than NAFTA and, in some respects, goes further than the agreement establishing the European Economic Area. This agreement brings Canada closer to the EU, and, indeed, its content is inspired by the idea and experience of the European Common Market, namely, to promote growth by the creation of a level playing field for all economic activity.

The innovative character of the CETA lies in the facilitation of a distinctive, integrative trade approach. By this, we mean that the agreement is a step up from export promotion and trade defence mechanisms,

towards internationalisation of trade through the promotion and facilitation of the creation of international value chains connecting Canada and
the EU through networks of activity. Protectionism is being discarded
and replaced by the active encouragement of inward and outward
Foreign Direct Investment (FDI), harmonisation serves to address the
issue of hidden – because "indistinctly applicable" obstacles to trade,
agreement is sought on the elimination of visa requirements, and the
recognition of professional qualifications, as well as on the content and
enforcement of proper IP regulations.

While the agreement is inspired by the Treaty of Rome and contains
many similar rules, in some respect, it is more modern and goes further
than that – unsurprisingly so because that treaty was and still is a
framework in need of further development. CETA is a further implementation of the Treaty of Rome, a step towards deepening of relations.
Still, it does not cover all trade between the parties. Some areas, considered sensitive, are expected to be excluded because of social or environmental concerns. In that sense, the agreement is, for better or worse,
not truly comprehensive.

The agreement is called CETA because of its holistic conception of
commerce. The adjective "comprehensive" seems to belong to the
nouns "economic" and "trade", rather than to the noun "agreement".
This is not a comprehensive agreement, but the approach to trade is.
Admittedly, other language versions of the agreement may not be that
accurate: in French it is *Accord économique et commercial global.*

Content of CETA

A brief description of the content of the CETA follows now, domain
per domain. E-commerce needs to be seen within this context.

Trade in Goods

The agreement will contain provisions on free movement of goods of
various kinds, including remaining customs duties, export subsidies and
state trading.

Both parties are of the view that tariff elimination should be ambitious in the sense that no tariff lines should be excluded, and the objective is to reach between a quarter and a third of the overall benefits of
any bilateral trade liberalisation.

Agriculture export subsidies and state trading enterprises (such as
Quebec's Société des Alcools du Québec – SAQ) will be addressed as
they create distortion of competition and barriers to trade and investment. The agreement will provide the necessary on emergency action
and trade remedies.

The parties are seeking to negotiate unambiguous provisions on rules of origin (ROO) that leave little room for administrative discretion, as well as provisions on customs procedures allowing for the effective and transparent administration of the ROO. Such procedures, (that will complement those of the existing Agreement between Canada and the European Community on Customs Cooperation and Mutual Assistance in Customs Matters) should help ensure compliance with rules of origin without creating unnecessary obstacles to trade.

There is an obvious relationship between the chapter on e-commerce and the chapters on the free movement of goods. Without the latter, e-commerce is severely restricted. Customs duties and procedures add costs to an electronic transaction, lead to market partitioning, and take away the ease of Internet shopping and part of the benefit of Internet selling. Whereas e-commerce stimulates the movement of goods (and diversification), the free movement of goods in turn favours e-commerce. This is true not only in relation to tariff barriers but also to nontariff barriers to trade and in relation to goods as well as services. The intention of the agreement is also to substantially reduce existing nontariff barriers to trade.

Sanitary and Phytosanitary Issues

Goods coming from abroad (ordered via the Internet or otherwise or sent as free samples) may be subject to inspections that are required for the protection of human or animal and plant health. These may or not be justified, but in all cases they create complications and delay the delivery of the items to their destination. They may entail additional cost for the addressee and red tape for the sender, which is difficult to accept, especially if the goods have already been tested in the country of origin and were adequately protected during the trip. The agreement pays attention to sanitary and phytosanitary issues in a special chapter, and the negotiating parties have agreed that the results should be tangible (Canada and European Union 2009). Provisions of the chapter on sanitary and phytosanitary (SPS) issues should go beyond those contained in the WTO Agreement on Sanitary and Phytosanitary Measures and the existing Canada-EU Veterinary Agreement.

Technical Barriers to Trade

A CETA chapter on provisions on technical barriers to trade (TBT) should enhance the provisions of the WTO in this domain too. The relevant agreement on Technical Barriers to Trade that will be reinforced by the CETA deals with issues such as transparency, international standards, technical regulations, and conformity assessment. There will, therefore, be a specific chapter on those issues in order to stimulate international transactions. Harmonisation already exists, but co-operation between the parties is necessary on an ongoing basis in order to ensure that newly created technical requirements will not interfere unduly with trade. The solution can be found in part in a regular sharing of experiences and the promotion of joint efforts to enhance good regulatory practice in implementing the TBT agreement, as well as the establishment of a mechanism to address specific TBT issues. It is evident that goods that do not comply with technical requirements and certifications in a country will be less traded. A holistic approach to commerce requires a chapter on TBTs as much as a chapter on e-commerce.

Trade Facilitation Measures

Trade facilitation measures equally stimulate growth. In complement to similar provisions under negotiation at the WTO as well as the existing Agreement between Canada and the European Community on Customs Cooperation and Mutual Assistance in Customs Matters, there will be provisions in a relevant chapter on trade facilitation, which would take account of the challenges faced by small and medium-sized enterprises and which would include as objectives efficiency, transparency, co-operation, and consultation. This would obviously be of relevance to e-commerce but would have a wider application.

Cross-Border Trade Services

In regard to services the CETA is equally ambitious. The liberalisation of trade in services should go further in terms of the number of sectors, the volume of trade, and modes of supply than the current WTO commitments and aim at achieving market access, non-discrimination, and compliance with Article V GATS (economic integration). Cross-border trade in services should be facilitated by regulatory provisions going beyond market access and non-discrimination. The agreement would apply to measures taken by all levels of government, as well as non-governmental bodies that exercise powers delegated by any level of government. Complementing the cross-border trade in services, any future agreement should include provisions to facilitate mutual recognition of professional qualifications in the field of services.

There is a growing market in e-services such as e-books, e-payments, e-recruitment services, and communication itself that is affected by this chapter, even if its provisions are more general.

Government Procurement

Considering the Government Procurement Agreement, public procurement markets on central and sub-central levels should be opened up to ensure equal access and transparency of rules and practices to the business community abroad.

Regulatory Co-Operation

There should be an intensification of regulatory co-operation beyond the goods sector and the central government level.

Investment

Whilst bilateral investment flows already represent a notable share of both parties' total foreign direct investment (FDI), it is agreed that there are opportunities for increasing bilateral investment flows (Canada and European Union 2009). The scope of the negotiations on investment covers pre- and post-establishment issues in all sectors in order to improve market access, to provide for the non-discriminatory treatment of investors and investments, and to improve transparency. The negotiations should deal with substantive and procedural obligations at both the central and sub-central government levels.

Competition Policy in the Broad Sense

The CETA would build upon and deepen the *acquis* of the Agreement between Canada and the European Communities regarding the Application of their Competition Law of 1999. It would improve exchange of information among competition authorities and address state aid, designated monopolies, and state/public enterprises to ensure that they do not distort competition and create barriers to trade and investment. This can be relevant to ensuring a level playing field not only in traditional commerce, but also in telecommunications and e-commerce.

Intellectual Property, including Geographical Indications

Another area of liberalization (and another one that is indirectly relevant for the success of e-commerce) is intellectual property law. The WTO Agreement on Trade-Related Aspects of Intellectual Property Rights (TRIPS) sets minimum levels of protection for intellectual property (IP) rights, and the parties were of the view that the EU-Canada agreement should substantially improve on all categories of IP rights where need for increased protection and/or enforcement could be identified. Furthermore, the CETA should establish and/or maintain very high standards of protection and enforcement of IP rights. Intellectual property provisions in CETA should cover, *inter alia*, a broad protection of geographical indications.

The Movement of Persons across Borders

The movement of persons is nowadays as relevant to the development of commerce as ever if not more so. The movement of people can be crucial for promotion of businesses (including e-commerce and related communication technology) at trade fairs, for after-sales services, and technical support for goods, construction, installation and programming, maintenance, and also for reception of services abroad and recruitment. The parties, recognising the mutual interest in facilitating the legitimate temporary movement of persons related to bilateral trade and investment, are agreed that provisions on such mobility (visas) should be included in the CETA.

Other

The above description gives an indication of the wide scope of the agreement that is expected to address many aspects of economic activity. The agreement covers other matters as well. It is not necessary for us to be complete in our description, since some aspects are more or less remote from our main concern (e-commerce). However, it is worth stressing one more area of negotiations as an example of just how comprehensive this agreement is. The scoping exercise reports that the parties intend to deal with sustainable development since this is a main concern of the parties (Canada and European Union 2009). Accordingly, it is expected that CETA will contain provisions favouring speedy market access of environment-friendly goods and services. Similarly, labour laws are a central issue, including the core labour standards embodied in the 1998 International Labour Organization (ILO) Declaration and in internationally recognized standards of corporate social responsibility. Principles that are likely to be covered in this section of the CETA include the right of contracting parties to regulate while aiming for high levels of protection, effective enforcement of environment and labour laws, a commitment to refrain from waiving such laws in a manner that affects trade or investment, a framework for cooperation, public involvement, and mechanisms to monitor and address disputes.

Whereas high standards in these areas can have an effect on trade and industry, these rules do not particularly affect e-commerce. However, they show that the intention of the parties is to conclude a comprehensive agreement that serves to create a level playing field for the parties and the absence of barriers to flows of goods, services, and investments. With only months to go until the final conclusion of the agreement, it is hoped that the agreement lives up to the expectations.

Benefits

Before we deal more particularly with e-commerce, the first chapter of the negotiations to be closed (see below), it is still appropriate to consider the benefits of Canada and the EU concluding a bilateral agreement. What is the advantage of concluding such a bilateral agreement if the WTO system is based on the principle of non-discrimination, and any concession granted to one trade partner should be available also to the other states that are parties to the GATT? The answer to this question is threefold:

First of all, to the extent that the issues are covered by WTO rules, they may come under the system of derogations or exceptions. Most prominently, customs unions covering substantially all trade among the parties (such as the EU or the EU-Turkey Customs Union) are entitled to an exception to the most favourite nation clause as regards tariffs, and the General Agreement on Trade Related Services (Article V) allows an exception for agreements that aim at economic integration in that sector, equally on the condition that substantially all transactions are covered by the clauses concerned.

It is suggested that the CETA is not entitled to an exception, and the Most Favoured Nation principle applies. Although it covers many matters, it does not cover substantially all trade between the EU and Canada. The name of the agreement may, in this respect, be misleading. Nevertheless the proposed agreement is innovative.

Second, to the extent that WTO rules do not allow for an exception, the advantage is one of time: Until other states invoke equal treatment, the EU and Canada still have the benefit of the early birds in that they can take advantage of a preferential treatment until similar agreements are concluded with other states. Indeed, the Harper government is keen on concluding similar agreements with many other countries in order to make up for the stalled progress in multilateral trade negotiations and to decrease its dependence on the US economy.

Finally, if there are any matters that are not governed by WTO restrictions, the regulation thereof is a distinct innovation and facilitation of trade from which the partners can draw exceptional benefit. CETA offers the parties a broad range of advantages which in part go beyond the WTO agreements. As a matter of fact, the chapter on e-commerce is one illustration of that finding.

The CETA and Electronic Commerce

As previously alluded to, the outcome of current negotiations relating to the Comprehensive Economic and Trade Agreement has yet to be officially made public. In fact, other than leaked documents published on the Trade Justice Network website (http://tradejustice.ca/en/section/3) in November 2010, we have little to go by – other than hearsay – as to the overall place electronic commerce has held in previous rounds of negotiation. All we do know is that sources claim that the agreement's chapter relating to electronic commerce was completed as of March 2011 (Canadian Conference of the Arts 2011), which would lead us to believe that the October 2010 draft is close to the final product. Although it is somewhat difficult to establish what exact framework the CETA will put forth regarding electronic commerce until the final draft of chapter G6 of the agreement (according to the October draft's numbering) is made publically available, we can suppose that the agreement will follow in the path of the 1999 Joint Statement on Electronic Commerce in the Global Information Society and the 2000 Electronic Commerce in the Global Information Society Work Plan (hereinafter the 2000 E-Commerce Work Plan), as this was the goal set out in 2004 when Canada and Europe agreed to a framework for a new Canada-EU Trade and Investment Enhancement Agreement (TIEA), a path that would lead to the current CETA negotiations: "Good progress was made on the TIEA until 2006 when Canada and the EU jointly decided to pause negotiations. With negotiations on a CETA, we have now moved beyond the TIEA toward an agreement with a much broader and more ambitious scope" (Foreign Affairs and International Trade Canada 2011). According to Foreign Affairs and International Trade Canada (2011), the TIEA's goal, as it related to electronic commerce was as follows:

> Canada and the EU agree to continue and reinforce co-operation on the basis of the 1999 Joint Statement on Electronic Commerce in the Global Information Society and the 2000 E-Commerce Work Plan, including new areas where Canada and the EU share common objectives. In particular, developments in sectors already identified in the current co-operation framework such as privacy, security and consumer protection should be taken into account, namely the fight against unsolicited communications (spam). This co-operation should take place, *inter alia*, bilaterally, in multilateral fora, or supporting and collaborating with the private sector and civil society.

As mentioned in the above quote, the final CETA draft should revolve around three main aspects relating to electronic commerce: (a) privacy, (b) information security, and (c) consumer protection. In fact, two of these three key points (privacy and consumer protection) are central to the electronic commerce chapter of the leaked draft of the agreement, while the third (information security) seems to constitute one of the main structural points of the chapter governing telecommunications. We will, therefore, focus on how Canadian/European legislation and treaties currently address these issues to establish whether the necessary legal framework has been put into place for the CETA to be effective.

Privacy

EU and Canada consider that legislative frameworks for the protection of privacy and personal information are a vital component of electronic commerce strategy and beneficial to the evolution of an information society. Internationally, EU and Canada will support a standards-based approach to complement national frameworks (European Union and Canada 1999).

According to the 2000 E-Commerce Work Plan, co-operation between Canada and Europe in the area of privacy had two closely linked objectives:

- Ensure the free flow of personal data between the EU and Canada on the basis of high data protection standards.
- Promote the development of compatible standards to complement national frameworks for the protection of personal data.

Let us see how both these objectives were addressed.

High Data Protection Standards

In 1995, when the first electronic commerce websites such as Amazon were still in their infancy (Amazon.com 2011), the European Parliament adopted Directive 95/46/EC of the European Parliament and of the Council of 24 October 1995 on the protection of individuals with regard to the processing of personal data and on the free movement of such data. Although the directive predated the rise of electronic commerce, its drafters had enough foresight to extend its reach to electronic data, as stated in Article 3(1): "This Directive shall apply to the processing of personal data wholly or partly by automatic means, and to the processing otherwise than by automatic means of personal data which form part of a filing system or are intended to form part of a filing system".

According to privacy specialists (Chassigneux 2004, p. 120), this broad scope implies that the directive applies to all personal data gathered and transferred electronically, including within the context of electronic commerce. This was further confirmed in 2002 when the European Parliament adopted Directive 2002/58/EC of the European Parliament and of the Council of 12 July 2002 concerning the processing of personal data and the protection of privacy in the electronic communications sector (Directive on privacy and electronic communications), which aimed to "particularise and complement Directive

95/46/EC" "with respect to the processing of personal data in the electronic communication sector and to ensure the free movement of such data and of electronic communication equipment and services in the Community" (Article 1 of Directive 2002/58/EC).

At the 1995 directive's core are a series of seven principles: data quality (Article 6), data processing legitimacy (Article 7), information must be given to the data subject (Articles 10 and 11), the data subject's right of access to data (Article 12), the data subject's right to object (Articles 14 and 15), confidentiality and security of processing (Articles 16 and 17), and transfer of personal data to third countries (Articles 25 and 26) (Chassigneux 2004, p. 120). This last principle, the one limiting the transfer of personal data to third countries, is fleshed out in section 25 of the 1995 Directive: "The Member States shall provide that *the transfer to a third country of personal data* which are undergoing processing or are intended for processing after transfer *may take place only if*, without prejudice to compliance with the national provisions adopted pursuant to the other provisions of this Directive, *the third country in question ensures an adequate level of protection*" (emphasis added).

The Article's second paragraph further explains that:

> The adequacy of the level of protection afforded by a third country shall be assessed in the light of all the circumstances surrounding a data transfer operation or set of data transfer operations; particular consideration shall be given to the nature of the data, the purpose and duration of the proposed processing operation or operations, the country of origin and country of final destination, the rules of law, both general and sectoral, in force in the third country in question and the professional rules and security measures which are complied with in that country.

Therefore, in order to reach the first objective of the 2000 E-Commerce Work Plan, Canada had to adopt and enact legislation that offered an "adequate level of protection" according to the Commission of the European Communities.

Shortly before the 26 June 2000 EU-Canada Summit (held in Lisbon) that would lead to the drafting of the 2000 E-Commerce Work Plan, the Canadian government had passed An Act to support and promote electronic commerce by protecting personal information that is collected, used or disclosed in certain circumstances, by providing for the use of electronic means to communicate or record information or transactions and by amending the Canada Evidence Act, the Statutory Instruments Act and the Statute Revision Act (better known under its short title, the Personal Information Protection and Electronic Documents Act or PIPEDA). The act, which came into force on 1 January 2001 (section 72):

> applies to all personal information collected, used or disclosed by private sector organisations engaged in commercial activities. [It] provides that organisations must obtain a person's consent before collecting, using or disclosing personal information about that person; that organisations are obliged to protect personal information by adopting appropriate security measures according to the degree of sensitivity of the information; and that individuals may have access to personal information about them that is held by an organisation and have it corrected if required. (European Commission and Government of Canada 2008, p. 101)

Within the context of the 2000 E-Commerce Work Plan, the European Union, therefore, took upon itself to "initiate an internal process under which the Commission will examine the privacy protection provisions of [PIPEDA], in light of the provisions of its Data Protection Directive, with a view to achieving a positive orientation for the next summit" (European Union and Canada 2000). Consequently, according to the powers given to it under Article 25(2) of the directive, the Commission of the European Communities studied whether PIPEDA could be considered to ensure an adequate level of protection to personal data held by a Canadian company. The outcome to the study was positive: In a decision of 20 December 2001 (C(2001) 4539), the Commission held that "Canada is considered as providing an adequate level of protection for personal data transferred from the Community to recipients subject to the Personal Information Protection and Electronic Documents Act".

Compatible Standards to Complement National Frameworks for the Protection of Personal Data

In order to reach this second objective, Canada and the European Union agreed to promote "a compatible standards-based approach to complement national frameworks" (European Union and Canada 2000). As a "starting point for discussion", the parties agreed to use the voluntary code developed by the Canadian Standards Association (CSA) (European Union and Canada 2000). Of course, considering that the key elements of said code were incorporated into PIPEDA and now form Schedule 1 of the Act (CSA Standards 2011), and that the Commission of the European Communities accepted that said law provided "an adequate level of protection for personal data transferred from the Community to recipients subject to the Personal Information Protection and Electronic Documents Act", one could submit that this objective was also reached, although the drafting and fine-tuning of standards remains an ongoing process, as alluded to in the 2000 E-Commerce

Work Plan: "The European Committee for Standardisation (CEN) could usefully continue its work to promote standards as an added value instrument to complement national and European frameworks".

It thus seems that collaborative efforts between Canada and the European Union, as they pertain to the protection of privacy and personal information, have met the objectives set by both parties in 2000. Therefore, if, as is suggested in the October 2010 draft of the CETA, the parties decide to include an article stating that:

Each Party should adopt or maintain laws, regulations or administrative measures for the protection of personal information of users engaged in electronic commerce and, when doing so, shall take into due consideration international standards *of data protection* of relevant international organisations of which both Parties are a member (Emphasis represents a modification suggested to the text by the European Union representatives).

It is our opinion that neither party will need to fundamentally change its current legislation and practices. At the most, we believe that some rules and regulation may need to be tweaked to follow technological changes and trends.

Information Security

EU and Canada agree on the necessity of policies to facilitate the use of technologies for authentication and for the conduct of secure electronic commerce. To this end, they will discuss the various technological options for providing authentication. EU and Canada will explore mechanisms to enhance international co-operation to combat illegal activities and to empower users with regards to potentially harmful content (European Union and Canada 1999).

According to the 2000 E-Commerce Work Plan, co-operation between Canada and Europe in the area of security revolves around two objectives:

- Promote mutual recognition of certificates and certification authorities' procedures;
- Facilitate cross-border recognition and use of electronic signatures.

To reach these objectives, it was agreed that:

- Canada [would] provide a working document for discussion by an experts group as a possible means of carrying out the work.
- European and Canadian experts would meet to:
  - identify the key elements for establishing trust in certification processes;

159

- map the existing schemes against these key elements; and
- identify potential obstacles to cross-border authentication (European Union and Canada 2000).

However, it seems that these actions, when taken, have not been as successful as those pertaining to privacy in the sense that they did not produce any noticeable changes in discourse. In fact, in a 2008 joint study assessing the costs and benefits of the CETA, the parties simply issued a reworded version of their 1999 joint statement:

> The EU and Canada agreed on the need to develop policies to facilitate the use of authentification [*sic*] technologies and to implement secure electronic commerce activities. In this regard, they are discussing various possible technological options as regards authentification [sic]. They are also analysing mechanisms to improve international cooperation to combat illegal activity and prompt users to exercise control themselves on potentially dangerous content. (European Commission and Government of Canada 2008, p. 104)

This is not to say that no legislative strides have been made in the fields of certification, cryptography, and cross-border authentication. However, they did not necessarily have tangible results. For example, in 2005, the World Customs Organization (WCO) – of which Canada, EU Member States, as well as European Communities, are members (WCO 2009) – adopted its SAFE Framework of Standards (WCO 2007), a document aimed at developing "a regime that will enhance the security and facilitation of international trade" (WCO 2007, p. 2). It should be noted that the SAFE Framework seems to have been an integral part of CETA negotiations. In fact, in a section on page 56 of the October 2010 draft, CETA states, "The Parties shall continue to cooperate in international fora, such as the World Customs Organization (WCO), to achieve mutually-recognized goals, such as those set out in the WCO Framework of Standards to Secure and Facilitate Global Trade".

With regards to security, the SAFE Framework (2007) explains that:

> The use of ICT [Information and Communication Technologies] in general and electronic exchange of information over open networks in particular requires a detailed ICT security strategy. ICT security therefore has to be seen as an integral part of any Customs supply chain security strategy. To arrive at an effective and efficient IT security strategy, Customs have to undertake risk assessment. The Kyoto ICT Guidelines outline ways in which a comprehensive ICT security strategy can ensure the availability, integrity and confidentiality of the information and of IT systems and the information they handle, including, for example, the avoidance of repudiation at origin or receipt. There are many ways to implement ICT security, for which purpose reference is made to the Kyoto ICT Guidelines.

With regards to electronic signatures, the SAFE Framework (2007) states:

> One essential ICT security element for a supply chain security strategy is related to digital signatures. Digital signatures, or Public Key Infrastructure arrangements, can play an important role in securing the electronic exchange of information. The integrated Customs control chain includes the possibility that traders can submit their declarations in advance to both the Customs administration at export and to the Customs administration at import. It would be beneficial if economic operators would also benefit from mutual recognition of digital certificates. This would allow the economic operator to sign all electronic messages to those Customs administrations having accepted to recognize this certificate. This crossborder recognition of digital certificates can help increase security but, at the same time, provide significant facilitation and simplification for the trader. For this purpose, Customs administrations are encouraged to apply the WCO Recommendation concerning the electronic transmission and authentication of Customs and other relevant regulatory information.

As noted in the above quotes, the SAFE Framework also refers to the Kyoto ICT Guidelines, i.e., the Kyoto Convention Guidelines on the Application of Information and Communication Technology, a document that goes into much more detail on how to address security issues using certification, electronic signatures, and other complementary technology. Of course, it must be pointed out that the SAFE framework and Kyoto ICT Guidelines are primarily aimed at customs agencies, not at those who rely on electronic commerce to purchase or sell goods. Nevertheless, the WCO has also drafted documents indirectly affecting electronic commerce. For example, Article 7.4 of the General Annex to the International Convention on the Simplification and Harmonization of Customs Procedures, a convention both Canada (Axworthy 2000) and the European Community (Council of the European Union 2003) have adhered to, states that:

New or revised national legislation shall provide for:

– electronic commerce methods as an alternative to paper-based documentary requirements;

– electronic as well as paper-based authentication methods; [...] (General Annex, p. 26)

In Europe, a number of directives satisfying those requirements have been adopted. Electronic commerce methods have in fact been governed by Directive 2000/31/EC of the European Parliament and of the Council of 8 June 2000 on certain legal aspects of information society services, in particular electronic commerce, in the Internal Market (Directive on electronic commerce) for more than a decade. As for electronic authentication methods, they are subject to Directive 1999/93/EC of the European Parliament and of the Council of 13 December 1999 on a Community framework for electronic signatures. The latter directive aims at facilitating "the use of electronic signatures and to contribute to their legal recognition" (Article 1). It also "establishes a legal framework for electronic signatures and certain certification-services in order to ensure the proper functioning of the internal market" (Article 1). On an international level, section 7 of the directive directly responds to the "promote mutual recognition of certificates and certification authorities' procedures" objective identified in the 2000 E-Commerce Work Plan by stating that:

1. Member States shall ensure that certificates which are issued as qualified certificates to the public by a certification-service-provider established in a third country are recognised as legally equivalent to certificates issued by a certification-service-provider established within the Community if:

a) the certification-service-provider fulfils the requirements laid down in this Directive and has been accredited under a voluntary accreditation scheme established in a Member State; or

b) a certification-service-provider established within the Community which fulfils the requirements laid down in this Directive guarantees the certificate; or

c) the certificate or the certification-service-provider is recognised under a bilateral or multilateral agreement between the Community and third countries or international organisations.

The Article goes on to state that:

2. In order to facilitate cross-border certification services with third countries and legal recognition of advanced electronic signatures originating in third countries, the Commission shall make proposals, where appropriate, to achieve the effective implementation of standards and international agreements applicable to certification services. In particular, and where necessary, it shall submit proposals to the Council for appropriate mandates for the negotiation of bilateral and multilateral agreements with third countries and international organisations. The Council shall decide by qualified majority.

3. Whenever the Commission is informed of any difficulties encountered by Community undertakings with respect to market access in third countries, it may, if necessary, submit proposals to the Council for an appropriate mandate for the negotiation of comparable rights for Community undertakings in these third countries. The Council shall decide by qualified majority.

Canada has also adapted its laws to facilitate the use of electronic signatures. For example, PIPEDA "provides for the formal recognition in law of digital signatures and electronic documents, through the amendment of more than 300 federal statutes relating to governmental transactions and information requirements" (Industry Canada 2009).

With regards to certification, however, although certain provinces such as Quebec have enacted legislation (see sections 47-62 of An Act to Establish a Legal Framework for Information Technology), the federal government has limited its involvement to the adoption of a series of principles: the Principles for Electronic Authentication (Industry Canada 2004).

All this goes to show that the legal framework is in place to allow those who wish to take advantage of electronic commerce to use electronic signatures and rely on third-party certification services. Therefore, when the 2010 draft CETA states that the parties "agree to maintain a dialogue on issues raised by electronic commerce, which will inter alia address: [...] the recognition of certificates of electronic signatures issued to the public and the facilitation of cross-border certification services", it simply reinforces current practices while restating what Canada and Europe have been agreeing to since 1999. Furthermore, it could be argued that lack of a legislative framework does not seem to have been the issue as to why these types of security measures are not as widespread as they could be. Rather, it would seem that there is a lack of interest from those who take part in electronic commerce, whether they be vendors or consumers.

Consumer Protection

EU and Canada believe that measures to provide consumers with a means to exercise choice, settle grievances and have lawful recourse to the resolution of disputes in an electronic environment (including online dispute settlement schemes) are central to the orderly development of electronic commerce. Consequently, they will discuss approaches to increase consumer confidence, protection and education (European Union and Canada 1999).

Ever since the first days of the Internet, the centrepiece to all online consumer protection discussions seems to have been online dispute resolution (ODR). In fact, the main objective to the 2000 E-Commerce Work Plan was to "[s]upport measures to promote consumer confidence in on-line markets, including consumer trustmarks and related extrajudicial dispute resolution mechanisms". This was to be done through a series of measures including the "promotion and implementation of the OECD guidelines on consumer protection in global electronic commerce", the "[p]romotion of mutual recognition of [...] national seal programmes for consumer protection developed on the basis of stakeholder collaboration", and the "[p]romotion of mutual recognition of [...] related extrajudicial dispute resolution mechanisms, such as the EU project ECODIR (European Consumer Dispute Resolution)".

Although there have been some efforts to honour these objectives, not the least of which is the adoption of Directive 2000/31/EC of the European Parliament and of the Council of 8 June 2000 on certain legal aspects of information society services, in particular electronic commerce, in the internal market (Directive on Electronic Commerce) that allows for out-of-court dispute settlements (see section 17 of the directive), national legislation in many European countries (for example, see section 2061 of France's Code civil), and provincial legislation in Canada (for example, see sections 3148 and 3159 of Quebec's Civil Code and section 11.1 of Quebec's Consumer Protection Act) (Dell Computer Corp. v. Union des consommateurs 2007) has somewhat hampered the recognition of international ODR decisions. Further, most of the initial investments into ODR did not result in any tangible results. Other than the aforementioned ECODIR platform, most projects funded by the European Commission were not seen through. As for ECODIR, although the platform was delivered (and is still functional), lack of sustained funding hindered its promotion and further deployment:

> Additional resources would have allowed ECODIR to enter into alliances and partnerships with major European commercial sites (and, possibly, with those based in North America also), and to envisage the inclusion of a requirement to use ECODIR in case of dispute as a condition for obtaining certain quality labels (Benyekhlef 2010, p. 89; translation provided by CRDP).

In the last year, the ODR debate has resurfaced in front of the United Nations Commission on International Trade Law (UNCITRAL). Member states, including Canada and European countries, are currently working to develop legal standards "in the field of online dispute resolution relating to cross-border electronic commerce transactions, including business-to-business (B2B) and business-to-consumer (B2C) transactions" (UNCITRAL 2010). The objective set forth in the 2000 E-Commerce Work Plan has, therefore, reached much further than a purely Canada-Europe partnership, and international guidelines should emerge in the coming years.

Although not explicitly mentioned in the 2000 E-Commerce Work Plan, unsolicited commercial email (also referred to as spam) has also become a focus point in Canada-Europe negotiations regarding online consumer protection. (The plan does, however, refer to the OECD guidelines on consumer protection in global electronic commerce (2000), a document that states: "Businesses should develop and implement effective and easy-to-use procedures that allow consumers to choose whether or not they wish to receive unsolicited commercial e-mail messages" (p. 14)). In fact, the draft CETA proposes that "the Parties agree to maintain a dialogue on issues raised by electronic commerce, which will inter alia address: [...] the treatment of unsolicited electronic commercial communications". Of course, spam legislation has existed in Europe for more than a decade now. Article 7 of the Directive on Electronic Commerce clearly states that:

> Member States which permit unsolicited commercial communication by electronic mail shall ensure that such commercial communication by a service provider established in their territory shall be identifiable clearly and unambiguously as such as soon as it is received by the recipient. [...] Member States shall take measures to ensure that service providers undertaking unsolicited commercial communications by electronic mail consult regularly and respect the opt-out registers in which natural persons not wishing to receive such commercial communications can register themselves.

Although Canada had not, at the time, followed suit, it has since worked on its own spam-related legislation. An Act to promote the efficiency and adaptability of the Canadian economy by regulating certain activities that discourage reliance on electronic means of carrying out commercial activities, and to amend the Canadian Radio-television and Telecommunications Commission Act, the Competition Act, the Personal Information Protection and Electronic Documents Act and the Telecommunications Act was assented to on 15 December 2010. It must, however, be emphasised that most of its dispositions have yet to come into force (see section 91 of the Act). Section 6 of the Act prohibits the transmission of unsolicited emails, except when a party falls within one of the numerous exceptions to the general rule. The Act also grants the Canadian Radio-Television and Telecommunications Commission (the CRTC) the power to make regulations regarding unsolicited email (see section 64 (2) of the Act). Draft regulations are currently available on the CRTC website (http://www.crtc.gc.ca/eng/archive/2011/2011-400.htm), and all signs point to them being enacted before CETA negotiations reach their ending point.

Evaluation

This succinct overview of legislative and collaborative efforts aimed – among other things – at favouring the growth of electronic commerce between Canada and Europe while ensuring the protection of consumers, their data, and their privacy, underlines the fact that much of what was at stake in the drafting of the 1999 Joint Statement on Electronic Commerce in the Global Information Society, the 2000 E-Commerce Work Plan, and the TIEA has been "settled" (in the sense that legislation on both sides of the Atlantic has been adopted pertaining to these issues) or is currently being addressed on a larger scale (such as the work currently being done by the UNCITRAL Working group III –

online dispute resolution). In sum, because the EU and Canada have co-operated to develop compatible and comparable (broadly speaking) legislation in the field of e-commerce, and because they have both participated in several international fora in which such issues are co-ordinated, such as the Organisation for Economic Co-operation and Development (OECD), United Nations Commission on International Trade Law (UNCITRAL), World Trade Organisation (WTO), and World Customs Organization (WCO), the CETA has benefitted from a solid base on which to build when it comes to regulating e-commerce practices between Canada and Europe.

The CETA is an ambitious agreement on many accounts and its chapter on e-commerce, the first one to be concluded, seems destined to consolidate and reinforce current practices. The existence of compatible legal provisions has allowed the negotiating parties of the CETA to come up with realistic and coherent promises and to agree relatively speedily regarding e-commerce practices. The chapter on e-commerce is a solid achievement that represents both a central element of the agreement and an incentive for negotiators to come up with comparable deliverables in other contexts. The chapter on telecommunications exudes the same constructive spirit. E-commerce issues are unlikely to be stumbling blocks when ratification by European and national parliaments is on the agenda on both sides of the Atlantic, mostly because the required legislation is already in place.

Obviously, e-commerce regulation is in constant evolution. In order to remain effective, the agreement would benefit from continued legislative co-operation between the parties. Furthermore, like in the case of the other chapters of the agreement, the effectiveness of the provisions will depend on the existence of adequate provisions on dispute resolution. Questions arise both in a general way and in a way that is quite specific to e-commerce. On a general level, choices will invariably have to be made concerning the level of centralisation of dispute resolution mechanisms: The available text did not allow us to draw conclusions on the modes of dispute resolution, whether intergovernmental/political or judicial. Needless to say, the more effective the enforcement, the more benefit the parties draw from the substantive provisions of the agreement. Of course, since this question is at the very heart of ongoing UNCITRAL negotiations regarding online dispute resolution mechanisms (UNCITRAL 2010), it would most probably be ill-advised for Canada and the European Union to hastily adopt a dispute resolution model for cyber consumers without taking the organisation's recommendations into account.

On a more specific level, e-commerce is a precious avenue for private individuals and small businesses to engage in cross-border transactions. Their protection is to be taken particularly seriously, not necessarily because of the sums involved but because of the vulnerability of the persons engaging in transnational transactions. Adequate dispute resolution procedures that are easy to use in a transnational context are, therefore, particularly important. On this account some progress is definitely needed.

Finally, it should be pointed out that other sections of the agreement that are not specifically linked to e-commerce – those that indiscriminately regulate all forms of commerce between Canada and Europe – will undoubtedly positively affect both B2B and B2C commercial transactions initiated online. Such is the case with the articles pertaining to the elimination of customs duties and nontariff barriers. Obviously, the elimination of trade barriers on goods delivered through classic means of freight transport yet purchased electronically will "help promote electronic trade between Europe and Canada, and develop a global environment for electronic commerce" (European Union and Canada 2000), since most e-commerce transactions still entail the purchase of tangible goods (books, electronics, clothing, etc.) that need to travel through customs before entering a country. As for intangible goods such as music downloads, e-books, software, and apps, according to the October 2010 draft, such products "shall not be subject to customs duties, fees or charges" (Canada and European Union 2010, p. 186). Although cynics might point to this being inevitable since control of online borders is at the very least impractical, if not impossible, without hampering citizens' rights, the confirmed lack of hidden transaction fees should serve as a positive incentive for online consumers.

References

Amazon.com (2011). *Media Kit: Timeline and History.* <http://phx.corporate-ir.net/phoenix.zhtml?c=176060&p=irol-corporateTimeline>. [Accessed 19 August 2011].

An Act to establish a legal framework for information technology, R.S.Q., chapter C-1.1. [Accessed 19 August 2011].

An Act to promote the efficiency and adaptability of the Canadian economy by regulating certain activities that discourage reliance on electronic means of carrying out commercial activities, and to amend the Canadian Radio-television and Telecommunications Commission Act, the Competition Act, the Personal Information Protection and Electronic Documents Act and the Telecommunications Act, S.C. 2010, c. 23. [Accessed 19 August 2011].

Axworthy, Lloyd (2000). Instrument of Accession. <http://www.wcoomd.org/files/1.%20Public%20files/PDFandDocuments/Procedures%20and%20Facilitation/RKC_Instruments/CA%2020008%20Instrument%20of%20accession.pdf>. [Accessed 19 August 2011].

Benyekhlef, Karim (2010). "La résolution en ligne des différends de consommation: un récit autour (et un exemple) du droit postmoderne", in Pierre-Claude Lafond (ed.), *L'accès des consommateurs à la justice*. Cowansville: Yvon Blais.

Canada and European Union (2009). Canada-European Union Joint Report: Towards a Comprehensive Economic Agreement. <http://www.international. gc.ca/trade-agreements-accords-commerciaux/agr-acc/eu-ue/can-eu-report-can-ue-rapport.aspx>. [Accessed 19 August 2011].

Canada and European Union (2010). Canada-EU CETA Draft Consolidated Text – Post Round IV. <http://fileserver.cfsadmin.org/file/tradejustice/ b743e1db9b85996e2ad1d3d3b99a6cda3c911853.pdf>. [Accessed 19 August 2011].

Canadian Conference of the Arts (2011). "An alliterated update: CRTC, C-470 and CETA", in CCA Bulletin 10/11 (21 March). <http://www.ccarts.ca/en/ advocacy/bulletins/2011/1011.htm#CETA>. [Accessed 19 August 2011].

Chassigneux, Cynthia (2004). *Vie privée et commerce électronique*. Montreal: Themis.

Civil Code of Quebec, LRQ, c C-1991.

Code civil (France).

Commission Decision of 20 December 2001 pursuant to Directive 95/46/EC of the European Parliament and of the Council on the adequate protection of personal data provided by the Canadian Personal Information Protection and Electronic Documents Act, C(2001) 4539.

Consumer Protection Act, RSQ, c P-40.1. [Accessed 19 August 2011].

Council of the European Union (2003). Instrument of Accession. <http://www. wcoomd.org/files/1.%20Public%20files/PDFandDocuments/Procedures%20a nd%20Facilitation/RKC_Instruments/EC%20200303%20Instrument%20of% 20accession.pdf>. [Accessed 19 August 2011].

CSA Standards (2011). Privacy Code. <http://www.csa.ca/cm/ca/en/privacy-code>. [Accessed 19 August 2011].

Dell Computer Corp. v. Union des consommateurs (2007). SCC 34, [2007] 2 SCR 801.

Directive 1999/93/EC of the European Parliament and of the Council of 13 December 1999 on a Community framework for electronic signatures.

Directive 2000/31/EC of the European Parliament and of the Council of 8 June 2000 on certain legal aspects of information society services, in particular electronic commerce, in the Internal Market (Directive on electronic commerce).

Directive 2002/58/EC of the European Parliament and of the Council of 12 July 2002 concerning the processing of personal data and the protection of privacy in the electronic communications sector (Directive on privacy and electronic communications).

Directive 95/46/EC of the European Parliament and of the Council of 24 October 1995 on the protection of individuals with regard to the processing of personal data and on the free movement of such data.

European Commission and Government of Canada (2008). Assessing the costs and benefits of a closer EU-Canada economic partnership, A Joint Study by the European Commission and the Government of Canada. ⟨http://www. international.gc.ca/trade-agreements-accords-commerciaux/assets/pdfs/EU-Canada_Joint_Study-Introduction_Executive_Summary.pdf⟩. [Accessed 19 August 2011].

European Union and Canada (1999). European Union-Canada Joint Statement: Electronic Commerce in the Global Information Society. <http://www.ic.gc. ca/eic/site/ecic-ceac.nsf/eng/gv00386.html>. [Accessed 19 August 2011].

European Union and Canada (2000). Electronic Commerce in the Global Information Society – EU-Canada Work Plan 2000/2001: Privacy, Security and Consumer Protection. <http://www.consilium.europa.eu/uedocs/cms_data/docs/pressdata/en/er/09549en-communiqu%C3%A9.htm#_Toc486671336>. [Accessed 19 August 2011].

Foreign Affairs and International Trade Canada (2011). Canada-European Union Trade and Investment Enhancement Agreement. <http://www. international.gc.ca/trade-agreements-accords-commerciaux/agr-acc/eu-ue/tiea.aspx>. [Accessed 19 August 2011].

H., Bill (2011). "History of E-commerce" in Sell it! on the Web. <http://sellitontheweb.com/blog/history-of-e-commerce/>. [Accessed 19 August 2011].

Industry Canada (2004). Principles for Electronic Authentication: A Canadian Framework. <http://www.ic.gc.ca/eic/site/ecic-ceac.nsf/eng/h_gv00240. html>. [Accessed 19 August 2011].

Industry Canada (2009). Legal and Regulatory Frameworks for Electronic Commerce. <http://www.ic.gc.ca/eic/site/ecic-ceac.nsf/eng/gv00086.html>. [Accessed 19 August 2011].

Organisation for Economic Co-operation and Development (OECD) (2000). Guidelines for Consumer Protection in the Context of Electronic Commerce. <http://www.oecdbookshop.org/oecd/get-it.asp?REF=9300023e.pdf& TYPE=browse>. [Accessed 19 August 2011].

Personal Information Protection and Electronic Documents Act, SC 2000, c. 5.

Plunkett Research (2011). E-commerce & Internet Business Overview. <http://www.plunkettresearch.com/ecommerce%20internet%20technology% 20market%20research/industry%20statistics>. [Accessed 19 August 2011].

Romano, Nicholas C. Jr. (2001). "Customer Relations Management Research: An assessment of Sub Field Development and Maturity". Proceedings of the 34th Hawaii International Conference on System Sciences: <http://doi. ieeecomputersociety.org/10.1109/HICSS.2001.927052>.

United Nations Commission on International Trade Law (UNCITRAL), Working Group III (Online Dispute Resolution) (2010). Online dispute resolution for cross-border electronic commerce transactions. <http://www.uncitral.org /uncitral/commission/working_groups/3Online_Dispute_Resolution.html>. [Accessed 19 August 2011].

Vermeys, Nicolas W., Karim Benyekhlef, and Vincent Gautrais (2004). "Réflexions juridiques autour de la terminologie associée aux places d'affaires électroniques". *Revue juridique Thémis*, 38(3), pp. 641-710.

World Customs Organization (WCO) (1999). International Convention on the Simplification and Harmonization of Customs Procedures. <http://www. wcoomd.org/Kyoto_New/Content/content.html>. [Accessed 19 August 2011].

World Customs Organization (WCO) (2004). Kyoto Convention Guidelines on the Application of Information and Communication Technology (Kyoto ICT Guidelines). <http://www.insw.go.id/images/public/kyoto-ict-guidelines-wco.pdf>. [Accessed 19 August 2011].

World Customs Organization (WCO) (2007). WCO SAFE Framework of Standards. <http://www.gumruk.gov.tr/tr-TR/emevzuat/Uluslararas%20 Szlemeler/SAFE%20Framework_EN_2007_for_publication.pdf>. [Accessed 19 August 2011].

World Customs Organization (WCO) (2009). World Customs Organization – 174 Members. <http://www.wcoomd.org/files/1.%20Public%20files/PDFand Documents/About%20Us/Members_table_174_EN.pdf>. [Accessed 19 August 2011].

The Other Transatlantic Relationship

The European Union and Latin America

Roberto DOMÍNGUEZ

Introduction

The study of the transatlantic relationship has been identified as a synonym for interactions between the United States and Europe. The North Atlantic area was the geopolitical centre of the world in the twentieth century, providing evidence of interdependence between both sides of the Atlantic and in some cases stimulating scholarly concepts such as the pluralistic security community (Deutsch *et al.* 1957). While this has led to intense academic research and analysis of the relationship between Europe and the United States, it has come at the cost of sidelining the other transatlantic relationship between Latin America and the European Union.

The endeavour of explaining the other transatlantic relationship is challenging due to the participation of numerous actors and various levels of intensity of regional, sub-regional or bilateral relationships in the economic and political areas. In order to provide an overview of the relationship between the EU and Latin America, the first step is to develop a taxonomy portraying three different levels of relationships between both regions, and the second is to explain the scope of each one of them. At the first level of region-to-region interaction, there is a clear lesson to be learnt from the six EU-Latin America and Caribbean summits held since 1999: Summits of sixty heads of state and government are broad frameworks to channel common denominators of co-operation, but they have produced limited results as is corroborated in the results of the summits in Guadalajara (2004), Vienna (2006), Lima (2008), and Madrid (2010).

The second level of relationship is between the EU and sub-regions in Latin America. Here both parties are able to narrow down their interests and reach more relevant mechanisms of co-operation such as the association agreement between Central America and the EU. While Europe has traditionally preferred this mechanism of co-operation, Latin America has faced problems to speak with one voice as sub-regions.

The third level, between the EU and individual countries, has proved to be quite dynamic with the conclusion and implementation of more tangible benefits such as the association agreements with Mexico and Chile or the strategic partnerships with Brazil and Mexico. This chapter examines these three levels of relationships between the EU and Latin America.

Inter-Regional Relations: Divergence of Views in the Summits

The region-to-region dialogue between the European Union and Latin America was institutionalized in 1999 when the first bi-regional summit took place in Rio de Janeiro (Roy and Domínguez 2005). Since then, six bi-regional meetings have been held, and all the meetings have emphasized the bilateral agenda. The second summit, held in Madrid in 2002, set the main areas of co-operation in the bilateral agenda, and the third, held in Guadalajara in 2004, brought about a sense of confidence in light of the recognition of social cohesion as the top priority in the summit agenda. The prospects of the social cohesion as the driving force of the bilateral relationship vanished because of the 2004 EU enlargement fatigue, the difficulties ratifying the Constitutional Treaty, and the rising scepticism on the free market of several left-leaning incoming governments in Latin America.

In May 2006, the fourth EU-Latin America summit took place in Vienna. The meeting had some positive outcomes. First, the European Commission published new communications to the Council on Latin America and the Caribbean replacing those of a decade earlier. Second, the European Parliament delivered its opinions in several documents about the bi-regional relationship. Third, EU was able to outline concrete financial commitments to buttress social cohesion policies in Latin America until 2013. Fourth, for the first time, a business summit took place in parallel with the political meeting (Schussel 2006). Despite the achievements of the Vienna summit, the unenthusiastic voice of one of its protagonists reveals the general perception of the scope of the summit: "But we must also ask ourselves in a mood of self-examination whether we have really done everything that we might have undertaken. And there, the answer can only be a self-critical no. And so here in Vienna, we cannot have a summit of self-satisfied, empty rhetoric; this must be a working meeting where we improve our own work" (Schussel 2006).

Along these lines, the political environment in Latin America also eroded the European enthusiasm to deepen co-operation, in the context of the strategic alliance, because of the emergence of populist governments and policies in the region (Sberro 2006). Particularly, the Venezuelan withdrawal from the Andean Community of Nations (ACN) shattered one of the historical objectives of the EU in the continent: the development of integration processes in Latin America. Likewise, Bolivian President Evo Morales' nationalization of the gas sector affected Spanish investments in that country, while the Venezuelan government announced plans for a new tax that had would have an impact on all foreign oil firms. In response to this challenge, the president of the European Commission, José Manuel Barroso, warned that European businesses had found some obstacles in Latin America: lack of predictability of the economic setting, market access difficulties (trade and on-trade barriers), political instability, excessive red tape, customs problems, insufficient regional infrastructures, corruption, and so forth. He emphasized that:

> On top of these obstacles, there is a worrisome new one: the tendency to understand European investment under a negative light. […] Make no mistake, whether this political attitude prospers, *European businesses will not be harmed as a consequence because there are abundant investment opportunities in other regions*, and the victims will be poor people in Latin America. […] In order to facilitate investment and trade in Latin America and the Caribbean, we need to guarantee predictability and safety for investments. (Barroso 2006, emphasis added)

The context for the 2008 summit in Lima was not quite conducive for reaching better results than the Vienna Summit. The international economy was affected by the economic crisis in the United States. While Europe was still focusing on the institutional reform of the Lisbon Treaty, the energy crisis, and the reconfiguration of the Balkans, South America faced a diplomatic crisis between Colombia and Ecuador-Venezuela who disagreed on how to approach the ACN negotiations with the EU.

Several events surrounding the Lima Summit strained the political environment. A number of European heads of government did not attend the meeting, such as the prime minister of the United Kingdom or French President Nicolas Sarkozy, who decided to cancel his official trip to Mexico and Peru because he was focused on the role of France as president of the EU in the second half of 2008, as well as on the project of a Mediterranean Union (Sberro 2008a). In spite of these absentees, one of the most visible actors was German Chancellor Angela Merkel. After an episode of verbal assaults from Hugo Chavez, she displayed a very active agenda in the region by visiting Colombia, Brazil, and Mexico. Likewise, in light of the diplomatic disputes between Venezuela-Ecuador and Colombia, Javier Solana, then High Representative of the EU, publicly endorsed the report of Director of Interpol Ronald

Noble, with regard to the unaltered computer files that the Colombian Army found in a FARC base in Ecuador on 1 March 2008 (El Universal 2008).

On the Latin American front, the position of the leaders was diverse. Evo Morales, the president of Bolivia, stated that "the way to eradicate poverty was by finishing the capitalist system" (AFP 2008), an argument diplomatically unwelcomed by the European Union. Likewise, the division within the ACN was evident during the summit. With regard to the negotiations between the ACN and the EU, the then President of Colombia Alvaro Uribe affirmed that his country would guarantee more time and flexibility for Ecuador and Bolivia in certain items of the agreement with the European Union, in order to disentangle the negotiation (Bosaans 2008).

With regard to the topics in the agenda, the Lima Declaration (Council of the European Union 2008b) focused on two main topics: (a) eradication of poverty, inequality, and exclusion and (b) sustainable development (environment, climate change, and energy). Certainly, both topics are quite important. However, energy was quite controversial, particularly, bio-fuels. While the EU leaders agreed that the EU should increase the use of bio-fuels in transport fuel to 10 per cent by 2020, some Latin American countries, international institutions, and environmental and development NGOs put pressure on the EU to abandon this policy, because of concerns that the controversial fuels contribute to global warming and food price rises (Phillips 2008).

The civil society was also present in a parallel summit. The People's Summit took place in Lima on 16 May 2008 (Transnational Institute 2008). In this alternative summit, there was a patent rejection of the association agreements proposed by the European Union as it was argued that they deepen and perpetuate the current system of domination. The participants in this summit also acknowledged the actions of nationalization of strategic companies and natural resources for national development, resources, which they contended belong to the people not multinationals, such as the nationalization of the Bolivian telecommunications company, ETI/ENTEL.

The Madrid Summit in May 2010 offered an important stimulus for the bi-regional relationship. Among others, the significant agreement reached at the bi-regional level is the Mechanism of Investment of Latin America, which seeks to promote projects of interconnectivity, energy infrastructure, transport systems, and social services. The expectations are that with resources originating from the Commission for €125 million until 2013, investments for more than €3 billion will be generated. In the first three projects, Central America has been the region that has benefitted the most. Moreover, as a result of the summit, the EU-

Latin America Foundation was created, to which the Commission provides €3 million until 2013, with contribution of resources from the members of the region (European Commission 2010).

The Madrid Declaration is divided in three parts. The first performs an exercise in rhetoric of the consensuses of both regions regarding the international scenario. Issues such as capital punishment, rejection of the Helms Burton Act, and gun trafficking, or the impulse for dialogue in international organizations about matters of financial architecture, gender violence, development, and climate change, are mentioned among others (Council of the European Union 2010).

The second part analyses ways to reinforce the bi-regional association. Aside from highlighting the advances in negotiations with countries of the regions, it attempts to relaunch the structured and global dialogue of the EU-LAC about migration and to continue with the EU-LAC dialogue on climate change and the environment. The third part addresses the principal theme of the summit. Among other elements, it was set as an objective to create an EU-LAC Space for Knowledge to facilitate the transfer of technology through a network of knowledge and innovation centres. Similarly, the integration of both regions in the Society of Information and the development of the information technology and communication (ITC) sectors are reinforced and backed, respectively.

The analysis of the summits contributes to understanding the priorities of both sides at the region-to-region level. The study of trade relations also sheds some light on identifying the interests of both parties. The general trend in trade is that the EU exerts a moderate influence on Latin America while the Latin American leverage in Europe is quite marginal. The situation is different in the North Atlantic relationship, namely, between the EU and the United States, wherein common history, legacies, and above all, shared challenges (security, migration, and economic growth) provide a firm and solid ground for mutual interdependence. However, when one shifts the attention to Latin America, one can see that the driving forces of interests and/or identities decrease, the relationship becomes asymmetrical, and the bilateral agenda becomes less relevant for the European Union while it remains quite important for Latin American countries.

As one can note on Table 1, as of 2010, Latin America trades three times more with the United States than with the EU; 35.1 and 13.5 per cent, respectively. Looking at the breakdown of numbers by subregions, the EU is the second largest trade partner of Central America and the Andean Community (AC), while for MERCOSUR it is the first trade partner. Table 2 indicates that the role of Latin America remains marginal for the EU by representing 6.3 per cent of the total EU trade.

Table 1
Latin America's Main Trade Partners (2010)

Imports from		Exports to		Major Trade Partners	
Country	%	Country	%	Country	%
Latin America		*Latin America*		*Latin America*	
1. United States	30.2	1. United States	40.3	1. United States	35.1
2. EU 27	14.0	2. EU 27	13.0	2. EU 27	13.5
3. China	12.4	3. China	7.2	3. China	9.9
Central America		*Central America*		*Central America*	
1. United States	41.6	1. United States	18.0	1. United States	56.0
2. China	13.1	2. EU 27	8.4	2. EU 27	8.5
3. EU 27	10.5	3 Canada	7.8	3. China	8.0
Andean Community		*Andean Community*		*Andean Community*	
1. United States	24.7	1. United States	30.0	1. United States	27.4
2. EU 27	13.1	2. EU 27	14.9	2. EU 27	14.0
3. China	11.4	3. Venezuela	6.9	3. China	9.1
MERCOSUR		*MERCOSUR*		*MERCOSUR*	
1. EU 27		1. EU 27	21.2	1. EU 27	20.9
2. United States	20.7	2. China	10.8	2. United States	12.0
3. China	15.1	3. United States	9.2	3. China	12.0
	13.3				

Source: Own Elaboration based upon EUROSTAT, DG Trade/Statistics, 18 March 2011.

EU and Latin American Sub-Regions: MERCOSUR, Andean Community, and Central America

The relationship with Latin American sub-regions has been one of the preferred strategies of the European Union. For decades, the EU found in sub-regional processes of integration the replication if its own model. In time, however, exporting the EU model produced limited results because of the obstacles the members of the Andean Community or the Central American process faced to pool sovereignty in community or supranational institutions. Thus, the balance in the case of the EU-sub-regions relationship is mixed with negotiations, with MERCOSUR stalled for a few years and the Andean Community divided. Central America is the exception as a result of the conclusion of an association agreement with the EU.

Table 2
EU's Main Trade Partners in Latin American (2010)

Imports from		Exports to		Major Trade Partners	
Country	%	Country	%	Country	%
1. China	18.9	1. United States	18.0	1. United States	14.5
2. United States	11.4	2. China	8.4	2. China	13.9
3. Russia	10.4	3. Switzerland	7.8	3. Russia	8.5
10. Brazil	2.2	9. Brazil	2.3	10. Brazil	2.2
24. Mexico	0.9	18. Mexico	1.6	20. Mexico	1.2
32. Chile	0.6	32. Argentina	0.5	33. Argentina	0.6
33. Argentina	0.6	36. Chile	0.3	34. Chile	0.5
40. Costa Rica	0.4	43. Venezuela	0.7	43. Colombia	0.3
42. Peru	0.3	45. Colombia	0.3	46. Venezuela	0.3
44. Colombia	0.3			49. Peru	0.3
48. Venezuela	0.3				
Latin America	6.0	Latin America	6.2	Latin America	6.1

Source: Own Elaboration based upon EUROSTAT, DG Trade/Statistics, 18 March 2011.

MERCOSUR

Due to its economic size, the relationship with MERCOSUR (Common Southern Market, including Argentina, Brazil, Paraguay, and Uruguay) has been a priority in the EU agenda. As a region, MERCOSUR ranks eighth among EU trading partners, accounting for 2.7 per cent of total trade in 2009. Negotiations for an inter-regional agreement between both parties were launched in 1999 but were suspended in October 2004. Both parties decided to resume negotiations in May 2010 with the aim of reaching a comprehensive and ambitious association agreement beyond the obligations of both sides to the WTO, extending to the coverage of products and services to be liberalized, ensuring respect for intellectual property rights, and establishing an effective dispute settlement mechanism (European Commission 2011). As of April 2011, the Bi-Regional Negotiations Committee has held four rounds of negotiation divided in eleven working groups in order to allow progress in the normative part of several areas of the negotiations, including rules of origin, public procurement, services and investment, competition, and dispute settlement, among others.

Andean Community/Colombia and Peru

Negotiations between the AC and the EU have been quite unusual because what started as a region-to-region association agreement turned into a region-two country free trade agreement. The EU-ACN negotiations were launched in June 2007, and four rounds took place (European Commission 2008b). In 2008, Bolivia distanced itself from other ACN members in four sensitive issues, namely services, investment, intellectual property, and public procurement. Ecuador, later supported by Bolivia, opposed the proposal of an ACN position on the chapter on trade and sustainable development. Such internal disagreement in the ACN led negotiators to water down the association agreement, and instead they suggested a free trade agreement with the AC members willing to move forward. Bolivia and Ecuador declined the new offer of negotiation.

In March 2011, the European Commission and the chief negotiators of Colombia and Peru initiated the final texts of the free trade agreement. In the case of Colombia, the protracted internal conflict raised several criticisms. In response, trade Commissioner De Gucht has reiterated that Colombia has not improved respect of human rights and democracy, and shortcomings in such areas will be denounced (Tatje 2010). From the economic standpoint, the free trade agreement sets market access for Peruvian and Colombian bananas and sugar to the European market while Europeans secured the access of their milk powder, cheese, whey, pork, meat, cereals, olive oil, wines, and spirits to Peruvian and Colombian markets (De Gucht 2010). The FTA also left a door open to Bolivia and Ecuador to join the agreement whenever they consider it appropriate.

Central America and the AC

Based on the results of the association agreements between the EU and Mexico and Chile, it could be said that such instruments should be seen not as a panacea but as a means to strengthen current processes of implementation of free market policies and democratization in Latin American countries. Following the pattern of Mexico and Chile, Central America signed a free trade agreement with the United States, which stimulated the prospects of a free trade agreement with the European Union. In addition, there was an improvement in the implementation of the Central American integration process, which was supported by an EU grant to the Central American countries for €7 million to consolidate their customs union.

Both parties started negotiations in 2007. While both parties made some progress in seven rounds of negotiation, they decided to postpone the eighth round due to the political instability in Honduras in 2009. Fortunately, the EU and Central America resumed and concluded negotiations for an association agreement in May 2010, during the EU-LAC Madrid Summit. The text was initiated in Brussels in March 2011. For the last decade, the EU's share in Central American trade has remained largely stable at around 10 per cent (8.5 per cent in 2009). Historically, the bulk of most Central American countries' trade is with the United States and Latin America, and it is only recently that the region has actively sought to increase its trade with Europe. EU imports from Central America are dominated by office and telecommunication equipment (53.9 per cent) and agricultural products (34.8 per cent in 2010). The most important exports from the EU to Central America are machinery and transport equipment (48.2 per cent) and chemicals (12.3 per cent).

EU and Individual Countries: Mexico, Chile, and Brazil

Brazil, Mexico, and Chile are the three main partners of the EU in Latin America. While Brazil has been negotiating as a MERCOSUR member in an association agreement with the EU for more than a decade, Mexico was the first Latin American country to reach an association agreement followed by Chile. Why were Mexico and Chile the first countries to sign these agreements? On a number of criteria ranging from the size of their economies to the nature of their political evolution, there are outstanding differences between Mexico and Chile. Nonetheless, both countries have undergone a simultaneous and gradual process of (a) erosion of political authoritarianism, (b) implementation of free market policies since the mid-1980s, and (c) conclusion of free trade agreements with the United States.

Mexico has gone through a process of steady electoral democratization and has become one of the most open economies in Latin America since the late 1980s. Chile, on the other hand, was welcomed to the family of democratic nations in the early 1990s and has made significant progress in the normalization of the relationship between the civil and political society on the one side and the military class on the other. In such processes, both countries implemented first a "perestroika" and later on in the 1990s, a "glasnost".

Mexico was the first and strongest candidate to launch a new generation of EU association agreements with Latin American countries. Due to their economic conditions, both parties pursued different objectives. On the Mexican side, the following objectives were crucial in the negotiations: (a) to deepen the process of economic modernization and trade liberalization, and (b) to improve the conditions for Mexican exporters' access to the European market. On the European side, three reasons seem quite relevant: (a) NAFTA as a catalyst for negotiations, (b) ending the discrimination in the Mexican market against European investors and exporters as a result of NAFTA, and (c) the prospects of a free trade area in the Americas as proposed in the 1994 Summit of the Americas (Zabludovsky and Lora 2005).

Chile managed to reinsert itself into the international community after years of relative isolation during the military regime and actually became a relevant actor in a number of international forays (European Commission 2006). Particularly in the economic realm, Chile has distinguished itself in Latin America by its good economic performance (high growth rates, low inflation, and public sector surplus). After a peaceful transition, Chile became the natural second candidate for an association agreement.

The relevance of the association agreements between the European Union and Mexico (2000) and the EU and Chile (2005) is based on the assumption that both agreements are significant for the EU-Latin American relationship due to two chief reasons: (a) They are the first comprehensive – political, economic, and co-operation – agreements with countries in the region, and (b) they set a precedent for future agreements with other countries or group of countries in the region. Certainly, the association agreements are not a solution for Latin America's problems. Instead, they complement the political and economic reforms in Mexico and Chile, and their overall impact is moderate.

Brazil: Strategic Partnership

Unlike Mexico and Chile, Brazil has not concluded an association agreement because it is a MERCOSUR member. Nonetheless, Brazil has elevated its profile in international relations during the last decade and has become one of the emerging powers in the new century, as a member of the informal BRIC group (Brazil, Russia, India, and China). Thus, the EU faced the situation whereby, on the one hand, the EU-MERCOSUR negotiations were suspended since 2004, and, on the other, the deepening of the relationship with the new emerging power in South America could not be ignored in the context of external relations of the EU. Against this backdrop, the EU launched a strategic partnership to further deepen its ties with Brazil, and the first ever EU-Brazil Summit was held in Lisbon in July 2007. The public statements of EU officials echoed the rationale of the new strategic partnership. President Barroso said that "Brazil's qualification as a 'key player' to join the restricted club of our strategic partners", and then Commissioner Ferrero Waldner stated, "I believe that by activating dialogue we will motivate Brazil to move forward towards more regional integration in Mercosur and encourage them to be more open in our negotiations" (European Commission 2007b).

As of 2011, four EU-Brazil summits have taken place. Central topics of the new partnership have included effective multilateralism, climate change, sustainable energy, the fight against poverty, the MERCOSUR's integration process, and Latin America's stability and prosperity. While the fruits of the strategic partnership can be observed in new agreements on technology or aviation, one important change is that the EU-MERCOSUR negotiations were resumed in 2010. The role of Brazil was pivotal in such achievement not only because it is the largest MERCOSUR member, but also because it is the tenth EU trade partner and the largest Latin American trade partner. Table 3 shows the relevance of Brazil in comparison to Mexico and Chile, second and third trade partners, respectively.

Table 3
EU trade with Brazil, Mexico and Chile

	Imports from EU	Exports to EU	Total Trade	Trade Balance
	(Euro Billions)			
Brazil	23.2	22.5	46.7	1.53
	(Primary 8.2; Manufacture 0.5)	(Primary 69.6; Manufacture. 4.1)		
Mexico	11.6	5	29.3	-12.7
	(Primary 14.4; Manufacture. 73.4)	(Primary 28.8; Manufacture. 66.5)		
Chile	15.6	18.5	11.6	2.2
	(Primary. 10.1; Manufacture 81.0)	(Primary 88.2; Manufacture. 7.4)		

Source: Own Elaboration based upon EUROSTAT, DG Trade/Statistics, 27 June 2011.

Mexico: New Formulas to Revitalize the Association Agreement

Along the lines of the EU-Brazil relationship, the EU agreed to launch a strategic partnership with Mexico in the Lima Summit in 2008. This partnership sought to revitalize the bilateral relationship eight years after the bilateral association agreement came into force. Bilateral relations between the EU and Mexico are governed by the Economic, Political and Co-operation Agreement (Global Agreement), which was signed in Brussels on 8 December 1997 and entered into force in October 2000.

The Free Trade Agreement (FTA), part of the Global Agreement, covers a broad spectrum of economic aspects and included a full liberalization of industrial products; substantial liberalization for agricultural and fisheries products; and, as regards rules of origin, a satisfactory balance between the EU's policy of harmonisation and market access considerations. The FTA has also provided EU operators with access to the Mexican procurement and services markets under equivalent conditions to the ones offered to NAFTA partners. Since the trade agreement came into force in 2000, bilateral trade grew 122 per cent, despite the negative consequences for the trade that the financial and economic world crisis has had since 2008 (Joint Committee Mexico-European Union 2010).

As to the political sphere of the agreement, the EU has contributed to strengthening the consolidation of Mexican democracy. The deeply atavistic and orthodox views about the meaning of sovereignty in Mexico postponed any major negotiation of an association agreement in the early 1990s because of the "implications" of the Democracy Clause to Mexican sovereignty. Once such clause was accepted by the Zedillo administration, the EU supported the decision of the Mexican government to prohibit the death penalty or the legitimacy of the contested electoral process in July 2006. Likewise, Mexico was one of three priority countries in Latin America for the 2002-2004 European Initiative on Democracy and Human Rights. By the same token, the association agreement facilitated the co-operation in a range of important areas such as tropical forests, NGOs, ECIP (European Community Investment Partners), ECHO (humanitarian aid), economic co-operation, demographic policies, and refugees and displaced persons.

The EU-Chile Association Agreement

Chile has been one of the most open economies in Latin America, which made it attractive for the negotiation of an association agreement. For instance, in 1975, Chile exported five hundred products while there were two hundred export companies. In 2004, four thousand products were exported, and six thousand companies are export oriented (Baeza 2004). It has also signed free trade agreements with thirty-seven countries.

In the context of the relations with Europe, Chile signed a co-operation framework agreement with the EU in 1996, which had as a final aim the establishment of a political and economic association between Chile and the European Community and its Member States (European Commission 2002). Indeed, the EU and Chile began these negotiations in April 2000, and after ten rounds of negotiations, the association agreement was signed on 18 November 2002.

The association agreement has been in force since 1 March 2005 while the trade provisions of the agreements entered into force on an interim basis on 1 February 2003. The association agreement covers the main aspects of EU-Chile relations, namely, political and trade relations and co-operation. Certainly, while the elimination of customs duties is clearly a major step forward, in view of the Commission, the agreements on services, market access, and investment are the areas where the most important liberalization has been made (Planistat 2002).

As a result of the bilateral co-operation, Chile has participated in Operation ALTHEA. In this regard, military co-operation is quite sensitive because the modernization of Chilean armed forces has contributed to shift them further away from the repressive role they played under Pinochet's regime, towards an international peacekeeping one (Sanchez 2006). Likewise, a recent agreement is in order to facilitate transportation co-operation between the two parties: The EU-Chile Horizontal Agreement in the field of air transport was reached, and there is a firm intention to move forward with Chile's request for liberalization of services in this area.

With regard to the trade area, it is still too early to assess the economic effects of the agreement on the Chilean economy, but there are already some trends in the bilateral exchange. The Chilean exports to the EU grew from €4.8 billion in 2002 to €11.6 billion in 2010. On the other hand, the EU exports to Chile presented in the same period a less dynamic change, increasing from €3.1 billion to €4.2 billion (European Commission 2007a).

However, the mere expectations of the association agreement since the end of the 1990s and the economic and political stability promoted confidence in investing and trading with that country. Unlike Mexico, Chile has a high degree of dependence on primary products that makes it vulnerable to external market fluctuations. This is the main challenge for Chile. Thus, traditional activities still have an important share in the country's GDP and export structure: During the first semester of 2003, mining (predominantly copper) still represented 46 per cent of total exports while agriculture, farming, forestry, and fishing products combined represented 13.02 per cent. In such a context, trade with the EU represents less than one-fourth of the overall Chilean external trade: 25 per cent of its exports go to the EU and 19 per cent of its imports come from the EU.

It is expected, nonetheless, that the specific areas covered by the trade chapter of the agreement will contribute to the diversification of the Chilean economy. In this regard, the agreement establishes a free trade area covering the progressive and reciprocal liberalization of trade in goods during a maximum transitional period of 10 years. It also establishes a free trade area in services and provides for the liberalization of investment and of current payments and capital movements. Likewise, it includes rules to facilitate trade in wines and spirits, animals and animal products, and plants, and provisions in areas such as customs and related procedures, standards, and technical regulations. Another important aspect is that it provides for the reciprocal opening of government procurement markets and for the adequate and effective protection of intellectual property rights.

In the context of the negotiations of the agreement, the co-operation offered by the EU to Chile is of the utmost relevance. Since 2000, 22 projects have been committed for a total amount of about €7,790,000. The bulk of the funds (87 per cent) committed so far has been allocated to NGO projects, 15 per cent of the funds went to pro-jects related to the European Initiative for Democracy and Human rights, and 3 per cent went to a project in favour of the environment. Similar to the Mexican experience, the political area of the agreement is significant. Having fresh memories of the recent past, the democracy clause in the agreement upholds the no return to authoritarian practices, or at least raises the political cost if such regression takes place in the future. Thus, the respect for democratic principles, human rights, and the rule of law are essential elements for Chile to be included in the agreement.

Looking to the future in EU-Chile relations and after three Councils of the Chile-EU troika summit, the parties agreed that bilateral co-operation will focus on the following areas of co-operation in the next four years: in innovation and competitiveness with a budget of €20.5 million; in social cohesion, €20.5 will be allocated; and higher education, for which the EU contribution amounts to €4.92 million (Council of the EU 2008c).

Final Considerations: Where Do We Find Ourselves in the 'Other Transatlantic Relationship'?

The bi-regional relationship between Europe and Latin America has been redefined in the last two decades. Two events are salient in the kaleidoscope of changes. The first relates to the redefinition of the strategies of both actors at the end of the Cold War. Since the beginning of the 1990s, the EU has constantly and progressively developed in-struments to project its voice in the world. The immediate effect of this strategy on Latin America was the opening of European Commission delegations and the development of common strategies towards the region. With different shades, Latin America adopted policies of eco-nomic and political openness that served as an incentive to attract investment and co-operation from Europe and elsewhere. The climax in the convergence of both strategies led to the development of the EU-Latin America summits and to association agreements with Mexico and Chile.

It would seem as though, as the bi-regional relationship strength-ened, a second moment was initiated where the scepticism and stagna-tion of programs and initiatives have been dominating characteristics. Carlos Malamud (2010) points out that, especially since the start of the twenty-first century, the discouragement in the bi-regional relationship is explained because Latin America is profoundly divided in two dis-tinct levels: The first is how the countries in the region perceive the way to relate to the globalized world; the second, which has brought forth as a consequence confrontations within the region, lies in the different ways of understanding the intraregional and bilateral relationships within the continent. In the same context, the European Union has concentrated on a process of internal reform that has led Europe to invest its political and economic capital in two principal fronts: the expansion from fifteen to twenty-seven members and the approval of the Lisbon Treaty.

This order of priorities has impacted the EU-Latin America relations. Added to that, the evaluation of the bi-regional relationships also finds structural limitations and externalities derived from the international economic structure. In the 1990s, there was a consensus in favour of the formation of regional blocs that even counted with the support of the United States. This led to a new regionalism that delineated the Europe-an Union's policy of negotiating with sub-regional groups in Latin America. Nonetheless, this strategy failed because of the fact that with the launching of the WTO and Doha, a limitation for regionalism at the systemic level was produced and, consequently, liberalization has taken a secondary role. It is this way that the path has been paved for bilateral strategies, which has translated into a sequence of proliferation of agreements in two different levels.

First, bilateralization of the commercial relations of the United States towards the region has led to different agreements with Latin American countries (Mexico, Chile, Central America, Colombia, and Peru). Second, once agreements are reached with the United States, or pro-spective agreements already exist, the EU initiates negotiations with those same countries, as was the case with Mexico and Chile and more recently at the conclusion of the negotiations with Central America, Colombia, and Peru. This sequence suggests that the presence of trade agreements between the United States and these countries is an incen-tive for the EU in view of (a) the loss of markets for the EU and (b) a consolidation of free trade rules in Latin American countries, which generates certainty and trust in European investors.

In this complicated context of a relationship that faces discourage-ment, a question that automatically emerges regarding the efficiency of the existing mechanisms for bi-regional co-operation – the mechanisms basically being the Ibero-American summits and the Latin American and the Caribbean-European Union summits. While both have developed alongside as spaces for interaction and interchange between Europe and Latin America, Spain and Portugal are the predominant actors, which is a limitation according to Anna Ayuso (2010), particularly because a heightened involvement by countries such as France or Germany is important. Even more relevant is to denote that it is pertinent and urgent to identify those areas where the summits' agendas tend to converge, despite both spaces being of a different nature. In that sense, there are at least six areas where said convergence is feasible, in which the following stand out: social agenda, governance, culture, investigation, migrations, and the environment. The seventh summit in Chile in 2012 will tell to what extent the EU and Latin America are able to revitalize the inter-regional biannual dialogue.

References

AFP (2008). "Morales denuncia demogogia y censura en la Cumbre de Lima", in *La Jornada*, 17 May.

Ayuso, A. (2010). "Espana y su papel en un espacion común bi-regional", in Roy, J. y R. Domínguez (eds.), *Espana, la Union Europea y la integración latinoamerica*. Miami: European Union Center, University of Miami.

Baeza, M. M. (2004). "Chile y los acuerdos de libre comercio", in G.B. García, P. Dardel and S. Monteverde (eds.), *La Experiencia Chilena. Negociaciones Económicas y Acuerdos de Libre Comercio*. Chile: Instituto de Relaciones Internacionales-Universidad de Vina del Mar.

Barroso, J.M. (2006). "Speech to Heads of State and Governments at the Fourth EU-Latin American and Caribbean Summit", Speech/06/297, 12 May.

Bosaans, T.A. (2008). "Cita en Perú deja evidencia quiebre en la Comunidad Andina de Naciones", in *El Mercurio*, 17 May.

Council of the European Union (2008a). Fourth Mexico EU Troika Summit, Presse 133, 9542/08, 17 May.

Council of the European Union (2008b). Lima Declaration, Presse 128, 9534/08, 16 May.

Council of the European Union (2008c). Third Chile-EU Troika Summit, Presse 131, 9540/1/08 REV 1, 17 May.

Council of the European Union (2010). Declaración de Madrid, 18 May.

De Gucht, K. (2010). "Speaking Points Before the International Trade Committee of the European Parliament", Speech /10/101, 16 March.

Deutsch, Karl W. *et al.* (1957). *Political Community and the North Atlantic Area: International Organization in the Light of Historical Experience*. Princeton: Princeton University Press.

Roberto Domínguez

European Commission (2002). Chile, Country Strategy Paper. <http://www. eeas.europa.eu/chile/csp/02_06_en.pdf>. [Accessed 6 May 2007].

European Commission (2006). "The EU's Relations with Chile. Overview". <http://europa.eu.int/comm/external_relations/chile/intro/index.htm>. [Accessed 6 March 2010].

European Commission (2007a). Chile: EU Bilateral Trade, Directorate General on Trade, 7 August.

European Commission (2007b). EU-Brazil: Commission Proposes Strategic Partnership, IP/07/725, 30 May.

European Commission (2008a). EU-Latin America/Caribbean trade in facts and figures, Memo/08/303, 14 May.

European Commission (2008b). Report on the Third Round of Negotiations between the EU and the Andean Community, External Relations Directorate General, RELEX G/3/MVS, 1 May.

European Commission (2010). EU and Latin America. http://www.eeas.europa. eu/la/index_en.htm. [Accessed 3 July, 2010].

European Commission (2011). Statement of the EU and MERCOSUR after the 4th round of negotiations, Directorate-General for Trade, Press Release, 18 March.

Joint Committee Mexico-European Union (2010) Joint Communique of the 10th Joint Committee Mexico-European Union, 27-28 October. <http://eeas. europa.eu/mexico/docs/10th_jtcommittee_1010_en.pdf>. [Accessed 4 April 2011].

Lagos, R. (2005). Presentation before the European Parliament, 25 October.

Malamud, C. (2010). "Las relaciones de España con América Latina entre la Cumbre Iberoamericana de Estoril y la ALCUE de Madrid", en Roy J. Domínguez y R. Domínguez (eds.), *Espana, la Union Europea y la integración latinoamerica*. Miami: European Union Center, University of Miami.

Notimex (2008). "Concluye Calderón gira con propuesta de Fondo Verde", in *El Universal*, 17 May.

Patten, C. (2003). "Prologue", in P. Leiva (ed.), *The Strategic Association Chile-European Union*, Chile: CELARE.

Phillips, L. (2008). "EU to Tussle with Latin America's Pink Tide at Lima Summit", in *EUobserver*, 15 May.

Planistat (2002). "Sustainable Impact Assessment (SIA) of the trade aspects of negotiations for an Association Agreement between the European Communities and Chile (specific agreement No. 1)", Final Report.

Roy, J. and R. Domínguez (eds.) (2005). *The European Union and Regional Integration. A Comparative Perspective and Lessons for the Americas*, Miami: European Union Center, University of Miami.

Roy, J. and R. Domínguez (eds.) (2010). *Espana, la Union Europea y la integración latinoamerica*. Miami: European Union Center, University of Miami.

Sanchez, M. (2006). "Bachelet, A Subtle Force", in *Washington Post*, 10 March.

Sberro, S. (2006). "Cartas desde Europa", in *El Universal*, 28 May.

Sberro, S. (2008a). "La decepción de Sarkozy", in *El Universal*, 11 May.

Sberro, S. (2008b). "La UE pide no echar en saco roto informe de Interpol de computadores de las FARC", in *El Universal*, 17 May.

Schussel, W. (2006). "Opening speech by Chancellor Schüssel at the EU/Latin American Summit in Vienna on 12 May 2006". 12 May. <http://www.eu 2006.at/en/News/Speeches_Interviews/1205RedeSchuessel.html>. [Accessed 18 March 2008].

Tatje, C. (2010). "We do not monitor any iPod", in *Zeit online*, 14 April.

Transnational Institute (2008). "People's Summit Linking Alternatives III Declaration", 16 May. <http://www.tni.org/detail_page.phtml?&act_id=182 87&menu=11a>. [Accessed 19 May 2008].

Universal El (2008). "La UE pide no echar en saco roto informe de Interpol de computadores de las FARC", Caracas, 17 May 2008.

Zabludovsky, J. and S. Lora (2005). "The European Window: Challenges in the Negotiation of Mexico's Free Trade Agreement with the European Union", Working Paper SITI-09, INTAL.

PART IV

TRANSATLANTIC RELATIONS, COMPETITION POLICY, AND THE ENVIRONMENT

In Search of a Coherent Transatlantic Antitrust Policy

Declan J. WALSH

Introduction

The historic enforcement of antitrust policy in the United States (US) and the European Union (EU) has witnessed divergent approaches to policy prioritisation, enforcement, and sanctions. However, recent years have witnessed infringements of antitrust rules on a global scale. When a cartel involving pharmaceutical corporations is formed, its effects are global. When a corporation such as Intel engages in monopolisation, competitors and consumers worldwide suffer the adverse consequences.

As a result, it is timely to question the maintenance of mutually exclusive policies and enforcement regimes. While co-operation exists through the International Competition Network and through bilateral agreements, there is a clear need for enhanced co-operation between the investigative branches of the European Commission and the Federal Trade Commission. While the pooling and sharing of information has assisted in the prosecution of some high profile cartel cases, it is suggested that a more coherent policy of enforcement is required to tackle antitrust behaviour that is now organised at a global level. Nonetheless, even an attempt at an enhanced level of co-operation may be difficult in the light of divergent approaches to sanctions and judicial application of antitrust rules.

Historically, the enforcement of economic laws remained the preserve of individual sovereign states. Antitrust laws first appeared in North America towards the end of the nineteenth century while in Europe competition law first appeared in the European Coal & Steel Community Treaty (ECSC) in 1951. Both the origins and evolution of these laws have reflected the divergent policy considerations of the relevant jurisdictions. Historically the US system was noted for its emphasis on efficiency in the market, its adoption of criminal sanctions as a deterrent, and private party actions to provide for damages for those who have suffered loss. In contrast, the development of EU Competition law and policy must be viewed in the light of the overriding objectives of the treaties, in particular, the achievement of a single market. Furthermore, enforcement at EU level is by means of administrative action with sanctions being solely civil in nature.

In certain areas of antitrust/competition, we have witnessed divergent views as to those matters that are considered to fall foul of existing rules. For example, there has been much debate in recent years as to the value of pursuing vertical agreements, with many American commentators believing that vertical restraints fall outside the classical scope of antitrust law (Bork 1978). In contrast, the European Commission, while not applying a rule of *per se* illegality to vertical restraints, nonetheless holds divergent views on vertical restraints, in particular in relation to price maintenance. Furthermore, both the Commission and the Court of Justice of the European Union (CJEU) view vertical restraints as a tool to distort the single market through attempts to partition markets based on national frontiers.

While there are divergent views on the extent of the ambit of antitrust laws and dissimilar approaches to sanctions and remedies, both the EU and the US concur on the importance of investigating and sanctioning cartels.

International Cartels

While both jurisdictions differ on approaches to a topic such as vertical restraints, there is less divergence with regard to cartels. Cartels, in various forms (price fixing, controlling output, market division, bid rigging) are outlawed in the United States under Section 1 of the Sherman Act and in the EU pursuant to Article 101 of the Treaty on the Functioning of the European Union (TFEU). Cartels have become the central focus of attention for antitrust authorities throughout the world in recent years. They remain in the words of the US Supreme Court "the supreme evil of antitrust".[1] Not only do both jurisdictions adopt a zero tolerance approach to cartels, they both acknowledge the difficulty in investigating cartels and bringing successful actions against participants in the cartels. Cartels by their nature are extremely secretive and are today often given effect on a global scale.

It is clear that cartels have become very sophisticated with regard to the avoidance of detection. This can be seen from various reports on cartel activity from the recent past. In 2007, the European Commission fined members of the Elevators & Escalators cartel a total of €992 million for operating cartels for the installation and maintenance of lifts

---

[1] *Verizon Communications v. Law Offices of Curtis V. Trinko*, 540 U.S. 398, 408 (2004).

and escalators in Germany, Belgium, Luxembourg, and the Netherlands. Evidence from the case illustrates the level of avoidance of detection:

> In all four cartels high-ranking national management (such as managing directors, sales and services directors and heads of customer service departments) participated in regular meetings and discussions. There is evidence that the companies were aware that their behaviour was illegal and they took care to avoid detection; they usually met in bars and restaurants, they travelled to the countryside or even abroad, and they used pre-paid mobile phone cards to avoid tracking. (European Commission 2007a)

This is further illustrated in the Insulated Gas Switchgear cartel where the Commission imposed fines totalling €770 million and noted that:

> Members of the cartel took sophisticated measures to keep their communications secret. Code names were used for both companies and individuals. In the last years of the cartel they relied on anonymous e-mail addresses for communication and used encryption for sending messages. According to a message sent by one cartel organiser to another, it was strictly forbidden to have "access to your [e-mail] from your home personal computer or any computer that can be easily linked to you. This will jeopardize the whole [cartel] network safety. Absolutely prohibit e-mails sending from your company computer to any AMB [i.e. anonymous mailbox]. This will also put the whole network security at risk. (European Commission 2007b)

The director general for competition at the European Commission (DGComp) has recently acknowledged that cartels are getting better at keeping a low profile with very detailed forensic IT support required during investigations into alleged cartel activity (Italianer 2011).

It is clear that not only do cartels pose a continuing threat to fair competition, the detection of such cartels is becoming increasingly difficult as cartel participants actively engage in detection avoidance measures. Moreover, the majority of cartel participants are corporations whose operations are global in nature. A decision to engage in price fixing or bid rigging in one territorial market is usually indicative of anticompetitive tendencies at a global level. Perhaps the most infamous cartel of recent years was the Vitamins cartel where all the major producers of vitamin products engaged in price fixing and market sharing on a global scale. The cartel was described at the time by the European Commission as "the most damaging series of cartels the Commission has ever investigated" (European Commission 2001). The cartel also led to investigations and sanctions (both criminal and civil) in the United States, but research has indicated that the cartel members paid less in fines and damages worldwide than the probable profit made from the overcharging by the cartel participants. Connor, in particular, has shown that despite a multiplicity of monetary sanctions including fines and awards of damages, the total penalties foregone by the Vitamins cartel participants fell short of the gain made as a result of the cartel over-charge. It is estimated that the total penalties paid by the participants amounted to between $6 billion and $7.5 billion, comprising criminal fines, administrative fines, and damages actions, both direct and indirect. Nonetheless the extra monopoly profit garnered by the participants is estimated at approximately $9 billion (Connor & Bush 2007). As has long been argued, the rational cartel member in such a situation will continue to engage in anticompetitive behaviour (Posner 2001). If cartels are being operated by multinational corporations in an era of globalization then the effects are clearly international, yet enforcement is not globalised. For example, in the Vitamins cartel, the majority of the fines and damages arose from actions, both public and private, taken in the United States, Canada, and the European Union. It is clear that a lack of strong antitrust enforcement in other parts of the world is a primary reason for the absence of an adequate dissuasive penalty against the cartel. This was further exacerbated by a decision of the United States Supreme Court to limit the calculation of damages in US courts to the actions of the cartel participants within the jurisdiction.[2]

The outcome of the Vitamins litigation is instructive on a number of points. First, although the cartel was truly global in nature, ineffective antitrust rules in certain parts of the world rendered effective enforcement impossible. Second, in the largest two markets, the United States and the European Union, public enforcement was strong but private enforcement haphazard, due to the constraints applied by the courts in the US and the absence at the time of an effective framework for private party actions at EU level. In contrast, it should be noted that criminal sanctions were applied in the United States with two executives from Hoffmann-La Roche serving terms of imprisonment as a result of a plea bargain agreement. The dissuasive effect of such a penalty is arguably greater than any monetary sanction (Wils 2005). However, the absence of equivalent criminal sanctions at EU level is a shortcoming in any attempt to ensure a uniform approach to enforcement globally. A further reason for the relative "success" of the Vitamins cartel was the absence of any evidence of cohesive and effective enforcement outside of the markets comprising the US and the EU. Indeed, the historic absence of effective antitrust measures outside of First World countries has ensured that global cartels can effectively profit from their activities despite the application of antitrust rules in the US and EU.

---

[2]   *F. Hoffmann-La Roche Ltd.v. Empagran S.A.* 542 U.S. 155 (2003).

Co-operation and Co-ordination

As former Competition Commissioner Mario Monti stated in 2004, "Undoubtedly, international cartels are the most damaging distortion of competition. Their prosecution requires a combination of resourceful enforcement domestically and of effective cooperation internationally" (Monti 2004). Furthermore, it has been pointed out that there is an inherent contradiction in having national economic laws despite the fact that economic problems transcend national boundaries (Fox 1999).

In 2008 the then EU Competition Commissioner Neelie Kroes stated that "while I firmly believe our systems are on a path of convergence, no-one has a monopoly on antitrust innovation" (Kroes 2008). It is probably an exaggeration to suggest that the US and EU systems are on a path of convergence, and such statements belie the fact that the EU has more recently engaged with other jurisdictions in an attempt to build global anti-cartel alliances. Nonetheless the level of co-operation and co-ordination between US and EU authorities is increasing incrementally.

While the level of co-operation to date between the US and the EU has been notable at agency level, one cannot discount the importance of cultural differences that inherently exist with regard to competition policy (Pape 1999). This is especially notable with regard to sanctions. One must question the likelihood of convergence in terms of sanctions. After all, if the EU and the US hold divergent views on whether or not certain forms of behaviour constitute an antitrust offence, it is only reasonable to accept that different schemes of sanctioning and restitution will remain. Divergences as to sanctions need not necessarily impede future convergence with regard to enforcement.

There are effectively three primary elements in modern antitrust enforcement, establishing the boundaries of illegality, the strength and resources of investigative authorities, and the nature and level of sanctions and penalties. It is in these three areas that we should question the need for a greater bilateral approach between the EU and the US. Despite the view of Commissioner Kroes that we are on a path of convergence it is contended that it is in the area of investigative powers that most convergence should occur. To go further in determining the scope of illegality from a policy standpoint and to attempt to introduce concurrent sanctions is to miss the point that the policy objectives are at best distant cousins.

In a globalised market, there is little doubt that would-be antitrust infringers take decisions that are often applied in the market worldwide. In challenging this behaviour, it is not only entirely sensible but imperative that closer co-operation occurs between the EU and the US. One cannot overemphasise the importance of co-ordinated investigations in both jurisdictions. In effect there is little point in the US Justice Department commencing an anti-cartel investigation if the end result is to forewarn the European branches of the same cartel members. Indeed a rational assessment of the situation would suggest that concurrent investigation by antitrust authorities in all markets is required to defeat the logic of a rational cartelist.

One particular case from the recent past illustrates the issues that arise in relation to enforcement prioritisation and co-operation.

Air Cargo Cartel

By its nature a cartel operating in the international air cargo market is going to lead to multijurisdictional investigation and enforcement, and in many ways the recent actions in this area can serve as a template for future co-operation and enforcement.

A large number of leading airlines have been investigated for operating a cartel in relation to pricing. The contacts on prices among the airlines concerned initially started with a view to discuss fuel surcharges. The carriers contacted each other so as to ensure that worldwide airfreight carriers imposed a flat rate surcharge per kilo for all shipments. The cartel members extended their co-operation by introducing a security surcharge and refusing to pay a commission on surcharges to their clients (freight forwarders).

The aim of these contacts was to ensure that these surcharges were introduced by all the carriers involved and that increases (or decreases) of the surcharge levels were applied in full without exception. By refusing to pay a commission, the airlines ensured that surcharges did not become subject to competition through the granting of discounts to customers. Such practices are in breach of the EU competition rules.

In 2006, the European Commission and the US Justice Department carried out concurrent raids on the offices of airlines suspected of operating a cartel in relation to air cargo (*Financial Times* 2006). Subsequently, the European Commission granted immunity to Lufthansa in return for assistance under its leniency programme. The matter concluded at EU level in November 2010 when the Commission imposed fines totalling €799 million against eleven air cargo carriers (European Commission 2010a). The decision is currently the subject of a number of recently lodged appeals at the General Court. There have also been significant fines imposed on cartel members in the US as well as Australia, Canada, and South Korea. At the time of writing, the effects of the initial investigation into the Air Cargo cartel continue to be seen with the imposition of fines by the High Court of New Zealand on Cargolux International Airlines and British Airways (Commerce Commission 2011).

To date, the total amount in fines imposed by public agencies worldwide against the Air Cargo cartel members totals €1.8 billion. There are also a series of private party claims for damages being pursued against cartel members in numerous jurisdictions.

The notable feature of the cartel investigation was the co-ordination and co-operation among the authorities. The subsequent sanctions have been criminal and civil, enforced publically and privately depending on the jurisdiction. The sanctions may vary depending on the jurisdiction, but they were made possible by the joint EU/US operation. The cases involving the airlines will run for many years, and the total worldwide cost will leave the companies concerned no doubt as to the effects of enforcement co-operation in the antitrust area. More important, future potential cartel participants who operate globally will realise the global effects of antitrust co-operation.

The investigation into and sanctioning of the air cargo cartel is as close as jurisdictions are likely to come in the search for optimal enforcement of antitrust rules at international level. Effective co-ordination and co-operation at the investigative level is of primary importance while a concurrence of sanctions is of secondary concern once the overall effect of these sanctions is sufficiently dissuasive.

Sanctions

At present there is a multiplicity of sanctions for infringements of competition laws depending on the jurisdiction. In the EU, the sanctions are civil in nature and are historically the subject of public enforcement. In the US, public enforcement may lead to criminal convictions while the majority of enforcement actions are made up of private party actions for damages, including class actions. There have been recent attempts to establish a private actions regime at EU level. In 2008, the Commission published a White Paper on private party actions and is currently engaged in a consultative process regarding the issue of collective redress. Vice President Almunia has indicated recently to the European Parliament that he is likely to bring forward legislative proposals in the area in early 2012 (Almunia, 2011). This author has previously contended that the current moves by the Commission are an attempt to *Americanise* EU Competition law (Walsh 2009). It is interesting to note that former Competition Commissioner Kroes, who actively worked towards the development of a private enforcement regime, is also the commissioner who speaks about the two jurisdictions being on a path of convergence (Kroes 2008). Separately, the European Commission has begun to move forward on an initiative regarding collective redress. This approach, while not exclusive to antitrust enforcement, indicates a more coherent level of thinking at EU level and may well lead to a conclusion that places redress for consumers at the heart of antitrust enforcement. It is significant that the Commission has emphasised that any proposal in the area of collective redress "fits well into the European legal tradition" (European Commission 2010b). The Commission stresses the need to avoid the risks inherent in "abusive litigation" and emphasises that "we therefore firmly oppose introducing 'class actions' along the US model into the EU legal order". It is difficult not to over-emphasise the importance of this statement from the Commission. It is apparent that the Commission has noted the comments received following previous proposals in the area, comments which at best could be described as cautioning against going down a road of US style actions for damages.

It is contended that a uniform or similar system of sanctions is not necessary for a coherent approach to antitrust enforcement. Sanctions by their nature reflect the differing attitudes to anticompetitive behaviour in differing cultures. While the US has actively pursued criminal cases against cartel members in recent years, individual Member States of the EU have been less inclined to move in this direction. Even in jurisdictions that have seen the adoption in legislation of criminalisation, there has been a reluctance to date to impose custodial sentences. In his ground-breaking study, Stephen (2008) highlights the public perception in the United Kingdom that while price fixing is viewed as wrong, it is not necessarily viewed as criminal activity. Others, notably Wils (2005), have contended that the EU should move towards the application of criminal sanctions via the decentralised application of Articles 101 and 102 TFEU. However, such a move should be at the behest of an intention to further deter cartel activity and recognise the futility of a system solely reliant on a fines-based approach rather than seeking to mimic the approach of the US authorities.

Do divergent policies and enforcement regimes reflect economic and cultural differences that inevitably require less homogeneity than that that is sometimes wished for? While sanctions for infringements of antitrust rules vary as a result of diverging cultural attitudes, it is clear that all sanctions serve as a means of deterring would-be cartel members from engaging in anticompetitive behaviour.

Deterrence Effect

Speaking in 2009, Commissioner Kroes attempted to put a general figure on the total amount of money saved through effective antitrust enforcement against cartels (Kroes 2009). She considered a wide-ranging study carried out in the United Kingdom by the Office of Fair Trade (OFT) that estimated that for every cartel discovered there were at least five others that were abandoned or which stalled before they could do real damage (Office of Fair Trading 2007). She then extrapolated that "If we apply the OFT's findings to our 18 decisions, the deterrence effect means we avoided 60 billion euros of consumer harm for the period 2005-2007. In other words: the deterrence effect of our policies may be in the order of 20 billion euros each year" (Kroes 2009). Clearly, increasing monetary penalties, through both fines and damages actions are likely to have a dissuasive effect if these penalties are applied concurrently in numerous jurisdictions.

A further issue for consideration is the likely deterrent effect of consecutive prison sentences in different jurisdictions. In principle, there is nothing to prevent executives being tried, convicted, and sentenced for the same cartel activity in different jurisdictions given that the offences relate only to the cartel activity on the specific market in question. In reality, it is likely that various enforcement agencies will work together to ensure that a convicted member of a cartel serves time in one jurisdiction and also ensures that the sentence served is at least as long as one which would have been imposed in the second jurisdiction. This is probably best illustrated by the various investigations into the Marine Hose Cartel. The cartel operated worldwide, and in 2007, co-ordinated raids by enforcement agencies took place at a number of locations worldwide. Concurrently, a number of senior executives of cartel participants were arrested in the United States. In 2009, the European Commission imposed a fine of €131 million against a number of the participants. However, it is the unprecedented level of co-operation at criminal investigation level that illustrates the effectiveness of closer co-ordination of enforcement proceedings.

A number of senior executives of one of the participants, Dunlop Oil & Marine, had been arrested in the US. In the face of potential incarceration of up to ten years, they entered a plea bargain arrangement with the Department of Justice and pleaded guilty to a breach of Section 1 of the Sherman Act. The plea bargain arrangement allowed the defendants to leave the US for the UK on condition that they stand trial and plead guilty on similar charges in the UK. Furthermore, the agreement with the US authorities included an undertaking that the defendants would return to the US to serve out their terms of imprisonment if the sentences handed down by the UK courts were less than those agreed to in the plea bargain agreement in the US. This level of unprecedented criminal enforcement co-operation is indicative of a new desire to ensure that minimum sentences are served between different jurisdictions where infringements of antitrust laws are criminalised. The effective deterrence value of such an approach is probably best illustrated by the acknowledgement by one of the Dunlop executives, Bryan Allison, of the effects of the transatlantic investigation. In an interview following his incarceration, Allison stated that "I think that people are much more frightened of the consequences. A jail term is a pretty chilling thought for anybody. In fairness, one has to say, I am much more conscious of it now than I was then" (O'Kane 2011). What is most notable about the level of transatlantic co-operation in the Marine Hose Cartel is not the co-ordination of the investigation by the US and EU authorities, but rather, the subsequent linking of the criminal investigations by the US and UK authorities so as to ensure that an adequate minimum term of imprisonment was served.

Future Directions

Effective antitrust enforcement against cartels requires effective deterrence across a range of competition systems appropriate to the legal traditions of each country (Kroes 2009).

Do divergent policies and enforcement regimes reflect economic and cultural differences that inevitably require less homogeneity than what is sometimes wished for? Historic co-operation at transatlantic level is now being replicated at a global level. There is evidence that the EU is beginning to play a lead role in fostering greater global enforcement of antitrust policy, particularly in the light of recent bilateral agreements with countries such as Brazil and South Korea. Furthermore, there is a growing reliance on a body such as the International Competition Network (ICN) to facilitate co-operation and convergence at a global level. The ICN already has a membership comprising enforcement agencies from one hundred-three jurisdictions. While the remit of the ICN extends to other aspects of antitrust activity, its emphasis on both procedural and substantive convergence is likely to impact greatly on anti-cartel enforcement in the coming years. It has recently set out a view of future convergence in the area of antitrust enforcement, and it is likely to play a central role on formulating proposals on both improved advocacy and communication (International Competition Network 2011).

There can be little doubt that co-operation in antitrust enforcement will continue to improve in the coming years. As stated earlier, a global cartel can only ever be effectively tackled by global enforcement. Sanctions need not be the same as long as they are effective. Rather than considering a convergence of substantive rules on antitrust, the global economy, and consumers in particular, may be best served by increased co-operation at investigative and sanctioning level. Optimum convergence of antitrust rules, between the EU and the US in particular, will have occurred when would-be cartelists desist from illegal activity out of a fear of international investigation and real and effective sanctions in a multiplicity of jurisdictions.

References

Almunia, Joaquin (2010). "New Transatlantic Trends in Competition Policy", in Friends of Europe, Brussels, 10 June, 2010. <http://europa.eu/rapid /pressReleasesAction.do?reference=SPEECH/10/305&format=HTML&aged =0&language=EN&guiLanguage=en>.

Almunia, Joaquin (2011). "SGEI reform and the application of competition rules to the financial sector: themes for dialogue with the European Parliament", European Parliament, ECON Committee Brussels, 22 March 2011. <http://europa.eu/rapid/pressReleasesAction.do?reference=SPEECH/11/197 &format=HTML&aged=0&language=EN&guiLanguage=en>.

Arena, Amedeo (2011). "The Relationship between Antitrust and Regulation in the US and the EU: An Institutional Assessment", IILJ Emerging Scholars Paper 19 (2011). <http://www.iilj.org/publications/documents/ESP19-2011 Arena.pdf>.

Barnett, Thomas O. (2007). "Global Antitrust Enforcement", Georgetown Law Global Antitrust Enforcement Symposium, 26 September 2007. <http://www.justice.gov/atr/public/speeches/226334.htm>.

Bork, Robert (1978). *The Antitrust Paradox.* Chicago: Free Press.

Commerce Commission (2011). "$7.6 million in Penalties imposed against two airlines in Cargo Cartel case", 5 April 2011. <http://www.comcom. govt.nz/media-releases/detail/2011/7-6-million-in-penalties-imposed-against-two-airlines-in-air-cargo-cartel-case>.

Connor, John M. and Darren Bush (2007). "Deterring International Cartels in the Face of Comity and Jurisdiction: A Legal, Economic, and Empirical Evaluation of the Extraterritorial Application of U.S. Antitrust Laws", 2 April. <http://ssrn.com/abstract=978846>.

Dabbah, Maher (2003). *The Internationalisation of Antitrust Policy.* Cambridge: Cambridge University Press.

European Commission (2001). "Commission imposes fines on vitamin cartels", DG Competition, 21 November. <http://europa.eu/rapid/press ReleasesAction.do?reference=IP/01/1625&format=HTML&aged=0& language=EN&guiLanguage=en>.

European Commission (2007a). "Competition: Commission fines members of lifts and escalators cartels over €990 million", DG Competition, 21 February. <http://europa.eu/rapid/pressReleasesAction.do?reference=IP/07/209&forma t=HTML&aged=0&language=EN&guiLanguage=en>.

European Commission (2007b). "Competition: Commission fines members of gas insulated switchgear cartel over 750 million euros", DG Competition,

24 January. <http://europa.eu/rapid/pressReleasesAction.do?reference=IP/07/80&format =HTML&aged=0&language=EN&guiLanguage=en>.

European Commission (2010a). "Antitrust: Commission fines 11 air cargo carriers €799 million in price fixing cartel", DG Competition, 9 November. <http://europa.eu/rapid/pressReleasesAction.do?reference=IP/10/1487&form at=HTML&aged=0&language=EN&guiLanguage=en>.

European Commission (2010b). "Towards a Coherent European Approach to Collective Redress: Next Steps – Joint Information Note by Vice President Viviane Reding, Vice President Joaquin Almunia and Commissioner John Dalli", SEC (2010) 1192, Brussels 5 October.

Federal Trade Commission (2011). "The FTC in 2011: Federal Trade Commission Annual Report", April.

Financial Times (2006). "Airlines raided in worldwide cargo cartel probe", 14 February.

Fox, Eleanor M. (1999). "Global Problems in a World of National Law", in *34 New Eng. L. Rev. 11* (1999-2000).

Ginsburg, Douglas H. and Joshua D. Wright (2010). "Antitrust Sanctions", in *Competition Policy International*, Volume 6, No. 2, Autumn, p. 3.

Harrington, Joseph (2010). "Comment on Antitrust Sanctions", in *Competition Policy International*, Volume 6, No. 2, Autumn, p. 40.

International Competition Network (2011). "The ICN'S Vision for its Second Decade", Presented at the 10th Annual Conference of the International Competition Network, The Hague, Netherlands, 17-20 May. <http://www. internationalcompetitionnetwork.org/library.aspx>.

Italianer, Alexander (2011). "Zero Tolerance for International Cartels", International Competition Network Cartel Workshop 2011, Bruges, Belgium 10-13 October.

Kroes, Neelie (2008). "EU & US antitrust policies – our shared belief in competitive markets", Opening remarks at 56th Annual Spring Meeting of The American Bar Association Section of Antitrust Law, Washington, D.C., 28 March. <http://europa.eu/rapid/pressReleasesAction.do?reference= SPEECH/08/154&format=HTML&aged=0&language=EN&guiLanguage=e n>.

Kroes, Neelie (2009). "Tackling cartels – a never-ending task. Anti-Cartel Enforcement: Criminal and Administrative Policy", Brasilia, 8 October. <http://europa.eu/rapid/pressReleasesAction.do?reference=SPEECH/09/454 &format=HTML&aged=0&language=EN&guiLanguage=en>.

Lowe, Philip (2006). "International Cooperation between Competition Agencies: Achievements & Challenges", 4th Seoul International Competition Forum, South Korea, 5 September. <http://ec.europa.eu/competition/speeches/ text/sp2005_021_en.pdf>.

Monti, Mario (2004). "International Antitrust – A Personal Perspective", Fordham Corporate Law Institute, New York, 7 October. <http://europa.

eu/rapid/pressReleasesAction.do?reference=SPEECH/04/449&format=HTM
L&aged=0&language=EN&guiLanguage=en>.

Montini, Massimiliano (1999). "Globalization and International Antitrust
Cooperation", Trade and Competition in the WTO and beyond, Venice, 4-
5 December. <http://www.feem.it/userfiles/attach/Publication/NDL1999/
NDL1999-069.pdf>,

Office of Fair Trading (2007). "The Deterrent Effect of Competition Enforcement by the OFT", Discussion document. <http://www.oft.gov.uk/
shared_oft/reports/Evaluating-OFTs-work/oft963.pdf>.

O'Kane, Michael (2011). "Does Prison Work for Cartelists? The View from
Behind Bars", in *The Antitrust Bulletin*, Vol. 56, No. 2, Summer.

Pape, Wolfgang (1999). "Socio-Cultural Differences and International Competition Law", *European Law Journal*, Vol. 5, No. 4, pp. 438-460.

Posner, Richard (2001). *Antitrust Law*, 2nd ed. University of Chicago Press,
p. 274.

Stephen, Andreas (2008). "Survey of Public Attitudes to Price-Fixing and Cartel
Enforcement in Britain", in *CompLRev*, Vol. 5, issue 1, pp. 123-145.

United States Department of Justice (2008). "Former US Executive of Italian
Marine Hose Manufacturer Agrees to Plead Guilty to Participation in
Worldwide bid-rigging Conspiracy", 17 April. 8. <http://www.
justice.gov/atr/public/press_releases/2008/232332.htm>.

Walsh, Declan J. (2009). "Carrots and Sticks: – leniency and fines in EC cartel
cases", *E.C.L.R.*, 30(1), pp. 30-35.

Wils, Wouter (2005). "Is Criminalisation of EU Competition Law the
Answer?", in *World Competition*, Vol. 28, No. 2, pp. 117-159.

Zingales, Nicolo (2008). "European and American Leniency Programmes: Two
Models towards Convergence", in *CompLRev*, Vol. 5, Issue 1, pp. 5-60.

EU and Canadian Merger Policy

Similar Origins and Divergent Regulations

Christian MARFELS and James SAWLER[1]

Should the ongoing trade talks between Canada and the EU produce an agreement, firms on both sides of the Atlantic will seek to restructure their operations to take advantage of new opportunities and respond to new competition. In many cases, this restructuring will be in the form of cross-border mergers between Canadian and European firms.[2] These proposed mergers will be subject to review in both Canada and the EU (and possibly in other jurisdictions as well). Multi-jurisdictional enforcement can impose significant costs on firms seeking to merge, particularly when there are divergent regulations. Therefore, an examination of Canadian and EU merger regulations is warranted. This chapter first reviews the development of Canadian and EU merger policy, highlighting certain parallels, and then examines current sources of divergence.

The Historical Background of Canada's Competition Act

The origins of Canadian merger control can be traced back to 1910 when the instruments and procedures for investigations of alleged restraints of trade were laid down in the Combines Investigation Act. Some 50 years thereafter, specific mention of anti-competitive mergers happened in an amendment of the Combines Investigation Act of 1960 when the anti-combines provisions of the Criminal Code were incorporated in the Act. Under the offenses of the Act were mergers and monopolies that may operate to the detriment of the public (Sec. 33).

Unfortunately, enforcement of the provisions of Sec. 33 was largely ineffective. Mergers and monopolies were formally treated the same way as conspiracies, i.e., a contested merger or monopoly was subject to criminal law procedures. Consequently, the undue lessening of competi-

---

[1] Financial support from a grant from the European Union Centre of Excellence (EUCE) at Dalhousie University is gratefully acknowledged.

[2] Following the Canada-US Free Trade Agreement, there was a spike in cross-border mergers (Long and Vousden 1995).

tion and the resulting detriment to the public had to be proven beyond a reasonable doubt. This was an almost insurmountable barrier for a challenge of monopolistic behaviour and even more so for a merger challenge. How could it ever be proven beyond a reasonable doubt that a merger would lead to public detriment? There were eleven monopoly and merger challenges brought forward for court action from 1910 to 1985 (West 2004). This was clearly a dismal record. The challenge of the acquisition of Manitoba Sugar Refining Co. by B.C. Sugar Refining Co. in 1960 was a case in point.[3] B.C. Sugar was a dominant firm, and Manitoba Sugar was the last independent sugar producer in Western Canada. With the exception of a 30 per cent market share of refineries from Eastern Canada in Manitoba, B.C. Sugar would hold 100 per cent of the market in Western Canada from Manitoba to British Columbia. The director of Investigation and Research, as the agency in charge under the Act, felt that this was a clear-cut case of an anti-competitive merger according to Sec. 33 of the Act. However, the court rejected the application to have the merger blocked. It was felt that the merger had not reduced competition beyond a reasonable doubt since there was still the competition in Manitoba from the refineries from Eastern Canada (Kilgour 1962). Likewise, the challenge against the acquisition of the last independent newspaper in New Brunswick, the *Fredericton Gleaner*, by the Irving Group in 1968 was not successful. This would be a merger to monopoly since the Irving Group already owned the other four English-language newspapers in the province. The merger-to-monopoly assessment was upheld by the Court of First Instance although it was felt that there was no proof of abuse of the monopoly position. However, the court underlined the Director's view that the complete dominance in itself was detrimental to the public. Alas, the Court of Appeal saw it differently and overturned the decision. To add one more, the Supreme Court followed the Appeal Court's view in a decision in 1976 and stated that a detriment to the public could not simply be concluded from the mere presence of a monopoly but that there had to be proof of detriment.[4] This decision in its finality was a serious blow to the Crown. If a merger to monopoly could not be successfully challenged there was virtually no place for an efficient merger control. Consequently, there were no more merger challenges under the Combines Investigation Act in the years to come.

Early on, the federal government had taken notice of the inability of the Combines Investigation Act to pursue an efficient control of mergers and abuse of market dominance. In 1966, the Economic Council of

---

[3]   *R. v. British Columbia Sugar Refining Co.* (1960), 129 C.C.C.7. (Man.Q.B).

[4]   *R. v. K.C. Irving* (1978), S.C.R. 408.

Canada (ECC) was asked to look into this matter and to provide proposals for new policy measures. Only three years later, the ECC presented its report (Economic Council of Canada 1969). This report can be safely regarded as a roadmap for an efficient competition policy in Canada. Most important were the following recommendations:

* the transition from the perception of the outdated Anti-Combines Policy to Competition Policy;
* the inclusion of the service economy;
* the replacement of the criminal law treatment of mergers and abuse of market power by a civil law treatment;
* the introduction of the Competitive Practices Tribunal in order to relieve the courts of the burden of the proceedings under civil law and rulings on joint ventures.

With the ECC recommendations on hand, the federal government wasted no time to prepare legislation based on the recommendations. The new legislation was introduced in Parliament as Bill C-256 in 1971. Unfortunately, the bill became the victim of mounting opposition from business interests. As a consequence, the government withdrew the bill only after first reading. In fact, it would take another fifteen years before the path-breaking and innovative ideas of the ECC would become reality in the Competition Act of 1986.

After the withdrawal of Bill C-256 in 1971, the federal government decided to proceed with the amendment of the Combines Investigation Act in two stages. The sensitive parts, i.e., mergers, abuse of market power and the Tribunal, referred to as "Stage II Amendments", would be postponed until more research and insight would be obtained from a commission to study these matters (Skeoch-McDonald Commission). The less controversial issues of Bill C-256 became law in 1976 (Stage I Amendments). Among them was the inclusion of the service economy into the realm of the Combines Investigation Act.

After receipt of the Skeoch-McDonald Report (1976), the federal government made several attempts to pass the slightly modified Stage II Amendments into law from 1976-1984 (Bills C-42, C-13, and C-29), but to no avail. Mention must be made that Bill C-29 of 1984 introduced a pre-notification requirement for larger mergers where the merger partners exceeded $500 million in sales or assets. Furthermore, banks would become subject to the new merger regulations as well. Unfortunately, Bill C-29 – which had received broad support – died on the agenda because of a change of government in 1984. Interestingly enough, the new government immediately continued on course towards introducing new legislation for a much-needed new competition policy based on the legacy of the ECC and on the provisions of earlier bills on the matter and, most notably, on the previous Bill C-29. When the new Bill C-91 was introduced in 1985, it took less than a year to have the new Competition Act under lock and key (Consumer and Corporate Affairs Canada 1985). And yes, the Act was virtually a blueprint of the recommendations of the ECC and of the subsequent Bill C-256 from almost two decades earlier.

The Long Way Towards EU Merger Control

To say that the EU Merger Regulation was a long time in the making is an understatement. As early as 1965, the EC-Commission (1965) concluded in a memorandum on concentration in the Common Market that merger control at the Community level was urgently needed. Since there was no specific rule regarding merger control in the Treaty of Rome of 1957, the Commission felt that Article 86 of the treaty, which referred to abuse of market power, would be the instrument to be applied to merger cases where a dominant firm acquired another firm, and competition would be annihilated through the merger. The Commission used this rule to issue an order of prohibition against the acquisition of the Dutch company Thomassen and Driyver-Verblifa by Continental Can's German subsidiary Schmalbach-Lubeca Werke in 1971. Both Schmalbach and Thomassen were competitors in the market of containers for meat and fish products and Continental Can was the dominant firm in the industry. Upon appeal to the European Court of Justice, the court approved the application of Article 86 to merger-to-monopoly cases, but it reversed the Commission's decision because of wrong market definitions in the case (European Court of Justice 1973). In the following years, the Commission investigated as many as nineteen merger cases, but in no case could market dominance prior to the merger be determined (Monopolkommission 1989).

The omission of a rule against anti-competitive mergers in the Rome Treaty of 1957 is surprising since there was such a rule in Article 66 of the Treaty of Paris of 1951 to establish the European Coal and Steel Community. Article 66 was directed at mergers that would prevent competition in coal and/or steel markets. This rule never gained momentum because of the existing hefty state subsidies in coal and steel. It is somewhat of an irony that the Treaty of Paris had a rule on mergers, which became almost obsolete, and the Treaty of Rome did not have such a rule although it was urgently needed.

In 1973, the EC-Commission saw the writing on the wall and introduced a proposal for an EC merger control (EC Commission 1973). The Commission was optimistic about the prospects of such merger control since both the Council of Ministers and the European Parliament had called for a comprehensive EC merger control in the mid- to late 1960s.

According to the proposal, merger control was directed at Community-wide mergers, which may endanger or impede trade among EC Member States. A Community-wide merger would be a merger that (a) included at least one EC company, (b) posted combined sales of the merger partners in excess of UA 200 million,[5] and (c) the combined market share of the merger partners would exceed 25 per cent in at least one and the same EC Member State. These criteria were indicative of the Commission's plan to establish a comprehensive merger control that would cover all large mergers and not just the ones in the realm of Article 86. Furthermore, the establishment of merger control at the Community level clearly set the agenda for a duality of merger control in the Common Market, *viz.*, Community-wide mergers in the realm of the Commission and national mergers in the realm of the EC Member States.

The European Parliament and the Economic and Social Committee of the EC approved of the proposed EC Merger Regulation, but the all-important Council of Ministers did not. This non-acceptance was surprising. Or was it? After all, the Council had indicated the desire to have an EC Merger Control established, and this position was reaffirmed at the Paris meetings of the European Council in October 1972 (Monopolkommission 1989). Yet, there was more to come. The Commission submitted a total of six further proposals for an EC merger control in the years to come, and the Council did not accept all of them.[6] It took a total of sixteen years before the regulation of December 1989 became the foundation of merger control in the Common Market. This long time period recalls the fate of the Canadian Competition Act from Bill C-256 in 1971 to the Act of 1986, i.e., fifteen years. In fact, there are more similarities between the developments of the Competition Act and the EC Merger Regulation. In Canada, it was next to impossible to pursue an effective merger control when mergers were still in the Criminal Code under Section 33. Likewise, merger control in the EC suffered from the application of Article 86 of the Rome Treaty with its rather stringent requirements of the existence of a dominant firm that would create a merger to monopoly in the post-merger constellation. In spite of these towering conditions, both the director of Investigation and Research in Canada and the EC-Commission made numerous efforts to challenge mergers. As was to be expected, it was an exercise in futility.

---

[5] The Unit of Account (UA) was replaced by the European Unit of Account (EUA) in 1975 that, in turn, was replaced by the European Currency Unit (ECU) in 1979.

[6] In 1981, 1984, 1986, 1988 (2), and 1989.

When it comes to the political aspects of achieving an effective merger control, the similarities between Canada and the EC come to an end. Canada is a nation state where new legislation needs its successful acceptance by Parliament. In contrast, the EC is a federation of independent states. Each Member State would send one representative to the Council of Ministers, which was the decision-making institution in the EC in the times of the "gestation period" of the EC Merger Regulation. Furthermore, decisions of the Council would have to be unanimous, a requirement which was difficult to achieve when it came to a complex phenomenon such as merger policy.

Consequently, there were substantive differences of opinion among EC Member States regarding merger policy. In fact, as of 1973, only two of the nine Member States had their own national merger control, *viz.*, Germany and Great Britain.[7] Obviously, Germany and Great Britain would see the merger regulation proposal from a different perspective than the other seven Member States by simply comparing their own merger regimes with the one of the proposal. For instance, Germany had established the issue of creation or strengthening of market dominance as the lead criterion in its appraisal of mergers (Marfels and Sawler 2009). Consequently, Germany wanted to see this criterion in an EC merger control rather than just the proposed more general criterion of an impediment of effective competition. Not surprisingly, market dominance found its way into the Commission Proposal of April 1988 (Monopolkommission 1989), and into the EC Merger Regulation of December 1989. Another aspect of concern for Germany and Great Britain was the rather low threshold of UA 200 million in the Commission's proposal. This would have extended the scope of EC merger control far too much into national merger control. In subsequent Commission proposals, the threshold was steadily increased until it reached ECU 1 billion in the 1989 Commission proposal.

It took fifteen years to reach a compromise solution of an EC merger control proposal that was unanimously accepted by the Council of Ministers. This led to Council Regulation No. 4064/89 of 21 December 1989 entitled "On the control of concentrations between undertakings". Such control was directed at concentrations with a Community dimension that would have (a) aggregate worldwide sales exceeding ECU 5 billion, (b) Community-wide sales of at least two of the merger partners in excess of ECU 250 million, and (c) sales of each of the merger partners not in excess of two-thirds of their Community-wide sales in one and the same EC Member State. The two-thirds rule was the divid-

---

[7] France got it in 1977 and the Republic of Ireland in 1988 (Monopolkommission 1989).

ing line between mergers in the realm of the EC and mergers that would be under national merger control as far as large mergers are concerned. This rule was indicative of the philosophy of the European Community. Whenever merger partners made the vast majority of their sales in one and the same Member State, then this Member State should be in charge, regardless of the size of the merger. The duality of EC merger control was further enhanced by the "German clause" in the regulation, i.e., a provision that a Member State could request a referral of a Community-wide merger when there was reason to believe that the merger would have a profound impact on the domestic market. It was up to the Commission whether a request for referral would be granted.

The appraisal of a Community-wide merger was based on a market-structure test of whether market dominance was created or strengthened by the merger. If this were not the case, the merger would be found as compatible with the Common Market.

There are interesting parallels in the development of Canadian and EU merger regulations. Most obvious is the timing of the regulations: The Canadian Competition Act (CCA), introduced in 1986, preceded the European Community Merger Regulation (ECMR) by only three years. More compelling is the fact that in both jurisdictions, specific merger regulations were introduced following failures by competition authorities to apply existing monopoly legislation towards merger control. Despite the parallels in their development, however, Canadian and EU merger policies differ significantly. These differences can impose costs on firms seeking to merge Canadian and EU firms.

The Costs of Divergent Merger Regulations

The principal objective of merger policy is to protect consumers by preserving competition. Therefore, while it is important to prevent anti-competitive mergers, it is equally important that regulations do not impose too great a cost on firms seeking to merge. Otherwise, firms may choose not to pursue mergers that could enhance competition or create efficiencies of benefit to consumers.[8]

There are numerous sources of efficiency that can result from mergers. Mergers can enhance productive efficiency by providing firms with economies of scale (declining average costs as output increases) and economies of scope (cost savings resulting from the joint production of two or more products). They can enhance innovation (dynamic efficiency) by allowing firms to share knowledge and combine research and development efforts and reduce transaction costs by eliminating

---

[8] The vast majority of mergers do not raise anti-competitive concerns.

rent-seeking behaviour of "middle men". Mergers can reduce procurement costs through volume discounts and reduce the cost of raising capital. Finally, it is argued that mergers can promote operational efficiency (X-efficiency) through the removal of ineffective management and a reallocation of an acquired firm's resources to more productive uses. Many of these efficiencies will ultimately lead to lower prices or higher quality products for consumers; thus, it is important that regulation does not impose too great a cost on such efficiency-enhancing mergers.

Unfortunately, divergent merger regulations can impose such costs (Marfels and Sawler 2004). Most immediate are the administrative costs associated with filing in two (or more) jurisdictions. These costs include fees for lawyers, economists, and translators, as well as the opportunity cost of management's time and attention being diverted away from ordinary business operations. These administrative costs are magnified when there is substantial divergence between the jurisdictions' regulations and procedures.

A more significant cost arising from divergent merger regulations is associated with a lack of timeliness. A merger is a strategic investment decision that is often a response to a changing competitive environment (such as trade liberalization) (Weston 2001). The modern global economy is characterized by rapid change that often requires an equally rapid strategic response. However, in dealing with two or more merger-control regimes, firms may have to wait months for a decision; the slowest regime delays the entire process. Meanwhile, even if the merger gains approval, the strategic opportunity may be lost.

The most significant cost of divergent merger regulations arises from uncertainty. When each of two or more merger-control regimes applies different sets of rules and tests, predicting the outcome of the review process becomes more difficult. Such uncertainty increases the opportunity cost of pursuing international mergers.

Thus, divergent merger regulations can impose significant costs on firms pursuing international mergers. How significant a problem is this for EU-Canadian mergers? Numerous sources of divergence are examined below.

Thresholds

In Canada, determining whether a merger is subject to review is relatively straightforward. The Competition Bureau must be given advance notice when the firm being acquired has Canadian assets of revenues greater than $73 million,[9] and when the combined Canadian assets or revenues of all parties is greater than $400 million (Canadian Competition Bureau 2011).

In the EU, this determination is more complicated. Notification is mandatory for all concentrations with a Community dimension, which occurs when the following conditions are met:

[T]he combined aggregate worldwide turnover [...] of all the undertakings concerned [...] is more than EUR 5,000 million,

and

the aggregate Community-wide turnover of each of at least two of the undertakings concerned is more than EUR 250 million,

unless

each of the undertakings concerned achieves more than two-thirds of its aggregate Community-wide turnover within one and the same Member State (European Commission 2010).

As mentioned earlier, these were the thresholds in the 1989 Merger Regulation. In later years, there were amendments to the Regulation in general and to the thresholds in particular. In case the original thresholds are not met, a concentration, nevertheless, has Community dimension, if

the combined aggregate worldwide turnover of all the undertakings concerned is more than EUR 2500 million,

and

in each of at least three Member States, the combined aggregate turnover of all the undertakings concerned is more than EUR 100 million,

and

in each of at least three Member States included for the purpose of the second point above, the aggregate turnover of each of at least two of the undertakings concerned is more than EUR 25 million,

and

the aggregate Community-wide turnover of each of at least two of the undertakings concerned is more than EUR 100 million,

unless

each of the undertakings concerned achieves more than two-thirds of its aggregate Community-wide turnover within one and the same Member State (EC Commission 2010).

---

[9] Provisions have been put in place that allow for automatic adjustment of this figure for inflation. This is the value for 2011.

Note the presence of the "two-thirds rule", which means that even a large merger may be reviewed, not at the EU level, but by a particular Member State.

Further complication arises from a potential for referrals. Pre-notification, the undertakings proposing to merge can request that a merger of a Community dimension be evaluated by a particular Member State, or that a merger that is not of a Community dimension be evaluated by the EU Commission. Post-notification, a Member State can request to evaluate a merger of Community dimension (the "German Clause"); conversely, it can also request that the Commission evaluate a merger not of a Community dimension.[10] These referrals add potential complication as merger review often differs among Member States and between Member States and the EU.

Authority

Canadian and EU merger regulations differ in terms of the authority of the respective agencies to review mergers and decide on a course of action. In Canada, mergers are reviewed by the Competition Bureau led by the competition commissioner. If the commissioner feels that a proposed merger is likely to substantially lessen or prevent competition, the case must be presented to the Competition Tribunal, a quasi-judicial body composed of both judicial and non-judicial members who provide business and economic expertise. The Tribunal has the authority to rule on the case.

In contrast, the EU Competition Commission has the authority not only to review mergers, but also to decide on the action to be taken. These decisions are subject to review by the Court of Justice.

Prohibitive Criteria

Another area of divergence between Canadian and EU merger policy is the application of different prohibition criteria. In Canada, the Tribunal can prohibit a merger which "prevents or lessens, or is likely to prevent or lessen, competition substantially" (Canadian Competition Bureau 2004). This substantially lessening of competition (SLC) test is used by the majority of merger control regimes outside the EU, including Australia and the Unites States. The SLC test is generally considered to be a relatively flexible criterion that allows for the inclusion of numerous competitive criteria in assessing the effects of the merger.

---

[10] For details on the referral process, see Articles 4, 9, and 22 of the ECMR and European Commission, "Commission Notice on Case Referral in Respect of Concentration", *Official Journal of the European Union*, 2005/C 56/02.

Prior to 2004, EU merger policy applied the market dominance (MD) test. Article 2.3 of the 1989 EC Merger Regulations describes the MD test as applied by the EU: "A concentration which creates or strengthens a dominant position as a result of which effective competition would be significantly impeded in the Common Market or in a substantial part of it shall be declared incompatible with the Common Market".

The MD test has been criticized on a number of fronts (particularly following the EU Commission's contentious blockage of the proposed GE-Honeywell merger in 2001). In particular, it has been argued that under the MD test, dominant firms seeking to merge could be penalized when the source of their dominance arises from efficiency. Furthermore, the ability of the MD test to handle issues of joint market power has been questioned (Marfels and Sawler 2009).

Partly in response to these criticisms, the EU moved somewhat closer to Canada (and the other jurisdictions using the SLC test) when it reformed its merger policies in 2004. Among the principal objectives of these reforms was the removal of uncertainty from the merger review process (European Commission 2001). Harmonising the EU's prohibition criterion with that of most other jurisdictions by dropping the MD test in favour of the SLC test would be a significant step in removing uncertainty. While this option was considered (European Commission 2001), the EU eventually settled for a hybrid of the two criteria. The new prohibition criterion described in Article 2(3) of the reformed EU Merger Regulation of 2004 is as follows: "A concentration which would significantly impede effective competition, in the Common Market or a substantial part of it, in particular as a result of the creation or strengthening of a dominant position, shall be declared incompatible with the Common Market". Thus, the EU's new prohibition criterion considers whether a merger results in dominance *and* whether there is a significant impediment (lessening) to competition in the market.

This change has moved the EU prohibition criterion closer to Canada's; however, it is still too early to tell exactly how it will be interpreted. For many merger cases in the immediate aftermath of the reforms, dominance continued to be the principal determinant of harm (Roller and Mano 2006). Many recent decisions, however, focus on whether the merger is likely to create a significant impediment to competition, and little mention is made of dominance. Nevertheless, a degree of uncertainty remains.

The Treatment of Efficiencies

Perhaps the most significant area of divergence is with respect to the treatment of efficiencies. While the EU is out of sync with the global majority with its prohibitive criteria, in terms of efficiencies, it is Canada which is the odd man out.

The EU's approach to evaluating efficiencies is relatively straight-forward and is summarized as follows:

> The EC will consider any substantiated claims of efficiency as part of the overall analysis of the merger to determine whether the merger will significantly impede effective competition in the Common Market. To the extent that the efficiencies may counteract the effects on competition – and in particular the harm to consumers – that the merger otherwise might have, those efficiencies may be taken into account as a factor pleading in favour of the merger being approved (Canadian Competition Bureau 2005).

Note that in the EU efficiencies are included as one factor among many to be considered in the analysis of the competitive effects. This practice is in line with that of the United States and with most other jurisdictions.

The EU Commission's approach to efficiencies can be examined in the contentious Ryanair/Aer Lingus case of 2007, which concerned a proposed merger between the two largest airlines in Ireland. Together, the two airlines accounted for roughly 80 per cent of the traffic to and from Dublin airport and 100 per cent of the traffic on numerous city-to-city routes. Additionally, the Commission found that there were substantial barriers to entry to the affected markets.

The Ryanair/Aer Lingus case also involved the most detailed examination of efficiencies up to that time (Gadas *et al.* 2007). Ryanair claimed that efficiencies would result from applying its low-cost business model and management practices to Aer Lingus. The Commission assessed whether the conditions for the acceptance of efficiencies under the Horizontal Merger Guidelines were met (European Commission 2004). The Commission rejected the first criterion, verifiability, because Ryanair's efficiency claim was based on applying its business model to Aer Lingus without taking into account the implications for Aer Lingus' product characteristics and revenue. The second criterion, merger specificity, was rejected because the Commission's analysis revealed that the proposed cost savings could be achieved without the merger. Finally, the third criterion, benefit to consumers, was rejected because the proposed savings would mostly be to Aer Lingus' fixed costs, making it uncertain they would be passed on to consumers (Gadas *et al.* 2007). Ultimately, the Commission rejected Ryanair's clam that there were substantial efficiencies to offset significant impediment to effective competition and prohibited the merger.[11]

While the EU includes efficiencies as one factor among many in assessing the competitive effects of a merger, Canadian merger legislation employs an "efficiency defence", outlined in section 96 of the Competition Act:

> The Tribunal shall not make an order under section 92 [prohibits mergers which prevent or lessen competition] if it finds that the merger or proposed merger [...] is likely to bring about gains in efficiency that will be greater than, and will offset, the effects of any prevention or lessening of competition that will result or is likely to result from the merger or proposed merger and that the gains in efficiency would not likely be attained if the order were made.

Canada's approach to evaluating efficiencies deviates from the EU's approach in two principal ways. First, while the EU considers efficiencies in the context of their potential to reverse the proposed merger's harm to consumers, Canada applies a balanced weights approach that attempts to weigh efficiency gains against loss in total surplus, adjusted for the distributional effects of lessened competition (Townley 1999). Note that in Canada, consumers are not required to be the ultimate beneficiaries of efficiencies. Second, while the EU evaluates efficiencies as one factor among many to be considered when assessing the overall anti-competitive effects of the merger (the factors approach), Canada does not evaluate efficiencies along with other factors relevant to assessing overall anti-competitiveness. Rather, once the anti-competitive effects have been established, it is determined *afterwards* whether enough efficiencies are generated by the merger to outweigh the anti-competitive effects.

The first (and so far only) instance where an otherwise anti-competitive merger was permitted under the efficiency defence was the Superior Propane Case. In 1998, Superior Propane's proposed acquisition of ICG Propane would create the largest national distributor of propane with a share of 70 per cent and virtual monopolies in numerous regional markets (Gudofsky and Gay 2000). Finding the merger likely to result in a substantial lessening of competition, the commissioner submitted an application to the Competition Tribunal to have it blocked. While the Tribunal agreed with the commissioner that the merger would likely result in a substantial lessening of competition, it nevertheless allowed the merger to proceed on the basis that the anticipated efficiencies arising from the merger would outweigh the anti-competitive

---

[11] The Commission's decision has since been upheld by the general court.

effects.[12] Upon appeal by the commissioner, the Tribunal's decision was upheld by the Federal Court of Appeal.

Thus, under Canadian merger policy, the presence of efficiencies can override all other potential anti-competitive effects of a merger, even if a merger leads to monopoly. Furthermore, the efficiency defence poses significant challenges to the Competition Bureau as post-merger efficiencies are extremely difficult to quantify – particularly dynamic efficiencies (Emberger 2003).

Conclusion

Despite certain interesting parallels in the development of Canadian and EU merger policies, there are numerous sources of divergence between the policies of the two merger control regimes. Such divergence can impose costs on firms seeking to use mergers to restructure or gain access to new markets. In turn, this could have negative implications for the gains expected from a Canada/EU free trade agreement.

References

Canadian Competition Bureau (2004). *Merger Enforcement Guidelines.*

Canadian Competition Bureau (2005). *Report of the International Roundtable on Efficiencies.*

Canadian Competition Bureau (2011). *2011 Pre-Merger Notification Transaction-Size Threshold.*

Consumer and Corporate Affairs Canada (1985). *Competition Law Amendments – Information.* Ottawa, December.

Emberger, G. (2003). "Canada's Merger Control System: A Perspective from the Inside", in *Competition Policy Newsletter* (European Commission), Vol. 2, pp. 43-49.

Economic Council of Canada (1969). *Interim Report on Competition Policy,* Ottawa.

EC Commission (1965). *Das Problem der Unternehmenskonzentration im Gemeinsamen Markt, Memorandum,* Brussels, December.

EC Commission (1973). Proposal for a Council Regulation on the Control of Concentrations between Undertakings, 16 O.J. EUR.COMM, No. C/92, Vol. 1

European Commission (2001). *Green Paper on the Review of Council Regulation (EEC),* No. 4064/89, Brussels.

---

[12] *The Commissioner of Competition v. Superior Propane Inc. and ICG Propane Inc.,* CT 1998 002, Reasons and Order, 30 August 2000.

European Commission (2004). *Guidelines on the Assessment of Horizontal Mergers Under the Council Regulation on the Control of Concentrations between Undertakings.*

European Commission (2005). "Commission Notice on Case Referral in Respect of Concentration", in *Official Journal of the European Union*, 2005/C 56/02.

European Commission (2010). *EU Competition Law: Rules Applicable to Merger Control, Situation as of April 1, 2010*, Brussels.

European Court of Justice (1973). *Judgement of the Court of 21 February, 1973: Europemballage Corporation and Continental Can Company Inc. v. Commission of the European Communities*, Case 6-72.

Gadas, R. *et al.* (2007). "Ryanair/Aer Lingus: Even 'Low-Cost' Monopolies Can Harm Consumers", in *Competition Policy Newsletter*, Vol. 70, No. 3, pp. 65-72.

Gudofsky, J.L. and P. Gay (2000). "Long Live the Merger Enforcement Guidelines? A Review of the Superior Propane Decision", in Canadian Competition Policy Record, Fall, pp. 46-84.

Kilgour, D.G. (1962). *Cases and Materials on Unfair and Restricted Trade Practices*. Toronto: University of Toronto Press.

Long, N.V. and N. Vousden (1995). "The Effects of Trade Liberalization on Cost-Reducing Horizontal Mergers", in *Review of International Economics*, Vol. 3, No. 2, pp. 141-155.

Marfels, C. and J. Sawler (2004). "The Case for Single-Jurisdictional Treatment of Transnational Mergers", in *Can. Comp. Rec.*, Vol. 22, No. 1, pp. 46-53.

Marfels, C. and J. Sawler (2009). "The Significance of EU Merger Policy to the Global Economy and the Persistence of the Criterion of Dominance", in *The EU in the Global Political Economy*, Finn Laursen (ed.). Brussels: P.I.E. Peter Lang, pp. 119-131.

Monopolkommission (1989). *Konzeption einer Europaeischen Fusionskontrolle*. Baden-Baden: Nomos.

Roller, L.H. and M. DeLa Mano (2006). "The Impact of the New Substantive Test in European Merger Control", in *European Competition Journal*, Vol. 2, No. 1, pp. 9-28.

Skeoch, A.P. and B. McDonald (1976), *Dynamic Change and Accountability in a Canadian Market Economy*. Ottawa: Queens Printer.

Townley, P. (1999). "Report, Exhibit A" (Expert affidavit submitted in *Commissioner of Competition v. Superior Propane Inc. and ICG Propane Inc.*), August.

West, D.S. (2004). *Modern Canadian Industrial Organization* (Supplement to Perloff, Carlton, *Modern Industrial Organization*, 2 e). New York: Harper Collins.

Weston, J.F. (2001). "Merger and Acquisitions as Adjustment Processes", in *Journal of Industry, Competition and Trade*, Vol. 1, No. 4, pp. 395-410.

The Role of the EU, the US, and China in Addressing Climate Change

Rafael LEAL-ARCAS

Introduction

Climate change is the most serious environmental threat to humankind (Richter 2001), the sustainability of the world's environment (Hardin 1968, p. 1243), the health and well-being of its people and the global economy. It is global, long-term, and accelerating, and in particular, will have a substantial impact on social, economic, and environmental systems and their interactions, and, thereby, on aspects of human security including water, food, and health. A valid, legal, and official definition of climate change appears in Article 1.2 of the United Nations Framework Convention on Climate Change (UNFCCC), which defines it as "a change of climate which is attributed directly or indirectly to human activity that alters the composition of the global atmosphere and which is in addition to natural climate variability observed over comparable time periods". The United Nations Development Program (UNDP) has characterized climate change as "the defining human development challenge for the 21st century" (UNDP, Human Development Report 2007/2008).

International law is not well-prepared to deal with these challenges. The Westphalian State system – dividing continents, regions, and the world into different territories and jurisdictions – is challenged by the fact that the global climate is an indivisible public good. Principles and tools of coexistence and co-operation in international law face the challenge of fragmentation and the need to bring about greater coherence in combating climate change. These are formidable challenges, and the international community is far from meeting them. Changing attitudes and more effective institutional designs are required to tackle the global sustainability challenges related to the use of our natural resources. Especially in the area of climate change, new legal foundations and linkages are called for.

The term "climate change" is sometimes used to refer to all forms of climatic inconsistency, but because the Earth's climate is never static, the term is more properly used to imply a significant change from one climatic condition to another. In some cases, climate change has been used synonymously with the term global warming;[1] scientists, however, tend to use the term in the wider sense to also include natural changes in climate. Calculations of climate change for specific areas are much less reliable than global ones, and it is unclear whether regional climate will become more variable (US Department of Transportation). Forests, deserts, rangelands, and other unmanaged ecosystems may face new climate stresses. As a result, many will decline or fragment, and individual species will be pushed to extinction (Moritz *et al.* 2008, p. 44; Ruhl 2009, p. 39). This projected change is larger than any climate change experienced during the last 10,000 years. It is based on current emissions[2] trends and assumes that no efforts are made to limit greenhouse gas (GHG) emissions.[3]

We are far from knowing the solution to climate change. The scientific community believes that global warming poses a crisis, and the longer we wait, the harder and more expensive it becomes to deal with climate change (Richter 2001; Edwards 2010; Stern Review). Although various steps have been taken to reach a solution, there are still many uncertainties about the scale and impacts of climate change (Global Commons Institute 2010; Spencer and Braswell 2011, p. 1603). Despite these uncertainties, climate change is a serious risk[4] worth combating through well-designed cost-effective policies (Stewart and Wiener 2003). Indeed, Sherwood Rowland, Nobel Prize winner for his research into the effects of chlorofluorocarbon gases on the ozone layer, asks: "What is the use of having developed a science well enough to make predictions if all we are willing to do is stand around and wait for them to come true?" (Brooks 2011). Furthermore, as the UK's climate envoy, John Ashton, put it, "We now need to stop talking about talking and

---

[1] Global warming is the progressive gradual rise of the Earth's surface temperature thought to be caused by the greenhouse effect and responsible for changes in global climate patterns. It is an increase in the near surface temperature of the Earth. Global warming has occurred in the distant past as the result of natural influences, but the term is most often used to refer to the warming predicted to occur as a result of increased emissions of greenhouse gases.

[2] Article 1.4 of the UNFCCC defines emissions as "the release of greenhouse gases and/or their precursors into the atmosphere over a specified area and period of time".

[3] Article 1.5 of the UNFCCC defines greenhouse gases as "those gaseous constituents of the atmosphere, both natural and anthropogenic, that absorb and re-emit infrared radiation". So greenhouse gas is any gas that absorbs infra-red radiation in the atmosphere. Greenhouse gases include water vapor, carbon dioxide (CO_2), methane (CH_4), nitrous oxide (N_2O), halogenated fluorocarbons (HCFCs), ozone (O_3), perfluorinated carbons (PFCs), and hydrofluorocarbons (HFCs).

[4] This raises the question of how much risk is socially acceptable.

start deciding about doing" (Reuters 2007). So the lack of evidence or uncertainty should not be a reason for inaction.

This chapter analyses the position of the three main players in climate change: China, the United States, and the European Union (EU). Although climate change is a truly global issue, for the purposes of this chapter only these three main players in the global climate change negotiations will be analysed. As shown in the chart below, they are the world's first, second, and third largest emitters of CO_2 respectively (Boden *et al.* 2007), and the EU has some of the strongest domestic support to address the climate change challenge. Each one of them is geographically and socially diverse, which is taken into account when analysing them.

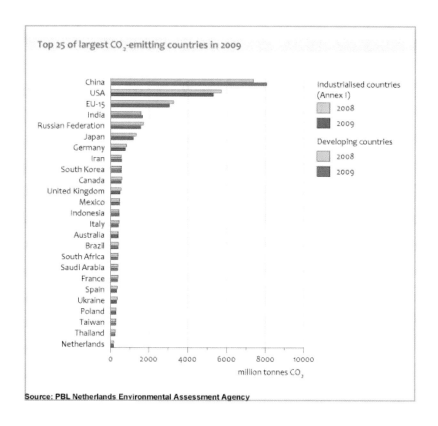

Source: PBL Netherlands Environmental Assessment Agency

US Position

Since 2007, the US has been the second largest source of GHG emissions, only behind China, and accounting for approximately 16 per cent of the world's total emissions as of 2006. However, per capita emissions remain extremely high in the US, with 18.376 tons of GHG emissions per year (OECD/IEA 2010) (compared to, for example, China with 4.916 tons of GHG emissions per year (OECD/IEA 2010)) as of 2008. The chart below illustrates the top CO_2-emitting countries and their per capita emissions as of 2004. One observes from the chart that per capita emissions in the US remain, by far, ahead of China's.

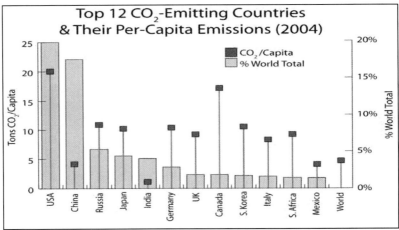

Source: World Resources Institute.

Concerning cumulative CO_2 emissions, the US remains responsible for 30 per cent during the period from 1900-2005 and the EU for 23 per cent, while China only counts for 8 per cent (OECD/IEA 2007). However, according to a high growth scenario during the period 2005-2030, the International Energy Agency predicts that the cumulative emissions for China since 1900 will be the same as those of the EU (OECD/IEA 2007). The map below shows that the US is one of the worst performers in the world based on its high CO_2 emissions from energy use.

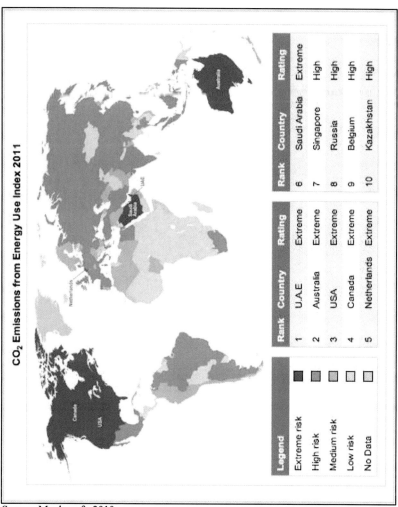

Source: Maplecroft, 2010.

The US uses fossil fuels inefficiently, in part because it has the lowest fuel taxes in the industrialized world, but also because its oil and coal industries are politically influential. One may also note that former US President G.W. Bush and Vice President Cheney are both former oil men, who still have close ties to oil-producing companies and regions (Reno 2000). President Obama, however, has proposed green energy tax incentives to encourage US businesses to upgrade their commercial buildings and make them more efficient (Kirchgaessner and Lemer 2011). As the chart shows, the main sources of energy in the US today are still oil, coal, and natural gas:

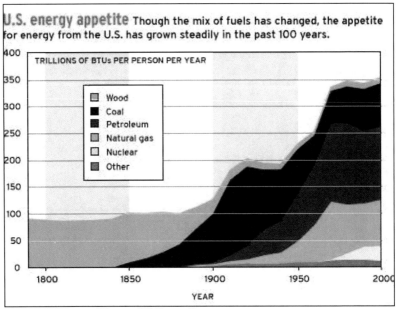

U.S. energy appetite Though the mix of fuels has changed, the appetite for energy from the U.S. has grown steadily in the past 100 years.

TRILLIONS OF BTUs PER PERSON PER YEAR

Legend:
- ☐ Wood
- ■ Coal
- ■ Petroleum
- ☐ Natural gas
- ☐ Nuclear
- ■ Other

YEAR

Sources: US Dept. of Energy, US Census Bureau.

Although former US President Clinton signed the Kyoto Protocol, former US President G.W. Bush publicly expressed scepticism, arguing that the Kyoto Agreement, as negotiated by the Clinton administration, represented a "lousy deal" (Forbes 2005) for the American people in general, and the US economy in particular, since the cost is too high. The G.W. Bush administration believed that the Kyoto Protocol would damage US industries. In fact, even if the G.W. Bush administration had made Kyoto its top priority (Ackerman 2007, p. 37), it would have needed perhaps quite some time to craft and adopt implementing legislation and win a difficult battle to ratify the treaty (Brewster 2010, p. 245). This means that the US government would have had only a few years before the Kyoto Protocol's limits on GHG emissions had taken full effect.

An interesting observation is that it was initially believed that if the US stayed on its present track, by the time we got to the period from 2008-2012, its GHG emissions would be perhaps 30 per cent higher than the 1990 levels. However, as can be seen in the chart below, the reality is that the US' actual CO_2 emissions for the period 1990-2008 was 14.9 to 15.3 per cent higher than the 1990 levels, therefore lower than the expectation in the early 2000s (OECD/IEA 2010). This, nevertheless, is far from reaching the mere 5 per cent-below-1990-levels target required by Kyoto.

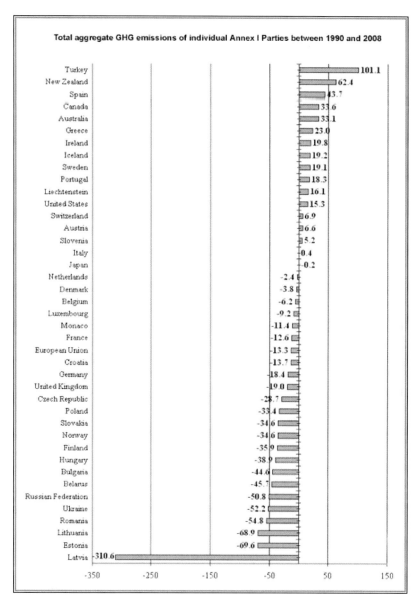

Total aggregate GHG emissions of individual Annex I Parties between 1990 and 2008

In a weekly policy meeting, former Vice President Cheney told a group of senators that the campaign pledge to control CO_2 was "a mistake", and that the administration was preparing a letter that would say CO_2 was not a pollutant (Office of the Press 2001).[5] G.W. Bush's opposition to climate control mechanisms and to the Kyoto Protocol was crystal clear in 2001:

As you know, I oppose the Kyoto Protocol because it exempts 80 percent of the world, including major population centers such as China and India, from compliance, and would cause serious harm to the US economy. The Senate's vote, 95-0, shows that there is a clear consensus that the Kyoto Protocol is an unfair and ineffective means of addressing global climate change concerns. As you also know, I support a comprehensive and balanced national energy policy that takes into account the importance of improving air quality. Consistent with this balanced approach, I intend to work with the Congress on a multi-pollutant strategy to require power plants to reduce emissions of sulfur dioxide, nitrogen oxides, and mercury. Any such strategy would include phasing in reductions over a reasonable period of time, providing regulatory certainty, and offering market-based incentives to help industry meet the targets. I do not believe, however, that the government should impose on power plants mandatory emissions reductions for carbon dioxide, which is not a "pollutant" under the Clean Air Act". (Office of the Press 2001)

In his opposition to the Kyoto Protocol, President G.W. Bush also referred to "the incomplete state of scientific knowledge of the causes of, and solutions to, global climate change" (Office of the Press 2001). In the US there has been vigorous debate on the reliability of climate change science, with some commentators accusing the Intergovernmental Panel on Climate Change (IPCC) of political bias. However, at the initiative of the Royal Society, a group of sixteen national academies of science from all parts of the world agreed to a statement in the US journal *Science*, saying that they recognized the IPCC as "the world's most reliable source of information on climate change" (The Royal Society 2001). In the same statement in *Science*, the academies criticized sceptics who question the need to mitigate climate change risks. "We do not consider such doubts justified", says the statement (The Royal Society 2001). The statement was signed by the scientific academies of Australia, Belgium, Brazil, Canada, the Caribbean, China, France, Germany, India, Indonesia, Ireland, Italy, Malaysia, New Zealand, Sweden, and the United Kingdom. Other members of the G.W. Bush administration have publicly shown their lack of interest in

---

[5] A letter dated 13 March 2001 from the US president to Senators Hagel, Helms, Craig, and Roberts in response to their letter of 6 March 2001, asking for the administration's views on global climate change, in particular the Kyoto Protocol, and efforts to regulate carbon dioxide under the Clean Air Act.

the Kyoto Treaty: "no, we have no interest in implementing that [Kyoto] treaty" (*Europe* 2001).[6]

In the 2000 presidential campaign, there was a division of position regarding the environment. Democrats believed that tackling global warming was not costly while Republicans believed it would be enormously costly. For example, the G.W. Bush administration argued that "in ruling out a plan to impose restrictions on power plants' emissions of carbon dioxide, [...] it is said such a step would be too costly to the economy and to American consumers" (Jehl 2001). Therefore, on the American side, there was a strong reluctance to impose rapid and severe cuts on energy consumption, especially by individual consumers (Anderson 2001, p. 11).

During the 2000 campaign, Bush showed some interest in the environment, but most likely only in order to gain votes. Once in office, Bush publicly mentioned that his campaign proposal had been in error, since CO_2 was not a "pollutant" according to the 1970 Clean Air Act (US Code 1990). He also referred to a December 2000 study by the Department of Energy, which, in his words, concluded that "caps on carbon dioxide emissions as part of a multiple emissions strategy would lead to an even more dramatic shift from coal to natural gas for electric power generation and significantly higher electricity prices" (Office of the Press 2001). These caps were a concern, he wrote, particularly in the West [of the US]: "At a time when California has already experienced energy shortages, and other Western states are worried about price and availability of energy this summer, we must be very careful not to take actions that could harm consumers" (Office of the Press). Yet, as Elizabeth Shogren of the *Los Angeles Times* immediately pointed out, California is "much less dependent on coal for power than most of the country" (Shogren 2001), with only about one-eighth of its power coming from coal-fired plants. Moreover, in a *New York Times* article published on 4 April 2001, it was noted that US administration officials had restated "a view that the 1997 treaty was unfair to the United States and that it was not worthy of American support" (Jehl 2001).

Arguments for Rejecting Kyoto

In 1997, the US Senate approved by a vote of 95-0 the Byrd-Hagel resolution (S. Res. 98, 105th Congress 1997), which urged the administration not to agree to a treaty that: (1) does not include developing countries (especially China) and (2) harms the US economy (Cohen

---

6 Christine Todd Whitman, administrator of the Environmental Protection Agency, discussing the US administration's decision to reject the Kyoto Treaty, in an interview.

2000, p. 10). Since according to the US Constitution, two-thirds of the US Senate (i.e., 67 votes) are needed for the ratification of a treaty (US Constitution), Kyoto's ratification by the US is far from becoming a reality. For years after the Byrd-Hagel resolution, President Clinton would frequently say, "Kyoto was the only bill I lost before I sent it to the Congress" (McGee and Taplin 2008, p. 19).

On what grounds did the US Senate argue, and continue to argue, the first point (i.e., not to agree to a climate change treaty that does not include developing countries)? (US Council of Economic Advisers 1998). According to the Netherlands Environmental Assessment Agency, since 2007, China has been the largest producer of CO_2 in the world (Netherlands Environmental Assessment Agency 2008). Since global warming is a long-term problem, China has to commit. Under the Kyoto Protocol, developing countries have no binding obligation, giving them a competitive advantage in marketing any product where energy costs are a key aspect to its manufacture (Pauwelyn 2007). The US Senate would ultimately reject any climate change treaty that does not include meaningful participation by developing countries (Strauss 2003).[7]

Since the 2009 COP-15 in Copenhagen resulted in an accord that resembles a pledge-and-review system, most observers now doubt that a framework built on emissions targets and timetables, as is the case of the Kyoto Protocol, is politically viable at all in the foreseeable future. A key issue is whether a pledge-and-review system suffices, at least for the time being. Will progress on the numbers (i.e., GHG emission rates or emission intensity) actually occur? If not, what other approach is feasible now or in the foreseeable future?

The climate change problem cannot be solved without developing country participation, but the industrialized countries have greater resources than most developing countries when it comes to tackling climate change. In the view of many people, as the biggest GHG polluters to date, the developed countries also have a moral obligation to act first. However, China is the major GHG emitting country since 2007, so its position as leader of a historically hurt G-77 is no longer credible.

As for the second point (i.e., not to agree to a climate change treaty that harms the US economy), the G.W. Bush administration argued that the overall cost of the Kyoto Protocol to the US economy would simply be too high. Moreover, West Virginia, among other states, opposed the

---

[7] Strauss argues that the recalcitrance of the US in global warming negotiations leads to the question of whether international litigation can viably contribute to encouraging the US to meet its global responsibilities regarding climate change. Strauss surveys and assesses the various potential international forums in which a climate change law suit might be brought against the US.

ratification of the Kyoto Protocol because West Virginia mainly produces coal. The same argument is used by Saudi Arabia and other Persian Gulf countries that are heavily reliant on the oil industry (Ebinger *et al.* 2011). Consumption of both coal and oil produces CO_2. Incidentally, Saudi Arabia is the only country to openly doubt the reality of human-caused climate change. Instead of ratification, G.W. Bush's national policy was to slightly slow the growth of GHG emissions by encouraging voluntary efficiency improvements by individuals and industries. It also supported subsidies and co-operative agreements for development of new low-carbon technologies. At other times, the G.W. Bush administration proposed adaptation as the only sensible climate policy. It is somewhat ironic that the Bush policy actually worked, not on its own, but because of the unanticipated steep rise in energy prices after 2001. The 2008 economic collapse further suppressed emissions.

Even under Barack Obama's administration, the US seems far from being committed to the Kyoto Protocol (Miller 2009). Although, at first, it seemed that the Obama administration was committed to, and displayed great enthusiasm for, the global negotiations on climate change (Lizza 2010), there is not much difference from G.W. Bush's administration (Thernstrom 2009). Political developments in the US have disillusioned this ambition. For example, congressional proposals for a domestic cap☐and☐trade regime for emissions limitations have failed (Larsen and Heilmayr 2009; Samaras *et al.* 2009; Luers *et al.* 2007). It is also interesting to note that, in May 1998, the Illinois General Assembly passed a bill condemning the Kyoto Protocol and forbidding state efforts to regulate greenhouse gases. The then state legislator Barack Obama voted for the bill (State of Illinois 1998). However, it was just a resolution, so even though it passed, it had no legal effect. The chart below shows the fact that climate change was not a top policy priority for the Obama administration in 2011:

Top Policy Priorities for 2011

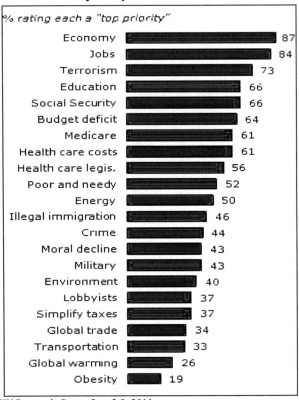

Source: PEW Research Center Jan. 5-9, 2011.

In fact, dealing with global warming as a top priority for the US president and Congress has been getting worse through the years since 2007, as the next chart clearly illustrates:

Public's Agenda for President and Congress 2001-2011

% considering each as a "top priority"	Jan 2001 %	Jan 2002 %	Jan 2003 %	Jan 2004 %	Jan 2005 %	Jan 2006 %	Jan 2007 %	Jan 2008 %	Jan 2009 %	Jan 2010 %	Jan 2011 %	10-11 change
Strengthening nation's economy	81	71	73	79	75	66	68	75	85	83	87	+4
Improving the job situation	60	67	62	67	60	65	57	61	62	81	84	+3
Defending against terrorism	--	83	81	78	75	80	80	74	76	80	73	-7
Improving education	78	66	62	71	70	67	69	66	61	65	66	+1
Securing Social Security	74	62	59	65	70	64	64	64	63	66	66	0
Reducing budget deficit	--	35	40	51	56	55	53	58	53	60	64	+4
Securing Medicare	71	55	56	62	67	62	63	60	60	63	61	-2
Reducing health care costs	--	--	--	--	--	--	68	69	59	57	61	+4
Revising health care legislation	--	--	--	--	--	--	--	--	--	--	56	--
Dealing with problems of the poor and needy	63	44	48	50	59	55	55	51	50	53	52	-1
Dealing with nation's energy problem	--	42	40	46	47	58	57	59	60	49	50	+1
Dealing with illegal immigration	--	--	--	--	--	--	55	51	41	40	46	+6
Reducing crime	76	53	47	53	53	62	62	54	46	49	44	-5
Dealing with moral breakdown in country	51	45	39	45	41	47	47	43	45	45	43	-2
Strengthening the military	48	52	48	48	52	42	46	42	44	49	43	-6
Protecting environment	63	44	39	49	49	57	57	56	41	44	40	-4
Reducing influence of lobbyists	--	--	--	--	--	--	35	39	36	36	37	+1
Simplifying tax system	--	--	--	--	39	40	--	--	--	--	37	--
Dealing with global trade	37	25	--	32	32	30	34	37	31	32	34	+2
Improving roads, bridges, and public transportation	--	--	--	--	--	--	--	--	--	--	33	--
Dealing with global warming	--	--	--	--	--	--	38	35	30	28	26	-2
Dealing w/ obesity	--	--	--	--	--	--	--	--	--	--	19	--

Source: PEW Research Center Jan 5-9, 2011. Q26.

To that can be added that, since 2008, Americans seem to be less worried about the threat of global warming, less convinced that its effects are already happening, and less sure that scientists themselves are certain about its occurrence (Newport 2010). Even some US policymakers deny that global warming is anthropogenic (CBS 2011).

If our aim is to move the world economy entirely away from fossil fuels, we would need to increase funding for research to find alternatives. Until we get there, we can gradually raise the efficiency of fossil-fuel consumption. The problem is that most of the technologies that use fossil fuels are long-lived (for example, the stock of automobiles has a lifetime of about two decades). This implies that even with clear policy signals to control emissions, manufacturers and consumers have only limited leverage over emissions in the short term. The US Climate Change Adaptation Task Force released an interagency report in October 2010 outlining recommendations to President Obama for how federal agency policies and programs can better prepare the US to respond to the impacts of climate change (White House Council on Environmental Quality 2010).

What Should the US Be Aiming at?

The US has long insisted that the most cost-effective way to reduce global emissions of greenhouse gases is through an international regime of emissions trading (Brewer 2010; Eizenstat 2009, p. 1). The Clinton administration had already said that it wanted explicit rules on international trading of emissions permits before ratifying the Kyoto Protocol, but the trading rules remain unclear (Anderson 2001, p. 11). Since Kyoto stipulates that emissions trading will be limited only to Annex I countries,[8] the US should try to renegotiate this limitation to expand it to trading emissions with developing countries.

The US (and other developed regions of the world, for this matter) should be willing to co-operate in technology transfer for the benefit of the environment globally (Stern and Antholis 2007-08, p. 175).[9] In fact, the US assumption during the Kyoto negotiations was that technology transfer from developed to developing countries could solve global warming and would also help the US have a greater market access to developing countries. As shown in the chart below, the contribution to GHG increase by 2025 coming from industrialized countries will be relatively modest, compared to that projected in developing countries. If we believe that in years to come, developing countries will be causing greater environmental damage than the developed world,[10] then this argument of environmental technology transfer makes perfect sense. While at a global level, it would be unfair to place the same burden on developing countries as on developed countries, developing countries must at least make a minimum of contribution.

---

[8] Annex I of the UNFCCC refers to developed countries and countries that are undergoing the process of transition to a market economy.

[9] The authors argue that the US will have no international credibility until it acts decisively domestically, and that the US should start seeing China as a partner on climate change.

[10] Indeed, since 2007, China is the largest emitter of CO_2 in the world. It is predicted that other major developing countries will increase their GHG emissions in the near future.

Projected Emissions of GHGs in 2025

Sources & Notes: Projections are based on US Energy Information Administration (EIA), 2003 (reference case, CO_2 from fossil fuels) and POLES (non-CO_2 gases) (EC, 2003). GHGs do not include CO_2 from land use change. 'FSU' is former Soviet Union.

Moreover, two steps need to be distinguished. First, US environmental policy is still hindered by the important economic consequences at stake. The US administration cannot ignore the economic interests linked to the soundness of the oil market, major firms rely on it, and a slowdown in their activity could hinder the US economic growth (Repetto 2001).[11] It makes it extremely difficult to pass an environmental bill through Congress. Second, the non-binding Copenhagen Accord, wished by the American president, acts as a compromise between flexibility ordered by the industry and the politically incorrect refusal of environmental policy changes.

On the domestic front, the Obama administration seems committed to implementing regulations on large GHG sources through its Clean Air Act authority (although how far it can go without causing a congressional backlash is unclear), and it has already tightened fuel economy standards across the motor vehicle fleet at the federal level. At the state and local level, greenhouse reduction plans are being implemented to cap or reduce emissions. In California, implementation of recent legislation to reduce GHG emissions from motor vehicles and other sources is providing a test case of the legal and political ability of states moving ahead without the federal government (California Global Warming

---

[11] In his book *America's Climate Problem*, Robert Repetto proposes a national policy for the US that can reduce GHG emissions and can bring about a transition to clean energy sources, while preserving healthy economic growth and high standards of living. Repetto addresses the controversial issue of fundraising as a root cause of the US Congress' failure to enact policies that set a price on carbon – even when the EU, Japan, Australia, New Zealand, several Canadian provinces, and even many US state governments have done so.

Solutions Act 2006). Success in California would provide some impetus to federal legislation (assuming costs of implementation are modest) as other states perhaps may do the same, and the industry may look to the US Congress for national uniformity. Previous examples of legislative success at the state level, which eventually turned into federal legislation, are urban air pollution, leading to the federal Clean Air Act of 1970, and acid rain, leading to the 1990 amendments.[12]

Several large companies such as General Electric and British Petroleum have made specific commitments over time to cut emissions in a way roughly consistent with the Kyoto obligations. Regarding the setting of emission caps, below is a sequence of decisions to be made: (1) determining a tolerable increase in temperatures; (2) calculating the CO_2 equivalent concentration in the atmosphere that leads to that increase; (3) calculating global emissions that lead to that CO_2 equivalent concentration; (4) dividing a global emissions budget among countries; and (5) dividing each country's emissions budget among sectors or otherwise controlling CO_2 emissions.

For the first time, in 2010, several large firms publicly endorsed an emission cap via the United States Climate Action Partnership.[13] One reason was their anticipation of ultimate CO_2 regulation and the competitive advantage that may reside in making appropriate investment decisions well in advance. Another was the opportunity to co-ordinate international operations because some companies will come under Kyoto's strictures through their foreign operations and will be participating in Kyoto's emissions trading market. A third reason was green image-making with the public. These motivations remain in place.

Consequences of the US Position for Foreign Affairs

The current situation is making the transatlantic relationship difficult. The issue of climate change has become a foreign policy problem for the US (Campbell *et al.* 2007). The G.W. Bush administration gradually understood that "this is about international relations as well, and other countries are reacting very strongly against the US" (Anderson 2001, p. 11).

---

[12] Section 812 of the 1990 Clean Air Act Amendments requires the US Environmental Protection Agency to develop periodic reports that estimate the benefits and costs of the Clean Air Act.

[13] The United States Climate Action Partnership (USCAP) is a group of business and leading environmental organizations that have come together to call on the federal government to quickly enact strong national legislation to require significant reductions of greenhouse gas emissions". For further information, see http://www.us-cap.org/.

Chinese Position

Climate change will have a significant impact on China (Gang *et al.* 2011). Conversely, China's impact on climate change is considerable. The size and rate of growth of China's economy, of its energy demand, of its energy imports, and of its atmospheric emissions of various types make this country an essential major partner in any regional or global discussions relating to climate change or the production and consumption of energy (Hallding and Olsson 2010). For example, China's coal-powered economic engine is overwhelming. In 2005, China produced 35 per cent of the world's steel, compared to just 13 per cent in 1996 (Economy 2007). A business-as-usual situation is not conducive to sustainable development neither at the national nor at the international level. If China continues on its business-as-usual path, predictions are that by 2030 its emissions will grow twice as fast as emissions from all the 30-member Organization for Economic Cooperation and Development (Brahic 2007). At the same time, as a Chinese vice minister of the State Environmental Protection Administration put it, China's economic "miracle will end soon because the environment can no longer keep pace" (Byrnes 2006).

China, a natural leader among developing countries, puts forward its counter-argument to the US position, that even if it is the largest producer of GHG emissions in cumulative terms since 2007 (Brahic 2007), its per capita GHG emissions were only about 25 per cent of US levels as of 2006. (See chart below regarding per capita CO_2 emissions.) Notwithstanding this, China recently questioned statistics published by the International Energy Agency, which is especially shocking given the unreliability of many of the statistical indicators published by the Chinese government (Yale Environment 360 2010).

China's position, therefore, is that global climate change must be addressed principally by wealthy industrial nations, which have not only the wealth and technology to provide solutions, but also the moral responsibility to do so because they have produced perhaps as much as 80 per cent of the GHG emissions to date (Netherlands Environmental Assessment Agency 2006), as shown in the chart below. China's refusal to agree to an internationally binding emissions target is commonly cited in the United States as an argument against US legislative action.

Per capital CO$_2$ emissions, 1980-2004

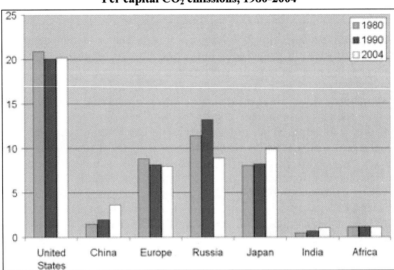

Source: Mongabay.com.

If the Kyoto commitment is not enough to solve the problem, developed countries should do more about GHG emission reductions before they ask developing nations for commitment. Large developing countries – such as China, India, and Brazil – will not commit internationally to material reductions in their emissions in the absence of some comparable commitment by, say, the US. Conversely, the US has not participated in the Kyoto Protocol and will not agree to mandatory emission reductions targets because of concerns about a loss of competitive advantage, relative to developing countries that are not subject to the same obligations.

This is a circular argument, bringing to mind the age-old question: What comes first, the chicken or the egg? The US is not willing to ratify an international multilateral environmental agreement on GHG emission reduction unless and until developing countries (especially China) are on board. On the other hand, China will only agree to being on board if the US complies with the Kyoto Protocol first.[14] As can be seen in the

---

[14] A large part of the relevant legal literature suggests that the main polluting nations can be held responsible under international law for the harmful effects of their greenhouse-gas emissions. As a result, affected countries may have a substantive right to demand the cessation of a certain amount of emissions. In some cases, they also have the procedural means to pursue intergovernmental litigation in an international judicial forum such as the International Court of Justice. Developing countries are understandably reluctant to challenge any of the big donor nations in an international court.

chart below, the Chinese argument seems pertinent in view of the projected per capita CO_2 emissions for major emitters by 2030:

Per capital CO_2 emissions for selected major Emitters

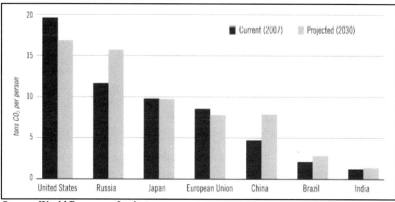

Source: World Resources Institute.

Regardless of what the US Congress does or does not legislate in climate change issues, with EU emissions probably having peaked and US emissions possibly having done so as well, at least for the foreseeable future, the fate of Article 2 of the UNFCCC[15] more and more resides in the actions of China, Brazil, India, and the other large developing country emitters. Conceivably, the US would eventually accept a Kyoto-like approach if means could be found to involve developing countries with specific obligations. However, the politics of negotiating subsequent steps and a long-term target for GHG emission reduction are full of difficulty as was obvious at the 2009 COP-15 in Copenhagen, where the US and the EU accused China of forcefully obstructing progress in the climate change negotiations (Helm and Hepburn 2009).

One wonders why China is so vehemently opposed to legally binding commitments under a strong multilateral climate regime and to international checks to verify that it is on track to slow down GHG

---

[15] Article 2 of the UNFCCC stipulates that:
The ultimate objective of this Convention and any related legal instruments that the Conference of the Parties may adopt is to achieve, in accordance with the relevant provisions of the Convention, stabilization of greenhouse gas concentrations in the atmosphere at a level that would prevent dangerous anthropogenic interference with the climate system. Such a level should be achieved within a time-frame sufficient to allow ecosystems to adapt naturally to climate change, to ensure that food production is not threatened and to enable economic development to proceed in a sustainable manner.

emissions. Not only are developing countries unlikely to assume binding obligations until industrialized countries have actually met some initial targets, but their potential assumption of obligations would raise the difficult question of equity (Ott *et al.* 2004). With per capita CO_2 emissions from fossil fuels in the US about four times those of China and twenty times those of India, questions of equity loom large when long-term limits are considered. Moreover, Article 3.1 of the UNFCCC expressly states:

> The Parties should protect the climate system for the benefit of present and future generations of humankind, on the basis of equity and in accordance with their *common* but differentiated responsibilities and respective capabilities. Accordingly, the *developed country Parties should take the lead* in combating climate change and the adverse effects thereof.[16]

Contributions to global warming

Source: World Resources Institute.

---

[16] Emphasis added.

This clearly means that all countries share responsibilities, although at different levels. Nevertheless, limited progress on this issue has occurred. Starting with the COP-13 in Bali in 2007 and culminating at the 2010 COP-16 in Cancun, developing countries enthusiastically embraced a plan for voluntary accession to limits and reduction crediting in the forest sector (dubbed Reducing Emissions from Deforestation and forest Degradation [REDD] program), predicated, however, on financial support from developed countries. On the financial aspect, the UNFCCC reminds us that "[p]olicies and measures to deal with climate change should be cost-effective so as to ensure global benefits at the lowest possible cost".[17]

At the same time, developing countries are watching this environmental negotiating process to ensure that it helps them cope with climate change without threatening their hopes of economic growth (Anderson 2001, p. 11), which is a right that every country has, albeit hope is green economic growth (Balme 2011, p. 44).[18] Officials are beginning to consider the possibility that a world climate change agreement might not be merely a crude attempt to cut off their economic growth, but rather a possible source of help in dealing with the air pollution that is emerging as a major threat to public health (Anderson 2001, p. 11). For instance, the health costs of air and water pollution in China account for an estimated 4.3 per cent of the nation's GDP (World Bank and State Environmental Protection Administration of the People's Republic of China 2007). Moreover, sixteen of the world's twenty most polluted cities are in China. Pollution in Beijing is six times higher than in New York City (Economy 2007). The ideal situation would be to have developing nations on board and the US Senate ratify the Kyoto Protocol. This is currently unrealistic. We need to find a compromise.

Rich countries generally favour the creation of a new climate pact to succeed the Kyoto Protocol, placing more responsibility on key developing country emitters such as China and India, whereas developing countries continue to favour an approach that would implement a second phase of the Kyoto Protocol, which allows them to opt out of emissions reductions if these pose a threat to development (International Centre for Trade and Sustainable Development 2010). In fact, the Chinese authorities have emphasized that the key to success in climate negotiations lies in commitments by rich countries to slash emissions and boost funding to developing countries in the form of aid and the

---

[17] Article 3.3 of the UNFCCC.

[18] Balme argues that without further significant changes in the structure of the political economy of developed countries, China will neither want, nor be able, to bring about any rapid change in its development path.

promotion of clean technology (International Centre for Trade and Sustainable Development 2010). China has concerns about emissions commitments because it expects GHG emissions levels to continue rising for some time. In fact, during the past decade, China's GHG emissions have more than doubled (International Centre for Trade and Sustainable Development 2010). This means that the EU's proposal to raise the bloc's target for cutting CO_2 emissions would have a limited impact on global warming, given that any benefit would be easily offset by China's rise in GHG emissions (Gallagher 2007, p. 389).

However, since the 2010 COP-16 in Cancun, China's attitude to combat climate change has been remarkable, by taking increasingly strong action to improve its energy efficiency, at both the national and subnational level. For example, China has set a 2020 carbon intensity target as part of its national policy and is taking aggressive steps to implement it (Watson *et al.* 2011). Moreover, China has prepared a five-year plan (2011-2015) that is the clearest indication of its determination to become a clean-energy powerhouse (Fulton 2011). This five-year plan puts emphasis on economic and industrial restructuring towards a greener, more efficient, and lower carbon economy (Gang *et al.* 2011). As part of this five-year plan, China is also developing regional domestic carbon trading programs and is also experimenting with emissions taxes.

There are both environmental and economic advantages and disadvantages to energy efficiency. Regarding the advantages, energy efficiency not only implies no GHGs, it saves money, it cannot be exported off-shore, and it has more potential than any other alternative. However, the disadvantages are that one must pay upfront as an investment, the oil industry wants more consumers to spend more energy, and there are tax incentives for energy use.

Climate change is one of the key drivers for China's fundamental shift. Investment in clean energy in China rose 30 per cent in 2010, to US $51.1 billion – by far the largest figure for a single country – and represented more than 20 per cent of the total global investment of US $243 billion, according to Bloomberg New Energy Finance (Kanter 2011). China's climate policy is largely motivated by factors other than concern about global warming, including energy security, the need to reduce local and regional atmospheric pollution from coal combustion that has caused serious health problems [see chart below for China's share of global coal consumption, which has steadily increased since 1965, to reach almost 50 per cent by 2009], and international competitiveness.[19] It has pushed development of renewable energy technology to become the market leader in production of wind and solar technology and adopted aggressive fuel economy standards for motor vehicles.

China % share of global coal consumption

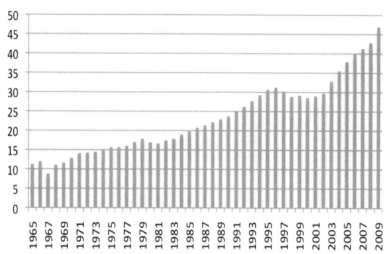

Source: Business Insider.

However, China has been, and would like to continue as, the *de facto* leader of the G-77 group of developing countries, which is the UNFCCC/Kyoto Protocol negotiating bloc for most developing countries. Accordingly, it would prefer not to take steps that would alienate other developing countries and jeopardize its role unless there are very large compensating economic or other gains to be had. At the same time, China is also a member of the BRIC group (Brazil, Russia, India, China, and South Africa) to co-ordinate climate and energy policies. Furthermore, China's interests, like those of Brazil and a few other developing countries, no longer align with the G-77 very well since some of these major developing countries are among the largest GHG polluters in the world today. Moreover, China is not only the largest GHG emitter, but the leading producer of wind turbines and solar panels. How will this aggressive move into renewable energy markets affect its climate positioning *versus* other countries?

---

[19] In 2011, China's environment minister issued an unusually stark warning about the effects of unbridled development on China's air and soil, arguing that the nation's current path could stifle long-term economic growth and feed social instability. See Jacobs, A. "China Issues Warning on Climate and Growth", *The New York Times*, 28 February 2011.

European Union Position

The European Union has long held a leadership position on climate change and has some of the strongest domestic support to address climate change (Oberthür and Pallemaerts 2010). Moreover, the EU has been a firm supporter of the Kyoto Agreement (Droege 2009, p. 2), and it has been among the foreign voices to react to former President G.W. Bush's decision to abandon the treaty. Its objective (and that of its then fifteen Member States) was to ratify Kyoto and have it in force by 2002 at the latest, which only happened in 2005 (Delegation of the European Commission to the US 2001, p. 14). In an encounter between officials of the EU and the US in Washington in early April 2001, European officials clearly said they were going to continue with the Kyoto process, even if the US was absent. In fact, some Europeans saw the COP-6 at The Hague as an opportunity for European governments to show leadership and initiative (Anderson 2001, p. 11). Among Europeans, there is a profound mistrust of the market mechanisms that the Americans propose in order to reduce the cost and impact of reductions (Anderson 2001, p. 11). On the other hand, the American view is that the European intransigence of asking parties to the Kyoto Protocol to accept Kyoto's commitments as they stand has killed the Kyoto Protocol because the current situation is unacceptable to the US. Europeans want a legally binding climate agreement with the US on board.

In response to former President G.W. Bush's decision to avoid his responsibility *vis-à-vis* the environment, former European Commission President Romano Prodi said to *La Repubblica* newspaper that "if one wants to be a world leader, one must know how to look after the entire Earth and not only American industry" (BBC News 2001).

Furthermore, Margot Wallström, former European commissioner for the environment, reacting to a statement from the US administration on their rejection of the Kyoto Protocol, said: "The US position is extremely worrying. The US must understand that this is not a marginal issue for the EU. It has implications for external relations including trade and economic affairs, and it cannot be played down" (Delegation of the European Union to Canada 2001). Kjell Larsson, Sweden's former environment minister, said in a statement following meetings with US administration officials on Kyoto: "Climate change is happening now and is a serious threat to the future of mankind. We are prepared if necessary to go forward without the US. We cannot allow one country to declare as dead the process for addressing this major global issue. However, we still hope to have the United States involved in the protocol as soon as possible" (*Europe* 2001). Also Gerhard Schröder, former chancellor of Germany, reacting to the US administration's decision to reject Kyoto, said, "Nobody should be relieved from his responsibility for climate control" (*Europe* 2001).

EU Emissions Cuts

Some people argue that in the EU there is much talk but little action concerning Kyoto. Even from a more technical view point, European finance and trade ministers are unlikely to let environmental ministers impose costly limits on emissions unless the US is also on board.

However, according to the UNFCCC, big EU economies such as the UK and Germany spewed smaller amounts of GHG into the atmosphere in 2008 than they did in 1990. Some of the biggest reductions of GHG emissions between 1990 and 2008 took place in former Soviet countries such as Ukraine, partly because their industries were very polluting before 1990. Moreover, a new report by the European Environment Agency (EEA) based on GHG emission data for 2008-2009 shows that a large drop in emissions during 2008 and 2009 gives the EU-15 a head start to reach and even overachieve its 8 per cent reduction target under the Kyoto Protocol (European Environment Agency 2010, p. 30). The EEA report also shows that the EU-27 is well on track towards achieving its 20 per cent reduction target by 2020 (European Environment Agency 2010, p. 30). Moreover, a report from the European Commission to the European Parliament and the EU Council shows the actual progress and determination in the EU to reduce emissions towards meeting the Kyoto target (European Commission 2010).

More recently, the EU has been arguing that emissions reduction is good for European business, thereby moving away from traditional reasons for deeper cuts in GHG emissions such as moral responsibility and survival of humankind (Chaffin 2010). Furthermore, a 2011 analysis by the European Commission shows

> That domestic emission reductions of the order of 40% and 60% below 1990 levels would be the cost-effective pathway by 2030 and 2040, respectively. In this context, it also shows reductions of 25% in 2020. This is illustrated in [the chart below]. Such a pathway would result in annual reductions compared to 1990 of roughly 1% in the first decade until 2020, 1.5% in the second decade from 2020 until 2030, and 2% in the last two decades until 2050. The effort would become greater over time as a wider set of cost-effective technologies becomes available. (European Commission 2011, p. 4)[20]

This means that GHG emissions would be reduced by a further 5 per cent.

---

[20] In a communication to the European Parliament, the Council, the European Economic and Social Committee and the Committee of the Regions.

EU GHG emissions towards an 80 per cent domestic reduction
(100%=1990)

Source: European Commission.

However, the only sector where the EU's GHG emissions continue to rise is in the transport sector. This may complicate the EU's target to reduce its GHG emissions between 80 per cent and 95 per cent by 2050 compared to the 1990 levels (Egenhofer 2011), since transport is one of the largest energy-consuming sectors in the EU, accounting for one-third of EU energy consumption. The chart below shows the projection of GHG emissions growth in the EU should things remain business as usual.

Projected EU GHG Emissions Growth:
Transport versus Non-Transport Sector

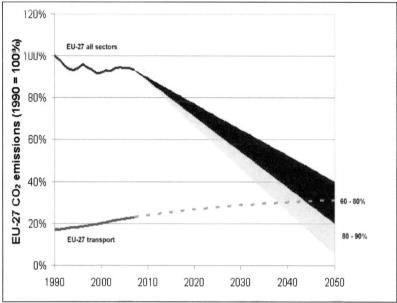

Source: European Commission.

EU Emissions Trading Scheme

The setup of transnational mitigation regimes is a challenging undertaking as is illustrated by the European Union's Emission Trading Scheme (EU ETS). The EU ETS[21] is the world's most important GHG emissions trading scheme (Pohlmann 2009, p. 337), with an estimated value of euro 63 billion of the overall euro 86 billion value of the global carbon market in 2008 (Capoor and Ambrosi 2009, p. 1). It is also the world's first mandatory cap-and-trade program for CO_2 emissions (Ellerman 2008), albeit the GHG emission caps remain too high (Egenhofer *et al.* 2011). Operational since 2005, the ETS's goal is to cut emissions by one-fifth from 1990 levels by 2020 (Cames 2011). It is the flagship policy covering half of the EU's carbon emissions,[22] and could turn intended restrictions on pollution into a trap that commits the EU to

---

[21] Directive 2003/87/EC, in force since 25 October 2003.

[22] On 20 December 2010, EU environment ministers agreed to bring Switzerland into the EU's ETS. The ETS already includes other non-EU European countries such as Norway, Liechtenstein, and Iceland. See EurActiv, "Switzerland moves to join Europe's carbon market". Available at: <http://bit.ly/ha7Mvu>.

247

increasing carbon emissions for much of the next decade, unless changes are swiftly introduced (Sandbag 2010).

A growing number of countries such as the United States, New Zealand, Australia, Canada, and Japan are integrating cap-and-trade schemes into their national climate policies. The EU ETS is the frontrunner in this development. The main features of the EU ETS are: (1) It is a classic cap-and-trade system with a highly decentralized implementation mechanism; (2) it is set up in sequential multiyear periods with a declining cap: Phase 1 was 2005-2007, phase 2 is 2008-2012, and phase 3 is 2013-2020; (Enzmann and Marr 2008); (3) offset is allowed up to 13 per cent of GHG emissions; and (4) there is a system of free allocation of emissions evolving to full auctioning (Weishaar 2008).

In the context of emissions trading, free allocation of emissions credits to energy-intensive industries has been considered a means to prevent "carbon leakage" to less regulated markets. Free allocation of emissions allowances may potentially have trade-related ramifications, with respect to the WTO and the Agreement on Subsidies and Countervailing Measures (SCM Agreement). New market mechanisms are set in place to allow developing countries to foster products with a low carbon footprint. The issuance of emission credits to host governments may be interpreted as unlawful subsidies under the SCM Agreement.

Among the achievements of the EU ETS are: (1) the pricing of carbon emission credits (CECs), the unutilized part of an emitter's allowance within a trading period that an emitter is permitted to trade within the EU ETS. Under the EU ETS, all emissions by European Economic Area (EEA) emitters must be covered by CECs. Where an EEA emitter has exhausted its allowance, it is required to purchase CECs, the price of which is set by the market in CECs according to demand and supply. As a consequence of the pricing of CECs, the cost of CECs is likely to discourage excessive GHG emissions. Furthermore, there was modest reduction in GHG emissions during 2008;[23] and (2) there is a mechanism in place for effecting further GHG emissions reductions as desired.

The European Commission sees the EU ETS as a blueprint for emerging schemes around the world and the nucleus for creating a global carbon market. It aims to establish full bilateral links to other ETS on the condition that these schemes are mandatory, are based on absolute caps, and do not contain price ceilings for GHG emission allowances. This vision includes achieving an OECD-wide carbon

---

[23] <http://europa.eu/rapid/pressReleasesAction.do?reference=IP/09/794>.

market by 2015 as well as the establishment and integration of trading systems in major emerging economies by 2020.

The principal regulatory techniques to reduce carbon emissions are regulating technology, regulating the quantity of GHG emissions, regulating the price for GHG emissions (Ellerman 2010), and regulating information (Chenevière and Nihoul 2009, p. 125).

Both the Fourth Assessment Report by the IPCC and the Stern Review on the Economics of Climate Change make clear the point that a price for GHG emissions is one of the most effective ways to mitigate climate change (Pachauri and Reisinger 2007, p. 18). The ETS is on course to require savings of, at best, a miniscule quantity of 32 million tons of emissions between 2008 and 2012, despite covering 12,000 installations and 1.9 billion tons of emissions annually.[24] Regulating a single power station during the same period could have had a greater impact.[25] An already weak cap for this period became a severe over-allocation of pollution permits when the 2008 economic recession caused a sharp drop in production and, therefore, carbon emissions (Ellerman 2007). These lower emissions, far from helping the EU towards a low carbon future, may actually trap it into continued high carbon economy because the ETS allows the huge volume of unused permits to be carried over into the next phase of the scheme that runs from 2013 to 2020. These permits would then be available for companies as the economy picks up again from the 2008 economic recession, removing a key driver for investment in low carbon options. The ETS in its current form, although a very powerful and effective policy in principle, is in danger of actually hindering a low carbon economy for years to come.[26]

---

[24] This estimated figure of 32 million tons saving during five years (2008-2012) assumes a rapid European economic recovery (to 2008 levels by 2011). This means that even if the economy recovers quickly from the 2008 financial crisis, caps will only be 32 million tons lower than the actual emissions in that period. A slower recovery would mean that the caps stayed above the carbon emissions, providing no constraint on emissions.

[25] Drax power station in the UK is estimated to have a cap on emissions 60 metric tons below its emissions in Phase 2. Caps like those given to Drax add up to an overall cap for large power installations that would have led to 1.1 billion expected savings, a genuine cap on pollution that could have driven emissions reductions and clean energy investment. However, this has been all but cancelled out by extravagant free allocations to heavy industry such as iron and steel, creating a billion more permits than are needed to cover their emissions.

[26] The volume of surplus permits in the trading scheme is now so high that the EU could increase emissions until as late as 2016 when they could reach almost a third higher than 2010 levels.

There are a few ways to solve the ETS and avoid the carbon trap (Ellerman and Joskow 2008). These involve compensating for the fact that too many permits have been put into the system, and include the following points:

1. Increasing the EU carbon reduction target from 20 per cent to 30 per cent by 2020. The EU has already achieved half the existing target, and a higher target would protect momentum towards low carbon future (Skea *et al.* 2010);

2. Setting caps for the next trading phase (2013-2020) based upon actual emissions and not on the permits allocated, which were too many (Reyes 2011). This would require holding back 1.4 billion tons of permits from the scheme from the start, whilst a political decision is reached to cancel the permits permanently. This decision must be reached as quickly as possible;

3. Amending the rules of the ETS (through a change in the directive)[27] to allow flexibility to respond to large drops in demand such as those caused by the 2008 economic recession, in order to prevent an inundation of permits undermining carbon savings.

These measures face some stiff resistance. While too many permits have been handed out overall, this was not done evenly across those companies covered by the scheme. Some companies received a cap lower than their emissions, but others higher. A few of the latter received an enormous over-allocation of permits, making millions from their sale. These are the "carbon fat cats", led by steel conglomerate ArcelorMittal, and a number of them are lobbying hard to keep the ETS broken.[28] If the international community manages to lower GHG emissions coming from the steel sector, climate change would largely be under control.

Millions of EU citizens are working hard to reduce their carbon emissions, saving a ton here, half a ton there. The ETS covers 1.9 billion tons annually, including those from electricity production (European Commission 2011). To allow the ETS to fail, providing miniscule carbon savings and allowing some "carbon fat cats" to make huge

---

[27] Directive 2003/87/EC of the European Parliament and of the Council of 13 October 2003 establishing a scheme for GHG emission allowance trading within the Community and amending Council Directive 96/61/EU, OJ L275, 25 October 2003; this directive has been amended most recently by Directive 2009/29/EC, so as to improve and extend the GHG emission allowance trading scheme of the Community, OJ L140/63, 5 June 2009.

[28] The surplus permits held by the top ten "carbon fat cats" in 2009 nearly quadrupled, growing from 33 million permits to 119 million. These would currently be worth roughly €1.7 billion if sold on the carbon market. ArcelorMittal is likely to accrue 102 million more permits than it needs.

profits through over-allocated permits would be a travesty (Holwerda 2010, p. 228).

Moreover, since the international negotiations for the creation of a global climate change agreement did not reach a conclusion in Copenhagen in 2009, the provisions of the Emissions Trading Directive on bilateral agreements have become more relevant than ever. International credits from projects or other emission-reducing activities in a third country are eligible for use in the EU ETS only if an agreement has been concluded between the EU and the respective third country.[29] Furthermore, the Emissions Trading Directive also stipulates that once an international agreement on climate change has been reached, from 2013 onwards, international credits are disqualified from use within the EU ETS if these credits are generated from projects from third countries that have not ratified the said agreement.[30]

The directive mentioned above establishing the EU ETS explicitly empowers the European Commission to negotiate linking agreements with Annex B countries that have ratified the Kyoto Protocol.[31] For the period beyond 2012, an amendment is foreseen that allows linking agreements to provide for the recognition of emission allowances between the EU ETS and mandatory GHGs trading systems with absolute emissions caps of any other country or regional entity.

EU law does not indicate whether the adoption of linking agreements should be accompanied by the establishment of new institutions entrusted with the regulation and supervision of linked carbon markets. Once the linking arrangement enters into force, disputes and irregularities may indeed arise across the link between participants in each emissions trading scheme, thereby necessitating adequate dispute settlement mechanisms and also raising the question of accountability by both participants and any institution or officials supervising the link's operation. As the implementation of the Kyoto Protocol's Clean Development Mechanism shows, these problems, if addressed insufficiently, raise important legitimacy concerns.

The carbon market is still largely unregulated, presenting opportunities for unscrupulous traders to trick customers. As the first phase of the EU ETS demonstrated, even where a supranational body acts in a supervisory function, widespread manipulation of the system can take

---

[29] Directive 2009/29/EC of 23 April 2009, amending Directive 2003/87/EC, Article 11a (5).

[30] Directive 2009/29/EC of 23 April 2009, amending Directive 2003/87/EC, Article 11a (7).

[31] Directive 2003/87/EC, para. 17.

place.[32] While the carbon market is seeing explosive growth, particularly in the EU, such growth will not be boundless, particularly if the market is perceived as ineffective in reducing actual emissions. In order for the carbon market to achieve long-term, sustainable success, it must be regulated, and where the right to increase emissions is being traded across international borders, the potential for affecting trade is heightened.

It is vital to assess what kind of institutions would be needed to supervise linked carbon markets and facilitate a smooth transition to a globally integrated carbon market. When exploring options for the improved governance of an integrated carbon market, the question of what could be learned from the trade field comes up. The international trading system, which started with bilateral free trade agreements, evolved into a comprehensive multilateral regime (i.e., the GATT) and finally resulted in the creation of a powerful new organization, the WTO (Leal-Arcas 2010; Leal-Arcas 2011a; Leal-Arcas 2011b).

Conclusions

Ideally, the conclusion of an effective and comprehensive global climate change agreement should be a priority, given that climate change is a global problem. Yet, the division in the UNFCCC between Annex I and non-Annex I countries has proven very resistant to evolution. If the international community wishes to continue with the current top-down architecture for international climate policy (UNFCCC/Kyoto Protocol), it would need to eliminate the UNFCCC's Annex I and provide an additional ingredient: a burden-sharing element, designed to produce a fair distribution of burdens across countries (beyond Annex I countries), while also giving priority to green economic development, addressing concerns about wealth inequality, and achieving emissions reductions consistent with limiting the expected increase in global average temperature to 2 degrees Celsius, without sacrificing economic growth.

However, there is no need to have a global solution/universal agreement to this global problem so long as the major GHG emitters reduce their emissions locally. In other words, if China's (or any other major emitter's) GHG emissions decrease, it will benefit the rest of the world, whereas if China's (or any other major emitter's) GHG emissions increase, it will affect the rest of the world. A local solution can, there-

---

[32] Regulation No. 2216/2004 for a standardized and secured system of registries pursuant to Directive 2003/87/EC was amended in July 2007 by Regulation No. 916/2007 to address problems regarding the registration of emissions under the EU ETS.

fore, have a global effect. So from an economic and environmental point of view, it is vital that China bring down its GHG emissions.

Pragmatism should be the crucial element in moving the climate agenda forward: plurilateral agreements instead of a universal climate agreement, flexibility instead of rigidity, and practical results instead of utopian ideals. Today, the UNFCCC is one actor among many in climate governance. Ideally, the international community should preserve the successes of the global regime and move on regionally or with coalitions of the willing. In the absence of such a global, universal agreement on climate change, it would make sense to explore, along with the current legal platform of UNFCCC/Kyoto Protocol, the "clubs approach" – such as the Major Economies Forum on Energy and Climate (MEF), the G-3, or the G-20 – given that the atmosphere does not care where emissions come from because GHG emissions mix globally in the atmosphere. This means that it does not matter where GHG emissions reduction takes place.

Regarding ways to move the climate change agenda forward, it is well known that equitable and efficient international co-operation is very difficult at the multilateral level. The geometries of power have fundamentally changed with the rising power of China and India. There is increasing international pressure on developing countries to reduce their GHG emissions. No breakthroughs will take place regarding a global climate change agreement until there is more political maturity and commitment on the side of the US regarding climate change and until rapidly emerging economies such as China and India indicate that they are ready to play their part in tackling climate change since they are part of the solution. Large emitters of GHG need to be involved for negotiations to come to a conclusion. Much progress is still needed until we reach an international agreement that covers all the world's countries and that is strong enough to tackle climate change effectively and equitable enough to gain the sympathy of all countries.

So long as the major GHG emitters are reducing their GHG emissions, not having the full UNFCCC membership on board does not really matter, given that the contribution to climate change by non-major emitters of GHGs is minimal. Every country in the world will benefit even in the case where only major GHG emitters reduce their emissions. *A sensu contrario*, the whole world will suffer if major GHG emitters increase their emissions as climate change is a global problem.

Moreover, the fact that perhaps only a club of major emitting countries may move the climate change agenda forward plurilaterally to limit GHG emissions – instead of the entire UNFCCC membership – is not as problematic as would be the case in the multilateral trading system, where issues of violation of the WTO law principle of non-discrimination would arise. Unlike the case of multilateral trade agreements, in the climate field, it may be preferable to have a minilateral climate change agreement (through clubs or coalitions of the willing) than no agreement at all, if that means making sure that the Earth's rising temperature is being addressed. There are clear costs and risks to not reaching a climate change agreement. Therefore, in the absence of a global climate change agreement, proceeding without the entire UNFCCC membership as the second best option appears to be a wise option.[33]

References

Ackerman, S. (2007). "What Are Lobbyists Saying on Capitol Hill? Climate Change Legislation as a Case Study for Reform", in *Envtl. L.*, 37, p. 137.

Anderson, J.W. (2001). "Climate Change Diplomacy: The Next Step", in *Resources*, Winter, No. 142, pp. 11-13.

Balme, R. (2011). "China's Climate Change Policy: Governing at the Core of Globalization", in *Carbon & Climate Law Review*, Vol. 5, No. 1, pp. 44-56.

BBC News (2001). "Europe Backs Kyoto Accord", 31 March. <http://news.bbc.co.uk/1/hi/world/europe/1252556.stm>.

Boden *et al.* (2007). "Ranking of the world's countries by 2007 total CO_2 emissions from fossil-fuel burning, cement production, and gas flaring", Carbon Dioxide Information Analysis Center, Oak Ridge National Laboratory. <http://cdiac.ornl.gov/trends/emis/top2007.tot>.

Brahic, C. (2007). "China's Emissions May Surpass US in 2007", *NewScientist.com*, 25 April.

Brewer, T. (2010). "US Government Policymaking on Climate Change: Recent Developments, Transitions, and Prospects for the Future", in *Oxford Energy and Environment Comment*, October.

Brewster, R. (2010). "Stepping Stone or Stumbling Block: Incrementalism in National Climate Change Legislation", in *Yale Law and Policy Review*, Vol. 28, No. 2, pp. 245-312.

Brooks, M. (2011). "Scientists finally get angry about indifference to climate change", in *The Guardian Online*, 5 July. <http://www.guardian.co.uk/science/2011/jul/05/scienceofclimatechange-climate-change>.

Byrnes, S. (2006). "The Man Making China Green", in *New Statesman*, 18 December.

California Global Warming Solutions Act (2006). Assembly Bill No. 32.

Cames, M. *et al.* (2011). "Functioning of the ETS and the Flexible Mechanisms", Brussels: European Parliament, March.

---

[33] In the meantime, the global economic crisis, which started in 2008, has resulted in mitigation of emissions because of low economic growth in major GHG emitters.

Campbell, K.M. *et al.* (2007). *The Age of Consequences: The Foreign Policy and National Security Implications of Global Climate Change*, Washington, DC: Center for Strategic & International Studies.

Capoor, K. and P. Ambrosi (2009). "State and Trends of the Carbon Market 2009", Washington, D.C.: The World Bank, May, pp. 1-2.

CBS News (2011). "New House Energy Chair. Global Warming Not Man-Made", 9 February. <http://www.cbsnews.com/8301-501465_162-20031180-501465.html>.

Chaffin, J. (2010). "EU warms to business of climate change", in *Financial Times*, 30 November.

Chenevière, C., and P. Nihoul (2009). "Les Règles Européennes Visant à Lutter Contre le Rechauffement Climatique", *Journal de Droit Européen*, 17(159), pp. 125-131.

Cohen, B. R. (2000). "Next Round in the Climate Debate", in *The Earth Times*, 30 October 30, pp. 10-15, at 14.

Competitive Enterprise Institute, "Carbon Dioxide Is Our Friend", <http://www.youtube.com/watch?v=0_VmMIbWKoo>; "Global Warming – 'Glaciers", <http://www.youtube.com/user/CEIdotorg#p/search/0/Wq_Bj-av3g0>.

Delegation of the European Union to Canada (2001). "Commission reacts to US statements on the Kyoto Protocol", 29 March. <http://www.delcan.ec.europa.eu/en/press_and_information/press_releases/2001/01PR004.shtml>.

Delegation of the European Commission to the US (2001). "Europe, The Green Issue", February, pp. 14-15.

Directive 2003/87/EC, Article 11a (5).

Droege, S. (2009). "Climate Policy and Economic Bust: The European Challenges to Create Green Stimulus", in *Carbon & Climate L. Rev.*, 2, 135.

Ebinger, C. *et al.* (2011). "Options for Low-Carbon Development in Countries of the Gulf Cooperation Council", Brookings Institution Policy Brief 11-02, June.

Economy, E. (2007). "The Great Leap Backward?", in *Foreign Affairs*, Vol. 86, No. 5, September-October.

Edwards, P. (2010a). *A Vast Machine: Computer Models, Climate Data, and the Politics of Global Warming.* Cambridge, MA: MIT Press.

Egenhofer, C. (2011). "The EU should not shy away from setting CO_2-related targets for transport", Policy Brief No. 229/January, Centre for European Policy Studies.

Egenhofer, C. *et al.* (2011). "The EU Emissions Trading System and Climate Policy towards 2050: Real Incentives to Reduce Emissions and Drive Innovation?" Centre for European Policy Studies.

Eizenstat, S. (2009). "The US Role in Solving Climate Change: Green Growth Policies Can Enable Leadership Despite the Economic Downturn", in *Energy Law Journal*, Vol. 30, No. 1, pp. 1-9.

Ellerman, A.D. (2008). "The EU Emission Trading Scheme: Prototype of a Global System?", Discussion Paper 2008-02, Cambridge, Mass: The Harvard Project on International Climate Agreements.

Ellerman, A.D. *et al.* (eds.) (2007). *Allocation in the European Emissions Trading Scheme: Rights, Rents and Fairness.* New York: Cambridge University Press.

Ellerman, A.D. *et al.* (2010). *Pricing Carbon: The European Union Emissions Trading Scheme.* New York: Cambridge University Press.

Ellerman, D. and P. Joskow (2008). "The European Union's Emission Trading System in Perspective", Pew Center on Global Climate Change.

Enzmann, J. and S. Marr (2008). "Moving Towards Phase III: Key Elements of the Review of the EU Emissions Trading Scheme", in *Journal of European Environmental & Planning Law*, 5(2), pp. 159-181.

Europe (2001). Europe Update, April, Vol. IX, No. 4.

European Commission (2010). "Progress Towards Achieving the Kyoto Objectives", COM, 569 final, 12 October.

European Commission (2011a). "A Roadmap for Moving to a Low Carbon Economy in 2050", COM, 112 final, 8 March, p. 4.

European Commission (2011b). "Investment Needs for Future Adaptation Measures in EU Nuclear Power Plants and Other Electricity Generation Technologies Due to Effects of Climate Change", March. <http://ec.europa.eu/energy/nuclear/studies/doc/2011_03_eur24769-en.pdf>.

European Environment Agency (2010). "Tracking Progress Towards Kyoto and 2020 Targets in Europe", EEA Report No. 7/2010, p. 30.

Forbes (2005). "Bush dubs Kyoto treaty 'lousy deal' for US economy", 7 April. <http://www.forbes.com/feeds/afx/2005/07/04/afx2122482.html>.

Fulton, M. (2011). "12th Five Year Plan – Chinese Leadership Towards a Low Carbon Economy", Deutsche Bank Group, 4 April.

Gallagher, K. (2007). "China Needs Help with Climate Change", in *Current History*, November, pp. 389-394.

Gang, F. *et al.* (eds.) (2011). *The Economics of Climate Change in China Towards a Low Carbon Economy.* London: Earthscan.

Global Commons Institute (2010). "Climate Uncertainty and Policymaking: A Policy Maker's View". <http://www.gci.org.uk/Documents/Uncertainty_Paper.pdf> (which examines the risks and uncertainties associated with the science, the scientists' tools and methods, and the policy-making process and considers how these might be integrated and communicated to policymakers).

Hallding, K. and M. Olsson (2010). "Balancing climate concerns and energy security: China searching for a new development pathway", *Stockholm Environment Institute Policy Brief.*

Hardin, G. (1968). "The Tragedy of the Commons", in *Science*, Vol. 162, No. 3859, pp. 1243-1248.

Helm, D. and C. Hepburn (2009). *The Economics and Politics of Climate Change*, Oxford: Oxford University Press.

Holwerda, M. (2010). "Subsidizing Carbon Capture and Storage Demonstration through the EU ETS New Entrants Reserve: A Proportionality Test", in *Carbon and Climate Law Review*, No. 3/2010, pp. 228-239.

International Centre for Trade and Sustainable Development (2010). "China Stands on Unconditional Climate Funding ahead of Cancún Talks", in *Bridges Trade*, Vol. 10, No. 1, 22 November.

Jacobs, A. (2011). "China Issues Warning on Climate and Growth", in *The New York Times*, 28 February.

Jehl, D. (2001). "US Rebuffs European Plea Not to Abandon Climate Pact", in *The New York Times*, 4 April.

Kanter, J. (2011). "China, Once Suspect on Emissions, Is Rapidly Becoming a Clean-Energy Power", in *The New York Times*, 26 January. <http://query.nytimes.com/gst/fullpage.html?res=9D05E0DF113EF935A157 52C0A9679D8B63>.

Kirchgaessner, S. and J. Lemer (2011). "Obama proposes 'green tax' incentives", in *Financial Times.com*, 3 February.

Larsen, J. and R. Heilmayr (2009). "Emission Reductions Under Cap-and-Trade Proposals in the 111th Congress", World Resources Institute, 22 June.

Leal-Arcas, R. (2010). *International Trade and Investment Law: Multilateral, Regional and Bilateral Governance*. Part 1. Cheltenham: Elgar.

Leal-Arcas, R. (2011a). "Proliferation of Regional Trade Agreements: Complementing or Supplanting Multilateralism?", in *Chicago Journal of International Law*, Vol. 11, No. 2, pp. 597-629.

Leal-Arcas, R. (2011b). "The Fragmentation of International Trade Law: Is Now the Time for Variable Geometry?" in *The Journal of World Investment and Trade*, Vol. 12, No. 2, pp. 145-195.

Lizza, R. (2010). "As the World Burns: How the Senate and the White House missed their best chance to deal with climate change", in *The New Yorker*, 11 October.

Luers, A. *et al.* (2007). "How to Avoid Dangerous Climate Change: A Target for US Emissions Reductions", Union of Concerned Scientists, September.

McGee, J. and R. Taplin (2008). "The Asia-Pacific Partnership and the United States' International Climate Change Policy", in *Colo. J. Int'l Envtl. L. & Pol'y*, 19, p. 179.

Miller, E.A. (2009). "Coordinating Government Agency Involvement in Climate Change", in *Working With Government Agencies in Climate Change Law*. Boston: Aspatore, pp. 103-120.

Moritz, A. *et al.* (2008). "Biodiversity Baking and Boiling: Endangered Species Act Turning Down the Heat", in *Tulsa L. Rev.* 44, p. 205.

Netherlands Environmental Assessment Agency (2008). "Global CO₂ emissions: increase continued in 2007", 13 June. <http://www.pbl.nl/en/publications/2008/GlobalCO₂emissionsthrough2007.html>.

Newport, F. (2010). "Americans' Global Warming Concerns Continue to Drop", in *Gallup*, 11 March. < http://www.gallup.com/poll/126560/americans-global-warming-concerns-continue-drop.aspx>.

Oberthür, S. and M. Pallemaerts (eds.) (2010). *The New Climate Policies of the European Union: Internal Legislation and Climate Diplomacy*. Brussels: Brussels University Press.

OECD/IEA (2007). *World Energy Outlook 2007-China and India Insights*, Paris, graph on p. 201.

OECD/IEA (2010). International Energy Agency Statistics, *CO₂ Emissions from Fuel Combustion: Highlights*, Paris.

Office of the Press (2001). "Text of a Letter from the President to Senators Hagel, Helms, Craig, and Roberts". The White House. <http://www.gcrio.org/OnLnDoc/pdf/bush_letter010313.pdf>.

Pachauri, R.K. and A. Reisinger, A. (eds.) (2007). "Summary for Policymakers", in *Climate Change 2007: Synthesis Report*. Cambridge: Cambridge University Press, p. 18.

Pohlmann, M. "The European Union Emissions Trading Scheme", in D. Freestone and C. Streck (eds.) (2009). *Legal Aspects of Carbon Trading: Kyoto, Copenhagen, and Beyond*. New York: Oxford University Press, pp. 337-366.

Ott, H. *et al.* (2004). "South-North Dialogue on Equity in the Greenhouse: A Proposal for an Adequate and Equitable Global Climate Agreement", Eschborn: Deutsche Gesellschaft für Technische Zusammenarbeit.

Pauwelyn, J. (2007). "US Federal Climate Policy and Competitiveness Concerns: The Limits and Options of International Trade Law", Nicholas Institute for Environmental Policy Solutions, *Working Paper 07-02*, Duke University.

Reno, R. (2000). "Bush, Cheney Are Oil Men and Oily Guys", *Newsday*, 21 September. <http://www.commondreams.org/views/092100-102.htm>.

Repetto, R. (2011). *America's Climate Problem: The Way Forward*. London: Earthscan.

Reuters (2007). *World's Biggest Polluters Start Climate Talks*, 20 September. <http://www.cnbc.com/id/21006799>.

Reyes, O. (2011). "EU Emissions Trading System: Failing at the Third Attempt", in *Carbon Trade Watch*, April.

Richter, B. (2001). "Learning What Fuel to Burn", in *The New York Times*, 17 April.

Ruhl, J.B. (2009). "Climate Change and the Endangered Species Act: Building Bridges to the No-Analog Future", in *Environmental Law Reporter* 39, August, 10735 p.

Samaras, C. *et al.* (2009). *Cap and Trade Is Not Enough: Improving US Climate Policy*. Pittsburgh: Carnegie Mellon University, March.

Sandbag (2010). "Cap or Trap? How the EU ETS Risks Locking-in Carbon Emissions", September. <http://sandbag.org.uk/files/sandbag.org.uk/caportrap.pdf>.

Schwarte, C. and R. Byrne (2010). "International Climate Change Litigation and the Negotiation Process", in *Oil, Gas & Energy*, November.

Shogren, E. (2001). "Bush Drops Pledge to Curb Emissions", in *Los Angeles Times*, 14 March. <http://articles.latimes.com/2001/mar/14/news/mn-37556>.

Skea, J., P. Ekins, and M. Winskel (eds.) (2010). *Energy 2050: Making the Transition to a Secure Low-Carbon Energy System*. London: Earthscan.

Spencer, R. and W. Braswell (2011). "On the Misdiagnosis of Surface Temperature Feedbacks from Variations in Earth's Radiant Eenrgy Balance", in *Remote Sensing*, Vol. 3, pp. 1603-1613.

State of Illinois (1998). Ninetieth General Assembly, House Joint Resolution No. 48, 22 May, p. 4313.

Stewart, R. and J. Wiener (2003). *Reconstructing Climate Policy: Beyond Kyoto*. Washington, DC: American Enterprise Institute.

Stern Review (2006). "The Economics of Climate Change, Summary of Conclusions", p. vi. <http://webarchive.nationalarchives.gov.uk/+/http://www.hm-treasury.gov.uk/media/3/2/Summary_of_Conclusions.pdf>.

Stern, T. and W. Antholis (2007-2008). "A Changing Climate: The Road Ahead for the United States", in *The Washington Quarterly*, 31:1, Winter, pp. 175-188.

Strauss, A. (2003). "The Legal Option: Suing the United States in International Forums for Global Warming", in *Environmental Law Reporter*, Vol. 33, pp. 10185-10191.

The Royal Society (2001). "The Science of Climate Change". <http://royalsociety.org/Report_WF.aspx?pageid=10028>.

Thernstrom, S. (2009). "The Quiet Death of the Kyoto Protocol", in *The American*, 5 November. <http://www.american.com/archive/2009/november/the-quiet-yet-historic-death-of-the-kyoto-protocol>.

UNDP (2007/2008). *Fighting Climate Change: Human Solidarity in a Divided World*, Human Development Report 2007/2008. <http://hdr.undp.org/en/reports/global/hdr2007-2008>.

UNFCCC, 9 May 1992, 31 ILM 849.

UNFCCC, *Kyoto Protocol*, Article 3.1.

US Code, Title 42, Chapter 85.

US Constitution, Article II, Section 2.

US Council of Economic Advisers (1998). *Economic Report of the President Transmitted to the Congress*, February. Washington, DC: US Government Printing Office, 1998.

US Department of Transportation, *Overview of Climate Change: An Introduction*. <http://climate.dot.gov/about/overview/science.html>.

US Environmental Protection Agency, Office of Air and Radiation (2011). "The Benefits and Costs of the Clean Air Act from 1990 to 2020. March.

Watson, J. *et al.* (2011). "UK-China Collaborative Study on Low Carbon Technology Transfer", Final Report, University of Sussex, April. <http://www.sussex.ac.uk/sussexenergygroup/documents/uk-china_final_report_-_april_2011.pdf>.

Weishaar, S. (2008). "The European Emissions Trading System: Auctions and their Challenges", in Faure, M. and M. Peeters (eds.), *Climate Change and European Emissions Trading: Lessons for Theory and Practice*. Cheltenham: Edward Elgar.

White House Council on Environmental Quality (2010). "Progress Report of the Interagency Climate Change Adaptation Task Force: Recommended Actions in Support of a National Climate Change Adaptation Strategy", 5 October.

World Bank and State Environmental Protection Administration of the People's Republic of China (2007). *Cost of Pollution in China: Economics Estimates of Physical Damages*, February. <http://siteresources.worldbank.org/INTEAPREGTOPENVIRONMENT/Resources/China_Cost_of_Pollution.pdf>.

Yale Environment 360 (2010). "China Said to Pass US as World's Biggest Energy Consumer". <http://www.e360.yale.edu/content/digest.msp?id=2511>.

Why Are Canada and the EU Attacking Each Other's Green-Energy Initiatives?
The Limits and Tensions of Ecological Modernization

Anders HAYDEN

Introduction

The European Union and Canada are widely seen to occupy different ends of the climate policy performance spectrum. The EU has been recognised for its efforts to achieve a global climate agreement at Kyoto and to try to keep the international process on track through the difficulties that followed. The EU was, by 2008, on track to meet its Kyoto Protocol target for greenhouse gas (GHG) emissions reductions (EEA 2008), even before the economic downturn cut emissions further. Also in 2008, EU Member States agreed on a wide-ranging climate and energy package, which by 2020 aims to cut GHG emissions 20 per cent below 1990 levels, reduce primary energy use 20 per cent through greater energy efficiency, and source 20 per cent of total energy from renewables. "Boosting growth and jobs by meeting our climate change commitments", was the message the European Commission (2008) chose to highlight when announcing proposals for the climate and energy package. These words illustrated a notable feature of European climate politics: the prominence – although not universal acceptance – of an ecological modernization or "green growth" discourse highlighting win-win opportunities to reduce emissions while expanding the economy.

In contrast, Canada is a repeat recipient of "colossal fossil" awards given by environmental NGOs to the nation doing the most to obstruct progress in international negotiations. It ranked 57 out of 60 countries – ahead only of Australia, Kazakhstan, and Saudi Arabia – on the 2011 Climate Policy Performance Index produced by two European NGOs, Germanwatch and Climate Action Network Europe. Canada's per-capita GHG emissions were not only high to start; they also grew at the fastest rate in the G8, up 24 per cent from 1990 to 2008, leaving the country 31 per cent above its Kyoto target (Environment Canada 2010). This record prompted the United Nations Development Programme to label

Canada "an extreme case" of failure to curb emissions (UNDP 2007, pp. 10, 43). In 2011, Canada announced its intention to withdraw from the Kyoto process – the only ratifying country to do so. Looking ahead, Canada has committed to very limited GHG reductions of 17 per cent below 2005 levels by 2020 – equivalent to a 2.5 per cent *increase* above 1990 levels. A main source of Canada's emissions growth, and a main political obstacle to stronger climate policy, has been the extraction and processing of oil from northern Alberta's tar sands.

Given its economic strategy based on oil exports, it is no surprise that Canada objected to proposals to categorise the tar sands as high-carbon fuel source in the EU's Fuel Quality Directive. Somewhat more surprising have been EU objections to one of Canada's flagship green policies, the Ontario Green Energy Act, which was inspired by success-ful ecological-industrial policies in Europe. This chapter will argue that Canada's resistance to the Fuel Quality Directive can be understood in light of its inability to reconcile its fossil-fuel-oriented growth strategy with GHG reductions through ecological modernization. Meanwhile the EU's objections to Ontario's green policy reflect the tensions within an ecological modernization strategy between ecological and commercial goals.

The Promise of Ecological Modernization

In many countries that have moved beyond inaction and a business-as-usual approach to climate change, a mainstream consensus has emerged around an ecological modernization (EM) project, which aims to decouple economic growth from rising emissions through improved efficiency and ecologically sound technologies. The "win-win" dis-course accompanying an EM project sees environmental management as "a positive-sum game: pollution prevention pays" (Hajer 1995; see also Murphy 2000; Revell 2005). Strong action to reduce GHGs is seen to provide opportunities for "green growth" and competitive advantage, as those who move first to develop low-carbon technologies can capture the rapidly expanding global market for emissions-reducing solutions (e.g., Jänicke and Jacob 2004). During its presidency of the EU in 2007, Germany promoted the EM-inspired idea of "ecological industrial policy" linking environmental and economic strategy (BMU 2008; Jänicke 2008, p. 558). EM thus transcends, at least rhetorically, the idea of an environment-economy conflict, enabling co-operation among government policy-makers, business leaders, moderate environmental-ists, and others.

Although conceptually distinct, EM as a *political project* and *dis-course* has an affinity with ecological modernization *theory*, which highlights positive environmental improvements and seeks to account for the processes behind them (e.g., Mol 2003; Mol *et al.* 2009). EM theory maintains that modern societies are increasingly influenced by ecological rationality, which is transforming key institutions including the state, business and the market, science, and technology. It is thus optimistic about reconciling economic growth and environmental sustainability and rejects the idea that capitalism's basic dynamics conflict with ecological limits.

An ecological modernization discourse is noteworthy not only within EU institutions, but also in Member States seen as climate leaders. A striking contrast to Canada is the embrace of a "green growth" language not only by the centre-left and Greens, but also by conservative-led governments in Europe's most influential states. For example, in an opinion piece in *The Financial Times* urging the EU to strengthen its emissions-reduction target to 30 per cent by 2020, the British, German, and French environment ministers warned, "If we stick to a 20 per cent cut, Europe is likely to lose the race to compete in the low-carbon world to countries such as China, Japan or the US – all of which are looking to create a more attractive environment for low-carbon investment" (Huhne *et al.* 2010). The ministers went on to add that "Europe's companies are poised to take advantage of the new opportunities".

EU Fuel Quality Directive

One complementary measure accompanying the EU's 2008 climate and energy package was a revised Fuel Quality Directive (FQD), which required fuel suppliers to reduce GHG emissions from the fuel production chain by 6 per cent by 2020. Since road transport was responsible for 20 per cent of EU GHGs, requiring use of lower carbon fuels was considered a key measure to meet the EU's overall carbon-reduction goal. It also represented, in the words of Environment Commissioner Stavros Dimas, "a concrete test of our political commitment to leadership on climate policy" (European Commission 2007).

The text of the FQD emphasised the controversial promotion of biofuels and creation of sustainability criteria for their use (European Union 2009). Indeed, neither "tar sands" nor "oil sands" – the cleanersounding term promoted by the oil industry and governments of Canada and Alberta – were mentioned in the directive itself. Canadians paid little attention until the European Commission (2009) released a consultation paper on calculating the life-cycle GHG intensity of fuels other than biofuels, which included a proposed default value for tar-sands-derived fuel of 107 grams of CO_2 per megajoule of fuel, 25 per cent higher than the 85.8 grams for conventional petrol. If this default value were confirmed, tar-sands fuel would become less competitive in the EU market – among other possible consequences, discussed below.

Canada's Response

A lobbying effort of unprecedented scale followed. Canada launched a "pan-European oil sands advocacy strategy" in December 2009, according to documents obtained through access to information requests by journalists and environmental groups (Lukacs 2011a; see also CAN Canada 2010; De Souza 2011; FoE Europe 2011). Activities included monitoring environmental groups, responding to negative media coverage, organising trips to Alberta for EU parliamentarians, and feverishly lobbying the European Commission and MEPs. Friends of the Earth documented 110 lobbying events organised by Canada in Europe from September 2009 to July 2011 – more than one per week. Participants included a number of federal and Alberta ministers. Lobbying took place at the highest levels, including a May 2010 meeting between Prime Minister Stephen Harper and EU Commission President Jose Manuel Barroso where the FQD was discussed (FoE Europe 2011, pp. 3, 13; Harrison & von Reppert-Bismarck 2011).

These European efforts were part of a wider Canadian strategy. The Climate Action Network (CAN Canada 2010) assembled evidence from internal government documents of an "Oil Sands Advocacy Strategy" that targeted climate and energy policies at the federal and state levels in the United States, as well as in Europe, that could limit Canada's ability to profit from tar-sands exports.

In addition to trying to ensure "non-discriminatory market access for oil sands derived products" in the EU, Canadian officials aimed to "defend Canada's image as a responsible energy producer and steward of the environment including climate change issues", according to government documents (FoE Europe 2011, p. 7). "Oil sands are posing a growing reputational problem [in Europe], with the oil sands defining the Canadian brand", stated one document. Concerns were also expressed about anti-tar-sands protests that "have become a regular occurrence in London" (Lukacs 2011a). Meanwhile, a diplomatic cable released by WikiLeaks revealed that Environment Minister Jim Prentice shared concerns with US Ambassador David Jacobson (2009) about the tar sands' impact on Canada's "historically 'green' standing on the world stage". Prentice expressed shock at the public sentiment he witnessed in Norway, where there was a debate over whether to invest in Alberta's "dirty oil".

A noteworthy element of Canada's strategy has been the cultivation of alliances with powerful non-state actors: European-based oil companies, who, despite trumpeting their green credentials at home, invested far more heavily in the tar sands than they did in renewable energy (WWF-UK & The Co-Operative 2010). One federal document from spring 2010 referred to a "meeting with like-minded allies" from BP and Shell (De Souza 2011). Other documents showed that Canada's mission in London maintained close contact with these firms and the Royal Bank of Scotland, a major source of tar-sands finance. Canada's Brussels bureau also co-operated with Shell in hosting complementary events. During a brief June 2010 visit to France, Prime Minister Harper found time to meet with the CEO of Total, which later announced plans to invest $20 billion in the tar sands by 2020. Meanwhile, Canada's mission in Oslo "holds regular meetings" with Statoil, the largely state-owned firm that invested upwards of $2 billion in the tar sands despite Norway's pledge to become "carbon neutral" (Lukacs 2011a; see also Arnott 2011; Lukacs 2011b; Macalister 2011a).

Canadian and Albertan officials attempted to promote a positive image of the tar sands as a clean and secure energy source. They highlighted the billions of dollars in planned expenditure to reduce GHGs through carbon capture and storage (CCS) (Alberta 2010; FoE Europe 2011, p. 11). Canada also promoted its democratic credentials and human rights record (FoE Europe 2011, p. 16; Macalister 2011a), which, according to an increasingly common argument, made the tar sands a source of "ethical oil" (Levant 2010). Meanwhile, *The Globe and Mail* revealed that Canada's EU ambassador privately promised EU politicians in 2010 that Canada would introduce regulations to reduce tar-sands GHG emissions – a promise that had not, by the time of writing, been kept.[1] For meetings with EU politicians, Canada's EU ambassador was advised to emphasise the tar sands' role in improving energy security for the West, as supplying the United States "alleviates demand pressures" on sources supplying Europe. The ambassador's briefing notes included the argument that "demonization" of the tar sands would "come at a high cost" to European firms BP, Total, Statoil, and Shell (McCarthy 2011a).

Canada also threatened the EU with trade conflict. Labelling the tar sands a high-carbon fuel source would "create barriers to trade", Canada's EU ambassador told the director-general of the EU's environment department in a letter (Harrison 2010). Contradicting

---

[1] In light of Canada's track record of continually delayed climate action, it would be surprising if this promise is fulfilled anytime soon. Indeed, Canadian Environment Minister Peter Kent emphasised in January 2011 that he would not introduce any GHG regulations that would discourage tar-sands investments, stating, "It is not our intention to discourage development of one of our great natural resources" (Chase 2011).

claims by Canada's trade minister that there was no link between trade talks and the tar-sands dispute, threats of trade conflict appeared in a Canadian letter in March 2011 to the EU commissioners for climate, trade, and energy (Harrison 2011). Briefing notes prepared by EU officials for the climate commissioner stated that Canada had raised the tar-sands issue during negotiations about a Comprehensive Economic and Trade Agreement (CETA) while Reuters cited sources saying that Canada at one point threatened to scrap CETA (Harrison & von Reppert-Bismarck 2011). Later reports suggested that Canada had shifted away from linking the issue to CETA talks but instead threatened the EU with a WTO challenge (*EurActiv* 2011b). Canadian officials warned that they would consider "singling out oil sands crude" as "unjustified discrimination" that is "not supported by the science", leaving EU officials with little doubt that this represented a threat to go to the WTO (Harrison 2011; Harrison & von Reppert-Bismarck 2011). Canada has already challenged other EU environment-related measures at the WTO, including policies related to seal-product imports, hormone-treated beef, and genetically modified food.

Should the final Canada-EU trade deal include a NAFTA-style investor-state dispute mechanism, as proposed by Canada in early drafts, CETA could also become a tool for oil firms operating in the tar sands to challenge and seek compensation from the EU for restrictions on their ability to sell into the European market. A parallel concern exists that EU-based oil firms could use CETA to challenge any future Canadian regulations to limit GHG emissions from tar-sands operations (Shrybman 2010; van der Zee 2011).

How 'Dirty' Is Tar Sands-Derived Fuel?

Canada also attempted to call into question the scientific basis for labelling the tar sands a source of GHG-intensive fuel. In response to the Commission's 2009 consultation paper, which suggested that the tar sands emit roughly one-quarter more carbon dioxide on a lifecycle basis than conventional petrol, Canada put forward its own numbers: 5 to 15 per cent greater emissions than conventional crude (FoE Europe 2011, p. 8; McCarthy 2011a). Based on these figures, produced by Cambridge Energy Research Associates (CERA), an oil industry consultancy, Canada argued that the differences with conventional oil were not large enough to justify special regulatory treatment.

To address the matter, the EU commissioned an analysis by Adam Brandt (2011) of Stanford University's department of energy resources engineering. Brandt concluded that a "most likely" estimate of average GHG emissions for tar-sands fuel was 107.3 grams of CO_2 per megajoule, 23 per cent more than the average 87.1 grams for conventional fuels – nearly identical to the Commission's original figures.[2] Brandt reviewed six previous studies, including the tar sands' defenders favoured CERA study, which he ruled out due to lack of methodological transparency (e.g., p. 32). He concluded that tar sands' GHG emissions "are significantly different enough from conventional oil emissions" to justify distinct treatment in regulatory frameworks (p. 3). Brandt's report was leaked the day after Alberta's energy minister, on a visit to Brussels, told reporters, "There is no evidence to discriminate against oil from oil sands by putting it in a separate category" (Rankin 2011b). A peer review of Brandt's study supported its core conclusions.

Why Such a Strong Canadian Reaction?

The EU imports minimal quantities of fuel that can be traced back to Alberta's tar sands, so the potential loss of the European market does not explain Canada's vehement reaction. Above all, Alberta and Canada have feared that the Fuel Quality Directive would set a precedent for others. "It is not because we are protecting a customer base [in Europe], but because we respect the fact that decisions in Europe find their way into other policies around the world", stated Alberta Environment Minister Rob Renner (Rankin 2010; see also Healing 2011).

The main jurisdiction of concern is the United States, the predominant export market for Canadian oil and home to considerable debate about low-carbon fuel standards similar to the EU FQD. California actually provided the model for the EU FQD with its establishment of a low-carbon fuel standard in 2007. Canada strongly opposed this initiative, intervening in the development of California's policy numerous times (CAN Canada 2010; Harrison 2010; Dembicki 2011b). California's example inspired eleven Northeast states, who agreed in 2009 to develop a regional low-carbon fuel standard. Even more worrying for Canada's petroleum interests were proposals for a similar federal standard, which Barack Obama endorsed during the 2008 presidential campaign and which appeared in versions of the defeated Lieberman-Warner and Markey-Waxman climate bills (Dembicki 2011b). Canada and Alberta also lobbied vigorously to exempt the tar sands from Section 256 of the Energy Independence and Security Act of 2007, which

---

[2] Critics often state that producing fuel from the tar sands is roughly three times more carbon intensive than conventional fuel – based on emissions linked to extraction, upgrading, and refining. Brandt reached a similar conclusion when only those activities are considered (2011, p. 4). The EU FQD, however, is based on lifecycle or "well-to-wheel" emissions including distribution and combustion. Since the lion's share of emissions occurs when fuel is burned in a vehicle, and combustion emissions are similar for tar sands and conventional fuels, defenders of the tar sands prefer such "well-to-wheel" figures that suggest a narrower differential.

prohibits US federal agencies, including the military and postal service, from buying alternative fuels with higher lifecycle GHG emissions than conventional petroleum (CAN Canada 2010; Dembicki 2011a).

Alberta officials expressed concern that the EU FQD could have an impact further afield, possibly in China and India, potential export markets that have copied past EU environmental measures (Dembicki 2010). "Our fear is that if something happens in the EU and it is spread in other countries – not only members of the EU – we could have roughly one-third of the world's population subscribing to regulation or legislation that mitigates against our oilsands", Alberta International and Intergovernmental Relations Minister Iris Evans told reporters (Gerein 2010).

EU confirmation that tar-sands fuel is "dirty oil" would also add to the wider reputational problem and make it even harder to sustain claims that the tar sands are an environmentally sound and "ethical" oil source. Canadian officials expressed concern that a high-carbon fuel classification would strengthen campaigns for European oil companies to disinvest from the tar sands (Lukacs 2011a).

More generally, to understand why the EU's effort to apply GHG emissions standards to the tar sands is seen as such a threat to Canada, two other factors need to be considered: the vast economic opportunities at stake and the practical impossibility in the foreseeable future of fully profiting from them while significantly lowering emissions. Canada's oil reserves of 175 billion barrels – more than 95 per cent of which are found in Alberta's tar sands – are the world's third largest. One study estimated the value of the oil in the tar sands at $1.4 trillion – equal to 18 per cent of Canada's tangible wealth (Sharpe *et al.* 2008). Canada's economy has become increasingly dependent on these resources as it has pursued its "energy superpower" ambitions. Crude bitumen production from the tar sands grew rapidly from 650,000 barrels per day in 1998 to 1.6 million in 2010 and was projected to reach 3.5 million by 2020. Squaring this drive for tar-sands expansion with GHG reductions is like "attempting to ride two horses galloping in opposite directions", as Canada's former Environment Minister Charles Caccia put it (Kolbert 2007).

Carbon capture and storage are often highlighted as the best hope for a technological solution. During EU lobbying, Canadian officials trumpeted their CCS investments as a sign of commitment to reducing tar-sands emissions; however, evidence suggests that CCS will likely be of very limited use for this purpose. A briefing note for federal and Alberta ministers, marked "secret" and revealed by the CBC (2008), said of the tar sands: "Only a small percentage of emitted CO_2 is 'capturable' since most emissions aren't pure enough. Only limited near-term opportunities exist in the oilsands and they largely relate to upgrader facilities". Meanwhile, the Royal Society of Canada (2010, pp. 91, 93) concluded that, since the geology of Northeastern Alberta is generally not suitable for storing CO_2, "the direct impact of CCS on reducing oil sands GHG emissions is not likely to be substantial" (see also WWF-UK & The Co-Operative 2009; Mech 2011, p. 53). Even in the limited situations where CCS is technically possible for tar-sands-related emissions, issues of cost arise. While the briefing notes for Canada's EU ambassador encouraged him to highlight Canada's CCS investments, they privately conceded that CCS may be prohibitively expensive (McCarthy 2011a). More generally, the Royal Society of Canada (2010, p. 4) concluded, "Technological solutions, such as carbon capture and storage (CCS), will not be sufficient to eliminate projected GHG increases from oil sands operations over the next decade".

Despite the industry's much-vaunted success in reducing GHG intensity, i.e., emissions *per barrel* of output, Canada forecast a tripling of total tar-sands GHG emissions from 30 to 92 million tonnes between 2005 and 2020 (Environment Canada 2011, p. 25), continuing the trend that saw GHGs from tar sands increase 165 per cent from 1990 to 2009 (Huot *et al.* 2011, p. 3). Projected tar-sands emission growth will counteract virtually all the benefits – a 65 million tonne reduction – expected from all current federal and provincial climate policies until 2020 (Environment Canada 2011). Clearly, rapid output growth has far outpaced emissions reductions per barrel of output – and signs are that it will continue to do so if tar-sands growth is not curbed.

In the future, it is questionable whether even per-barrel emissions reductions can be sustained. While the Royal Society of Canada (2010, p. 89) concluded that "there is some promise for further reductions in GHG intensity", it added that an increasing share of future output will come from "*in situ*" production, used to extract bitumen that is too far below the surface to be mined and which results in greater GHG emissions. In fact, from 2006 to 2010, the tar sands' GHG intensity stopped declining and actually increased by 4 per cent, according to the industry's own figures (CAPP 2011; see also Huot *et al.* 2011, pp. 5-6).

The evidence suggests that technology and efficiency are not up to the task of allowing Canada to continue to pursue rapid tar-sands expansion without generating vast quantities of additional emissions, which threaten its ability to meet its very modest Copenhagen accord commitments. Simply to avoid large future emissions increases, let alone reduce emissions below current levels, would require slowing or stopping this particular form of growth and leaving a great deal of oil – and a large part of a trillion dollar-plus economic opportunity – in the ground (at least until some distant future when low-carbon extraction methods might become available). Ideas of ecological modernization suggest that such trade-offs can be transcended, but they have been at the core of Canada's climate difficulties. Canada and, especially, Alberta have not been prepared to forego their high-carbon pot of gold, opting instead for weak climate targets and policies at home, while attacking climate policies abroad that threaten their growth strategy.

Impact of Canadian Efforts

Canada's intense lobbying produced initial results, but it was not clear at the time of writing if it would ultimately achieve its aims. The default value for tar-sands-derived fuel, proposed in the Commission's July 2009 consultation paper, did not appear in a revised draft in early 2010. References to the tar sands were dropped, and a single GHG value for all oil-based transport fuels remained, prompting reports that the EU had yielded to Canadian pressure (Harrison 2010). In response, environmental campaigners from Europe, Canada, and the US demanded reinsertion of separate default values for the tar sands and other sources of heavy crude (FoE Europe *et al.* 2010; Macalister 2011b). In March 2011, Connie Hedegaard, the climate action commissioner, told MEPs that the Commission did, in fact, intend to include separate default values for tar sands and other unconventional fuel sources (European Parliament 2011b; Macalister 2011b).

The issue produced tensions within EU institutions. In the Commission, the climate action commissioner faced resistance from Trade Commissioner Karel De Grucht, who was concerned the tar-sands provisions would affect CETA negotiations and provoke a WTO challenge. Trade officials also expressed doubts about whether scientific studies on the tar-sands' impacts were strong enough to withstand WTO criteria for measures to be "proportional, non-discriminatory, and based on solid scientific evidence" (Brand 2011; Rankin 2011a). Joining the trade commissioner in opposing a separate tar-sands default value were the energy and competition commissioners (Taylor 2011). However, in October 2011, Hedegaard won a victory as the Commission approved a default value for tar-sands fuel of 107 grams CO_2 equivalent per megajoule.

The European Parliament was a source of considerable criticism of the Commission, and especially the trade commissioner, for delays in finalising the tar-sands provisions, while MEPs also insisted that the scientific basis for action was more than adequate (Brand 2011; Rankin 2011a; Taylor 2011). During parliamentary debate in April 2011, MEPs from across the political spectrum backed the call for a separate default value for the tar sands. In June, a European Parliament (2011a) resolution on Canada-EU trade relations reiterated MEPs' "concern about the impact of the extraction of oil sand on the global environment due to the high level of CO_2 emissions during its production process", while stating that "CETA negotiations should not affect the EU's right to legislate in the fuel quality directive or inhibit the ability of the Canadian authorities to introduce future environmental standards concerning the extraction of oil sands". For many MEPs, the dispute was a credibility test for the EU's much-vaunted commitment to climate action (Rankin 2011a).

The ultimate decision would come down to the Member States in the Council. The UK played a particularly important role in delaying EU action on the FQD, as it called for more consultation and research while pushing back a final vote (*EurActiv* 2011a). The UK's position was a product not only of oil-company lobbying, but also high-level communications with Canadian officials, including discussions between David Cameron and Stephen Harper (Carrington 2011). A vote at a committee meeting of technical experts in February 2012 ended in a stalemate, with neither enough votes to defeat or approve the separate default value for tar-sands fuel. While Spain, Italy, Poland, and some other new Member States voted against the measure, equally important in blocking approval (at least temporarily) were the abstentions of the UK, Netherlands, and France – home to BP, Shell, and Total – as well as Germany (CBC 2012). The Commission subsequently decided to undertake a further impact assessment of the FQD, with a final vote in the Council expected no earlier than 2013.

Whatever the final outcome, Canada had succeeded in delaying EU action as the Commission missed the original January 2011 deadline for confirming default values for different fuel sources. Intense Canadian lobbying also provoked criticism from some MEPs and environmental groups. "The government of Canada has been lobbying us in a manner that is not acceptable", said Finnish Green MEP Satu Hassi, vice chair of the European Parliament's environment committee (McCarthy 2011c). Likewise, British Labour MEP Linda McAvan stated, "I find it unacceptable that a country which has not even tried to meet their Kyoto emission reduction target should be lobbying to water down the EU's environmental legislation" (Morrison 2011). Meanwhile, Climate Action Network Canada's executive director found it "appalling" that his government was "attacking clean energy policy in other countries" (Council of Canadians 2011).

Although the circumstances were not identical, the EU was simultaneously attacking clean energy policy in Canada.

Ontario's Green Energy Act

While Canada's dominant approach has been to pursue a high-carbon economic path, some provinces have taken significant steps to reconcile carbon reduction and economic strategy. One of the most noteworthy ecological modernization-oriented initiatives is Ontario's Green Energy Act (GEA). The province of Ontario (2009) passed the Act with much fanfare, proclaiming its intention "to attract new investment, create new green economy jobs and better protect the environment". At the core of the Act was a feed-in-tariff (FIT) system to encourage green investment by providing guaranteed, premium prices for renewable energy. These premium prices would lead to small increases in electricity bills, but in return they would generate, according to the government, upwards of 50,000 green jobs over three years.

The GEA was inspired by European successes – notably in Denmark, Germany, and Spain – in stimulating economic activity through FITs. Ontario Energy Minister George Smitherman travelled to Europe in 2008 to learn lessons for transforming the province's struggling, automobile-centred manufacturing sector into a hub of green industry. Of particular inspiration was Germany's Renewable Energy Sources Act, which was credited with stimulating rapid expansion of solar and wind power and creating large numbers of manufacturing jobs. In one sense, Ontario's Act is an even more ambitious carbon-reduction initiative than Germany's, as one of its goals is to help the province close its remaining coal-fired power plants, while Germany is still building new coal-fired facilities (and phasing out nuclear power instead).

Shortly after the GEA's approval, Ontario signed a deal with Samsung of South Korea on a $7 billion plan to build four factories to make wind and solar equipment and employ 16,000 people. Other renewable technology makers that announced manufacturing investments in the province included Siemens AG and Bosch Solar of Germany, Siliken of Spain, Silifab of Italy, SunEdison of the US, Dago Group of China, and Ontario-based Canadian Solar.

The GEA had significant potential to alter the balance of political forces by bringing more businesses and employees into a coalition favouring strong climate action.[3] Germany's renewable energy laws encouraged the growth of a green industrial sector whose firms and workers became part of the advocacy coalition backing strong climate

---

[3] The GEA also had the potential to bring aboriginal people into the climate action coalition as it included specific measures to support renewable energy projects in First Nations and Métis communities.

policies and an important counterweight to industries resisting action (Jacobsson and Lauber 2006; Hey 2010). Canada, until now, has lacked such a green counterweight to its dominant petroleum sector.

The GEA received backing from some influential external observers for its transformational possibilities. Achim Steiner, executive director of the United Nations Environment Programme, defended the GEA from criticism that it was driving up power prices and highlighted the policy's potential to stimulate a green economic transition. He added that Canada was putting itself at risk by overemphasising fossil fuels. "If you want to build Canada's economy on the premise that you are going to stick with a fuel of the 20th century as the central engine of innovation, investment and infrastructure development, then that's a high-risk choice", said Steiner (Blackwell 2011b). Meanwhile, John Podesta, former advisor to Barack Obama and chief of staff to Bill Clinton, argued that it would be a mistake to repeal the Act, as proposed by Ontario's Conservative opposition. The GEA "has put Ontario on the map not just as a leader in Canada but as a model for the world as well", Podesta said (McCarthy 2011b).

One contentious aspect of the GEA has been its domestic content requirements. To ensure that Ontario receives economic benefits and new green jobs, all projects that receive premium feed-in-tariffs must source a minimum percentage of their goods and services within the province. For solar energy, 40 to 50 per cent of the costs of developing a project had to be spent on Ontario products or services, rising to 60 per cent in 2011, while for wind, the figures were 25 per cent, rising to 50 per cent in 2012.

Reaction by the EU and Others

Japan, home to solar panel suppliers such as Sanyo, Kyocera, and Sharp, was the first state to object officially to Ontario's GEA. In September 2010, it filed a complaint with the WTO, arguing that the GEA's domestic content requirements discriminate against producers outside Ontario. It further argued that premium FIT rates are a prohibited subsidy since they are contingent on using domestic over imported goods (Weber 2010; Herman 2011). As a first step to resolve the dispute, Japan asked for consultations with Canada. The United States and the EU soon asked to join these consultations. After consultations failed to resolve the matter, Japan asked the WTO in June 2011 to form a legal panel to rule on the issue.

The EU used the CETA negotiations to try to remove the GEA's domestic content requirements. A main objective of the EU and European-based corporations in these talks has been to restrict the widespread use by Canadian federal, provincial, and municipal governments of procurement policies to promote local economic development and other social and environmental objectives. Ontario's Green Energy Act has been the EU's most visible target (Sinclair 2010, pp. 3, 11). A position paper tabled by EU negotiators specifically highlighted Ontario's GEA as the type of "protectionist" legislation that prevents European access to Canadian markets (Saunders 2010; see also Hamilton 2009; McCarthy 2010b). Other provinces including Quebec and Prince Edward Island also reward renewable energy producers that purchase local goods and services while green procurement measures include municipal "buy local" food policies in Toronto and other cities, which seek to reduce carbon emissions from long-distance transport while supporting local farmers.

In August 2011, the EU issued its own request for WTO negotiations, officially becoming a complaining party on the grounds that the GEA was "in clear breach of the WTO rules that prohibit linking subsidies to the use of domestic products". In filing its complaint, the European Commission (2011) stated that it "welcomes" Ontario's commitment to promote green energy. "However, the promotion of renewable energies must be done in a manner consistent with international trade rules", the Commission added. The EU appeared to have concluded that CETA negotiations alone, without additional pressure through the WTO, would be insufficient to resolve the issue in its favour (Greenberg 2011).

Interpreting the EU Challenge to Ontario's Green Energy Act

The EU's action against the GEA can be understood as a combination of ideas, interests, and institutions. It illustrates the EU's commitment – a selective one, as discussed in more detail below – to a neoliberal trade orthodoxy that insists on open, competitive markets as the best way to achieve economic as well as environmental ends (see Finbow, this volume). The influence of institutions embodying neoliberal ideas – the WTO and the still emerging CETA – are clearly key factors in the story. For the purposes of this chapter, the most significant factor is the EU's effort to defend and advance its economic interests – in ways that illustrate tensions within the ecological modernization paradigm that has guided EU climate policy.

The EU's economic interests and commitment to neoliberal ideas and institutions were evident in its letter to the WTO asking to be part of the Japan-Canada consultations on the GEA. In it, the European Union (2010) stated: "The renewable energy generation sector is of key interest for the EU importers, exporters and investors. [...] Therefore the EU has a substantial trade interest in the present dispute as well as a systemic interest in the correct implementation of [global trade agreements]". In its subsequent request to the WTO for its own consultations with Canada, the EU highlighted its "significant" exports to Canada of wind power and photovoltaic equipment, ranging from 300 to 600 million euros from 2007-2009. "These figures could be higher should the local content requirements be removed from the legislation in question", according to the European Commission (2011).

Germany's influential solar firms were one of the voices to which the Commission was responding. These beneficiaries of generous German feed-in-tariffs were among the first to express displeasure with Ontario's approach to promoting renewable energy. Shortly after the GEA's approval, BSW-Solar, the German solar industry association that represents more than 800 companies in a sector employing some 60,000 people, urged its members to protest Ontario's "local protectionism" (Hamilton 2009).

Similar to Canada's motivation for objecting to the Fuel Quality Directive, the EU wanted to prevent such policies from spreading to other jurisdictions. A leaked memo for EU negotiators in the CETA talks refers to the objectives regarding the GEA: "In the short term, to convince the governments of Ontario and Canada to abandon the requirement to use domestically produced equipment to produce renewable electricity in order to benefit from high feed-in tariffs. In the medium term, to avoid the Ontario initiative becoming a precedent for other provinces some of which are on the verge of implementing similar schemes" (Berthiaume 2010; Sinclair 2010, p. 11). Elsewhere, the European Commission (2011) stated that it is "increasingly concerned by such measures taken by other trading partners".

Tensions within an ecological modernization perspective are revealed by such actions. Recall that one of EM's main promises is that companies and countries that move first to develop green technologies will profit from exports to markets that will eventually demand their products. The EU's challenge to Ontario's GEA represents a case of first movers seeking to ensure that they do, in fact, realise the export profits that are part of the EM vision. However, the risk, in environmental terms, is of undermining an innovative policy effort designed to enable a late mover to move beyond inaction on climate change and to find a politically viable path reconciling green action with economic opportunity.

Is the Green Energy Act Unfair?

In its defence, Ontario argued that the GEA was consistent with its WTO obligations. The province maintained that its domestic content rules were designed to ensure that, in addition to producing economic and environmental benefits for Ontario, foreign companies could also gain from the new opportunities created by the policy. "Our conclusion is that the domestic content rules have been developed in a way that welcomes investment from outside Ontario, because only a portion of the costs are required to be spent in Ontario", a government spokesperson stated (Hamilton 2009). Ontario Premier Dalton McGuinty said of the GEA, "We believe we have struck the right balance in terms of ensuring that companies and businesses from outside Ontario, and outside of Canada, can in fact participate in our feed-in-tariff program" (Diebel 2010). Ultimately, the WTO will decide the issue on the basis of a number of different questions: Do renewable energy purchases through the Ontario Power Authority represent a form of government procurement that is exempt under the WTO? Is the policy actually discriminatory or neutral in its effect by making the same demands on energy producers, regardless of national origin, in return for the premium FIT? Does a FIT contract fall under the definition of a subsidy (Herman 2011)?

Beyond these specific issues, the GEA raises broader questions about what governments can do to encourage a green-energy transition at a time when there is a widely recognized need for deep and rapid GHG reductions. These questions have become entangled in the intensifying battle among jurisdictions about their respective shares of the renewable energy market. Other examples of this conflict include a dispute between the United States and China about the latter's subsidies to wind turbine and solar manufacturers that use domestic parts, which ended in 2011 when China agreed to withdraw such policies. Meanwhile, German solar producers experienced growing angst about their declining global market share as China and Taiwan brought cheaper products onto the market (Dohmen *et al.* 2010).

One position on these issues is that the best way to promote renewable energy is through open, competitive markets that reduce the prices of green technology, make it more competitive with fossil energy, and lead to its more rapid deployment. That position was put forward, for example, by WTO Director-General Pascal Lamy, who called on governments to liberalise trade in renewable technologies, stating, "We all would agree barriers to trade in these areas do penalise the planet". A related argument is that manufacturers can best reduce costs by concentrating production in a small number of facilities that serve many markets, rather than building facilities in each jurisdiction to meet local content rules. "We need scale to bring down costs and free trade is critical to achieving scale", according to John Krenicki, vice chairman of General Electric, who noted with concern that many US states have included local content requirements in their renewable energy promotion policies (McCarthy 2010b).[4]

A counterargument to the trade liberalization perspective is that domestic content rules help build public support for the introduction and continuation of policies that expand the renewables market. In the absence of such rules, or other ways to guarantee domestic job creation, it becomes much more difficult for late-moving jurisdictions to justify pro-renewable policies. Without local content requirements, Ontario saw a risk of subjecting its citizens to higher power prices to pay for premium feed-in-tariffs while jobs and profits went to more established producers in Europe, Japan, and the US, or emerging low-cost producers in China. In other words, for Ontario, domestic content requirements were considered necessary for the GEA to have "win-win" potential in line with the promise of ecological modernization. As one defender of Ontario's policy put it: "Jobs are a large part of what has driven the Green Energy Act. And indeed, it may not exist without the jobs" (Estill 2010).

The EU's drive to increase exports by removing the GEA's domestic content requirements seemed to assume that Ontario would continue its considerable support for green energy if it were not guaranteed a percentage of the economic development benefits. An alternative possibility is that EU "success" on this issue would undermine the economic case for Ontario to continue such high levels of support for renewable energy while bolstering the position of the GEA's conservative opponents. EU renewable equipment producers could ultimately lose out on opportunities to provide the 40 to 50 per cent of supplies for green-energy projects that do not have to be sourced within Ontario under the GEA. Failure of Ontario's initiative in producing local green jobs would also undermine the case for other provinces to try to significantly expand the role of renewable electricity. A dynamic rather than static analysis, one which takes into account the need to construct and maintain a political coalition that can defend and advance green energy policies, could lead to very different conclusions about how to expand EU renewable-energy exports to Canada. More important, it would lead to different conclusions about how to encourage climate laggard nations such as Canada to take stronger action in the fight against climate change, a battle which is a stated priority of the EU.

---

[4] Even some GEA defenders had doubts about local content rules. One was former Obama advisor John Podesta, who stated, "I think that ultimately you want access to the most innovative products at the cheapest costs to make sure prices are low" (McCarthy 2011c).

An additional point to consider is that Europe's own renewable industry did not emerge by adhering strictly to neoliberal trade principles. Denmark's successful wind industry was built through a range of supportive policies, including "a discriminatory tariff that privileged purchases of electricity from locally-owned cooperatives, a policy inconsistent with the principle of national treatment" (Cho & Dubash 2003, pp. 2, 28-30). With the Danish case in mind, Sinclair (2010, p. 11) writes, "Ironically, if the CETA had been in place in the 1980s and 1990s, the European wind industry might not be the world leader it is today". Meanwhile, Gamesa, one of the world's largest wind turbine manufacturers, is a product of local content requirements in Spain (Lewis & Wiser 2007, p. 1851). While Germany did not have domestic content requirements, it did use generous subsidies to lure foreign companies, including Ontario's Arise Technologies, which received a €25-million grant to build a solar cell factory near Dresden (Reguly 2008). In the words of Sven Krug from the Stuttgart-based company Sinosol, "Take a look at the German map and where most of the solar companies are. They are in East Germany where there were massive state subsidies so as to attract the companies" (Zhang 2010).

Which state initiatives are most effective and justifiable in promoting green energy is a matter worthy of debate. As noted above, legitimate objections to domestic content requirements exist as do strong points in their favour. A question arises as to the most appropriate institutions to resolve such issues. Critics of the EU and Japanese turn to the WTO to argue that these questions should be resolved in other forums where trade liberalization does not have ultimate priority over the need for rapid responses to urgent environmental problems (e.g., Council of Canadians 2010).

Impact of the EU's Challenge

Since the WTO process moves slowly, it could take years before the full impact of the EU and Japanese challenges to the GEA becomes clear. A more immediate effect was to add to the uncertainty for investors that threatened to slow Ontario's transition to green energy while compounding the provincial government's problems in defending its flagship green policy from concerted opposition. Climate sceptic and conservative columnist Lorne Gunter (2011) was among those who celebrated the EU's filing of its WTO complaint, proclaiming, "Another wheel falls off [Ontario's] green-energy bus".

As noted above, criticisms of the GEA included its impact on electricity prices. Local opposition also emerged to planned construction of nearby wind turbines while the government also had to backtrack on plans to rapidly expand offshore wind power in Lake Ontario. There were significant delays in approving the vast numbers of new projects for connection to the overloaded transmission grid, which was not built with decentralized, renewable generation in mind. Meanwhile, in addition to the EU and Japanese WTO complaints, the GEA faced a NAFTA challenge from Texas energy tycoon T. Boone Pickens, who sought $775 million in compensation for alleged discrimination against his wind energy company, Mesa Power Group, with regard to access to the transmission grid.

Ontario's Conservative Party seized on such difficulties as it attacked the GEA. Had the Conservatives won the 2011 provincial election and fulfilled their campaign promises, the EU would have been able to drop its WTO challenge as the entire FIT programme – not just the domestic content requirements – would have been scrapped. These opposition promises caused some companies to reconsider their green-energy investments for a time, but the European and Japanese WTO complaints left a more lasting uncertainty. Trade lawyer Lawrence Herman noted that their WTO actions "are not helpful to the investment climate" for renewable energy in Ontario (Blackwell 2011a; see also Wallace 2011).

Some actors within EU institutions shared the view that Brussels was not playing a constructive role in opposing the GEA's domestic content rules. A report "on international trade policy in the context of climate change imperatives" by the European Parliament's Committee on International Trade (2010b) called on the Commission "not to systematically oppose local content clauses in its partners' climate policies, as in the case of the Ontario Green Energy Act", adding that "such clauses do in fact ensure that these policies are accepted by citizens and companies". The European Parliament's (2010a) subsequent resolution on the issue did not ultimately contain this language; however, in June of the following year, MEPs did call on the Commission, "as a sign of good will, to drop its challenges against the Ontario Green Energy Act's local content requirements" (2011a).

Conclusion

Although the overall climate records of the EU and Canada are very different, some similarity is evident in their respective efforts to block green energy policies introduced by the other. Canada's attempt to stop European proposals to identify the tar sands as a source of high-carbon fuel can be understood as an effort to defend an economic growth strategy based on the full development of the country's vast fossil-fuel resources. For the foreseeable future, this strategy cannot be reconciled with the need for large cuts in GHG emissions and ideas of ecological modernization. There has been no sign of an absolute decoupling of growth and GHG emissions in the tar sands, where reductions in emissions per barrel of output to date have been dwarfed by much faster output growth. Looking ahead, the evidence suggests that the most talked about technological solution, carbon capture and storage can only play a small role in limiting emissions growth. Plans for further rapid expansion of tar-sands output come at a time when the trend toward declining emissions per barrel of output has stalled, and the Canadian government projects a tripling of total tar-sands-related emissions from 2005 to 2020. Avoiding such large emissions increases would require not only technology and efficiency, the staples of EM reform, but also limiting the rate of growth in this sector and leaving oil and profits in the ground – ideas that fall outside the boundaries of EM. Undoubtedly, Canada could find other ways to maintain a comfortable level of prosperity; however, they are unlikely to be as profitable as extracting the world's second largest oil reserves. Canada faces significant trade-offs – of the kind that ecological modernization's "win-win" discourse does not readily acknowledge. Canada's response has been to adopt weak climate policies at home and to lobby against measures in the EU and elsewhere that threaten its high-carbon growth strategy.

In contrast, the EU has embraced ideas of ecological modernization, but its challenge to Ontario's Green Energy Act reveals tensions within an EM project. The EU and several Member States have linked development of renewable energy and carbon reduction to job creation and business growth. Ontario sought to follow these examples through its Green Energy Act. Since "first movers" in Europe and elsewhere were already well-established, Ontario saw a need to include domestic content requirements to ensure that it could capture a share of the economic spinoffs in return for its willingness to accept the higher short-term cost of green energy. The EU and Europe's eco-industrial lobby saw – rightly or wrongly – Ontario's action as a threat to its ability to maximise renewable-energy-related exports. The EU has sought to defend its commercial interests through neoliberal trade institutions, even at the risk of undermining one of the green initiatives with the greatest transformative potential in a climate laggard nation struggling to move beyond inaction. These actions reflect the tension between ecological and economic rationalities, which an EM project promises to reconcile. Also noteworthy is that EU green energy firms, which have been agents of ecological reform in Europe and backed stronger climate action in line with EM theory, have played a very different and contradictory role from an Ontario perspective, acting as forces of resistance to the province's most significant green policy even as some of them also invested in the province.

Ecological modernization still has a very important role to play in addressing environmental problems. The promise of win-win ecological action that simultaneously serves the goals of job creation and economic prosperity can be quite powerful in enabling significant climate action to begin. However, these cases illustrate limits to EM and tensions within it that also must be acknowledged.

References

Alberta (2010). European meetings on responsible development key to advancing Alberta's competitiveness. News release, 10 March. Edmonton: Government of Alberta. <http://alberta.ca/home/NewsFrame.cfm?ReleaseID=/acn/201003/2796248FCB3D8-9007-F182-8C5BC60FC004C78F.html>. [Accessed 16 August 2011].

Arnott, S. (2011). "RBS faces AGM protests over tar sands cash", in *The Independent*, 19 April.

Berthiaume, L. (2010). "EU takes aim at Canada Post, Ontario Green Energy Act", in *Embassy*, 24 February. <http://www.embassymag.ca/page/view/eu-02-24-2010>. [Accessed 20 August 2011].

Blackwell, R. (2011a). "Ontario urged to stick with green energy program", in *The Globe and Mail*, 10 May.

Blackwell, R. (2011b). "EU targets Ontario's green energy subsidies in WTO complaint", in *The Globe and Mail*, 12 August.

BMU (2008). *Ecological Industrial Policy: Sustainable Policy for Innovation, Growth, and Employment*. Berlin: Federal Ministry for the Environment, Nature Conservation, and Nuclear Safety.

Brand, C. (2011). MEPs challenge Commission over green status of tar sands", in *European Voice*, 7 April. <http://www.europeanvoice.com/article/imported/meps-challenge-commission-over-green-status-of-tar-sands/70754.aspx>. [Accessed 14 August 2011].

Brandt, A.R. (2011). "Upstream greenhouse gas (GHG) emissions from Canadian oil sands as a feedstock for European refineries". <https://circabc.europa.eu/d/d/workspace/SpacesStore/db806977-6418-44db-a464-20267139b34d/Brandt_Oil_Sands_GHGs_Final.pdf>. [Accessed 9 August 2011].

CAN Canada (2010). *The Tar Sands' Long Shadow: Canada's Campaign to Kill Climate Policies Outside Our Borders*. Ottawa: Climate Action Network Canada.

CAPP (2011). *2010 Responsible Canadian Energy Data: Overview*. Calgary: Canadian Association of Petroleum Producers. <http://rce2010.ca/assets/CAPP_AggregateDataGraph.pdf>. [Accessed 22 December 2011].

CBC (2008). "Secret advice to politicians: oilsands emissions hard to scrub", *CBC News*, 24 November. <http://www.cbc.ca/canada/story/2008/11/24/sands-trap.html>. [Accessed 21 August 2011].

CBC (2012). "EU at stalemate on Canada's oilsands ranking", *CBC News*, 22 February. <http://www.cbc.ca/news/world/story/2012/02/22/oilsands-european-union-vote.html>. [Accessed 24 April 2012].

Carrington, D. (2011). "UK secretly helping Canada push its oil sands project", in *The Guardian*, 28 November.

Chase, S. (2011). "Peter Kent's plan to clean up the oil sands' dirty reputation", in *The Globe and Mail*, 7 January.

Cho, A.H. and N.K. Dubash (2003). *Will Investment Rules Shrink Policy Space for Sustainable Development? Evidence from the Electricity Sector.* Washington, DC: World Resources Institute.

Council of Canadians (2010). "Japan's WTO complaint against Green Energy Act baseless but dangerous, says Council of Canadians", media release, 13 September. <http://www.canadians.org/media/trade/2010/13-Sep-10.html>. [Accessed 10 August 2011].

Council of Canadians (2011). "Canadian lobbying against EU climate policy must end, says joint letter ahead of trade talks", media release, 8 April. <http://www.canadians.org/media/trade/2011/08-Apr-11.html>. [Accessed 16 August 2011].

Dembicki, G. (2010). "Why Europe Could Decide Fate of Canada's Oil Sands", in *The Tyee*, 20 October. <http://thetyee.ca/News/2010/10/20/EuropeDecidesFate/>. [Accessed 15 August 2011].

Dembicki, G. (2011a). Canada Teams with Oil Lobby to Fight US Clean Energy Clause", in *The Tyee*, 16 March. <http://thetyee.ca/News/2011/03/16/Canada_Teams_With_Oil_Lobby/>. [Accessed 15 August 2011].

Dembicki, G. (2011b). "The Battle to Block Low Carbon Fuel Standards", in *The Tyee*, 17 March. <http://thetyee.ca/News/2011/03/17/LowCarbonFuel Fight/>. [Accessed 15 August 2011].

De Souza, M. (2011). "Ottawa considers PR firm for oilsands", in *Calgary Herald*, 31 May.

Diebel, L. (2010). "Move by Japan seen derailing green programs", in *Toronto Star*, 14 September.

Dohmen, F., N. Klawitter and W. Reuter (2010). "Solar Industry Fights to Save Subsidies", in *Der Spiegel*, 22 April. <http://www.spiegel.de/international/germany/0,1518,690297,00.html>. [Accessed 22 August 2011].

EEA (2008). "EU-15 on target for Kyoto, despite mixed performances", press release, 16 October. Copenhagen: European Environment Agency. <http://www.eea.europa.eu/pressroom/newsreleases/eu-15-on-target-for-kyoto-despite-mixed-performances>. [Accessed 27 September 2010].

Environment Canada (2010). *National Inventory Report 1990-2008: Greenhouse Gas Sources and Sinks in Canada, Part 1.* Ottawa: Environment Canada.

Environment Canada (2011). *Canada's Emissions Trends.* Ottawa: Environment Canada.

Estill, G. (2010). "Japan takes Green Energy Act to the WTO", in *Theenergycollective*, 18 September. <http://theenergycollective.com/glenestill/43710/japan-takes-green-energy-act-wto>. [Accessed 22 August 2011].

EurActiv (2011a). "Britain accused of stalling EU tar sands regulation", in *EurActiv*. <http://www.euractiv.com/climate-environment/britain-accused-stalling-eu-tar-sands-regulation news 508576>. [Accessed 22 November 2011].

EurActiv (2011b). "Canada's tar sands lobbying gets murky", in *EurActiv*. <http://www.euractiv.com/climate-environment/canada-tar-sands-lobbying-gets-murky-news-509489>. [Accessed 7 December 2011].

European Commission (2007). "Stricter fuel standards to combat climate change and reduce air pollution", press release, 31 January. Brussels: European Commission. IP/07/120. <http://europa.eu/rapid/pressReleasesAction.do?reference=IP/07/120>. [Accessed 14 August 2011].

European Commission (2008). "Boosting growth and jobs by meeting our climate change commitments", press release, 23 January. Brussels: European Commission. IP/08/80. <http://europa.eu/rapid/pressReleasesAction.do?reference=IP/08/80>. [Accessed 12 March 2010].

European Commission (2009). Directive 2009/30/EC amending Directive 98/70/EC on fuel quality: Consultation paper on the measures necessary for the implementation of Article 7a(5). Brussels: European Commission. <http://ec.europa.eu/environment/air/transport/pdf/art7a.pdf>. [Accessed 14 August 2011].

European Commission (2011). "The EU requests WTO consultations with Canada over Ontario's renewable energy policy", press release, 11 August. Brussels: European Commission. <http://trade.ec.europa.eu/doclib/press/index.cfm?id=732>. [Accessed 20 August 2011].

European Parliament (2010a). European Parliament resolution of 25 November 2010 on international trade policy in the context of climate change imperatives. Brussels: European Parliament. P7_TA(2010)0445. <http://www.europarl.europa.eu/sides/getDoc.do?type=TA&reference=P7-TA-2010-0445&language=EN>. [Accessed 21 August 2011].

European Parliament (2010b). *Report on international trade policy in the context of climate change imperatives*. Brussels: European Parliament. A7-0310/2010. <http://www.europarl.europa.eu/sides/getDoc.do?type=REPORT&reference=A7-2010-0310&language=EN>. [Accessed 21 August 2011].

European Parliament (2011a). European Parliament resolution of 8 June 2011 on EU-Canada trade relations. Brussels: European Parliament. P7_TA(2011)0257. <http://www.europarl.europa.eu/sides/getDoc.do?type=TA&language=EN&reference=P7-TA-2011-0257>. [Accessed 15 August 2011].

European Parliament (2011b). Implementation of the Fuel Quality Directive (debate). Brussels: European Parliament. <http://www.europarl.europa.eu/sides/getDoc.do?pubRef=-//EP//TEXT+CRE+20110323+ITEM-021+DOC+XML+V0//EN>. [Accessed 14 August 2011].

European Union (2009). Directive 2009/30/EC of the European Parliament and of the Council of 23 April 2009. Brussels: European Union. <http://eurlex.europa.eu/LexUriServ/LexUriServ.do?uri=OJ:L:2009:140:0088:0113:EN :PDF>. [Accessed 14 August 2011].

European Union (2010). Canada – Certain Measures Affecting the Renewable Energy Sector: Request to Join Consultations. 27 September. <http://www.seia.org/galleries/pdf/EU_request.pdf>. [Accessed 19 August 2011].

Finbow, R. (forthcoming). "Embedding Liberalisation: Will CETA Undermine the Social Dimension of Transatlantic Integration?", in F. Laursen (ed.), *The EU and the Political Economy of Transatlantic Relations*. Brussels: P.I.E. Peter Lang.

FoE Europe (2011). *Canada's dirty lobby diary: Undermining the EU Fuel Quality Directive*, Brussels: Friends of the Earth Europe. <http://www.foeeurope.org/publications/2011/FOEE_Report_Tar_Sands_Lobby_Final_July82011.pdf>. [Accessed 15 August 2011].

FoE Europe *et al.* (2010). Letter to Commissioner Hedegaard on the implementation of Fuel Quality Directive. 22 March. <http://www.foeeurope.org/corporates/Extractives/letter_Hedegaard_FQD_March2010.pdf>. [Accessed 16 August 2011].

Gerein, K. (2010). "EU delegation visit crucial to oilsands", in *Edmonton Journal*, 2 November.

Greenberg, L. (2011). "European Union launches formal challenge to Ontario power payments", in *Ottawa Citizen*, 11 August.

Gunter, L. (2011). "Still another wheel falls off Ont.'s green-energy bus", in *National Post*, 12 August.

Hajer, M.A. (1995). *The Politics of Environmental Discourse: Ecological Modernization and the Policy Process*. Oxford: Oxford University Press.

Hamilton, T. (2009). "Germany fuming over solar policy", in *Toronto Star*, 24 October.

Harrison, P. (2010). "EU yields to Canada over oil trade barriers: sources", in *Reuters Canada*. <http://ca.reuters.com/article/idCATRE62N3T920100324? sp=true>. [Accessed 15 August 2011].

Harrison, P. (2011). "Canada warns EU over oil sands", in *Edmonton Journal*, 5 April.

Harrison, P. and J. von Reppert-Bismarck (2011). "Tar sand row threatens Canada-EU trade deal – sources", in *Reuters*, 21 February. <http://www.reuters.com/article/2011/02/21/us-eu-canada-trade-idUSTRE71K2FL20110 221>. [Accessed 5 June 2011].

Healing, D. (2011). "EU report warns of oilsands emissions", in *Calgary Herald*, 9 February.

Herman, L. (2011). *Green Energy Act – Japan's Challenge in the WTO*. Toronto: Cassels Brock & Blackwell LLP. <http://www.casselsbrock.com/CBNewsletter/Green_Energy_Act___Japan_s_Challenge_in_the_WTO>. [Accessed 20 August 2011].

Hey, C. (2010). "The German Paradox: Climate Leader and Green Car Laggard", in *The New Climate Policies of the European Union: Internal Legislation and Climate Diplomacy*, S. Oberthür and M. Pallemaerts (eds.). Brussels: VUB Press, pp. 211-230.

Huhne, C., N. Röttgen and J.-L. Borloo (2010). "Europe needs to reduce emissions by 30%", in *Financial Times*, 15 July.

Huot, M., L. Fischer and N. Lemphers (2011). *Oilsands and Climate Change: How Canada's oilsands are standing in the way of effective climate action.* Drayton Valley, AB: Pembina Institute. <pubs.pembina.org/reports/oilsands-and-climate-briefing-note-201109.pdf>. [Accessed 24 September 2011].

Jacobson, D. (2009). Ottawa: Ambassador Jacobson and Environment Minister Prentice discuss continental carbon market and oil sands. Diplomatic cable released by Wikileaks. <http://www.aftenposten.no/nyheter/iriks/article3959849.ece>. [Accessed 17 August 2011].

Jacobsson, S. and V. Lauber (2006). "The politics and policy of energy system transformation – explaining the German diffusion of renewable energy technology", in *Energy Policy*, 34, pp. 256-276.

Jänicke, M. (2008). "Ecological modernisation: new perspectives", in *Journal of Cleaner Production*, 16(5), pp. 557-565.

Jänicke, M. and K. Jacob (2004). "Lead Markets for Environmental Innovations: A New Role for the Nation State", in *Global Environmental Politics*, 4(1), pp. 29-46.

Kolbert, E. (2007). "Unconventional crude: Canada's synthetic-fuels boom", in *New Yorker*, 12 November, pp. 46-51.

Levant, E. (2010). *Ethical Oil: The Case for Canada's Oil Sands.* Toronto: McClelland & Stewart.

Lewis, J.I. and R.H. Wiser (2007). "Fostering a renewable energy technology industry: An international comparison of wind industry policy support mechanisms", in *Energy Policy*, 35(3), pp. 1844-1857.

Lukacs, M. (2011a). "Canada on Secret Oil Offensive: Documents", in *The Dominion*, 25 May. <http://www.dominionpaper.ca/articles/3991>. [Accessed 15 August 2011].

Lukacs, M. (2011b). "Canada's crude politics on oil sands", in *The Guardian*, 31 May. <http://www.guardian.co.uk/commentisfree/cifamerica/2011/may/31/oil-sands-oil>. [Accessed 15 August 2011].

Macalister, T. (2011a). "UK undermining Europe's tar sands ban, say campaigners", in *The Guardian*, 31 May, p. 25.

Macalister, T. (2011b). "Canadian government accused of 'unprecedented' tar sands lobbying", in *The Guardian*, 4 August. <http://www.guardian.co.uk/environment/2011/aug/04/canada-tar-sands-lobbying>. [Accessed 15 August 2011].

McCarthy, S. (2010a). "Ontario green policy comes under attack", in *The Globe and Mail*, 17 September.

McCarthy, S. (2010b). "Ontario's green policy cited in EU talks", in *The Globe and Mail*, 19 October.

McCarthy, S. (2011a). "Oil sands emissions rules stalled, despite vows to EU", in *The Globe and Mail*, 22 March.

McCarthy, S. (2011b). "Ottawa fights EU's dirty fuel label on oil sands", in *The Globe and Mail*, 28 March.

McCarthy, S. (2011c). "Ontario urged not to scrap renewable energy policy", in *The Globe and Mail*, 13 July.

Mech, M. (2011). *A Comprehensive Guide to the Alberta Oil Sands: Understanding the Environmental and Human Impacts, Export Implications, and Political, Economic, and Industry Influences.* <http://greenparty.ca/files/attachments/a_comprehensive_guide_to_the_alberta_oil_sands_-_may_20111.pdf>. [Accessed 17 August 2011].

Mol, A.P.J. (2003). *Globalization and Environmental Reform: The Ecological Modernization of the Global Economy.* Cambridge, MA: MIT Press.

Mol, A.P.J., D.A. Sonnenfeld and G. Spaargaren (2009). *The Ecological Modernisation Reader: Environmental Reform in Theory and Practice.* London: Routledge.

Morrison, S. (2011). "Pollution fears as UK blocks European ban on fuel from tar sands", in *The Independent*, 1 June. <http://www.independent.co.uk/environment/green-living/pollution-fears-as-uk-blocks-european-ban-on-fuel-from-tar-sands-2291598.html>. [Accessed 17 August 2011].

Murphy, J. (2000). "Ecological modernisation", in *Geoforum*, 31(1), pp. 1-8.

Ontario (2009). "McGuinty Government's Plan Will Lead to Green Jobs and Green Energy", press release, 14 May. Toronto: Ontario Ministry of Energy and Infrastructure. <http://http://news.ontario.ca/mei/en/2009/05/ontario-legislature-passes-green-energy-act.html>. [Accessed 13 August 2009].

Rankin, J. (2010). "A very sticky situation", in *European Voice*, 27 May. <http://www.europeanvoice.com/article/imported/a-very-sticky-situation/68076.aspx>. [Accessed 15 August 2011].

Rankin, J. (2011a). "Row over green status of oil from tar sands", in *European Voice*, 3 February. <http://www.europeanvoice.com/article/imported/row-over-green-status-of-oil-from-tar-sands/70112.aspx>. [Accessed 14 August 2011].

Rankin, J. (2011b). "Tar sands 'more polluting than other fuels'", in *European Voice*, 3 February. <http://www.europeanvoice.com/article/2011/february/tar-sands-creates-more-pollution-than-other-fossil-fuels-/70152.aspx>. [Accessed 18 August 2011].

Reguly, E. (2008). "Lessons from Germany's Energy Renaissance", in *The Globe and Mail*, 22 March.

Revell, A. (2005). "Ecological Modernization in the UK: Rhetoric or Reality?", in *European Environment*, 15, pp. 344-361.

Royal Society of Canada (2010). *Environmental and Health Impacts of Canada's Oil Sands Industry.* Ottawa: Royal Society of Canada.

Saunders, D. (2010). "Ontario foot-dragging imperils Canada-EU trade pact, officials say", in *The Globe and Mail*, 31 March.

Sharpe, A. *et al.* (2008). *The Valuation of the Alberta Oil Sands*. Ottawa: Centre for the Study of Living Standards. <http://www.csls.ca/reports/csls2008-7.pdf>. [Accessed 28 August 2011].

Shryhman, S. (2010). *Potential Impacts of the Proposed Canada-European Union Comprehensive Economic and Trade Agreement (CETA) on the Pace and Character of Oil Sands Development*. Toronto: Sack Goldblatt Mitchell. <http://canadians.org/trade/documents/CETA/legal-opinion-CETA-tarsands.pdf>. [Accessed 17 August 2011].

Sinclair, S. (2010). *Negotiating from Weakness: Canada-EU trade treaty threatens Canadian purchasing policies and public services*. Ottawa: Canadian Centre for Policy Alternatives.

Taylor, S. (2011). "Split over emissions from tar sands", in *European Voice*, 14 July. <http://www.europeanvoice.com/CWS/Index.aspx?PageID=191&articleID=71624&lg=1>. [Accessed 14 August 2011].

UNDP (2007). *Human Development Report 2007/2008 – Fighting Climate Change: Human Solidarity in a Divided World*. New York: United Nations Development Programme.

Wallace, K. (2011). "Solar layoffs heat political sparring", in *Toronto Star*, 9 July.

Weber, A.M. (2010). "Japan, US and the EU Face-Off against Ontario's Renewable Energy Program at the WTO", in *Canadian Energy Law*, 20 December. <http://www.canadianenergylaw.com/2010/12/articles/regulatory/japan-us-and-the-eu-faceoff-against-ontarios-renewable-energy-program-at-the-wto/>. [Accessed 20 August 2011].

WWF-UK and The Co-Operative (2009). *CCS in the Alberta Oil Sands – A Dangerous Myth*, London and Manchester: WWF and the Co-Operative.

WWF-UK and The Co-Operative (2010). *Opportunity cost of tar sands development*. London and Manchester: WWF and the Co-Operative.

van der Zee, B. (2011). "Trade talks could wreck climate change measures, campaigners warn", in *The Guardian*, 31 January. <http://www.guardian.co.uk/environment/2011/jan/31/alberta-tar-sands-trade-agreement>. [Accessed 17 August 2011].

Zhang, D. (2010). "German energy firms try to benefit from China's green revolution", in *Deutsche Welle*, 26 October. <http://www.dw-world.de/dw/article/0,,6151346,00.html>. [Accessed 22 August 2011].

By Way of Conclusions

Explaining Transatlantic Economic Relations and Looking Towards the Future

Finn LAURSEN

The global political economy is changing rapidly. The industrialized part of the world, including North America and Europe, has been going through financial crises in recent years. Low and even negative economic growth has produced high unemployment, which in turn puts pressure on governments to introduce protectionist measures. Overall, however, the countries in the North Atlantic area have largely succeeded in resisting calls for protectionism. They even engage in bilateral free trade negotiations with selected countries, partly to offset the lack of progress in the Doha Development Round of the World Trade Organization (WTO). But low growth and high unemployment remain serious problems for the Atlantic area countries. And there is no agreed strategy on how to deal with the crises. Political leaders disagree on how to increase competitiveness and create jobs and find it difficult to get the required reforms adopted.

Some countries were less affected by the financial crises than others. These include a number of emergent economies, especially the so-called BRICS (Brazil, Russia, India, China, and now also including South Africa). They have been able to continue with impressive economic growth rates, thereby gradually accounting for a greater share of world production as well as trade. How co-operation between the Atlantic countries and the emerging powers will develop in the future is of great importance to the welfare of the Atlantic area countries, even if growth may also slow down in the BRICS.

There is of course already some co-operation between the industrialized and emerging economies inside global institutions, including the WTO and the International Monetary Fund (IMF). Recently, the co-operation between finance ministers and central bank governors that emerged at the time of the Asian financial crisis in 1997 in the form of the Group of 20 (G20) has been extended to include summit meetings to deal with the financial crisis that started in the United States in 2008 and subsequently spread to other parts of the world, including the EU. These

G20 meetings allow leaders, ministers, and central bank officials to compare notes, possibly learn from each other, and make commitments at least at the rhetorical level.

What Went Wrong with Finance?

Efforts to explain the recent and still ongoing financial crisis will take us in different directions (See chapters by DioGuardi, Brunet, and Pooran). The world is multivariate. There is no generally accepted model that can explain financial crises. The phenomenon is over-determined, explainable by imprudent domestic economic policies, inadequate international financial management as well as other factors (Gilpin 2001, pp. 266-67).

Arguably, the current crisis started in the United States, but who knows whether the sovereign debt crisis in Europe would have happened anyway, maybe with some further delay. Explaining the financial crisis in the United States is now a hot topic in the presidential election campaign, with Republicans blaming the Barak Obama administration, but with defenders of the president saying that he inherited the crisis from the George W. Bush administration, possibly because of military overstretches in Iraq, Afghanistan, etc., but also because of nefarious roles played by private actors, the banks, and Wall Street. This, in turn, raises questions of regulation of private actors. What role should governments play? Again, we see a split between most Republicans and most Democrats, the former wanting the market to take care of the problems and the latter arguing that the government must play an active role. We see a clash of economic doctrines.

The problem with the argument that the capitalist system will solve the problems, if we reduce government, is, of course, that there is such a phenomenon as market failure. If we think in terms of simple game theory, it is known that there are many situations where independent rational actors have problems producing optimal collective outcomes (Stein 1990). This is really why government was invented in the first place.

The response to the financial crisis on both sides of the Atlantic was to increase the governmental oversight by creating new institutions. But the moment a crisis starts spreading from one country to another, the collective action problem becomes an international problem. This explains why international institutions, especially the IMF, got involved. As a corollary development, the Group of 8 (G8) delegated its work to a beefed up G20, involving also emergent economies, such as the BRICS countries in global financial management. Transatlantic economic relations are clearly very much embedded in wider international economic relations and regimes, and the Atlantic countries increasingly face competitors from outside the region, first of all the emerging economies, which also request a greater say in existing institutions (BRICS 2012, G20 Information Centre 2012).

The EU responded to the financial crisis with a series of steps that are still ongoing, suggesting a bit of a trial-and-error process. Here too, as in the United States, the steps taken were politically controversial, but given the EU's basic confederal structure, the controversies were partly and largely among the Member States. These interstate disagreements in turn depended on domestic politics. The countries that needed to bail out their banks or needed bailouts themselves because of unsustainable public debt, the PIIGS (Portugal, Ireland, Italy, Greece and Spain) in particular, were blamed for irresponsible fiscal policies, and other countries were not eager to step in.

The European Central Bank did assist the private sector, but a no-bailout clause in the Treaty of Maastricht created problems especially for assisting Greece but potentially also for other eurozone countries with high public debt, such as Italy and Spain. These latter countries have much larger economies than Greece. Germany, arguably the regional paymaster in the EU, set strict conditions for assistance, which first led to the creation of a temporary bailout fund, the European Financial Stabilisation Mechanism (EFSM) and then a permanent bailout fund, The European Stability Mechanism (ESM). This was referred to as a firewall in the debate. In parallel, private investors also had to take a loss. This, in turn, was referred to as a haircut. The ESM required an amendment of the Lisbon Treaty. Further, a Fiscal Stability Treaty involving all eurozone members and most other EU Member States, except the UK and the Czech Republic, has been adopted. It is hoped that these and other measures will reduce the risks in the future. But many observers remain sceptical. And the challenge of competitiveness and growth remains to be addressed adequately.

The eurozone crisis clearly demonstrated the asymmetrical nature of the Economic and Monetary Union (EMU), which had been established by the Maastricht Treaty creating the EU in 1993. The EMU has a centralized monetary policy, with a single currency for the 17 countries that have adopted the single currency, the euro, as well as a European Central Bank (ECB) in charge of monetary policy. But fiscal policy has remained decentralised, with Member States retaining the main responsibilities for taxation and expenditures (Verdun 2011, p. 254). Only about 1 per cent of the EU's Gross Domestic Product (GDP) goes through the EU budget, so the possibilities for autonomous EU anti-cyclical policies are tiny, basically limited to money from the so-called Structural Funds, including the Cohesion Fund, which has transferred money to the poorer countries in the EU in the past, especially Greece, Spain, Portugal, and Ireland until the Eastern enlargements in 2004 and 2007. The new Member States from Central and Eastern Europe have now become the major recipients of money from the Structural Funds (Sbragia and Stolfi 2008).

Post-Lisbon Treaty Amendments for Fiscal Stability[1]

Dealing with the fiscal crisis in the EU has required some treaty making. In the minds of many actors and observers, the Lisbon Treaty was to be the last reform for many years. But the EU is still a work in progress, and we have already seen a couple of small amendments to the EU treaty, one dealing with membership of the European Parliament, the other one allowing for the permanent bailout mechanism.

The European Stability Mechanism

The sovereign debt crisis, with especially Greece being unable to finance or refinance its debt, created problems for the eurozone. The crisis exposed the asymmetrical nature of EMU, with a centralized monetary policy and decentralized fiscal policy. To make things worse, the Maastricht Treaty had a no-bailout clause (Art. 104b in the Maastricht Treaty, now Art. 125 TFEU), so rules had to be adapted to assist Greece. The situation was further complicated by the strong political resentment against the southern members of the eurozone who faced the debt crisis: Portugal, Italy, Greece, and Spain especially. The idea behind the no-bailout clause was to avoid so-called "moral hazard", i.e., a temptation to engage in imprudent fiscal policies (Verhelst 2011, pp. 9-10).

A rescue package of €750 billion was approved by the Economic and Financial Affairs Council of Ministers (EcoFin) in May 2010. It was to be paid out through the new temporary bailout fund, the EFSF.[2] It was established on the basis of Article 122 TFEU, which allows for financial assistance "where a Member State is in difficulties or is seriously threatened with severe difficulties caused by natural disasters or exceptional occurrences beyond its control". In the adopted regulation, "the unprecedented global financial crisis and economic downturn that have hit the world over the last two years" was seen as constituting such an "exceptional situation beyond the control of the Member States" (Council of the EU 2010).

---

[1] This section partly relies on the concluding chapter in Laursen, forthcoming.

[2] "About EFSF", <http://www.efsf.europa.eu/about/index.htm>. [Accessed 19 February 2012].

On 16 December 2010, the European Council agreed to amend the Lisbon Treaty to allow for the creation of a permanent bailout mechanism, the ESM to replace the temporary EFSF that would expire in 2013. According to the European Council decision, the following paragraph would be added to Article 136 of the TFEU:

The Member States whose currency is the euro may establish a stability mechanism to be activated if indispensable to safeguard the stability of the euro as a whole. The granting of any required financial assistance under the mechanism will be made subject to strict conditionality. (European Council 2010c)

The treaty change was designed as a small change under the Lisbon Treaty's "special revision clause" (Article 48(6) TEU). This clause is limited to Part Three of the TFEU dealing with policies and action of the Union. The decision in the European Council must be unanimous, and it must not increase the competences of the Union (Phillips 2010).

Subsequently, the Member States taking part in the euro worked out the EMS treaty. A first version was signed by the eurozone countries on 11 July 2011. On 22 March 2011, it was approved by the European Parliament (European Parliament 2011). The European Council approved the treaty at its meeting on 24-25 March 2011 (European Council 2011a). A new improved version was signed on 2 February 2012. It duly referred to the additional paragraph added to Article 136 TFEU allowing for such a mechanism to be established (Treaty Establishing the European Stability Mechanism 2012). In the meantime, the eurozone countries and some other EU countries had also agreed to a so-called stability pact.

The European Fiscal Stability Treaty

The financial crisis led to calls for fiscal union, where the eurozone countries would give up some sovereignty over taxation and budgetary policy and accept enforcement mechanisms through the European Commission. Especially German Chancellor Angela Merkel demanded such a fiscal union. On the other hand, however, she was not willing to accept the idea of Eurobonds issued by the ECB to mutualise part of the sovereign debt. Commission President José Manuel Barroso on 21 November 2011 suggested that Eurobonds, which he called "stability bonds", could be a good way to deal with the crisis (Taylor 2011).

On 9 December 2011, the European Council had a meeting dealing with the financial crisis.[3] All seventeen members of the eurozone as well

---

[3] For conclusions, see: <http://europa.eu/rapid/pressReleasesAction.do?reference= DOC/11/8&type=HTML>. [Accessed 18 February 2012].

as most other EU Member States agreed to work out an intergovernmental treaty creating a fiscal compact (European Council 2011b). Given a veto from the British Prime Minister David Cameron, this would not be a revision of the EU treaty but a new separate treaty.[4]

In the end, the Treaty on Stability, Coordination and Governance in the Economic and Monetary Union was signed by all EU Member States expect the UK and the Czech Republic on 2 March 2012 (Mahony 2012; BBC News 2012). It will enter into force on 1 January 2013 if it has been ratified by 12 eurozone countries by then, otherwise the first of the month following the deposit of the 12th instrument of ratification (Treaty on Stability, Coordination and Governance in the Economic and Monetary Union 2012, Article 14(2)). Letting it enter into force before all members have ratified is an interesting feature of the treaty. Given the fact that Ireland has decided to have a referendum on the treaty and the fact that the leading Socialist candidate in the upcoming French presidential elections is very critical of the treaty suggest that more interesting politics may lie ahead.

Since the new Fiscal Stability Treaty does not increase the size of the EU budget, it will not help the EU develop an active growth and employment policy. Greece *et al.* must pull themselves up from the desperate situation they brought themselves into, with a little help from their friends.

Towards More Bilateralism in Trade

Turning to trade, you face the old question: Is the bottle half full or is it half empty? As we have noticed, Mexico got a free trade agreement (FTA) with the EU in 2000, partly as a response to the creation of the North American Free Trade Area (NAFTA) in the early 1990s (see chapter by Dominguez). We now have free trade among the three North American countries through NAFTA and free trade among the 27 Member States of the EU in Europe. With the exception of the EU-Mexican agreement, the transatlantic trade relations are governed by the WTO regimes, including the General Agreement on Tariffs and Trade (GATT) and General Agreement on Trade in Services (GATS), which basically means most-favoured nation treatment in respect to tariffs and national treatment in respect to taxation, i.e., non-discrimination in trade relations. Through GATT trade negotiation rounds, the tariffs have gradually been reduced to the point that they are no longer very important. But a number of nontariff barriers to trade (NTBs) remain, and

---

[4]   For an account of the meeting, see: "Eurozone crisis live: Germany wins battle on tighter fiscal rules for the euro", <http://www.guardian.co.uk/business/2012/jan/30/debt-crisis-greece>. [Accessed 18 February 2012].

there have been efforts through bilateral negotiations between the European Union and the United States to reduce these. In the case of Canada, the approach is now more radical, with ongoing efforts to negotiate a Comprehensive Economic and Trade Agreement (CETA) (see chapter by Finbow). If the negotiations succeed in reaching an agreement, it will change the rules of the game for the EU-USA economic relations as well, especially if cumbersome and costly rules of origin have to be avoided.

It is too early to tell where we will end up on this. Economic theory suggests that free trade is normally a good thing (Gilpin 2001, Ch. 8). It produces economic gains. From that perspective, it is strange that we do not already have a vast Transatlantic FTA. The explanation for this absence is a typical political economy explanation. Only competitive parts of industry are in favour of free trade. Non-competitive parts of industry will favour and demand protection. The potential loss of jobs gives non-competitive industries strong political arguments. The consumers who should normally favour free trade, to find more and cheaper products and greater variety of goods on the market, tend to be poorly organized. Still, various citizens groups do get involved in lobbying trade policy decision-makers. Trade unions tend to be sceptical of freer trade, seeing increased foreign competition as a threat to jobs. This is why trade policy has usually been very controversial in the United States, with presidents needing fast-track authorizations to engage in international trade negotiations. With the European Parliament now getting more involved in trade policy, thanks to the Lisbon Treaty, it remains to be seen whether that will politicize trade policy in Europe more in the future (Meunier and Nicolaïdis 2011; Niemann 2012).

Given the current focus on bilateral FTAs, the multilateral WTO regimes face challenges (see chapter by Behrens). It raises the question whether the Doha Development Round can be rescued. An agreement will require willingness to compromise. Both the industrialized North and the emerging South will have to open up further, not only at the border but also behind the borders. The rich countries will have to continue reforming their agricultural policies – not just the EU Common Agricultural Policy – and open up their markets for agricultural products. Developing countries in return must also be willing to include public procurement, competition, and investments on the agenda and engage with these broader issues. The problem for multilateralism is that bilateral negotiations create the possibility of more selective approaches to these issues, thus creating an increasingly complex international political economy in the area of trade.

Tackling Global Warming

Much of the trade political agenda nowadays is about behind-the-border issues, including product standards, other NTBs, competition rules, and increasingly, also environmental standards, from hormone-treated meat to pollution from tar sands. Concerning environmental standards, there are disagreements on both sides of the Atlantic and between the two sides (see chapters by Leal-Arcas and Hayden). It makes a difference whether Canada has a Conservative or a Liberal government and presumably also whether the US has a Democratic or Republican administration. On the EU side, there are leaders and lag-gards among the Member States, the former including especially the Northern Member States and the latter the Southern – and now also Eastern – Member States (Sbragia 2000). The European countries and the EU can and have sometimes played a role of leadership, as for instance, in connection with the Kyoto Protocol negotiations in the 1990s (Bretherton and Vogler 2006; Vogler 2011). In connection with efforts to renew the Kyoto Protocol, the European side has been disap-pointed by its North American partners, including the way President Obama negotiated directly with the BASIC countries (Brazil, South Africa, India, and China) at the Copenhagen summit on climate change in December 2009, thus marginalizing the EU, and reaching an agree-ment that the EU found inadequate (Eppstein *et al.* 2010; Smith and Steffenson 2011). More recently in December 2011, Canada decided to pull out of the Kyoto Protocol (CBC News 2011). So global warming remains a hot issue in transatlantic relations.

As for money and trade, the world also faces collective action prob-lems in respect to the environment. It is tempting to let the neighbour pay part of the price of pollution. Much pollution is trans-boundary in nature. In the long run, non-co-operation will be self-defeating. The world needs to build good international institutions to deal with these issues. Many of these institutions will have to be global. Commitments must be legally binding. Otherwise, defection becomes too easy. Since the rich developed countries pollute more than the less developed countries, the former have a special responsibility to show global lead-ership. If such leadership could be a shared co-operative transatlantic leadership, the chances of success would increase. Needless to say, given the fast growth in the BRICS countries, it is important to get these countries on board too. Especially China has become a heavy polluter.

The Shifting Power Relations

What this adds up to is a new situation. The Atlantic world can no longer dominate the world. China is clearly becoming an actor in the global political economy, and it expects to be listened to, with India following closely afterwards. That Russia is an important actor is not completely new, partly for security reasons, but also because the EU has become heavily dependent on energy imports from Russia. That Brazil, South Africa, and other countries in the South are becoming more important actors completes the picture of a world with more actors than in the past, where the US and EU could dominate in GATT – assisted by Japan – and where these same countries could dominate the other Bretton Woods institutions, the World Bank, and the IMF. It is not surprising that the BRICS countries now demand changes in the voting rights in the Washington-based Bretton Woods institutions. As they put it in the Delhi Declaration from their fourth summit in New Delhi on 29 March 2012:

> We recognize the importance of the global financial architecture in main-taining the stability and integrity of the global monetary and financial sys-tem. We therefore call for a more representative international financial ar-chitecture, with an increase in the voice and representation of developing countries and the establishment and improvement of a just international monetary system that can serve the interests of all countries and support the development of emerging and developing economies. Moreover, these economies having experienced broad-based growth are now significant con-tributors to global recovery. (BRICS 2012)

The emerging actors may not fully share the liberal doctrines of the old powers, even if most of them joined the WTO from the beginning in 1995 (Brazil, India, and South Africa). China joined in December 2001, and Russia is now finally in the process of ratifying accession. These countries may be less willing to protect Intellectual Property Rights (IPR) and more willing to protect domestic production or distribution of goods. For these reason, the global economy will remain politicized. Conflicts and friction will keep emerging in the future. Creating global institutions where solutions can be negotiated and disputes settled is, therefore, of great importance.

The fact that the BRICS themselves are a strange group of countries with very different perspectives on many issues will not make things easier. The start of G20 summits may be a useful beginning, but more is needed. G20 is still a deliberative body. It may draw up conclusions with individual commitments, but it does not make decisions, nor does it engage in monitoring and sanctioning. So how credible are the com-mitments? As long as the institutions are based on classical international law, it is fair to say that commitments will remain weak at best. In such a situation, the Atlantic world will still have to use its economic power to defend its interests. Given the size of its economies, those of the United States and the EU in particular, it still has such power. The US remains the largest economy in the world. And the EU can also be an economic superpower if it pulls its act together.

References

Apart from the chapters in the book the following sources have been useful:

BBC News (2012). "EU summit: All but two leaders sign fiscal treaty", 2 March. <http://www.bbc.co.uk/news/world-europe-17230760>. [Accessed 15 March 2012].

Bretherton, Charlotte and John Vogler (eds.) (2006). *The European Union as a Global Actor.* 2nd ed. London: Routledge.

BRICS (2012). "Fourth BRICS Summit – Delhi Declaration". <http://www.mea.gov.in/mystart.php?id=190019162>. [Accessed 2 April 2012].

CBC News (2011). "Canada pulls out of Kyoto Protocol", 12 December. <http://www.cbc.ca/news/politics/story/2011/12/12/pol-kent-kyoto-pullout.html>. [Accessed 4 April 2012].

Council of the European Union (2010). "Council Regulation establishing a European financial stabilisation mechanism", Brussels 10 May. <http://register.consilium.europa.eu/pdf/en/10/st09/st09606.en10.pdf>. [Accessed 15 March 2012].

Eppstein, Gloria, Sina Gerlach, and Maren Huser (2010. "The EU's Impact in International Climate Change Negotiations – The Case of Copenhagen". <http://dseu.lboro.ac.uk/members/Maastricht/DSEU%20Epstein%20Gerlach%20Huser%20paper.pdf >. [Accessed 3 April 2012].

European Council (2010a). Protocol No. 36 on transitional provisions concerning the composition of the European Parliament for the rest of the 2009-2014 parliamentary term, see: Decision of the European Council of 19 May 2010 (EUCO 11/10). <http://register.consilium.europa.eu/pdf/en/10/st00/st00011.en10.pdf>. [Accessed January 2012].

European Council (2010b). Brussels European Council 28-29 October, Presidency Conclusions, Brussels (Euco 25/1/10 Co Rev 1 Eur18 Concl 4). <http://www.consilium.europa.eu/uedocs/cms_data/docs/pressdata/en/ec/117496.pdf.> [Accessed January 2012].

European Council (2010c). Brussels European Council 16/17 December, Presidency Conclusions, Brussels (Euco 30/10 Co Eur 21 Concl 5). <http://www.consilium.europa.eu/uedocs/cms_data/docs/pressdata/en/ec/118578.pdf>. [Accessed January 2012].

European Council (2011a), European Council 24/25 March, Conclusions, Brussels (Euco 10/1/11 Co Eur 6 Concl 3). <http://www.consilium.europa.eu/uedocs/cms_data/docs/pressdata/en/ec/120296.pdf>. [Accessed 15 March 2012].

European Council (2011b). "European Council concludes discussion on the new fiscal compact". <http://www.european-council.europa.eu/homepage/highlights/european-council-concludes-discussion-on-the-new-fiscal-compact>. [Accessed 15 March 2012].

European Parliament (2011). "Parliament approves Treaty change to allow stability mechanism". http://www.europarl.europa.eu/news/en/pressroom/content/20110322IPR16114/html/Parliament-approves-Treaty-change-to-allow-stability-mechanism>. [Accessed 15 March 2012].

G20 Information Centre. "The G20", http://www.g20.utoronto.ca/g20whatisit.html>. [Accessed 3 April 2012]

Gilpin, Robert (2001). *Global Political Economy: Understanding the International Economic Order.* Princeton: Princeton University Press.

Keukeleire, Stephan and Hans Bruyninckx (2011). "The European Union, the BRICs, and the Emerging New World Order", in Christopher Hill and Michael Smith (eds.), *International Relations and the European Union.* 2nd ed. Oxford: Oxford University Press, pp. 380-403.

Laursen, Finn (ed.) (2009). *The EU in the Global Political Economy.* Brussels: P.I.E. Peter Lang.

Laursen, Finn (ed.) (2010). *Comparative Regional Integration: Europe and Beyond.* Farnham: Ashgate.

Laursen, Finn (ed.) (forthcoming). *Designing the European Union: From Paris to Lisbon.* Houndmills: Palgrave Macmillan.

Mahony, Honor (2012). "Twenty five EU leaders sign German-model fiscal treaty", in *EUobserver*, 2 March. <http://euobserver.com/843/115460>. [Accessed 3 March 2012].

Meunier, Sophie and Kalypso Nicolaïdis (2011). "The European Union as a Trade Power", in Christopher Hill and Michael Smith (eds.), *International Relations and the European Union.* 2nd ed. Oxford: Oxford University Press, pp. 275-298.

Niemann, Arne (2012). "The Common Commercial Policy: From Nice to Lisbon", in Finn Laursen (ed.), *The EU's Lisbon Treaty: Institutional Choices and Implementation.* Farnham: Ashgate, pp. 205-227.

Peterson, John (2008). "The EU as a Global Actor", in Elizabeth Bomberg, John Peterson and Alexander Stubb (eds.), *The European Union: How Does it Work?* 2nd ed. Oxford: Oxford University Press, pp. 201-221.

Phillips, L. (2010). "'Small, small, small' EU treaty change to deliver 'quantum leap'", in *EUobserver*, 29 October. <http://euobserver.com/18/31163>. [Accessed 15 March 2012].

Sbragia, Alberta (2000). "Environmental Policy: Economic Constraints and External Pressures", in Helen Wallace and William Wallace (eds.), *Policy-Making in the European Union.* 4th ed. Oxford: Oxford University Press, pp. 293-316.

Sbragia, Alberta and Francesco Stolfi (2008). "Key Policies", in Elizabeth Bomberg, John Peterson and Alexander Stubb (eds.), *The European Union: How Does it Work?* 2nd ed. Oxford: Oxford University Press, pp. 115-137.

Smith, Michael and Rebecca Steffenson (2011), "The EU and the United States", in Christopher Hill and Michael Smith (eds.), *International Relations and the European Union.* 2ⁿᵈ ed. Oxford: Oxford University Press, pp. 404-431.

Stein, Arthur A. (1990). *Why Nations Cooperate: Circumstance and Choice in International Relations.* Ithaca: Cornell University Press.

Taylor, Simon (2011). "Barroso says Eurobonds will 'be seen as natural'", in *European Voice*, 17 November. <http://www.europeanvoice. com/article/imported/barroso-says-eurobonds-will-be-seen-as-natural- /72630.aspx>. [Accessed 18 February 2012].

"Treaty establishing the European Stability Mechanism..." (2012). 2 February. <http://www.european-council.europa.eu/media/582311/05-tesm2.en12. pdf>. [Accessed 12 March 2012].

"Treaty on Stability, Coordination and Governance in the Economic and Monetary Union..." (2012). 2 March. http://european-council.europa. eu/media/639235/st00tscg26_en12.pdf>. [Accessed 15 March 2012].

Verdun, Amy (2011). "The EU and the Global Political Economy", in Christopher Hill and Michael Smith (eds.), *International Relations and the European Union.* 2ⁿᵈ ed. Oxford: Oxford University Press, pp. 246-274.

Verhelst, Stijn (2011). *The Reform of European Economic Governance: Towards a Sustainable Monetary Union?* Egmont Paper 47. Brussels: Royal Institute for International Relations.

Vogler, John (2011). "The Challenge of the Environment, Energy, and Climate Change", in Christopher Hill and Michael Smith (eds.), *International Relations and the European Union.* 2ⁿᵈ ed. Oxford: Oxford University Press, pp. 349-379.

List of Contributors

Maria Behrens has held a Chair for International Relations and Comparative Politics since 2008, and is speaker of the Institute of Political Science at the University of Wuppertal. From 2005 until 2007 she was Deputy Professor of International Relations at the Johann Wolfgang Goethe-University in Frankfurt/Main (Germany). Her professional expertise in international political economy and foreign policy focuses on: political coordination and regulation of conflicts in international relations, interrelations of international organizations, uni- or bilateral strategies in foreign economic policy, the relation between political institutions, and economic resources and societal interests in the national and international arena.

Ferran Brunet is Doctor of Economics, and Professor of European Studies at the Universitat Autònoma de Barcelona, Spain. He teaches and researches on European integration, European economy, and economic policy. He did predoctoral studies at the Institut d'Études Politiques (Paris), Université catholique de Louvain (Belgium), and postdoctoral work at Kobe University (Japan), Renmin University of China (Beijing), and Harvard University. He is author of the reference textbook *Curso de Integración Europea* (second edition, Madrid, Alianza Editorial, 2010) and has published on economic regulation, competition, productivity, euroimbalances, and European socio-economic model(s). Dr. Brunet is currently working on a project that analyses the Europeanization and the quality of regulation, the need for Europe and the place of the European Union as state-builder.

Joe DioGuardi served for twenty-two years, twelve of them as a partner with the international accounting firm of Arthur Andersen & Co., one of the first public advocates of governmental fiscal responsibility. In January 1985, he brought his extensive professional and volunteer experience to Congress when he became the first practicing certified public accountant to serve in the US House of Representatives. As a new Member of the House, DioGuardi took the lead in sounding the call for truth in federal budgeting, accounting and reporting, and in bringing financial accountability to Capitol Hill. He was the original author of the Chief Financial Officer's Act, signed by President George Bush in 1990, which mandated the assignment of a CFO to each major department and agency of the US government. Since leaving Congress in 1989, DioGuardi has established several nonpartisan organizations, including Truth in Government, through which he continues his crusade for federal fiscal reforms. He has written widely on the need for fiscal responsibility and public accountability in government and been a keynote speaker at the annual conferences of the Association for Government Accountants, the American Accounting Association, and the Institute of Management Accountants. Almost twenty years ago, in 1992, DioGuardi published *Unaccountable Congress: It Doesn't Add Up (Regnery Gateway)*, sounding the alarm about the lack of fiscal responsibility in government and our massive national debt and calling for reform. Now, in the wake of the financial crisis that is gripping the United States, he has issued a new edition of the book, identifying the changes that the federal government must make to stop out-of-control government spending and borrowing, and to put America back on the road to a fiscally sustainable future.

Roberto Domínguez is Associate Professor in the Department of Government at Suffolk University. He holds a PhD in International Studies from University of Miami and an M.A. from Ortega y Gasset Foundation, Spain, as well as a Diploma on US Studies at the University of California in San Diego. He was professor of International Relations at UNAM, México as well as editor of the Journal Relaciones Internacionales (UNAM). He has been a visiting Professor at University of Quintana Roo (México) and Teikyo University (Maastricht, Netherlands) and is currently a research associate at the European Union Centre of Excellence at the University of Miami. Dr. Dominguez's research interests are security governance and regional integration. He is currently member of the funded tri-national project PIERAN, conducting an evaluation on "NAFTA: 20 Years After". His recent publications include: *Security Governance and Regional Organizations* (with Emil Kirchner, Abingdon, 2011); *European Union Foreign Policy* (New York: Edwing Mellen Press, 2008) and *Lisbon Fado: The European Union under Reform* (with Joaquin Roy, Miami European Union Center, 2009).

Robert G. Finbow, Professor and Chair of Political Science at Dalhousie University, received his doctorate from the London School of Economics. A recipient of SSHRC and Fulbright fellowships, he has published books and articles on trade, labour and environmental policies in NAFTA and the EU, comparative political cultures, health care and social policy in North America, and regionalism in Atlantic Canada.

Anders Hayden is Assistant Professor of Political Science at Dalhousie University. He holds a PhD in sociology from Boston College. In 2010, he was a visiting researcher with the Environmental Policy Group, Wageningen University, the Netherlands. His primary research interest is the social and political responses to climate change, particularly the evolving balance between efforts to promote ecological modernization (green growth) and sufficiency-based challenges to the endless growth of production and consumption. One related stream of work examines the successes and limits of the European Union and the United Kingdom as relative leaders in ecological modernization and climate action. He is the author of the book *Sharing the Work, Sparing the Planet: Work Time, Consumption & Ecology*.

Finn Laursen received his PhD from the University of Pennsylvania in 1980. In 2008, he received an ad personam Jean Monnet Chair, and he currently holds a Canada Research Chair (Tier 1) of EU Studies at Dalhousie University, Halifax, Nova Scotia, Canada where he directs the EU Centre of Excellence. He has been a lecturer at the London School of Economics, 1985-1988, Professor at the European Institute of Public Administration (EIPA), Maastricht, 1988-1995, and Professor of International Politics at the University of Southern Denmark, Odense, 1999-2006. Recent edited books include: *The Rise and Fall of the EU's Constitutional Treaty* (Nijhoff, 2008), *The EU as a Foreign and Security Policy Actor* (Republic-of-Letters Publishing, Dordrecht, 2009), *The EU in the Global Political Economy* (PIE Peter Lang, 2009), *Comparative Regional Integration: Europe and Beyond* (Ashgate, 2010), *The EU and Federalism: Polities and Policies Compared* (Ashgate, 2011), *The Making of the Lisbon Treaty: the Role of Member States* (PIE Peter Lang, 2012), and *The EU's Lisbon Treaty: Institutional Choices and Implementation* (Ashgate, 2012).

Rafael Leal-Arcas is Senior Lecturer, Queen Mary University of London, Senior Research Fellow at the World Trade Institute (University of Bern), and is the author of more than 70 scholarly publications on international and European economic law. Among his publications are the books *International Trade and Investment Law: Multilateral, Regional and Bilateral Governance* (Edward Elgar, 2010) and *Theory and Practice of EC External Trade Law and Policy* (Cameron May, 2008). Dr. Leal-Arcas has previously taught at the Academy of WTO Law and Policy of Georgetown University Law Center (Washington, D.C.), the University of Vienna School of Law Summer School, Nankai University (China), the National Law School of India University (Bangalore, India), where he was POROS Chair in European Union law, the Universidade Federal Minas Gerais School of Law (Brazil), the Universidade Federal de Pernambuco, School of Law (Brazil), and various Turkish universities. Dr. Leal-Arcas's previous employers include the World Trade Organization, the US Court of International Trade, the European Court of Justice, the European Commission, the EU Council of Ministers Legal Service, the European Parliament, the United Nations Secretariat, and the European Commission Delegation to the United Nations. A member of the Madrid Bar, he has been a Fellow at NYU Law School, the American Society of International Law, the Australian National University, Scholar at Georgetown's Institute of International Economic Law, the University of Wisconsin-Madison Law School, and Researcher at Harvard Law School and NYU Law School. He received his graduate legal education at Stanford, Columbia, the London School of Economics, and the European University Institute, in Florence, Italy.

Christian Marfels received his doctorate from the Free University of Berlin in Germany. For the past 30 years, his main research interest has been the economics of the European Union. In the 1980s he published several industry studies under the auspices of the EC Competition Directorate and has published widely on competition policy matters in the European Union, Canada, and the United States. In more recent years, this research was done jointly with Dr. James Sawler.

Nanette Neuwahl (PhD, EUI) is Jean Monnet Professor of European Union Law at Université de Montréal and Researcher at the Centre de Recherche en Droit public. She currently co-directs the *European Foreign Affairs Review* (with Joerg Monar) and has published widely on matters related to the constitutional law of the European Union, external relations law of the European Union, international migration, and access to justice.

Priya Nandita Pooran, Attorney-at-Law, received her Master of Laws (LL.M) in Corporate and Commercial Law from the London School of Economics (1996), and was admitted to the bar in England & Wales in 1997 and in New York in 2003. Her areas of expertise include banking law and regulation, insurance law and regulation, systemic risk, financial markets governance, international financial systems, and international organizations.

James Sawler received his PhD from Dalhousie University and is Associate Professor of Economics at Mount Saint Vincent University. His research interests include the teaching of economics, strategic decision-making involving alliances, and competition policy. His recent publications include articles appearing in *The Journal of Economic Education*, *Managerial and Decision-Making Economics*, and *The Canadian Competition Record*.

Nicolas W. Vermeys, LL. M., LL. D., CISSP, is a professor at the Université de Montréal, Faculté de droit, a researcher at the Centre de recherche en droit public (CRDP), the co-director of the maîtrise en commerce électronique (an e-commerce masters' program) and the Associate Director of the Cyberjustice Laboratory. He also serves as a legal advisor for the law firm of Legault Joly Thiffault, and as a board member for the Société québécoise d'information juridique (SOQUIJ). He is a Certified Information System Security Professional (CISSP) as recognised by (ISC)2, and is the author of numerous publications relating to the impact of technology on the law, including *Actes illicites sur Internet: Qui et comment poursuivre?* (Yvon Blais, 2011), *Responsabilité civile et sécurité informationnelle* (Yvon Blais, 2010), and *Virus informatiques: Responsables et responsabilité* (Thémis, 2006). He is also a columnist for a number of online publications and blogs (*Slaw*, *La Référence*, etc.) and serves as a member of the Scientific Panel of different law journals, including *Lex Electronica*, for which he served as editor-in-chief from 2001 to 2003. Mr. Vermeys' research focuses on legal issues pertaining to information security, developments in the field of cyberjustice, and other questions relating to the impact of technological innovations on the law.

Declan J. Walsh is Lecturer in European Union Law at the Faculty of Law, U.C.C., Cork, Ireland. He is a graduate of the University of Limerick and University College London. He has worked as special ministerial advisor to the Minister of State for the Marine, attending and advising at numerous Council of Ministers meetings. He has written extensively on issues relating to EU competition law and policy and on European Union law generally. He is a regular contributor to both *The Irish Times* and *The Irish Examiner* on matters relating to the European Union and is a regular commentator on RTE radio on matters relating to the European Union. He is a committee member of the Irish Society of European Law and a member of the Irish Centre for European Law, the Competition Law Scholars Forum and the University Association for Contemporary European Studies. In 2009 he acted as a spokesperson for Ireland for Europe during the successful referendum campaign on the Lisbon Treaty. He has twice been Acting Head of the Department of Law, UCC.

Index

"European Policy"

"European Policy" is an interdisciplinary series devoted to the study of European integration in a broad sense. Although mostly focusing on the European Union, it also encourages the publication of books addressing the wider, pan-European context, as well as comparative work, including other forms of regional integration on the world scene. The core disciplines are politics, economics, law, and history. While being committed to high academic standards, "European Policy" seeks to be accessible to a wide readership, including policymakers and practitioners, and to stimulate a debate on European issues. Submissions will normally undergo a thorough peer-review process. The series publishes both in English and in French.

Series Editor: **Pascaline WINAND,**
Professor/Director, Monash European and EU Centre
(Monash University, Australia)

Recent Titles

• No.51: *The EU and the Political Economy of Transatlantic Relations,* Finn LAURSEN (ed.), 2012, 321 p., ISBN 978-90-5201-900-0

• No.50: *Obama, US Politics, and Transatlantic Relations. Change or Continuity?,* Giles SCOTT-SMITH (ed.), 2012, 332 p., ISBN 978-90-5201-876-8

• No.49: *The Making of the EU's Lisbon Treaty. The Role of Member states,* Finn LAURSEN (ed.), 2012, 324 p., ISBN 978-90-5201-812-6

• No.48: *Energy and the Environmental Challenge. Lessons from the European Union and Australia,* Lillian WYLIE and Pascaline WINAND (eds.), 2011, 415 p., ISBN 978-90-5201-765-5

• No.47: *New Europe, New World? The European Union, Europe and the Challenges of the 21st Century,* Alfonso MARTÍNEZ ARRANZ, Natalie J. DOYLE & Pascaline WINAND (eds.), 2010, 283 p., ISBN 978-90-5201-604-7

• No.46: *Switzerland – European Union. An Impossible Membership?,* René SCHWOK, 2009, 155 p., ISBN 978-90-5201-576-7

• No.45: *The EU in the Global Political Economy,* Finn LAURSEN, 2009, 352 p., ISBN 978-90-5201-554-5

• No.44: *America, Europe, Africa / L'Amérique, l'Europe, l'Afrique. 1945-1973,* Éric REMACLE & Pascaline WINAND (eds./dir.), 2009, 329 p., ISBN 978-90-5201-529-3

• N° 43: *Le paysage européen de la sécurité intérieure,* Pierre BERTHELET, 2009, 573 p., ISBN 978-90-5201-473-9

• No.42: *In Pursuit of Influence. The Netherlands' European Policy during the Formative Years of the European Union, 1952-1973,* Anjo G. HARRYVAN, 2009, 284 p., ISBN 978-90-5201-497-5

• N° 41: *Les États-Unis et l'unification monétaire de l'Europe,* Dimitri GRYGOWSKI, 2009, 472 p., ISBN 978-90-5201- 489-0

• N° 40: *Le Traité de Rome : histoires pluridisciplinaires. L'apport du Traité de Rome instituant la Communauté économique européenne,* Sandrine DEVAUX, René LEBOUTTE & Philippe POIRIER (dir.), 2009, 210 p., ISBN 978-90-5201-500-2

• No.39: *European Integration from Rome to Berlin: 1957-2007. History, Law and Politics,* Julio BAQUERO CRUZ & Carlos CLOSA MONTERO (eds.), 2009, 286 p., ISBN 978-90-5201-464-7

• No.38: *European and Turkish Voices in Favour and Against Turkish Accession to the European Union,* Christiane TIMMERMAN, Dirk ROCHTUS & Sara MELS (eds.), 2008, 149 p., ISBN 978-90-5201-428-9

• N° 37: *Centre et centrisme en Europe aux XIXe et XXe siècles. Regards croisés,* Sylvie GUILLAUME et Jean GARRIGUES (dir.), 2006, 288 p., ISBN 978-90-5201-317-6

• N° 36: *Vers une Europe fédérale ? Les espoirs et les actions fédéralistes au sortir de la Seconde Guerre mondiale,* Bertrand VAYSSIÈRE, 2006 (2nd printing 2007), 416 p., ISBN 978-90-5201-353-4

• N° 35: *Institutionnaliser l'évaluation des politiques publiques. Étude comparée des dispositifs en Belgique, en France, en Suisse et aux Pays-Bas,* Steve JACOB, 2005, 271 p., ISBN 978-90-5201-078-6

• No.34: *Visions, Votes and Vetoes. The Empty Chair Crisis and the Luxembourg Compromise Forty Years On,* Jean-Marie PALAYRET, Helen WALLACE & Pascaline WINAND (eds.), 2006, 344 p., ISBN 978-90-5201-031-1

• No.33: *Networks of Empire. The US State Department's Foreign Leader Program in the Netherlands, France, and Britain 1950-70,* Giles SCOTT-SMITH, 2008, 516 p., ISBN 978-90-5201-256-3

• N° 32: *Le droit institutionnel de la sécurité intérieure européenne,* Pierre BERTHELET, 2003, 324 p., ISBN 978-90-5201-193-6

Peter Lang—The website

Discover the general website of the Peter Lang publishing group:

www.peterlang.com